The **UNIX**™ System User's Manual

AT&T

The UNIX™ System User's Manual

AT&T Information Systems

PRENTICE-HALL, Englewood Cliffs, New Jersey 07632

Published by Prentice-Hall
A Division of Simon & Schuster, Inc.
Englewood Cliffs, New Jersey 07632

IMPORTANT NOTE TO USERS

While every effort has been made to ensure the accuracy of all information in this document, AT&T assumes no liability to any party for any loss or damage caused by errors or omissions or by statements of any kind in *The UNIX* System User's Manual*, its updates, supplements, or special editions, whether such errors are omissions or statements resulting from negligence, accident, or any other cause. AT&T further assumes no liability arising out of the application or use of any product or system described herein; nor any liability for incidental or consequential damages arising from the use of this document. AT&T disclaims all warranties regarding the information contained herein, whether expressed, implied or statutory, including implied warranties of merchantability or fitness for a particular purpose.

AT&T makes no representation that the interconnection of products in the manner described herein will not infringe on existing or future patent rights, nor do the descriptions contained herein imply the granting of license to make, use or sell equipment constructed in accordance with this description.

AT&T reserves the right to make changes without further notice to any products herein to improve reliability, function, or design.

This document was set on an AUTOLOGIC, Inc. APS-5 phototypesetter driven by the `troff` formatter operating on UNIX System V on an AT&T 3B20 computer.

---

* UNIX is a trademark of AT&T.
APS-5 is a trademark of AUTOLOGIC, Inc.

Printed in the United States of America

10 9 8 7 6 5 4 3 2 1

ISBN 0-13-938242-9 025
SELECT CODE NO. 320-041

Prentice-Hall International (UK) Limited, *London*
Prentice-Hall of Australia Pty. Limited, *Sydney*
Prentice-Hall Canada Inc., *Toronto*
Prentice-Hall Hispanoamericana, S.A., *Mexico*
Prentice-Hall of India Private Limited, *New Delhi*
Prentice-Hall of Japan, Inc., *Tokyo*
Prentice-Hall of Southeast Asia Pte. Ltd., *Singapore*
Editora Prentice-Hall do Brasil, Ltda., *Rio de Janeiro*
Whitehall Books Limited, *Wellington, New Zealand*

To the many users
past, present and future
whose programming contributions
built and sustain
the UNIX System

Table of Contents

Preface

The UNIX System User's Manual* addresses itself to the needs of all users of UNIX System V, but especially to those of application-developers building C language application-programs whose source-code must be portable from one UNIX System V environment to another. *The UNIX System User's Manual* serves the following major purposes:

- To provide a single reference defining operating system components provided by computer systems supporting UNIX System V.
- To define the feature/functionality that application-programs and end-users can expect from those components. (This does *not* include the details of how the operating system implements these components.)
- To assist in porting software between computer systems supporting UNIX System V. (This assumes the source is recompiled for the proper target hardware.)

The UNIX System User's Manual is based on Issue 2 of the *System V Interface Definition*, which corresponds to functionality in UNIX System V Release 1.0 and UNIX System V Release 2.0. The *System V Interface Definition* applies to computer systems ranging from personal computers to mainframes, and specifies a computing environment for creating applications software independent of any particular computer hardware. Applications conforming to the *System V Interface Definition* allow users to take advantage of changes in technology and to choose the computer system that best meets their needs from among many manufacturers while retaining a common computing environment.

The UNIX System User's Manual describes operating system components available to both end-users and application-programs. *The UNIX System User's Manual* specifies the source-code or command-level interfaces of each operating system component as well as the run-time behavior an application-program or an end-user should expect. *The UNIX System User's Manual* specifies the functionality of components without stipulating the implementation. The emphasis is on defining a common computing environment for application-programs and end-users; not on the internals of the operating system, such as the scheduler or memory manager.

* UNIX is a trademark of AT&T.

The **UNIX**™ System User's Manual

Introduction

Scope and Field of Application

The UNIX System User's Manual defines the source-code interfaces and the run-time behavior for components of UNIX System V. These components include operating system routines, general library routines, system data files, special device files and end-user utilities (commands). *The UNIX System User's Manual* follows the *System V Interface Definition* by grouping the components of UNIX System V into a Base System plus a series of Extensions to that Base System. This does not change the definition of UNIX System V. Instead it recognizes that the entire feature/functionality of UNIX System V may be unnecessary in certain environments, especially on small hardware configurations. It also recognizes that different computing environments require some functions that others do not.

The Base System includes the components that all computer systems supporting UNIX System V provide, but a system may provide some or none of the Extensions. Extensions to the Base System may not be present on a computer system supporting UNIX System V, but when a component is present it will have the specified functionality. All the components of an Extension are present on a system that meets the requirements of the Extension. This does not preclude a system from including only a few components from some Extension, but the system would *not* then meet the requirements of that Extension. Some Extensions require other Extensions to be present (e.g., the Advanced Utilities require the Basic Utilities).

This partitioning into the Base System and Extensions allows an application-program to be built using a basic set of components that are consistent across all computer systems supporting UNIX System V. Where necessary, an application-developer can choose to use components from an Extension and require the run-time environment to support that Extension in addition to the Base System. To execute, many application-programs will require only the components in the Base System. Other application-programs will need one or more Extensions.

The Extensions to the Base System provide a growth path in natural functional increments, which leads to a full UNIX System V configuration. The division into a Base System and Extensions allows system builders to create machines tailored for different purposes and markets in an orderly fashion. Thus, a small business/professional computer system designed for novice single-users might include only the Base System and the Basic Utilities. A system for advanced business/professional users might add to this the Advanced Utilities. A system designed for high-level language software development would include the Base System, the Kernel Extension and the Basic Utilities, Advanced Utilities and Software Development Extension. Although the Extensions are not meant to specify the physical packaging of UNIX System V for a particular product, it is expected that the Extensions will lead to a fairly consistent packaging scheme.

The run-time behavior of the components defined in *The UNIX System User's Manual* is supported by computer systems supporting UNIX System V. However, the source-code libraries themselves may not be present on a system that supports only the Base System. The Base System supports only the *execution* of application-programs; the Software Development Extension supports the *compilation* of those application-programs. A computer system that supports only the Base

System provides only a run-time environment; it is assumed that an application-program targeted to *execute* on such a system would be *compiled* on a computer system that supports the Software Development Extension.

The Base System defines a basic set of UNIX System V components needed to support a minimal, stand-alone run-time environment for executable application-programs originally written in a high-level language, such as C. An example of such a system would be a dedicated-use system; that is, a system devoted to a single application, such as a vertically-integrated application-package for managing a legal office. In this environment, the end-user would not interact directly with the traditional UNIX System V shell and commands.

The Base System excludes end-user level utilities (commands). Executable application-programs designed for maximum portability should use Base Library Routines instead of any Commands and Utilities. For example, an application-program written in C would use the *function* `chown` [see CHOWN(BA_SYS)] to change the owner of a file rather than using the *command* `chown` [see CHOWN(AU_CMD)]. This does not say that an application-program running in a target environment that supports only the Base System cannot execute another application-program. Using the SYSTEM(BA_SYS) routine, one application-program can execute another application-program.

Features or side-effects that are not explicitly defined should not be used by application-programs that require portability. Some Extensions may add features to components defined in the Base System. The additional features supported in an extended environment are described in **Environment** in a section titled EFFECTS(XX_ENV) (e.g., EFFECTS(KE_ENV) in **Kernel Extension Environment**).

The UNIX System User's Manual defines source-code interfaces for the C language. The following two references define the C language for UNIX System V Release 1.0 and UNIX System V Release 2.0 respectively:

- *UNIX System V Programming Guide*, Issue 1, February 1982.
- *UNIX System V Programming Guide*, Issue 2, April 1984.

The UNIX System User's Manual describes each component's run-time behavior, but does not specify its implementation.

Structure

Each component definition follows the same structure. The sections are listed below, but not all of them appear in each description. Sections entitled **EXAMPLE**, **APPLICATION USAGE** and **USAGE** are not considered part of the formal definition of a component.

- **NAME** — name of component
- **SYNOPSIS** — summary of source-code or user-level interface
- **DESCRIPTION** — functionality and run-time behavior
- **RETURN VALUE** — value returned by the function
- **ERRORS** — possible error conditions
- **FILES** — names of files used
- **APPLICATION USAGE** or **USAGE** — guidance on use
- **EXAMPLE** — examples and sample usage
- **SEE ALSO** — list of related components
- **CAVEATS** — future directions

In general, commands and utilities lack a **RETURN VALUE** section. Except as noted in the detailed definition for a particular command or utility, they return a zero exit code for *success* and non-zero for *failure*.

The component definitions are similar in format to traditional AT&T UNIX System V manual pages, but have been extended or modified as follows:

- All machine-specific or implementation-specific information has been removed, and all implementation-specific constants have been replaced by symbolic names, defined in a separate section [see **Implementation-specific constants** in **Definitions**]. When these symbolic names are used they always appear in curly brackets (e.g., {PROC_MAX}). The symbolic names correspond to those the November 1985 draft of the **IEEE P1003** Standard defines to be in a `<limits.h>` header file; however, in this document, they are *not* to be read as symbolic constants defined in header files.
- A section entitled **CAVEATS** has been added to indicate how a component may evolve. The information ranges from specific changes in functionality to more general indications of proposed development.
- A section entitled **APPLICATION USAGE** or **USAGE** has been added to guide application-developers on the expected or recommended usage of certain components. Detailed definitions of System and Library routines have an **APPLICATION USAGE** section while Utilities have a **USAGE** section.

While System and Library routines are used only by application-programs, Utilities may be used by application-programs, by end-users or by system-administrators. The **USAGE** section indicates which of these three is appropriate for a particular utility (this is not meant to be prescriptive, but rather to give guidance).

The **USAGE** section uses the following terms:

- *application-program*
- *end-user*
- *system-administrator*
- *general*

The term *general* indicates that the utility might be used by all three: *application-programs*, *end-users* and *system-administrators*.

When referred to individually, component definitions are identified by a suffix of the form (XX_YYY), where XX identifies the Base System or the Extension the component belongs to and YYY identifies the type of component. Possible types are:

ENV — environmental components

SYS — system service routines

LIB — general library routines

CMD — commands or utilities

For example, component definitions in **Base System Routines** are identified by (BA_SYS), those in **Base Library Routines** are identified by (BA_LIB) and those in **Kernel Extension Routines** are identified by (KE_SYS).

Contents

Chapter 1. — Basic Utilities (BU_CMD) defines basic user-level functions like:

- the `sh` (shell) command interpreter,
- shell programming aids,
- facilities for basic directory and file manipulation,
- facilities for text file editing and processing.

Basic Utilities require Base System Routines and Base Library Routines.

Chapter 2. — Advanced Utilities (AU_CMD) defines the next logical expansion step up from Basic Utilities. Advanced Utilities require Base System Routines, Base Library Routines and Basic Utilities.

Chapter 3. — Administered Systems Utilities (AS_CMD) defines utilities used for system administration; most of which are restricted to super-users. Administered Systems Utilities require Base System Routines, Base Library Routines, Kernel Extension Routines, Basic Utilities and Advanced Utilities.

Chapter 4. — Software Development Utilities (SD_CMD) defines facilities for compiling and maintaining C language software. Principal components are the C compiler `cc` and related utilities, program development aids `yacc` and `lex`, and Source Code Control System (SCCS) utilities. Software Development Utilities require Base System Routines, Base Library Routines, Basic Utilities and Advanced Utilities.

Chapter 5. — Base System Routines (BA_SYS) defines operating system components that provide application-programs access to basic system resources (e.g., allocating dynamic storage). Base System Routines provide access to and control over system resources such as memory, files and process execution. The Base System excludes some UNIX System V components that provide operating system services. An application-program using any of these requires an *extended* environment.

Chapter 6. — Kernel Extension Routines (KE_SYS) defines operating system components that support process-accounting tools, software-development tools and application-programs requiring more sophisticated inter-process communication than provided by Base System Routines.

Chapter 7. — Base Library Routines (BA_LIB) defines general-purpose library routines that perform a wide range of useful functions including:

- mathematical functions,
- string and character-handling routines,
- sorting and searching routines,
- standard I/O routines.

Chapter 8. — Software Development Library (SD_LIB) defines facilities for compiling and maintaining C language software. The standard C library is automatically included in the Software Development Library (that is, searched to resolve undefined external references). This includes all Base System Routines (BA_SYS), Kernel Extension Routines (KE_SYS) and Base Library Routines (BA_LIB) listed above. They must be present (that is, compilation of programs that use these routines must be supported) to satisfy the requirements of the Software Development Library.

Inclusion of other libraries requires specific loader options on the C compiler `cc` command line. For example, the mathematical library ("Mathematical Functions" in Base Library Routines) is searched by including the option `-lm` on the command line:

`cc` *file*`.c -lm`

Notes on other libraries:

- The `lex` library (`cc` option `-ll`) is required for the compilation of programs generated by `lex` [see LEX(SD_CMD)].
- The object file library (`cc` option `-lld`) contains routines used for the manipulation of object files. The only such routines required for the Software Development Library are `sputl` and `sgetl` [see SPUTL(SD_LIB)].
- The `yacc` library (`cc` option `-ly`) facilitates the use of `yacc` [see YACC(SD_CMD)].

Chapter 9. — Base System Environment (BA_ENV) defines error conditions, environmental variables, directory tree structures, system data files and special device files present in the Base System.

Chapter 10. — Kernel Extension Environment (KE_ENV) defines Kernel Extension error conditions and other extensions to the Base System Environment, including additional behavior of Base System Routines when Kernel Extension Routines are present on a system [see EFFECTS(KE_ENV)].

Chapter 11. — Administered Systems Environment (AS_ENV) defines the process of initializing UNIX System V on a computer system.

Chapter 12. — Base System Definitions (BA_DEF) defines terms used in the Base System; these definitions also apply to the Extensions because the Base System is a prerequisite for any Extension.

Chapter 13. — Kernel Extension Definitions (KE_DEF) defines terms relating to message-queues, semaphores, shared-memory and the inter-process communication mechanisms introduced by the Kernel Extension.

Commands and Utilities

In the following tables, utilities marked with * are Level 2: 1 January defined in the *System V Interface Definition* and those marked with ** are 1 December 1985. The utilities marked with † are new in UNIX System V Re 2.0 and those marked with # are optional.

TABLE 1. Basic Utilities

ar	AR(BU_CMD)	nl	NL(BU_CMD)
awk	AWK(BU_CMD)	nohup	NOHUP(BU_CMD)
banner	BANNER(BU_CMD)	pack	PACK(BU_CMD)
basename	BASENAME(BU_CMD)	paste	PASTE(BU_CMD)
cal	CAL(BU_CMD)	pcat	PACK(BU_CMD)
calendar	CALENDAR(BU_CMD)	pg†	PG(BU_CMD)
cat	CAT(BU_CMD)	pr	PR(BU_CMD)
cd	CD(BU_CMD)	ps	PS(BU_CMD)
chmod	CHMOD(BU_CMD)	pwd	PWD(BU_CMD)
cmp	CMP(BU_CMD)	red	ED(BU_CMD)
col	COL(BU_CMD)	rm	RM(BU_CMD)
comm	COMM(BU_CMD)	rmail	MAIL(BU_CMD)
cp	CP(BU_CMD)	rmdir	RM(BU_CMD)
cpio	CPIO(BU_CMD)	rsh	SH(BU_CMD)
cut	CUT(BU_CMD)	sed	SED(BU_CMD)
date	DATE(BU_CMD)	sh	SH(BU_CMD)
df	DF(BU_CMD)	sleep	SLEEP(BU_CMD)
diff	DIFF(BU_CMD)	sort	SORT(BU_CMD)
dirname	BASENAME(BU_CMD)	spell	SPELL(BU_CMD)
du	DU(BU_CMD)	split	SPLIT(BU_CMD)
echo	ECHO(BU_CMD)	sum	SUM(BU_CMD)
ed	ED(BU_CMD)	tail	TAIL(BU_CMD)
expr	EXPR(BU_CMD)	tee	TEE(BU_CMD)
false	TRUE(BU_CMD)	test	TEST(BU_CMD)
file	FILE(BU_CMD)	touch	TOUCH(BU_CMD)
find	FIND(BU_CMD)	tr	TR(BU_CMD)
grep	GREP(BU_CMD)	true	TRUE(BU_CMD)
kill	KILL(BU_CMD)	umask	UMASK(BU_CMD)
line	LINE(BU_CMD)	uname	UNAME(BU_CMD)
ln	CP(BU_CMD)	uniq	UNIQ(BU_CMD)
ls	LS(BU_CMD)	unpack	PACK(BU_CMD)
mail	MAIL(BU_CMD)	wait	WAIT(BU_CMD)
mkdir	MKDIR(BU_CMD)	wc	WC(BU_CMD)
mv	CP(BU_CMD)		

TABLE 2. Advanced Utilities

[illegible]	AT(AU_CMD)	newgrp	NEWGRP(AU_CMD)
batch	AT(AU_CMD)	news	NEWS(AU_CMD)
cancel	LP(AU_CMD)	od	OD(AU_CMD)
chgrp	CHOWN(AU_CMD)	passwd	PASSWD(AU_CMD)
chown	CHOWN(AU_CMD)	shl†	SHL(AU_CMD)
cron	CRON(AU_CMD)	stty	STTY(AU_CMD)
crontab†	CRONTAB(AU_CMD)	su	SU(AU_CMD)
csplit	CSPLIT(AU_CMD)	tabs	TABS(AU_CMD)
cu	CU(AU_CMD)	tar	TAR(AU_CMD)
dd	DD(AU_CMD)	tty	TTY(AU_CMD)
dircmp	DIRCMP(AU_CMD)	uucp	UUCP(AU_CMD)
egrep**	EGREP(AU_CMD)	uulog	UUCP(AU_CMD)
ex†	EX(AU_CMD)	uuname	UUCP(AU_CMD)
fgrep**	EGREP(AU_CMD)	uupick	UUTO(AU_CMD)
id	ID(AU_CMD)	uustat	UUSTAT(AU_CMD)
join	JOIN(AU_CMD)	uuto	UUTO(AU_CMD)
logname	LOGNAME(AU_CMD)	uux	UUX(AU_CMD)
lp	LP(AU_CMD)	vi†	VI(AU_CMD)
lpstat	LPSTAT(AU_CMD)	wall	WALL(AU_CMD)
mailx†	MAILX(AU_CMD)	who	WHO(AU_CMD)
mesg	MESG(AU_CMD)	write	WRITE(AU_CMD)

TABLE 3. Administered Systems Utilities

acctcms	ACCTCMS(AS_CMD)	mkfs	MKFS(AS_CMD)
acctcom	ACCTCOM(AS_CMD)	mknod	MKNOD(AS_CMD)
acctcon1	ACCTCON(AS_CMD)	monacct	ACCT(AS_CMD)
acctcon2	ACCTCON(AS_CMD)	mount	MOUNT(AS_CMD)
acctdisk	DISKUSG(AS_CMD)	mvdir	MVDIR(AS_CMD)
acctmerg	ACCTMERG(AS_CMD)	ncheck**	NCHECK(AS_CMD)
accton	ACCT(AS_CMD)	nice	NICE(AS_CMD)
acctprc1	ACCTPRC(AS_CMD)	prctmp	ACCTCON(AS_CMD)
acctprc2	ACCTPRC(AS_CMD)	prdaily	ACCT(AS_CMD)
acctwtmp	ACCT(AS_CMD)	prtacct	ACCT(AS_CMD)
chargefee	ACCT(AS_CMD)	pwck	PWCK(AS_CMD)
ckpacct	ACCT(AS_CMD)	runacct	RUNACCT(AS_CMD)
clri**	CLRI(AS_CMD)	sa1	SA1(AS_CMD)
devnm	DEVNM(AS_CMD)	sadc	SA1(AS_CMD)
diskusg	DISKUSG(AS_CMD)	sadp	SADP(AS_CMD)
dodisk	ACCT(AS_CMD)	sar	SAR(AS_CMD)
fsck	FSCK(AS_CMD)	setmnt	SETMNT(AS_CMD)
fsdb	FSDB(AS_CMD)	shutacct	ACCT(AS_CMD)
fuser	FUSER(AS_CMD)	startup	ACCT(AS_CMD)
fwtmp	FWTMP(AS_CMD)	sync	SYNC(AS_CMD)
grpck	PWCK(AS_CMD)	sysdef	SYSDEF(AS_CMD)
init	INIT(AS_CMD)	timex	TIMEX(AS_CMD)
ipcrm	IPCRM(AS_CMD)	turnacct	ACCT(AS_CMD)
ipcs	IPCS(AS_CMD)	umount	MOUNT(AS_CMD)
killall	KILLALL(AS_CMD)	unlink	LINK(AS_CMD)
labelit	VOLCOPY(AS_CMD)	volcopy	VOLCOPY(AS_CMD)
lastlogin	ACCT(AS_CMD)	whodo	WHODO(AS_CMD)
link	LINK(AS_CMD)	wtmpfix	FWTMP(AS_CMD)

TABLE 4. Software Development Utilities

`admin`	ADMIN(SD_CMD)	`make`	MAKE(SD_CMD)
`as#`	AS(SD_CMD)	`nm`	NM(SD_CMD)
`cc`	CC(SD_CMD)	`prof`	PROF(SD_CMD)
`cflow`	CFLOW(SD_CMD)	`prs`	PRS(SD_CMD)
`chroot`	CHROOT(SD_CMD)	`rmdel`	RMDEL(SD_CMD)
`cpp`	CPP(SD_CMD)	`sact`	SACT(SD_CMD)
`cxref`	CXREF(SD_CMD)	`sdb`	SDB(SD_CMD)
`delta`	DELTA(SD_CMD)	`size`	SIZE(SD_CMD)
`dis#`	DIS(SD_CMD)	`strip`	STRIP(SD_CMD)
`env`	ENV(SD_CMD)	`time`	TIME(SD_CMD)
`get`	GET(SD_CMD)	`tsort`	TSORT(SD_CMD)
`ld`	LD(SD_CMD)	`unget`	UNGET(SD_CMD)
`lex`	LEX(SD_CMD)	`val`	VAL(SD_CMD)
`lint`	LINT(SD_CMD)	`what`	WHAT(SD_CMD)
`lorder`	LORDER(SD_CMD)	`xargs`	XARGS(SD_CMD)
`m4`	M4(SD_CMD)	`yacc`	YACC(SD_CMD)

System Routines

All the routines in Table 5, except those marked with † or ††, are common to UNIX System V Release 1.0 and UNIX System V Release 2.0. Those marked with † first appeared in UNIX System V Release 2.0. The function `lockf`, marked with ††, is a post UNIX System V Release 2.0 component.

TABLE 5. Base System Routines

abort	ABORT(BA_SYS)	getuid	GETUID(BA_SYS)
access	ACCESS(BA_SYS)	ioctl	IOCTL(BA_SYS)
alarm	ALARM(BA_SYS)	kill	KILL(BA_SYS)
calloc	MALLOC(BA_SYS)	link	LINK(BA_SYS)
chdir	CHDIR(BA_SYS)	lockf††	LOCKF(BA_SYS)
chmod	CHMOD(BA_SYS)	mallinfo†	MALLOC(BA_SYS)
chown	CHOWN(BA_SYS)	malloc	MALLOC(BA_SYS)
clearerr	FERROR(BA_SYS)	mallopt†	MALLOC(BA_SYS)
dup	DUP(BA_SYS)	mknod	MKNOD(BA_SYS)
exit	EXIT(BA_SYS)	pause	PAUSE(BA_SYS)
fclose	FCLOSE(BA_SYS)	pclose	POPEN(BA_SYS)
fcntl	FCNTL(BA_SYS)	pipe	PIPE(BA_SYS)
fdopen	FOPEN(BA_SYS)	popen	POPEN(BA_SYS)
feof	FERROR(BA_SYS)	realloc	MALLOC(BA_SYS)
ferror	FERROR(BA_SYS)	rewind	FSEEK(BA_SYS)
fflush	FCLOSE(BA_SYS)	setgid	SETGID(BA_SYS)
fileno	FERROR(BA_SYS)	setpgrp	SETPGRP(BA_SYS)
fopen	FOPEN(BA_SYS)	setuid	SETUID(BA_SYS)
fread	FREAD(BA_SYS)	signal	SIGNAL(BA_SYS)
free	MALLOC(BA_SYS)	sleep	SLEEP(BA_SYS)
freopen	FOPEN(BA_SYS)	stat	STAT(BA_SYS)
fseek	FSEEK(BA_SYS)	stime	STIME(BA_SYS)
fstat	STAT(BA_SYS)	system	SYSTEM(BA_SYS)
ftell	FSEEK(BA_SYS)	time	TIME(BA_SYS)
fwrite	FWRITE(BA_SYS)	times	TIMES(BA_SYS)
getcwd	GETCWD(BA_SYS)	ulimit	ULIMIT(BA_SYS)
getegid	GETGID(BA_SYS)	umask	UMASK(BA_SYS)
geteuid	GETUID(BA_SYS)	uname	UNAME(BA_SYS)
getgid	GETGID(BA_SYS)	unlink	UNLINK(BA_SYS)
getpgrp	GETPID(BA_SYS)	ustat	USTAT(BA_SYS)
getpid	GETPID(BA_SYS)	utime	UTIME(BA_SYS)
getppid	GETPID(BA_SYS)	wait	WAIT(BA_SYS)
close	CLOSE(BA_SYS)	fork	FORK(BA_SYS)
creat	CREAT(BA_SYS)	lseek	LSEEK(BA_SYS)
execl	EXEC(BA_SYS)	mount	MOUNT(BA_SYS)
execle	EXEC(BA_SYS)	open	OPEN(BA_SYS)
execlp	EXEC(BA_SYS)	read	READ(BA_SYS)
execv	EXEC(BA_SYS)	umount	UMOUNT(BA_SYS)
execve	EXEC(BA_SYS)	write	WRITE(BA_SYS)
execvp	EXEC(BA_SYS)		
_exit	EXIT(BA_SYS)	sync	SYNC(BA_SYS)

Table 5 shows three sets of routines in order to reflect recommended u
application-programs.

- The first set of routines (from `abort` to `wait`) should fulfill the needs most application-programs.
- The second set of routines (from `close` to `write`) should be used by application-programs only when some special need requires it. For example, application-programs, when possible, should use the function `system` rather than the functions `fork` and `exec` because it is easier to use and supplies more functionality. The corresponding Standard Input/Output, *stdio* routines [see **stdio-routines** in **Definitions**] should be used instead of the functions `close`, `creat`, `lseek`, `open`, `read`, `write` (e.g., the *stdio* routine `fopen` should be used rather than the function `open`).
- The third set of routines (`_exit` and `sync`), although defined as part of the basic set of UNIX System V components, are not expected to be used by application-programs. These routines are used by other Base System Routines.

TABLE 6. Kernel Extension Routines

acct	ACCT(KE_SYS)	ptrace	PTRACE(KE_SYS)
chroot	CHROOT(KE_SYS)	semctl	SEMCTL(KE_SYS)
msgctl	MSGCTL(KE_SYS)	semget	SEMGET(KE_SYS)
msgget	MSGGET(KE_SYS)	semop	SEMOP(KE_SYS)
msgrcv	MSGOP(KE_SYS)	shmctl#	SHMCTL(KE_SYS)
msgsnd	MSGOP(KE_SYS)	shmget#	SHMGET(KE_SYS)
nice	NICE(KE_SYS)	shmat#	SHMOP(KE_SYS)
plock	PLOCK(KE_SYS)	shmdt#	SHMOP(KE_SYS)
profil	PROFIL(KE_SYS)		

Optional. These routines are hardware-dependent and will only appear on machines with the appropriate hardware.

...ry Routines

...e routines in Table 7, except those marked with † are in both UNIX System ...Release 1.0 and UNIX System V Release 2.0. Those marked with * are Level-2 ...n the *System V Interface Definition*; those marked with # are optional.

TABLE 7. Base Library Routines

Mathematical Functions			
abs	ABS(BA_LIB)	j0	BESSEL(BA_LIB)
acos	TRIG(BA_LIB)	j1	BESSEL(BA_LIB)
asin	TRIG(BA_LIB)	jn	BESSEL(BA_LIB)
atan2	TRIG(BA_LIB)	ldexp	FREXP(BA_LIB)
atan	TRIG(BA_LIB)	log10	EXP(BA_LIB)
ceil	FLOOR(BA_LIB)	log	EXP(BA_LIB)
cos	TRIG(BA_LIB)	matherr	MATHERR(BA_LIB)
cosh	SINH(BA_LIB)	modf	FREXP(BA_LIB)
erf	ERF(BA_LIB)	pow	EXP(BA_LIB)
erfc	ERF(BA_LIB)	sin	TRIG(BA_LIB)
exp	EXP(BA_LIB)	sinh	SINH(BA_LIB)
fabs	FLOOR(BA_LIB)	sqrt	EXP(BA_LIB)
floor	FLOOR(BA_LIB)	tan	TRIG(BA_LIB)
fmod	FLOOR(BA_LIB)	tanh	SINH(BA_LIB)
frexp	FREXP(BA_LIB)	y0	BESSEL(BA_LIB)
gamma	GAMMA(BA_LIB)	y1	BESSEL(BA_LIB)
hypot	HYPOT(BA_LIB)	yn	BESSEL(BA_LIB)

String and Character Handling Routines			
_tolower	CONV(BA_LIB)	memccpy	MEMORY(BA_LIB)
_toupper	CONV(BA_LIB)	memchr	MEMORY(BA_LIB)
advance	REGEXP(BA_LIB)	memcmp	MEMORY(BA_LIB)
asctime	CTIME(BA_LIB)	memcpy	MEMORY(BA_LIB)
atof	STRTOD(BA_LIB)	memset	MEMORY(BA_LIB)
atoi	STRTOL(BA_LIB)	setkey#	CRYPT(BA_LIB)
atol	STRTOL(BA_LIB)	step	REGEXP(BA_LIB)
compile	REGEXP(BA_LIB)	strcat	STRING(BA_LIB)
crypt#	CRYPT(BA_LIB)	strchr	STRING(BA_LIB)
ctime	CTIME(BA_LIB)	strcmp	STRING(BA_LIB)
encrypt#	CRYPT(BA_LIB)	strcpy	STRING(BA_LIB)
gmtime	CTIME(BA_LIB)	strcspn	STRING(BA_LIB)
isalnum	CTYPE(BA_LIB)	strlen	STRING(BA_LIB)
isalpha	CTYPE(BA_LIB)	strncat	STRING(BA_LIB)
isascii	CTYPE(BA_LIB)	strncmp	STRING(BA_LIB)
iscntrl	CTYPE(BA_LIB)	strncpy	STRING(BA_LIB)
isdigit	CTYPE(BA_LIB)	strpbrk	STRING(BA_LIB)
isgraph	CTYPE(BA_LIB)	strrchr	STRING(BA_LIB)
islower	CTYPE(BA_LIB)	strspn	STRING(BA_LIB)
isprint	CTYPE(BA_LIB)	strtod†	STRTOD(BA_LIB)
ispunct	CTYPE(BA_LIB)	strtok	STRING(BA_LIB)
isspace	CTYPE(BA_LIB)	strtol	STRTOL(BA_LIB)
isupper	CTYPE(BA_LIB)	toascii	CONV(BA_LIB)
isxdigit	CTYPE(BA_LIB)	tolower	CONV(BA_LIB)
localtime	CTIME(BA_LIB)	toupper	CONV(BA_LIB)
		tzset	CTIME(BA_LIB)

Sorting and Searching Routines			
bsearch	BSEARCH(BA_LIB)	mktemp	MKTEMP(BA_LIB)
clock	CLOCK(BA_LIB)	mrand48	DRAND48(BA_LIB)
drand48	DRAND48(BA_LIB)	nrand48	DRAND48(BA_LIB)
erand48	DRAND48(BA_LIB)	perror*	PERROR(BA_LIB)
ftw	FTW(BA_LIB)	putenv†	PUTENV(BA_LIB)
getenv	GETENV(BA_LIB)	qsort	QSORT(BA_LIB)
getopt	GETOPT(BA_LIB)	rand	RAND(BA_LIB)
gsignal*	SSIGNAL(BA_LIB)	seed48	DRAND48(BA_LIB)
hcreate	HSEARCH(BA_LIB)	setjmp	SETJMP(BA_LIB)
hdestroy	HSEARCH(BA_LIB)	srand48	DRAND48(BA_LIB)
hsearch	HSEARCH(BA_LIB)	srand	RAND(BA_LIB)
isatty	TTYNAME(BA_LIB)	ssignal*	SSIGNAL(BA_LIB)
jrand48	DRAND48(BA_LIB)	swab	SWAB(BA_LIB)
lcong48	DRAND48(BA_LIB)	tdelete	TSEARCH(BA_LIB)
lfind†	LSEARCH(BA_LIB)	tfind†	TSEARCH(BA_LIB)
longjmp	SETJMP(BA_LIB)	tsearch	TSEARCH(BA_LIB)
lrand48	DRAND48(BA_LIB)	ttyname	TTYNAME(BA_LIB)
lsearch	LSEARCH(BA_LIB)	twalk	TSEARCH(BA_LIB)

Standard I/O Routines			
ctermid	CTERMID(BA_LIB)	puts	PUTS(BA_LIB)
fgetc	GETC(BA_LIB)	putw	PUTC(BA_LIB)
fgets	GETS(BA_LIB)	scanf	SCANF(BA_LIB)
fprintf	PRINTF(BA_LIB)	setbuf	SETBUF(BA_LIB)
fputc	PUTC(BA_LIB)	setvbuf†	SETVBUF(BA_LIB)
fputs	PUTS(BA_LIB)	sprintf	PRINTF(BA_LIB)
fscanf	SCANF(BA_LIB)	sscanf	SCANF(BA_LIB)
getc	GETC(BA_LIB)	tempnam	TMPNAM(BA_LIB)
getchar	GETC(BA_LIB)	tmpfile	TMPFILE(BA_LIB)
gets	GETS(BA_LIB)	tmpnam	TMPNAM(BA_LIB)
getw	GETC(BA_LIB)	ungetc	UNGETC(BA_LIB)
printf	PRINTF(BA_LIB)	vfprintf†	VPRINTF(BA_LIB)
putc	PUTC(BA_LIB)	vprintf†	VPRINTF(BA_LIB)
putchar	PUTC(BA_LIB)	vsprintf†	VPRINTF(BA_LIB)

TABLE 8. Software Development Library

a64l	A64L(SD_LIB)	getutent	GETUT(SD_LIB)
assert	ASSERT(SD_LIB)	getutid	GETUT(SD_LIB)
endgrent	GETGRENT(SD_LIB)	getutline	GETUT(SD_LIB)
endpwent	GETPWENT(SD_LIB)	l64a	A64L(SD_LIB)
endutent	GETUT(SD_LIB)	MARK	MARK(SD_LIB)
fgetgrent	GETGRENT(SD_LIB)	monitor	MONITOR(SD_LIB)
fgetpwent	GETPWENT(SD_LIB)	nlist	NLIST(SD_LIB)
getgrent	GETGRENT(SD_LIB)	putpwent	PUTPWENT(SD_LIB)
getgrgid	GETGRENT(SD_LIB)	pututline	GETUT(SD_LIB)
getgrnam	GETGRENT(SD_LIB)	setgrent	GETGRENT(SD_LIB)
getlogin	GETLOGIN(SD_LIB)	setpwent	GETPWENT(SD_LIB)
getpass	GETPASS(SD_LIB)	setutent	GETUT(SD_LIB)
getpwent	GETPWENT(SD_LIB)	sgetl	SPUTL(SD_LIB)
getpwnam	GETPWENT(SD_LIB)	sputl	SPUTL(SD_LIB)
getpwuid	GETPWENT(SD_LIB)	utmpname	GETUT(SD_LIB)

Part I

Commands and Utilities

Chapter 1

Basic Utilities

NAME

ar — archive and library maintainer for portable archives

SYNOPSIS

`ar` *option* [*posname*] *afile* [*name*]...

DESCRIPTION

The `ar` command maintains groups of files combined into a single archive file. It is used to create and update library files as used by the link editor [see LD(SD_CMD)]. It can be used, however, for any similar purpose. If an archive file is created from printable files, the entire archive file is printable.

Archives of text files created by `ar` are portable between implementations of UNIX System V.

When `ar` creates an archive file, it creates administrative information in a format that is portable across all machines. When there is at least one object file (that `ar` recognizes as such) in the archive, an archive symbol table is created in the archive file and maintained by `ar`. The archive symbol table is never mentioned or accessible to the user. (It is used by the link editor to search the archive file.) Whenever the `ar` command is used to create or update the contents of such an archive, the symbol table is rebuilt. The `s` modifier character described below forces the symbol table to be rebuilt.

The *option* is a – followed by one character from the set `drqtpmx` which may be optionally concatenated with one or more characters to modify the action. These modifier characters are taken from the set `vuabicls` but not all modifiers make sense with all options. See below for further explanation. The argument *posname* is the name of a file in the archive file, used for relative positioning; see options `-r` and `-m` below. The argument *afile* is the archive file. The *names* are constituent files in the archive file.

The meanings of the *option* characters are:

`-d` Delete the named files from the archive file. Valid modifiers are `vl`.

`-r` Replace the named files in the archive file. Valid modifiers are `vuabicl`. If the modifier `u` is used, then only those files with dates of modification later than the archive files are replaced. If an optional positioning character from the set `abi` is used, then the *posname* argument must be present, and specifies that new files are to be placed after (`a`) or before (`b` or `i`) *posname*. Otherwise new files are placed at the end.

`-q` Quickly append the named files to the end of the archive file. Valid modifiers are `vcl`. In this case `ar` does not check whether the added members are already in the archive. This is useful to bypass the searching otherwise done, when creating a large archive piece-by-piece.

`-t` Print a table of contents of the archive file. If no names are given, all files in the archive are listed. If names are given, only those files are listed. Valid modifiers are `vs`. The `v` modifier gives a long listing of all information about the files.

`-p` Print the named files from the archive. Valid modifiers are `vs`.

`-m` Move the named files to the end of the archive. Valid modifiers are `vabil`. If a positioning modifier from the set `abi` is present, then the *posname* argument must be present, and, as with the option character `r`, it specifies where the files are to be moved.

`-x` Extract the named files. If no names are given, all files in the archive are extracted. The archive file is not changed. Valid modifiers are `vs`.

The meanings of the modifier characters are:

`v` Give verbose output. When used with the option characters `d`, `r`, `q`, or `m`, this gives a verbose file-by-file description of the making of a new archive file from the old archive (if one exists) and the constituent files. When used with `x`, this precedes each file with its name.

`c` Suppress the message that is produced by default when the archive file `afile` is created.

`l` Place temporary files in the local current working directory, rather than in the directory specified by the environment variable `TMPDIR` or in the default directory.

`s` Force the regeneration of the archive symbol table even if `ar` is not invoked with a command which will modify the archive file contents. This command is useful to restore the archive symbol table after it has been stripped [see STRIP(SD_CMD)].

SEE ALSO

LD(SD_CMD), STRIP(SD_CMD).

USAGE

General.

NAME

awk — pattern-directed scanning and processing language

SYNOPSIS

`awk` [`-F`*c*] [`-f` *progfile*] [`'`*program*`'`] [*parameters*] [*file* ...]

DESCRIPTION

The `awk` command executes programs written in the awk programming language, which is specialized for data manipulation. An `awk` program is a sequence of patterns and corresponding actions. When input is read that matches a pattern, the action associated with that pattern is carried out.

The *file* arguments contain the input to be read. If no files are given or the filename `-` is given, the standard input is used.

Each line of input is matched in turn against the set of patterns in the program. The `awk` program may either be in a file *progfile* or may be specified in the command line as a string enclosed in single quotes.

Each line of input is matched in turn against each pattern in the program. For each pattern matched, the associated action is executed.

The command `awk` interprets each input line as a sequence of fields where, by default, a field is a string of non-blank, non-tab characters. This default whitespace field delimiter can be changed by using the `-F`*c* option, or the variable `FS`; see below. The command `awk` denotes the first field in a line `$1`, the second `$2`, and so forth; `$0` refers to the entire line. Setting any other field causes the re-evaluation of `$0`.

Pattern-action statements in an `awk` program have the form:

pattern { *action* }

In any pattern-action statement, either the pattern or the action may be omitted. A missing action means print the input line to the standard output; a missing pattern is always matched, and its associated action is executed for every input line read.

Patterns

Patterns are *special patterns* or arbitrary Boolean combinations (`!`, `||`, `&&` and parentheses) of regular-expressions and relational expressions. The operator `!` has the highest precedence, then `&&` and then `||`. Evaluation is left to right and stops when truth or falsehood has been determined.

Boolean Operator	*Meaning*
`!`	negation
`&&`	and
`||`	or

Special Patterns

The awk command recognizes two special patterns, BEGIN and END. BEGIN is matched once and its associated action executed before the first line of input is read. END is matched once and its associated action executed after the last line of input has been read. (See examples 4 and 5). These two patterns must have associated actions.

Relational Expressions

A pattern may be any expression that compares strings of characters or numbers. A relational expression is either an

expression relational-operator expression

or an

expression matching-operator regular-expression

The six relational operators are listed below; regular-expression matching operators are described later. If both operands are numeric, a numeric comparison is made, otherwise, a string comparison is made.

Relational Operator	*Meaning*
<	less than
<=	less than or equal to
>	greater than
>=	greater than or equal to
!=	not equal to
==	equal to

Regular Expressions

A regular-expression must be surrounded by slashes. If *re* is a regular-expression, then the pattern

/re/

matches any line of input that contains a substring specified by the regular-expression. A regular-expression comparison may be limited to a specific field by one of the two regular-expression matching operators: ~ and !~.

$4 ~ */re/*

matches any line whose 4th field matches the regular-expression */re/*.

$4 !~ */re/*

matches any line whose 4th field *fails* to match the regular-expression */re/*.

Regular-expressions recognized by awk are those recognized by the ed [see ED(BU_CMD)] except for \(and \) and the addition of the special characters +, ?, |, and ( ). The meaning of a special character can be turned off by preceding the character with a \. The special characters *, + and ? have the highest precedence, then concatenation, then alternation; all are left-associative.

Regular-expressions recognized by `awk` are listed below:

Regular Expression	*Pattern Matched*
c	the character *c* where *c* is not a special character.
c	the character *c* where *c* is any character.
^	the beginning of the string being compared.
$	the end of the string being compared.
.	any character in the input but newline.
[*s*]	any character in the set *s* where *s* is a sequence of characters and/or a range of characters, *c*-*c*.
[^*s*]	any character not in the set *s*, where *s* is defined as above.
*r**	zero or more successive occurrences of regular-expression *r*.
r+	one or more successive occurrences of regular-expression *r*.
r?	zero or one occurrence of regular-expression *r*.
(*r*)	the regular-expression *r*. (Grouping)
rx	the occurrence of regular-expression *r* followed by the occurrence of regular-expression *x*. (Concatenation)
r¦*x*	the occurrence of regular-expression *r* or the occurrence of regular-expression *x*.

Pattern Ranges

A pattern may consist of two patterns separated by a comma; in this case, the action is performed for all lines between an occurrence of the first pattern and the following occurrence of the second pattern.

Variables and Special Variables

Variables may be used in an `awk` program by assigning to them. They do not need to be declared. Like *field* variables, all variables are treated as string variable unless used in a clearly numeric context (see **Relational Expressions**). Field variables are designated by a `$` followed by a number or numerical expression. New field variables may be created by assigning a value to them. Other special variables set by `awk` are listed below:

Special Variable	*Meaning*
$*n*	The string read as field *n*.
FS	Input field separator. Set to whitespace by default.
FILENAME	Name of the current input file.
NF	Number of fields in the current record.
NR	Ordinal number of the current record from start of input.
OFMT	The `print` statement output format for numbers. `%.6g` by default.
OFS	The `print` statement output field separation. One blank by default.
ORS	The `print` statement output record separator. Newline by default.

Actions

An action is a sequence of statements. A statement can be one of the following. Square brackets indicate optional elements. Keywords are shown in constant-width font.

```
if ( expression ) statement [ else statement ]
while ( expression ) statement
for ( expression ; expression ; expression ) statement
break
continue
{ [ statement ] ... }
variable = expression
print [ expression-list ] [ >expression ]
printf format [ , expression-list ] [ >expression ]
next
exit ( expression )
```

Any single statement may be replaced by a statement list enclosed in curly braces. The statements in a statement list are separated by newlines or semicolons. The character # anywhere in a program line begins a comment, with is terminated by the end of the line.

Statements are terminated by semicolons, newlines, or right braces. A long statement may be split across several lines by ending each partial line with a `\`. An empty expression-list stands for the whole input line. Expressions take on string or numeric values as appropriate, and are built using the operators + (addition), - (subtraction), * (multiplication), / (division), % (modulus operator), and concatenation (indicated by a blank between strings in an expression). The C language operators `++`, `--`, `+=`, `-=`, `*=`, `/=` and `%=` are also available in expressions. Variables may be scalars, array elements (denoted `x[i]`) or fields. Variables are initialized to the null-string. Array subscripts may be any string, not necessarily numeric.

String constants are surrounded by double quotes ("..."). A string expression is created by concatenating constants, variables, field names, array elements, functions and other expressions.

The *expression* acting as the conditional in an `if` statement can include the relational operators, the regular-expression matching operators, logical operators, juxtaposition for concatenation and parentheses for grouping. The *expression* is evaluated and if it is non-zero and non-null, *statement* is executed, otherwise if `else` is present, the statement following the `else` is executed. The `while`, `for`, `break` and `continue` statements are as in the C language.

The `print` statement prints its arguments on the standard output (or on a file if >*expression* is present), separated by the current output field separator (see variable `OFS` below), and terminated by the output record separator (see variable `ORS` below). The `printf` statement formats its expression list according to *format* [see PRINTF(BA_LIB)].

The `next` statement causes the next input line to be scanned, skipping the remaining characters on the current input line. The `exit` statement causes the termination of the `awk` program, skipping the rest of the input.

The built-in function `length(s)` returns the length of its arguments taken as a string, or of the whole line, `$0`, if there is no argument. There are also built-in functions `exp(x)` (the exponential function of `x`), `log(x)` (natural logarithm of `x`), `sqrt(x)` (square root of `x`), and `int(x)` (truncates its argument to an integer). The call `substr(s, p, n)` returns the at most `n`-character substring of `s` that begins at position `p`.

The function `sprintf(fmt, expr, expr ...)` formats the expressions according to the PRINTF(BA_LIB) format given by `fmt` and returns the resulting string.

EXAMPLES

The following are examples of simple `awk` programs:

Print on the standard output all input lines for which field 3 is greater than 5.

```
$3 > 5
```

Print every 10th line.

```
(NR % 10) == 0
```

Print any line with a substring matching the regular-expression.

```
/(G|D)(2[0-9][a-zA Z]*)/
```

Print the second to the last and the last field in each line. Separate the fields by a colon.

```
{OFS=":";print $(NF-1), $NF}
```

Print the line number and number of fields in each line. The three strings representing the line number, the colon and the number of fields are concatenated and that string is printed.

```
BEGIN {line = 0}
    {line = line + 1
    print line ":" NF}
```

Print lines longer than 72 characters.

```
length > 72
```

Print first two fields in opposite order separated by the `OFS`.

```
{ print $2, $1 }
```

Add up first column, print sum and average.

```
{s += $1 }
END  {print "sum is ", s, " average is", s/NR}
```

Print fields in reverse order:

```
{ for (i = NF; i > 0; --i) print $i }
```

Print all lines between occurrences of the strings `start` and `stop`:

```
/start/, /stop/
```

Print all lines whose first field is different from the previous one:

```
$1 != prev { print; prev = $1 }
```

Print file, filling in page number starting at 5:

```
/Page/ { $2 = n++; }
    { print }
```

command line:

```
awk -f program n=5 input
```

USAGE

General.

There are no explicit conversions between numbers and strings. To force an expression to be treated as a number add 0 to it; to force it to be treated as a string concatenate the null string (`""`) to it.

NAME

banner — make large letters

SYNOPSIS

`banner` *strings*

DESCRIPTION

The command `banner` prints each argument in large letters (across the page) on the standard output, putting each argument on a separate "line". Spaces can be included in an argument by surrounding it with quotes. The maximum number of characters that can be accomodated in a line is implementation dependent; excess characters are simply ignored.

SEE ALSO

ECHO(BU_CMD)

USAGE

General.

NAME

basename, dirname — deliver portions of path names

SYNOPSIS

`basename` *string* [*suffix*]
`dirname` *string*

DESCRIPTION

The command `basename` deletes any prefix ending in / and the *suffix* (if present in *string*) from *string*, and prints the result on the standard output. It is normally used inside substitution marks (``) within command procedures.

The command `dirname` delivers all but the last level of the path name in *string*.

EXAMPLES

The following example moves the named file to a file named `xyz` in the current directory:

```
mv abc `basename /p/q/xyz.c '.c'`
```

The following example will set the variable `NAME` to `/usr/src/cmd`:

```
NAME=`dirname /usr/src/cmd/xyz.c`
```

SEE ALSO

SH(BU_CMD)

USAGE

General.

NAME

cal — print calendar

SYNOPSIS

`cal` [[*month*] *year*]

DESCRIPTION

The `cal` command prints a calendar for the specified year. If a month is also specified, a calendar just for that month is printed. If neither is specified, a calendar for the present month is printed. The argument *year* can be between 1 and 9999. (Note that "`cal` 83" refers to 83 A.D., not 1983.) The *month* is a number between 1 and 12.

USAGE

End-user.

NAME

calendar — reminder service

SYNOPSIS

`calendar`

DESCRIPTION

The command `calendar` consults the file `calendar` in the current directory and prints out lines that contain today's or tomorrow's date anywhere in the line. Month-day date formats such as "Aug. 24," "august 24," "8/24," are recognized. On weekends, "tomorrow" extends through Monday.

USAGE

End-user.

NAME

cat — concatenate and print files

SYNOPSIS

`cat [ -s ]` *file* . . .

DESCRIPTION

The command `cat` reads each *file* in sequence and writes it on the standard output. Thus:

`cat` *file*

prints the file, and:

`cat` *file1 file2* >*file3*

concatenates the first two files and places the result in the third.

If no input file is given, or if the argument — is encountered, `cat` reads from the standard input file. The `-s` option makes `cat` silent about non-existent files.

USAGE

General.

Command formats such as

`cat` *file1 file2* >*file1*

will cause the original data in *file1* to be lost.

NAME

cd — change working directory

SYNOPSIS

`cd` [*directory*]

DESCRIPTION

If *directory* is not specified, the value of the environmental variable `HOME` is used as the new working directory. If *directory* specifies a complete path starting with /, ., or .., *directory* becomes the new working directory. If neither case applies, `cd` tries to find the designated directory relative to one of the paths specified by the `CDPATH` environmental variable. `CDPATH` has the same syntax as, and similar semantics to, the `PATH` variable [see SH(BU_CMD)]. The command `cd` must have execute (search) permission in *directory*.

SEE ALSO

PWD(BU_CMD), SH(BU_CMD), CHDIR(BA_SYS)

USAGE

General.

NAME

chmod — change mode

SYNOPSIS

`chmod` *mode files*

DESCRIPTION

The permissions of the named *files* are changed according to *mode*, which may be absolute or symbolic.

An *absolute-mode* is a four octal-digit number constructed from the logical *OR* (sum) of the following modes:

4000	set user-ID on execution
2000	set group-ID on execution
1000	Reserved
0400	read by owner
0200	write by owner
0100	execute (search in directory) by owner
0040	read by group
0020	write by group
0010	execute (search) by group
0004	read by others
0002	write by others
0001	execute (search) by others

A *symbolic-mode* has the form:

[*who*] *op permission* [*op permission*]

The *who* part is a combination of the letters `u` (user), `g` (group) and `o` (other). The letter `a` stands for `ugo`, the default if *who* is omitted.

The argument *op* can be `+` to add permission to the file-mode, `-` to take away permission, or `=` to assign permission absolutely (all other bits will be reset).

The argument *permission* is any combination of the letters `r` (read), `w` (write), `x` (execute), and `s` (set owner or group-ID); `u`, `g`, or `o` indicate that permission is to be taken from the current mode. Omitting *permission* is only useful with `=` to take away all permissions.

Multiple symbolic-modes separated by commas may be given. Operations are performed in the order specified. The letter `s` is only useful with `u` or `g`.

Only the owner of a file (or the super-user) may change its mode. In order to set set-group-ID, the group of the file must correspond to the user's current group-ID.

EXAMPLES

The first example denies write permission to others, the second makes a file executable:

```
chmod o-w file

chmod +x file
```

SEE ALSO

LS(BU_CMD), CHMOD(BA_SYS).

USAGE

General.

CAVEATS

The command `chmod` will be used to specify mandatory locking (enable/disable) on a file. This will be done as follows:

> An absolute mode of `20#0` specifies *set-group-ID* if # is `1`, `3`, `5`, or `7`; specifies *enable mandatory locking* if # is `0`, `2`, `4`, or `6`.
>
> A symbolic-mode of `l` specifies mandatory locking, `+` to enable, `-` to disable.

It will not be possible to have set-group-ID set and mandatory locking enabled on a file simultaneously.

NAME

cmp — compare two files

SYNOPSIS

`cmp [ -l ] [ -s ]` *file1 file2*

DESCRIPTION

The command `cmp` compares two files. (If *file1* is −, the standard input is used.) Under default options, `cmp` makes no comment if the files are the same; if they differ, it announces the byte and line number at which the difference occurred. If one file is identical to the first part of the other, then it is reported that end-of-file was reached in the shorter file (before any differences were found).

Options:

`-l` Print the byte number (decimal) and the differing bytes (octal) for each difference.

`-s` Print nothing for differing files; return codes only.

ERRORS

Exit code 0 is returned for identical files, 1 for different files, and 2 for an inaccessible or missing argument.

SEE ALSO

COMM(BU_CMD), DIFF(BU_CMD)

USAGE

General.

NAME

col — filter reverse line-feeds

SYNOPSIS

`col [ -bfpx ]`

DESCRIPTION

The command `col` reads from the standard input and writes onto the standard output. It performs the line overlays implied by reverse line feeds, and by forward and reverse half-line feeds.

If the `-b` option is given, `col` assumes that the output device in use is not capable of backspacing. In this case, if two or more characters are to appear in the same place, only the last one read will be output.

Although `col` accepts half-line motions in its input, it normally does not emit them on output. Instead, text that would appear between lines is moved to the next lower full-line boundary. This treatment can be suppressed by the `-f` (fine) option; in this case, the output from `col` may contain forward half-line feeds, but will still never contain either kind of reverse line motion.

Unless the `-x` option is given, `col` will convert white space to tabs on output wherever possible to shorten printing time.

The **ASCII** control characters **SO** and **SI** are assumed by `col` to start and end text in an alternate character set. The character set to which each input character belongs is remembered, and on output **SI** and **SO** characters are generated as appropriate to ensure that each character is printed in the correct character set.

On input, the only control characters accepted are space, backspace, tab, return, newline, **SI**, **SO**, **VT**, reverse line feed, forward half-line feed, and reverse half-line feed. The **VT** character is an alternate form of full reverse line-feed, included for compatibility with some earlier programs of this type. All other non-printing characters are ignored.

The **ASCII** codes for the control functions and line-motion sequences mentioned above are as given in the table below. ESC stands for the ASCII "escape" character, with the octal code 033; ESC-*x* means a sequence of two characters, ESC followed by the character *x*.

reverse line feed	ESC-7
reverse half-line feed	ESC-8
forward half-line feed	ESC-9
vertical tab (VT)	013
start-of-text (SO)	016
end-of-text (SI)	017

Normally, `col` will remove any escape sequences found in its input that are unknown to it; the `-p` option may be used to force these to be passed through unchanged. The use of this option is discouraged unless the user is aware of the consequences.

USAGE

General.

Local vertical motions that would result in backing up over the first line of the document are ignored. As a result, the first line must not have any superscripts.

NAME

comm — select or reject lines common to two sorted files

SYNOPSIS

`comm [ -[ 123] ]` *file1 file2*

DESCRIPTION

The command `comm` reads *file1* and *file2,* which should be ordered in **ASCII** collating sequence [see SORT(BU_CMD)], and produces a three-column output: lines only in *file1;* lines only in *file2;* and lines in both files. The file name − means the standard input.

Flags 1, 2, or 3 suppress printing of the corresponding column. Thus `comm -12` prints only the lines common to the two files; `comm -23` prints only lines in the first file but not in the second; `comm -123` is a no-op.

SEE ALSO

CMP(BU_CMD), DIFF(BU_CMD), SORT(BU_CMD), UNIQ(BU_CMD).

USAGE

General.

NAME

cp, ln, mv — copy, link or move files

SYNOPSIS

`cp` *file1* [*file2* ...] *target*
`ln` [`-f`] *file1* [*file2* ...] *target*
`mv` [`-f`] *file1* [*file2* ...] *target*

DESCRIPTION

These commands respectively copy, link, or move files; *file1* and *target* may not be the same. If *target* is not a directory, then only one file may be specified before it; if *target* is an existing file, its contents are destroyed, otherwise (*target* is neither an existing file nor a directory) the file *target* is created. If *target* is a directory, then more than one file may be specified before it; the specified files are respectively copied, linked, or moved to that directory.

cp

If *target* is not a directory, `cp` copies *file1* to *target*. If *target* exists, its contents are overwritten, but the mode, owner, and group are not changed. If *target* is a link to a file, all links remain (the file is changed).

If *target* is a directory, then the specified files are copied to that directory. For each file named, a new file, with the same mode, is created in the target directory; the owner and the group are those of the user making the copy.

ln

If *target* is not a directory, `ln` links *file1* to *target*, that is, the name *target* is linked to the file *file1*. If *target* exists, and its mode forbids writing, the mode is printed, and the user asked for a response; if the response begins with a `y`, (and the user is permitted) then the `ln` occurs. No questions are asked and the `ln` is done where permitted when the `-f` option is used or if the standard input is not a terminal.

If *target* is a directory, then the specified files are linked to that directory. That is, files with the same names are created in the directory, linked to the specified files.

mv

If *target* is not a directory, `mv` moves (renames) *file1* as directed. If *target* does not exist, and has the same parent as *file1*, *file1* may be a directory: this allows a directory rename.

If *target* is a directory, then the specified files are moved to that directory.

If *file1* is a file and *target* is a link to another file with links, the other links remain and *target* becomes a new file.

If *target* is a file, and its mode forbids writing, the mode is printed, and the user asked for a response; if the response begins with a `y`, (and the user is permitted) then the `mv` occurs. No questions are asked and the `mv` is done where permitted when the `-f` option is used or if the standard input is not a terminal.

SEE ALSO

CPIO(BU_CMD), RM(BU_CMD), CHMOD(BU_CMD).

USAGE

General.

If *file1* and *target* lie on different file systems, `mv` may achieve the move by copying the file and deleting the original. In this case any linking relationship with other files is lost.

`ln` will not link across file systems.

NAME

cpio — copy file archives in and out

SYNOPSIS

`cpio -o[acBv]`

`cpio -i[Bcdmrtuvf]` [*patterns*]

`cpio -p[adlmruv]` *directory*

DESCRIPTION

The command `cpio -o` (copy out) reads the standard input to obtain a list of path names and copies those files onto the standard output together with path name and status information. Output is padded to a 512-byte boundary.

The command `cpio -i` (copy in) extracts files from the standard input, which is assumed to be the product of a previous `cpio -o`. Only files with names that match *patterns* are selected. The arguments *patterns* are simple regular expressions given in the name-generating notation of the shell [see SH(BU_CMD)]. In *patterns*, meta-characters ?, *, and [...] match the / character. Multiple *patterns* may be specified and if no *patterns* are specified, the default for *patterns* is * (i.e., select all files). The extracted files are conditionally created and copied into the current directory tree based upon the options described below. The permissions of the files will be those of the previous `cpio -o`. The owner and group of the files will be that of the current user unless the user is super-user, which causes `cpio` to retain the owner and group of the files of the previous `cpio -o`.

The command `cpio -p` (pass) reads the standard input to obtain a list of path names of files that are conditionally created and copied into the destination *directory* tree based upon the options described below.

Archives of text files created by `cpio` are portable between implementations of UNIX System V.

The meanings of the available options are:

- `a` Reset access times of input files after they have been copied. [When option `-l` (see below) is also specified, the linked files do not have their access times reset.]
- `B` Input/output is to be blocked 5120 bytes to the record (does not apply to the `pass` option; meaningful only with data directed to or from character special files).
- `d` Directories are to be created as needed.
- `c` Write header information in ASCII character form for portability.
- `r` Interactively rename files. If the user types a null line, the file is skipped.
- `t` Print a table of contents of the input. No files are created.
- `u` Copy unconditionally (normally, an older file will not replace a newer file with the same name).
- `v` Verbose: causes the names of the affected files to be printed. With the `t` option, provides a detailed listing.

- `l` Whenever possible, link files rather than copying them. Usable only with the `-p` option.
- `m` Retain previous file modification time. This option is ineffective on directories that are being copied.
- `f` Copy in all files except those in *patterns*.

EXAMPLES

The first example below copies the contents of a directory into an archive; the second duplicates a directory hierarchy:

```
ls | cpio -oc >/dev/mt/0m
```

```
cd olddir
find . -depth -print | cpio -pdl newdir
```

SEE ALSO

AR(BU_CMD), FIND(BU_CMD), LS(BU_CMD), TAR(AU_CMD).

USAGE

General.

Only the super-user can copy special files.

NAME

cut — cut out selected fields of each line of a file

SYNOPSIS

`cut -c`*list*[*file1 file2* `...`]
`cut -f`*list* [`-d`*char*] [`-s`] [*file1 file2* `...`]

DESCRIPTION

The command `cut` cuts out columns from a table or fields from each line of a file. The fields specified by *list* can be of fixed length, specified by character position (`-c` option), or the length can vary and be marked with a field delimiter character like `tab` (`-f` option). The command `cut` can be used as a filter; if no files are given, the standard input is used. The option qualifier *list* (see options `-c` and `-f` below) is a comma-separated list of integers (in increasing order), with optional `-` to indicate ranges; e.g., `1,4,7;` `1-3,8;` `-5,10` (short for `1-5,10`); or `3-` (short for third through last).

The meanings of the options are:

`-c`*list* The *list* following `-c` (no space) specifies character positions (e.g., `-c1-72` would pass the first 72 characters of each line).

`-f`*list* The *list* following `-f` lists fields assumed to be separated in the file by a delimiter character (`-d`); e.g., `-f1,7` copies the first and seventh field only. Lines with no field delimiters remain intact (useful for table subheadings), unless `-s` is specified.

`-d`*char* The character following `-d` is the field delimiter (used with the `-f` option only). Default is the tab character. Space or other characters with special meaning to the command interpreter must be quoted.

`-s` Suppresses lines with no delimiter characters when used with the `-f` option. Unless specified, lines with no delimiters will be passed through untouched.

Either the `-c` or the `-f` option must be specified.

EXAMPLES

The following maps user IDs to names:

```
cut -d: -f1,5 /etc/passwd
```

SEE ALSO

GREP(BU_CMD), PASTE(BU_CMD), SH(BU_CMD).

USAGE

General.

Use `grep` to make horizontal "cuts" (by context) through a file, or `paste` to put files together column-wise (i.e., horizontally). To reorder columns in a table, use `cut` and `paste`.

NAME

date — print or set the date

SYNOPSIS

`date` *mmddhhmm* [*yy*]

`date` [+*format*]

DESCRIPTION

The first form of `date` sets the current date and time; it is usable only by the super-user. The first *mm* is the month (number); *dd* is the day (number) of the month; *hh* is the hour (number, 24-hour system); the second *mm* is the minute (number); *yy* is the last 2 digits of the year and is optional. For example:

```
date 10080045
```

sets the date to Oct 8, 12:45 AM. The current year is the default if no year is given. The system operates in GMT; `date` takes care of the conversion to and from local standard and daylight time. (The environment variable `TZ` specifies the local time-zone; therefore its value affects the conversion between the internal GMT clock and the local time.)

In the second form, if no argument is given, the current date and time are printed. (As above, the environment variable `TZ` specifies the local time-zone, and therefore its value affects the output.) If an argument beginning with `+` is given, the output of `date` is under the control of the user. The format for the output is similar to that of the first argument to the `printf` routine [see PRINTF(BA_LIB)]. All output fields are of fixed size (zero padded if necessary). Each field descriptor is preceded by `%` and will be replaced in the output by its corresponding value. A single `%` is encoded by `%%`. All other characters are copied to the output without change. The string is always terminated with a newline character.

Field Descriptors:

`n`	insert a newline character
`t`	insert a tab character
`m`	month of year — 01 to 12
`d`	day of month — 01 to 31
`y`	last 2 digits of year — 00 to 99
`D`	date as mm/dd/yy
`H`	hour — 00 to 23
`M`	minute — 00 to 59
`S`	second — 00 to 59
`T`	time as *HH*:*MM*:*SS*
`j`	day of year — 001 to 366
`w`	day of week — Sunday = 0
`a`	abbreviated weekday — Sun to Sat
`h`	abbreviated month — Jan to Dec
`r`	time in AM/PM notation

EXAMPLE

```
date '+DATE: %m/%d/%y%nTIME: %H:%M:%S'
```

generates the output:

```
DATE: 08/01/76
TIME: 14:45:05
```

SEE ALSO

PRINTF(BA_LIB).

USAGE

General.

It is a bad practice to change the date while the system is running multi-user.

NAME

df — report free disk space

SYNOPSIS

`df [ -t ] [` *file-system* `... ]`

DESCRIPTION

The command `df` prints out the free space (in 512-byte units) and the number of free file slots ("inodes") available for on-line file systems. The argument *file-system* may be specified either by device name (e.g., `/dev/dsk/0s1`) or by mounted directory name (e.g., `/usr`). If no *file-system* is specified, the free space on all of the mounted file systems is printed.

The `-t` option causes the total allocated space figures to be reported as well.

USAGE

General.

NAME

diff — differential file comparator

SYNOPSIS

`diff` [`-efbh`] *file1 file2*

DESCRIPTION

The command `diff` tells what lines must be changed in two files to bring them into agreement. If *file1* (*file2*) is `-`, the standard input is used. If *file1* (*file2*) is a directory, then a file in that directory with the name *file2* (*file1*) is used. The normal output contains lines of these forms:

```
n1 a n3,n4

n1,n2 d n3

n1,n2 c n3,n4
```

These lines resemble `ed` commands to convert *file1* into *file2*. The numbers after the letters pertain to *file2*. In fact, by exchanging **a** for **d** and reading backward one may ascertain equally how to convert *file2* into *file1*. As in `ed`, identical pairs, where `n1 = n2` or `n3 = n4`, are abbreviated as a single number.

Following each of these lines come all the lines that are affected in the first file flagged by <, then all the lines that are affected in the second file flagged by >.

The `-b` option causes trailing blanks (spaces and tabs) to be ignored and other strings of blanks to compare equal.

The `-e` option produces a script of **a**, **c**, and **d** commands for the editor `ed`, which will recreate *file2* from *file1*.

The `-f` option produces a similar script, not useful with `ed`, in the opposite order.

Option `-h` does a fast, half-hearted job. It works only when changed stretches are short and well separated, but does work on files of unlimited length.

Options `-e` and `-f` are unavailable with the `-h` option.

SEE ALSO

CMP(BU_CMD), COMM(BU_CMD), ED(BU_CMD).

ERRORS

Exit status is:

0 no differences

1 some differences

2 errors

USAGE

General.

Editing scripts produced under the `-e` or `-f` option may be incorrect when dealing with lines consisting of a single period.

NAME

du — estimate file space usage

SYNOPSIS

du [-ars] [*file* ...]

DESCRIPTION

The command du gives an estimate, in 512-byte units, of the file space contained in all the specified files. Whenever a directory is named, all files within it are reported; sub-directories are traversed recursively. If no file is specified, the current directory is used.

The option −s causes only the grand total (for each of the specified files) to be given. The option −a causes a report to be generated for each file. With no options, a report is given for each directory only.

du is normally silent about directories that cannot be read, files that cannot be opened, etc. The −r option will cause du to generate messages in such instances.

A file with two or more links is only counted once.

USAGE

General.

If the −a option is not used, non-directories given as arguments are not listed.

Files with holes in them may get an incorrect (high) estimate.

NAME

echo — echo arguments

SYNOPSIS

`echo` [*arg*] ...

DESCRIPTION

The command `echo` writes its arguments separated by blanks and terminated by a newline on the standard output. It also understands the following escape conventions.

`\b`	backspace
`\c`	print arguments up to this point, without newline; ignore remainder of command line
`\f`	form-feed
`\n`	newline
`\r`	carriage return
`\t`	tab
`\v`	vertical tab
`\\`	backslash
`\0`*n*	*n* must be a 1-, 2- or 3-digit octal number; specifies the corresponding **ASCII** character

SEE ALSO

SH(BU_CMD).

USAGE

General.

The command `echo` is useful for producing diagnostics in command scripts and for sending known data into a pipe.

Arguments containing blanks and escape sequences must be enclosed in double quotes.

NAME

ed, red — text editor

SYNOPSIS

`ed` [`-`] [`-p` *string*] [*file*]

`red` [`-`] [`-p` *string*] [*file*]

DESCRIPTION

The command `ed` is a text editor. If the *file* argument is given, `ed` simulates an `e` command (see below) on the named file; that is to say, the file is read into the `ed` buffer so that it can be edited.

The option `-` suppresses the printing of character counts by `e`, `r`, and `w` commands, of diagnostics from `e` and `q` commands, and of the `!` prompt after a `!`*command.*

The `-p` option allows the user to specify a prompt string. (This option is new in UNIX System V Release 2.0.)

`ed` operates on a copy of the file it is editing; changes made to the copy have no effect on the file until a `w` (write) command is given. The copy of the text being edited resides in a temporary file called the *buffer.* There is only one buffer.

The command `red` is a restricted version of `ed`. It will only allow editing of files in the current directory, and prohibits executing commands via `!`*command.* Attempts to bypass these restrictions result in an error message.

Commands to `ed` have a simple and regular structure: zero, one, or two *addresses* followed by a single-character *command*, possibly followed by parameters to that command. These addresses specify one or more lines in the buffer. Every command that requires addresses has default addresses, so that the addresses can very often be omitted.

In general, only one command may appear on a line. Certain commands allow the input of text. This text is placed in the appropriate place in the buffer. While `ed` is accepting text, it is said to be in *input mode*. In this mode, no commands are recognized; all input is merely collected. Input mode is left by typing a period (`.`) alone at the beginning of a line.

`ed` supports a limited form of *regular-expression* notation; regular expressions are used in addresses to specify lines and in some commands (e.g., *s*) to specify portions of a line that are to be substituted. A regular-expression (*RE*) specifies a set of character strings. A member of this set of strings is said to be **matched** by the *RE*. The *RE*s allowed by `ed` are constructed as follows:

The following *one-character-RE*s match a *single* character:

1.1 An ordinary character (**not** one of those discussed in 1.2 below) is a *one-character-RE* that matches itself.

1.2 A backslash (`\`) followed by any special character is a *one-character-RE* that matches the special character itself. The special characters are:

a. ., *, [, and \ (period, asterisk, left square bracket, and backslash, respectively), which are always special, *except* within square brackets ([ ]; see 1.4 below).

b. ^ (caret or circumflex), which is special at the *beginning* of an *entire-RE* (see 3.1 and 3.2 below) or immediately after the open square bracket of a pair ([ ]; see 1.4 below).

c. $ (currency symbol), which is special at the *end* of an *entire-RE* (see 3.2 below).

d. The character used to bound (i.e., delimit) an *entire-RE*, which is special for that *RE* (for example, see how slash (/) is used in the g command, below).

1.3 A period (.) is a *one-character-RE* that matches any character except newline.

1.4 A non-empty string of characters enclosed in square brackets ([ ]) is a *one-character-RE* that matches **any one** character in that string. If, however, the first character of the string is a caret (^), the *one-character-RE* matches any character **except** newline and the remaining characters in the string. The ^ has this special meaning **only** if it occurs first in the string. The minus (-) may be used to indicate a range of consecutive **ASCII** characters; for example, [0-9] is equivalent to [0123456789]. The - loses this special meaning if it occurs first (after an initial ^, if any) or last in the string. The right square bracket ( ]) does not terminate such a string when it is the first character within it (after an initial ^, if any); e.g., [ ]a-f] matches either a right square bracket ( ]) or one of the letters a through f inclusive. The four characters listed in 1.2.a above stand for themselves within such a string of characters.

The following rules may be used to construct *RE*s from *one-character-RE*s:

2.1 A *one-character-RE* is a *RE* that matches whatever the *one-character-RE* matches.

2.2 A *one-character-RE* followed by an asterisk (*) is a *RE* that matches *zero* or more occurrences of the *one-character-RE*. If there is any choice, the longest leftmost string that permits a match is chosen.

2.3 A *one-character-RE* followed by \{*m*\}, \{*m*,\}, or \{*m*,*n*\} is a *RE* that matches a *range* of occurrences of the *one-character-RE*. The values of *m* and *n* must be non-negative integers less than 256; \{*m*\} matches **exactly** *m* occurrences; \{*m*,\} matches **at least** *m* occurrences; \{*m*,*n*\} matches **any number** of occurrences between *m* and *n* inclusive. Whenever a choice exists, the *RE* matches as many occurrences as possible.

2.4 The concatenation of *RE*s is a *RE* that matches the concatenation of the strings matched by each component of the *RE*.

2.5 A *RE* enclosed between the character sequences `\(` and `\)` is a *RE* that matches whatever the unadorned *RE* matches.

2.6 The expression `\n` matches the same string of characters as was matched by an expression enclosed between `\(` and `\)` *earlier* in the same *RE*. Here *n* is a digit; the sub-expression specified is that beginning with the *n*-th occurrence of `\(` counting from the left. For example, the expression `^\(.*\)\1$` matches a line consisting of two repeated appearances of the same string.

Finally, an *entire-RE* may be constrained to match only an initial segment or final segment of a line (or both).

3.1 A circumflex (`^`) at the beginning of an *entire-RE* constrains that *RE* to match an *initial* segment of a line.

3.2 A currency symbol (`$`) at the end of an *entire-RE* constrains that *RE* to match a *final* segment of a line.

The form `^`*entire-RE*`$` constrains the *entire-RE* to match the entire line.

The null *RE* (e.g., `//`) is equivalent to the last *RE* encountered.

To understand addressing in `ed` it is necessary to know that at any time there is a **current line**. Generally speaking, the current line is the last line affected by a command; the exact effect on the current line is discussed under the description of each command. Addresses are constructed as follows:

1. The character `.` addresses the current line.
2. The character `$` addresses the last line of the buffer.
3. A decimal number *n* addresses the *n*-th line of the buffer.
4. '*x* addresses the line marked with the mark name character *x*, which must be a lower-case letter. Lines are marked with the `k` command described below.
5. A *RE* enclosed by slashes (`/`) addresses the first line found by searching **forward** to the end of the buffer from the line after the current line and stopping at the first line with a string matching the *RE*. If necessary, the search wraps around to the beginning of the buffer and continues up to and including the current line, so that the entire buffer is searched.
6. A *RE* enclosed in question marks (`?`) addresses the first line found by searching **backward** to the beginning of the buffer from the line before the current line and stopping at the first line with a string matching the *RE*. If necessary, the search wraps around to the end of the buffer and continues up to and including the current line.
7. An address followed by a plus sign (`+`) or a minus sign (`-`) followed by a decimal number specifies that address plus (respectively minus) the indicated number of lines. The plus sign may be omitted.

8. If an address begins with `+` or `-`, the addition or subtraction is taken with respect to the current line; e.g, `-5` is understood to mean `.-5`.

9. If an address ends with `+` or `-`, then 1 is added to or subtracted from the address, respectively. As a consequence of this rule and of rule 8 immediately above, the address `-` refers to the line preceding the current line. Moreover, trailing `+` and `-` characters have a cumulative effect, so `--` refers to the current line less 2.

10. For convenience, a comma (`,`) stands for the address pair `1,$`, while a semicolon (`;`) stands for the pair `.,$`.

Commands may require zero, one, or two addresses. Commands that require no addresses regard the presence of an address as an error. Commands that accept one or two addresses assume default addresses when an insufficient number of addresses is given; if more addresses are given than such a command requires, the last one(s) are used.

Typically, addresses are separated from each other by a comma (`,`). They may also be separated by a semicolon (`;`). In the latter case, the current line (`.`) is set to the first address, and only then is the second address calculated. This feature can be used to determine the starting line for forward and backward searches (see rules 5. and 6. above). The second address of any two-address sequence must correspond to a line that follows, in the buffer, the line corresponding to the first address.

In the following list of `ed` commands, the default addresses are shown in parentheses. The parentheses are **not** part of the address; they show that the given addresses are the default.

It is generally illegal for more than one command to appear on a line. However, any command (except `e`, `f`, `r`, or `w`) may be suffixed by `l`, `n`, or `p` in which case the current line is either listed, numbered or printed, respectively, as discussed below under the `l`, `n`, and `p` commands.

[.]a
<text>
.

The append command reads the given text and appends it after the addressed line; the **current line** becomes the last inserted line, or, if there were none, the addressed line. Address 0 is legal for this command: it causes the "appended" text to be placed at the beginning of the buffer. The maximum number of characters that may be entered from a terminal is 256 per line (including the newline character).

[.]c
<text>
.

The change command deletes the addressed lines, then accepts input text that replaces these lines; `.` is left at the last line input, or, if there were none, at the first line that was not deleted.

[. , .]d
The delete command deletes the addressed lines from the buffer. The line after the last line deleted becomes the current line; if the lines deleted were originally at the end of the buffer, the new last line becomes the current line.

e *file*
The edit command causes the entire contents of the buffer to be deleted, and then the named *file* to be read in; . is set to the last line of the buffer. If no file-name is given, the currently-remembered file-name, if any, is used (see the f command). The number of characters read is typed; the name *file* is remembered for possible use as a default file-name in subsequent e, r, and w commands. If *file* is replaced by !, the rest of the line is taken to be a command whose output is to be read. Such a command is *not* remembered as the current file-name.

E *file*
The E (edit) command is like *e*, except that the editor does not check to see if any changes have been made to the buffer since the last w command.

f *file*
If *file* is given, the file-name command changes the currently-remembered file-name to *file*; otherwise, it prints the currently-remembered file-name.

[1 , $]g/*RE*/*command-list*
In the global command, the first step is to mark every line that matches the given *RE*. Then, for every such line, the given *command-list* is executed with . initially set to that line. A single command or the first of a list of commands appears on the same line as the global command. All lines of a multi-line list except the last line must be ended with a \; a, i, and c commands and associated input are permitted. The . terminating input mode may be omitted if it would be the last line of the *command-list*. An empty *command-list* is equivalent to the p command. The g, G, v, and V commands are **forbidden** in the *command-list*.

[1 , $]G/*RE*/
In the interactive global command, the first step is to mark every line that matches the given *RE*. Then, for every such line, that line is printed, . is changed to that line, and any **one** command (other than one of the a, c, i, g, G, v, and V commands) may be input and is executed. After the execution of that command, the next marked line is printed, and so on; a newline acts as a null command; an & causes the re-execution of the most recent command executed within the current invocation of G. Note that the commands input as part of the execution of the G command may address and affect **any** lines in the buffer. The G command can be terminated by an interrupt signal (**ASCII DEL** or **BREAK**).

`h`

The help command gives a short error message that explains the reason for the most recent `?` diagnostic.

`H`

The help command causes `ed` to enter a mode in which error messages are printed for all subsequent `?` diagnostics. It will also explain the previous `?` if there was one. The `H` command alternately turns this mode on and off; it is initially off.

`[.]i`
<text>
.

The insert command inserts the given text before the addressed line; `.` is left at the last inserted line, or, if there were none, at the addressed line. This command differs from the `a` command only in the placement of the input text. Address 0 is not legal for this command. The maximum number of characters that may be entered from a terminal is 256 per line (including the newline character).

`[.,.+1]j`

The join command joins contiguous lines by removing the appropriate newline characters. If exactly one address is given, this command does nothing.

`[.]k`*x*

The mark command marks the addressed line with name `x`, which must be a lower-case letter. The address `'x` then addresses this line; `.` is unchanged.

`[.,.]l`

The list command prints the addressed lines in an unambiguous way: a few non-printing characters (e.g., **tab, backspace**) are represented by (hopefully) mnemonic overstrikes. All other non-printing characters are printed in octal, and long lines are folded. An `l` command may be appended to any other command other than `e`, `f`, `r`, or `w`.

`[.,.]m`*a*

The move command repositions the addressed line(s) after the line addressed by *a*. Address 0 is legal for *a* and causes the addressed line(s) to be moved to the beginning of the file. It is an error if address *a* falls within the range of moved lines; `.` is left at the last line moved.

`[.,.]n`

The number command prints the addressed lines, preceding each line by its line number and a tab character; `.` is left at the last line printed. The `n` command may be appended to any other command other than `e`, `f`, `r`, or `w`.

[. , .]p
The print command prints the addressed lines; . is left at the last line printed. The p command may be appended to any other command other than e, f, r, or w. For example, dp deletes the current line and prints the new current line.

P
The editor will prompt with a * for all subsequent commands. The P command alternately turns this mode on and off; it is initially off.

q
The quit command causes ed to exit.

Q
The editor exits without checking if changes have been made in the buffer since the last w command.

[$]r *file*
The read command reads in the given file after the addressed line. If no file-name is given the currently-remembered file-name, if any, is used (see e and f commands). The currently-remembered file-name is **not** changed unless *file* is the very first file-name mentioned since ed was invoked. Address 0 is legal for r and causes the file to be read at the beginning of the buffer. If the read is successful, the number of characters read is typed; . is set to the last line read in. If *file* is replaced by !, the rest of the line is taken to be a command whose output is to be read. Such a command is **not** remembered as the current file-name.

[. , .]s/*RE*/*replacement*/ or
[. , .]s/*RE*/*replacement*/g or
[. , .]s/*RE*/*replacement*/*n* *n* = 1–512
The substitute command searches each addressed line for an occurrence of the specified *RE*. In each line in which a match is found, all (non-overlapped) matched strings are replaced by the *replacement* if the global replacement indicator g appears after the command. If the global indicator does not appear, only the first occurrence of the matched string is replaced. If a number *n* follows the command, only the *n*-th occurrence of the matched string on each addressed line is replaced. It is an error when the substitution fails on **all** addressed lines. Any character other than space or newline may be used instead of / to delimit *RE* and *replacement*; . is the last line on which a substitution occurred.

An ampersand (&) appearing in the *replacement* is replaced by the string matching the *RE* on the current line. The special meaning of & in this context may be suppressed by preceding it by \. As a more general feature, the characters *n*, where *n* is a digit, are replaced by the text matched by the *n*-th regular subexpression of the specified *RE* enclosed between \(and \). When nested parenthesized subexpressions are present, *n* is determined by counting occurrences of \(starting from the left. When the character % is the only character in the *replacement*, the *replacement* used in the most recent substitute command is used as the *replacement* in the current substitute command. The % loses its special meaning when it is in a replacement string of more than one character or is preceded by a \.

A line may be split by substituting a newline character into it. The newline in the *replacement* must be escaped by preceding it by \. Such substitution cannot be done as part of a g or v *command-list*.

[. , .]t*a*

This command acts just like the m command, except that a **copy** of the addressed lines is placed after address *a* (which may be 0); . is left at the last line of the copy.

u

The undo command nullifies the effect of the most recent command that modified anything in the buffer, namely the most recent a, c, d, g, i, j, m, r, s, t, v, G, or V command.

[1 , $]v/*RE*/*command-list*

This command is the same as the global command g except that the *command-list* is executed with . initially set to every line that does **not** match the *RE*.

[1 , $]V/*RE*/

This command is the same as the interactive global command G except that the lines that are marked during the first step are those that do **not** match the *RE*.

[1 , $]w *file*

The write command writes the addressed lines into the named file. The currently-remembered file-name is **not** changed unless *file* is the very first file-name mentioned since ed was invoked. If no file-name is given, the currently-remembered file-name, if any, is used (see e and f commands); . is unchanged. If the command is successful, the number of characters written is typed. If *file* is replaced by !, the rest of the line is taken to be a command whose standard input is the addressed lines. Such a command is **not** remembered as the current file-name.

[$]=

The line number of the addressed line is typed; . is unchanged by this command.

! *command*

The remainder of the line after the ! is sent to the command interpreter to be interpreted as a command. Within the text of that command, the unescaped character % is replaced with the remembered file-name; if a ! appears as the first character of the command, it is replaced with the text of the previous command. Thus, !! will repeat the last command. If any expansion is performed, the expanded line is echoed; . is unchanged.

[.+1]

An address alone on a line causes the addressed line to be printed. A newline alone is equivalent to .+1p; it is useful for stepping forward through the buffer.

If an interrupt signal (**BREAK**) is sent, ed prints a ? and returns to its command level.

If the closing delimiter of a *RE* or of a replacement string (e.g., /) would be the last character before a newline, that delimiter may be omitted, in which case the addressed line is printed. The following pairs of commands are equivalent:

```
s/s1/s2 s/s1/s2/p
g/s1 g/s1/p
?s1 ?s1?
```

If changes have been made in the buffer since the last w command that wrote the entire buffer, ed warns the user if an attempt is made to destroy the editor buffer via the e or q commands. It prints ? and allows the user to continue editing. A second e or q command at this point will take effect. The - command-line option inhibits this feature.

ERRORS

? for command errors.

?*file* for an inaccessible file.

[see the h and H (help) commands for detailed explanations].

FILES

ed.hup work is saved here if the terminal is hung up.

SEE ALSO

GREP(BU_CMD), SED(BU_CMD), SH(BU_CMD).

USAGE

General.

A ! command cannot be subject to a g or a v command.

The sequence \n in a *RE* does not match a newline character.

If the editor input comes from a command file, for example:

```
ed file < ed-cmd-file
```

the editor exits at the first failure of a command in the command file.

CAVEATS

The option - will be replaced by -s, in order to conform to the syntax standard. The old form of the option will continue to be accepted for some time.

NAME

expr — evaluate expression

SYNOPSIS

`expr` *expression*

DESCRIPTION

The command `expr` evaluates an expression and writes the result on the standard output. Terms of the expression must be separated by blanks. Characters special to the command interpreter must be escaped. Note that **0** is returned to indicate a zero value, rather than the null string. Strings containing blanks or other special characters should be quoted. Integer-valued arguments may be preceded by a unary minus sign.

The operators are listed below. Characters that need to be escaped are preceded by \. The list is in order of increasing precedence, with equal precedence operators grouped within {} symbols. The symbol *arg* represents an argument.

arg* \| *arg
: returns the first *arg* if it is neither null nor **0**, otherwise returns the second *arg*.

arg* \& *arg
: returns the first *arg* if neither *arg* is null or **0**, otherwise returns **0**.

arg* { =, \>, \>=, \<, \<=, != } *arg
: returns the result of an integer comparison if both arguments are integers, otherwise returns the result of a lexical comparison.

arg* { +, − } *arg
: addition or subtraction of integer-valued arguments.

arg* { *, /, % } *arg
: multiplication, division, or remainder of the integer-valued arguments.

arg* : *arg
: The matching operator : compares the first argument with the second argument which must be a regular expression. Regular expression syntax is the same as that of `ed`, except that all patterns are "anchored" (i.e., begin with ^) and, therefore, ^ is not a special character, in that context. Normally, the matching operator returns the number of characters matched (0 on failure). Alternatively, the **\(...\)** pattern symbols can be used to return a portion of the first argument.

EXAMPLES

1. `` a=`expr $a + 1` ``

   adds 1 to the variable **a**.

2. For $a equal to either */usr/abc/file* or just *file*

```
expr  $a  :  '.*/\(.*\)'  \|  $a
```

returns the last segment of a path name (i.e., `file`). Watch out for / alone as an argument: `expr` will take it as the division operator.

3. A better representation of example 2.

```
expr  //$a  :  '.*/\(.*\)'
```

The addition of the // characters eliminates any ambiguity about the division operator and simplifies the whole expression.

4. `expr  $VAR  :  '.*'`

   returns the number of characters in $VAR.

SEE ALSO

ED(BU_CMD), SH(BU_CMD).

ERRORS

As a side effect of expression evaluation, `expr` returns the following exit values:

0 if the expression is neither null nor **0**

1 if the expression is null or **0**

2 for invalid expressions.

USAGE

General.

After argument processing [see SH(BU_CMD)], `expr` cannot tell the difference between an operator and an operand except by the value. If **$a** is **=**, the command:

```
expr  $a  =  '='
```

looks like:

```
expr  =  =  =
```

as the arguments are passed to `expr` (and they will all be taken as the **=** operator). The following works:

```
expr  X$a  =  X=
```

NAME

file — determine file type

SYNOPSIS

`file [ -f` *lfile* `]` *file* `...`

DESCRIPTION

The command `file` performs a series of tests on each specified *file* in an attempt to classify it. If it appears to be a text file, `file` examines an initial segment and makes a guess about its language. (The answer is not guaranteed to be correct.) If an argument is an executable (*a.out*) file it is identified as such, and any other available information is reported.

If the `-f` option is given, the next argument is taken to be a file containing the names of the files to be examined.

USAGE

General.

NAME

find — find files

SYNOPSIS

`find` *path-name-list expression*

DESCRIPTION

The command `find` recursively descends the directory hierarchy for each path name in the *path-name-list* (i.e., one or more path names) seeking files that match a boolean *expression* written in the primaries given below. In the following descriptions, the argument *n* is used as a decimal integer where +*n* means more than *n*, −*n* means less than *n* and *n* means exactly *n*.

The *expression* argument is made up of:

`-name` *file* — True if *file* matches the current file name. The argument syntax of `sh` [see SH(BU_CMD)] may be used if escaped (especially note **[, ? and ***)).

`-perm` *onum* — True if the file permission flags exactly match the octal number *onum* [see CHMOD(BU_CMD)] If *onum* is prefixed by a minus sign, more flag bits (017777) [see STAT(BA_SYS)] become significant and the flags are compared.

`-type` *c* — True if the type of the file is *c*, where *c* is **b**, **c**, **d**, **p**, or **f** for block special file, character special file, directory, fifo (named pipe), or plain file respectively.

`-links` *n* — True if the file has *n* links.

`-user` *uname* — True if the file belongs to the user *uname*. If *uname* is numeric and does not appear as a login name in the `/etc/passwd` file, it is taken as a user ID.

`-group` *gname* — True if the file belongs to the group *gname*. If *gname* is numeric and does not appear in the `/etc/group` file, it is taken as a group ID.

`-size` *n*[**c**] — True if the file is *n* "blocks" long (block = 512 bytes). If *n* is followed by a **c**, the size is in characters.

`-atime` *n* — True if the file has been accessed in *n* days. The access time of directories in *path-name-list* is changed by `find` itself.

`-mtime` *n* — True if the file has been modified in *n* days.

`-ctime` *n* — True if the file inode has been changed in *n* days.

`-exec` *cmd* — True if the executed *cmd* returns a zero value as exit status. The end of *cmd* must be punctuated by an escaped semicolon. A command argument `{}` is replaced by the current path name.

`-ok` *cmd* — Like `-exec` except that the generated command line is printed with a question mark first, and is executed only if the user responds by typing **y**.

`-print` — Always true; causes the current path name to be printed.

`-newer` *file* — True if the current file has been modified more recently than the argument *file*.

`-depth` — Always true; causes descent of the directory hierarchy to be done so that all entries in a directory are acted on before the directory itself. This can be useful when `find` is used with `cpio` [see CPIO(BU_CMD)] to transfer files that are contained in directories without write permission.

(*expression*) — True if the parenthesized expression is true (parentheses must be escaped if they are special to the command interpreter).

The primaries may be combined using the following operators (in order of decreasing precedence):

1) The negation of a primary (**!** is the unary *not* operator).

2) Concatenation of primaries (the *and* operation is implied by the juxtaposition of two primaries).

3) Alternation of primaries (**-o** is the *or* operator).

EXAMPLE

To remove all files named `tmp` or ending in `.xx` that have not been accessed for a week:

```
find / \( -name tmp -o -name '*.xx' \) -atime +7
-exec rm {} \;
```

FILES

```
/etc/passwd
/etc/group
```

SEE ALSO

CHMOD(BU_CMD), CPIO(BU_CMD), SH(BU_CMD), TEST(BU_CMD), STAT(BA_SYS).

USAGE

General.

NAME

grep — search a file for a pattern

SYNOPSIS

`grep` [*options*] *expression* [*files*]

DESCRIPTION

The command `grep` searches the input *files* (standard input default) for lines matching a pattern. Normally, each line found is copied to the standard output. The patterns are limited regular *expressions* in the style of `ed`.

The following options are recognized:

- `−v` All lines but those matching are printed.
- `−c` Only a count of matching lines is printed.
- `−i` Ignore upper/lower case distinction during comparisons. (This option is new in UNIX System V Release 2.0.)
- `−l` Only the names of files with matching lines are listed (once), separated by newlines.
- `−n` Each line is preceded by its relative line number in the file.
- `−s` The error messages produced for nonexistent or unreadable files are suppressed.

In all cases, the file name is output if there is more than one input file. Care should be taken when using characters in *expression* that may also be meaningful to the command interpreter. It is safest to enclose the entire *expression* argument in single quotes '...'.

ERRORS

Exit status is 0 if any matches are found, 1 if none, 2 for syntax errors or inaccessible files (even if matches were found).

SEE ALSO

ED(BU_CMD), EGREP(AU_CMD), SED(BU_CMD).

USAGE

General.

CAVEATS

The functionality of `egrep` and `fgrep` [see EGREP(AU_CMD)] will eventually be provided in `grep`, and those two commands discontinued.

NAME

kill — send signal to a process

SYNOPSIS

`kill` [*-signal*] *PID*

DESCRIPTION

The command `kill` sends the specified *signal* to the specified processes (or process groups). If process number 0 is specified, all processes in the process group are signaled. Process numbers can be found by using `ps` [see PS(BU_CMD)].

The argument *signal* must be specified as a numeric value; these values are implementation dependent. (See **CAVEATS** below.)

If no signal is specified, `kill` sends SIGTERM (terminate). This will normally kill processes that do not catch or ignore the signal.

The specified process(es) must belong to the user unless the user is super-user.

Further details are described in KILL(BA_SYS).

SEE ALSO

PS(BU_CMD), KILL(BA_SYS), SIGNAL(BA_SYS).

USAGE

General.

CAVEATS

The command `kill` will be changed to use symbolic names rather than numeric values of signals. The old form will continue to be accepted for some time.

NAME

line — read one line

SYNOPSIS

`line`

DESCRIPTION

The command `line` copies one line (up to a newline) from the standard input and writes it on the standard output. It returns an exit code of 1 on **EOF** and always prints at least a newline. It is often used within command scripts to read from the user's terminal.

SEE ALSO

SH(BU_CMD).

USAGE

General.

NAME

ls — list contents of directory

SYNOPSIS

`ls` [*options*] [*file* . . .]

DESCRIPTION

For each *file*, if it is directory `ls` lists the contents of the directory; if it is a file, `ls` repeats its name and gives any other information requested. The output is sorted alphabetically by default. When no *files* are specified, the current directory is listed. When several arguments are given, the arguments are first sorted appropriately, but files appear before directories and their contents.

Note that the following options are new in UNIX System V Release 2.0: `-C`, `-F`, `-R`, `-m`, `-n`, `-q`, and `-x`.

There are three major listing formats. The default format is to list one entry per line; the options `-C` and `-x` enable multi-column formats; and the `-m` option enables stream output format in which files are listed across the page, separated by commas.

In order to determine output formats for the `-C`, `-x`, and `-m` options, `ls` uses the environmental variable `COLUMNS` to determine the number of character positions available on one output line. If this variable is not set, the `terminfo` database is used to determine the number of columns, based on the environmental variable `TERM`. If this information cannot be obtained, 80 columns is assumed.

There are a large number of options:

`-C` Multi-column output with entries sorted down the columns.

`-F` Put a slash (/) after each filename if that file is a directory and put an asterisk (*) after each filename if that file is executable.

`-R` Recursively list subdirectories encountered.

`-a` List all entries; usually entries whose names begin with a period (.) are not listed.

`-c` Use time of last modification of the i-node (file created, mode changed, etc.) for sorting (`-t`) or printing (`-l`).

`-d` If an argument is a directory, list only its name (not its contents); often used with `-l` to get the status of a directory.

`-f` Force each argument to be interpreted as a directory and list the name found in each slot. This option turns off `-l`, `-t`, `-s`, and `-r`, and turns on `-a`; the order is the order in which entries appear in the directory.

`-g` The same as `-l`, except that the owner is not printed.

`-i` For each file, print the inode number in the first column of the report.

`-l` List in long format, giving mode, number of links, owner, group, size in bytes, and time of last modification for each file (see below). If the file is a special file, the size field will instead contain the major and minor device numbers rather than a size.

`-m` Stream output format; files are listed across the page, separated by commas.

`-n` The same as `-l`, except that the owner's **UID** and group's **GID** numbers are printed, rather than the associated character strings.

`-o` The same as `-l`, except that the group is not printed.

`-p` Put a slash (/) after each filename if that file is a directory.

`-q` Force non-printing characters (in file names) to be displayed as the character (?).

`-r` Reverse the order of sort to get reverse alphabetic or oldest first as appropriate.

`-s` Give size of each file in 512-byte units.

`-t` Sort by time modified (latest first) instead of by name.

`-u` Use time of last access instead of last modification for sorting (with the `-t` option) or printing (with the `-l` option).

`-x` Multi-column output with entries sorted across rather than down the page.

The mode printed under the `-l` option consists of 10 characters that are interpreted as described below.

The first character is:

d if the entry is a directory;
b if the entry is a block special file;
c if the entry is a character special file;
p if the entry is a fifo (named pipe) special file;
- if the entry is an ordinary file.

The next 9 characters are interpreted as three sets of three bits each. The first set refers to the owner's permissions; the next to permissions of others in the user-group of the file; and the last to all others. Within each set, the three characters indicate permission to read, to write, and to execute the file as a program, respectively. For a directory, "execute" permission is interpreted to mean permission to search the directory for a specified file.

The permissions are indicated as follows:

r if the file is readable;
w if the file is writable;
x if the file is executable (also see below);

- if the indicated permission is *not* granted.

The group-execute permission character is given as **s** if the file has set-group-ID mode; likewise, the user-execute permission character is given as **s** if the file has set-user-ID mode. These are given as **S** (capitalized) if the corresponding execute permission is NOT set. (See, however, **CAVEATS** below.)

FILES

`/etc/passwd`	to get user IDs for `ls -l` and `ls -o`.
`/etc/group`	to get group IDs for `ls -l` and `ls -g`.
`/usr/lib/terminfo/*/*`	*terminfo* terminal information database

SEE ALSO

CHMOD(BU_CMD), FIND(BU_CMD).

USAGE

General.

CAVEATS

The group execute permission will be shown as **l** if mandatory locking is enabled for the file. It will not be possible to set-group-ID without also turning on group execute permission; therefore the group execute permission character will have one of the following values: **-**, **x**, **s**, or **l**; (**S** will not be possible).

NAME

mail, rmail — send or read mail

SYNOPSIS

`mail [-epqr] [-f` *file*`]`

`mail [-t]` *name* `...`

`rmail [-t]` *name* `...`

DESCRIPTION

The command `mail` without arguments prints a user's mail, message-by-message, in last-in first-out order. For each message, the user is prompted with a **?**, and a line is read from the standard input to determine the disposition of the message:

`<newline>`	Go on to next message.
`+`	Same as <newline>.
`d`	Delete message and go on to next message.
`p`	Print message again.
`–`	Go back to previous message.
`s [`*file*`]`	Save message in the named *file* (`mbox` is default).
`w [`*file*`]`	Save message, without its header, in the named *file* (`mbox` is default).
`m [`*name* ...`]`	Mail the message to the named users (names are user login names; the default is the user).
`q`	Put undeleted mail back in the *mailfile* and stop.
`EOF`	(Usually control-D.) Same as **q.**
`x`	Put all mail back in the *mailfile* unchanged and stop.
`!`*command*	Escape to the command interpreter to execute *command.*
`*`	Print a command summary.

The optional arguments alter the printing of the mail:

`−e`	causes mail not to be printed. An exit value of 0 is returned if the user has mail; otherwise, an exit value of 1 is returned.
`−p`	causes all mail to be printed without prompting for disposition.
`−q`	causes `mail` to terminate after interrupts. Normally an interrupt only causes the termination of the message being printed.
`−r`	causes messages to be printed in first-in, first-out order.
`−f`*file*	causes `mail` to use *file* (e.g., `mbox`) instead of the default *mailfile*.

When *names* (user login names) are given, `mail` takes the standard input up to an end-of-file (or up to a line consisting of just a .) and adds it to each user's *mailfile.* The message is preceded by the sender's name and a postmark. Lines in the message that begin with the word "From" are preceded with a >. The **−t** option causes the message to be preceded by all users the `mail` is sent to. If a user being sent mail is not recognized, or if `mail` is interrupted during input, the file `dead.letter` will be saved to allow editing and resending. Note that this is regarded as a temporary file in that it is recreated every time needed, erasing the previous contents of `dead.letter`.

To denote a recipient on a remote system, *name* is the user's login name prefixed by the system name and an exclamation mark. Everything after the first exclamation mark is interpreted by the remote system. In particular, if *name* contains additional exclamation marks, it can denote a sequence of machines through which the message is to be sent on the way to its ultimate destination. For example, specifying **a!b!cde** as a recipient's name causes the message to be sent to user **b!cde** on system **a.** System **a** will interpret that destination as a request to send the message to user **cde** on system **b.** This might be useful, for instance, if the sending system can access system **a** but not system **b,** and system **a** has access to system **b.**

The *mailfile* may also contain the first line:

Forward to *person*

which will cause all mail sent to the owner of the *mailfile* to be forwarded to *person.* This is especially useful to forward all of a person's mail to one machine in a multiple machine environment. In order for forwarding to work properly the *mailfile* should have "mail" as group ID, and the group permission should be read-write.

The command `rmail` only permits the sending of mail.

FILES

`/etc/passwd`	to identify sender and locate persons
`$HOME/mbox`	saved mail
`dead.letter`	unmailable text

USAGE

General.

NAME

mkdir — make a directory

SYNOPSIS

`mkdir` *dirname* `...`

DESCRIPTION

The command `mkdir` creates the specified directories. Standard entries, ., for the directory itself, and .., for its parent, are made automatically.

The command `mkdir` requires write permission in the parent directory.

ERRORS

The command `mkdir` returns exit code 0 if all directories were successfully made; otherwise, it prints a diagnostic and returns non-zero.

SEE ALSO

RM(BU_CMD).

USAGE

General.

NAME

nl — line numbering filter

SYNOPSIS

`nl` [`-h`*type*] [`-b`*type*] [`-f`*type*] [`-v`*start#*] [`-i`*incr*] [`-p`] [`-l`*num*] [`-s`*sep*] [`-w`*width*] [`-n`*format*] [`-d`*delim*] [*file*]

DESCRIPTION

The command `nl` reads lines from the named `file` or the standard input if no `file` is named and reproduces the lines on the standard output. Lines are numbered on the left in accordance with the command options in effect.

`nl` views the text it reads in terms of logical pages. Line numbering is reset at the start of each logical page. A logical page consists of a header, a body, and a footer section. Empty sections are valid. Different line numbering options are independently available for header, body, and footer (e.g., no numbering of header and footer lines while numbering blank lines only in the body).

The start of logical page sections are signaled by input lines containing nothing but the following delimiter character(s):

Line	*Start of*
\:\:\:	header
\:\:	body
\:	footer

Unless otherwise specified, `nl` assumes the text being read is in a single logical page body.

Options may appear in any order and may be intermingled with an optional file name. Only one file may be named. The options are:

`-b`*type* Specifies which logical page body lines are to be numbered. Recognized *types* and their meaning are: `a`, number all lines; `t`, number lines with printable text only; `n`, no line numbering; `p`*string*, number only lines that contain the regular expression specified in *string*. Default *type* for logical page body is `t` (text lines numbered).

`-h`*type* Same as `-b`*type* except for header. Default *type* for logical page header is `n` (no lines numbered).

`-f`*type* Same as `-b`*type* except for footer. Default for logical page footer is `n` (no lines numbered).

`-p` Do not restart numbering at logical page delimiters.

`-v`*start#* The initial value used to number logical page lines. Default is `1`.

`-i`*incr* The increment value used to number logical page lines. Default is `1`.

−s*sep* The character(s) used in separating the line number and the corresponding text line. Default *sep* is a tab.

−w*width* The number of characters to be used for the line number. Default *width* is 6.

−n*format* The line numbering format. Recognized values are: `ln`, left justified, leading zeroes suppressed; `rn`, right justified, leading zeroes supressed; `rz`, right justified, leading zeroes kept. Default *format* is `rn` (right justified).

−l*num* The number of blank lines to be considered as one. For example, `−l2` results in only the second adjacent blank being numbered (if the appropriate `−ha`, `−ba`, and/or `−fa` option is set). Default is 1.

−d*xx* The delimiter characters specifying the start of a logical page section may be changed from the default characters (\:) to two user-specified characters. If only one character is entered, the second character remains the default character (:). No space should appear between the **−d** and the delimiter characters. To enter a backslash, use two backslashes.

EXAMPLE

The command:

```
nl −v10 −i10 −d!+ file1
```

will number file1 starting at line number 10 with an increment of ten. The logical page delimiters are !+.

USAGE

General.

SEE ALSO

PR(BU_CMD).

NAME

nohup — run a command immune to hangups and quits

SYNOPSIS

`nohup` *command* [*arguments*]

DESCRIPTION

The command `nohup` executes *command* with the signals SIGHUP and SIGQUIT ignored. If output is not re-directed by the user, both standard output and standard error are sent to `nohup.out`. If `nohup.out` is not writable in the current directory, output is redirected to `$HOME/nohup.out`.

EXAMPLE

It is frequently desirable to apply `nohup` to pipelines or lists of commands. This can be done only by placing pipelines and command lists in a single file; this procedure can then be executed as *command*, and the `nohup` applies to everything in the file.

USAGE

General.

SEE ALSO

SH(BU_CMD), SIGNAL(BA_SYS).

NAME

pack, pcat, unpack — compress and expand files

SYNOPSIS

`pack [ - ] [ -f ]` *name* `...`

`pcat` *name* `...`

`unpack` *name* `...`

DESCRIPTION

The command `pack` attempts to store the specified files in a compressed form. Wherever possible (and useful), each input file *name* is replaced by a packed file *name.z* with the same access modes, access and modified dates, and owner as those of *name*. The option **-f** will force packing of *name*. This is useful for causing an entire directory to be packed even if some of the files will not benefit. If `pack` is successful, *name* will be removed. Packed files can be restored to their original form using `unpack` or `pcat`.

The command `pack` uses Huffman (minimum redundancy) codes on a byte-by-byte basis. If the − argument is used, an internal flag is set that causes the number of times each byte is used, its relative frequency, and the code for the byte to be printed on the standard output. Additional occurrences of − in place of *name* will cause the internal flag to be set and reset.

The amount of compression obtained depends on the size of the input file and the character frequency distribution. Because a decoding tree forms the first part of each file, it is usually not worthwhile to pack files smaller than three blocks, unless the character frequency distribution is very skewed, which may occur with printer plots or pictures.

Typically, text files are reduced to 60-75% of their original size. Load modules, which use a larger character set and have a more uniform distribution of characters, show little compression, the packed versions being about 90% of the original size.

The command `pack` returns a value that is the number of files that it failed to compress.

No packing will occur if:

the file appears to be already packed;
the file name has more than {NAME_MAX}-2 characters;
the file has links;
the file is a directory;
the file cannot be opened;
the file is empty;
no disk storage blocks will be saved by packing;
a file called *name.z* already exists;
the **.z** file cannot be created;
an I/O error occurred during processing.

The last segment of the file name must contain no more than {NAME_MAX}-2 characters to allow space for the appended **.z** extension.

The command `pcat` does for packed files what `cat` does for ordinary files, except that `pcat` cannot be used as a filter. The specified files are unpacked and written to the standard output. Thus to view a packed file named *name.z* use:

```
pcat name.z    (or pcat name)
```

To make an unpacked copy, called `abc`, of a packed file named *name.z* (without destroying *name.z*) use the command:

```
pcat name >nnn
```

The command `pcat` returns the number of files it was unable to unpack. Failure may occur if:

the file name (exclusive of the **.z**) has more than {NAME MAX}-2 characters;
the file cannot be opened;
the file does not appear to be the output of `pack`.

The command `unpack` expands files created by `pack`. For each file *name* specified in the command, a search is made for a file called *name.z* (or just *name*, if *name* ends in **.z**). If this file appears to be a packed file, it is replaced by its expanded version. The new file has the **.z** suffix stripped from its name, and has the same access modes, access and modification dates, and owner as those of the packed file.

The command `unpack` returns a value that is the number of files it was unable to unpack. Failure may occur for the same reasons that it may in `pcat`, as well as for the following:

a file with the "unpacked" name already exists;
the unpacked file cannot be created.

USAGE

General.

SEE ALSO

CAT(BU_CMD).

NAME

paste — merge same lines of several files or subsequent lines of one file

SYNOPSIS

`paste` *file1 file2* `. . .`
`paste −d`*list file1 file2* `. . .`
`paste −s [-d`*list*`]` *file1 file2* `. . .`

DESCRIPTION

In the first two forms, `paste` concatenates corresponding lines of the given input files *file1*, *file2*, etc. The file-name − means standard input. It treats each file as a column or columns of a table and pastes them together horizontally (parallel merging). In the last form above (`−s` option), `paste` combines subsequent lines of the input file (serial merging).

In all cases, lines are glued together with the `tab` character, unless the `−d` option is used (see below).

Output is to the standard output, so that `paste` can be used as the start of a pipe, or as a filter, if − is used in place of a file name.

Without the `−d` option, the newline characters of each but the last file (or last line in case of the `−s` option) are replaced by a `tab` character.

When this option is used, a character from the *list* immediately following `−d` replaces the default `tab` as the line concatenation character. The list is used circularly, i.e., when exhausted, it is reused. In parallel merging (i.e., no `−s` option), the lines from the last file are always terminated with a newline character, not from the *list*. The list may contain the special escape sequences: **\n** (newline), **\t** (tab), **** (backslash), and **\0** (empty string, not a null character). Quoting may be necessary, if characters have special meaning to the command interpreter.

EXAMPLES

```
ls | paste − − − −
```
list directory in four columns

```
paste −s −d"\t\n" file
```
combine pairs of lines into lines

USAGE

General.

SEE ALSO

CUT(BU_CMD), GREP(BU_CMD), PR(BU_CMD).

NAME

pg — file perusal filter for soft-copy terminals

SYNOPSIS

pg [-*number*] [-p *string*] [-cefns] [+*linenumber*] [+/*pattern*/] [*files*. . .]

DESCRIPTION

The command pg is a filter that allows the examination of *files* one screenful at a time on a soft-copy terminal. (The file name − and/or null arguments indicate that pg should read from the standard input.) Each screenful is followed by a prompt. If the user types a carriage return, another page is displayed; other possibilities are enumerated below.

This command is different from previous paginators in that it allows the user to back up and review something that has already passed. The method for doing this is explained below.

In order to determine terminal attributes, pg scans the *terminfo* data base for the terminal type specified by the environmental variable TERM. If TERM is not defined, the terminal type *dumb* is assumed.

The command line options are:

−*number*
: An integer specifying the size (in lines) of the window that pg is to use instead of the default. (On a terminal containing 24 lines, the default window size is 23).

−p *string*
: Causes pg to use *string* as the prompt. If the prompt string contains a "%d", the first occurrence of "%d" in the prompt will be replaced by the current page number when the prompt is issued. The default prompt string is \`\`:''.

−c Home the cursor and clear the screen before displaying each page. This option is ignored if **clear_screen** is not defined for this terminal type in the *terminfo* data base.

−e Causes pg *not* to pause at the end of each file.

−f Normally, pg splits lines longer than the screen width, but some sequences of characters in the text being displayed (e.g., escape sequences for underlining) generate undesirable results. The −f option inhibits pg from splitting lines.

−n Normally, commands must be terminated by a newline character. This option causes an automatic end of command as soon as a command letter is entered.

−s Causes pg to print all messages and prompts in standout mode (usually inverse video).

+*linenumber*
Start up at *linenumber*.

+*/pattern/*
Start up at the first line containing the regular expression pattern.

The responses that may be typed when `pg` pauses can be divided into three categories: those causing further perusal, those that search, and those that modify the perusal environment.

Commands which cause further perusal normally take a preceding address, an optionally signed number indicating the point from which further text should be displayed. This address is interpreted in either pages or lines depending on the command. A signed address specifies a point relative to the current page or line, and an unsigned address specifies an address relative to the beginning of the file. Each command has a default address that is used if none is provided.

The perusal commands and their defaults are as follows:

(+1)`<newline>` or `<blank>`
This causes one page to be displayed. The address is specified in pages.

(+1) `l`
With a relative address this causes `pg` to simulate scrolling the screen, forward or backward, the number of lines specified. With an absolute address this command prints a screenful beginning at the specified line.

(+1) `d` or ^D
Simulates scrolling half a screen forward or backward.

The following perusal commands take no address.

. or ^L
Typing a single period causes the current page of text to be redisplayed.

$
Displays the last windowful in the file. Use with caution when the input is a pipe.

The following commands are available for searching for text patterns in the text. The regular expressions described in ED(BU_CMD) are available. They must always be terminated by a `<newline>`, even if the `-n` option is specified.

`i`*/pattern/*
Search forward for the `i`*th* (default `i=1`) occurrence of *pattern*. Searching begins immediately after the current page and continues to the end of the current file, without wrap-around.

`i`^*pattern*^
`i`?*pattern*?
Search backwards for the `i`*th* (default `i=1`) occurrence of *pattern*. Searching begins immediately before the current page and continues to

the beginning of the current file, without wrap-around. (The ^ notation is useful for terminals that do not properly handle the ?.)

After searching, `pg` will normally display the line found at the top of the screen. This can be modified by appending `m` or `b` to the search command to leave the line found in the middle or at the bottom of the window from now on. The suffix `t` can be used to restore the original situation.

The user of `pg` can modify the environment of perusal with the following commands:

`in` Begin perusing the `i`*th* next file in the command line. The `i` is an unsigned number, default value is 1.

`ip` Begin perusing the `i`*th* previous file in the command line. `i` is an unsigned number, default is 1.

`iw` Display another window of text. If `i` is present, set the window size to `i`.

`s` *filename*
Save the input in the named file. Only the current file being perused is saved. The white space between the `s` and *filename* is optional. This command must always be terminated by a `newline`, even if the `-n` option is specified.

`h` Help by displaying an abbreviated summary of available commands.

`q` or `Q`
Quit `pg`.

! *command*
The argument *command* is passed to the command interpreter, whose name is taken from the `SHELL` environmental variable. If this is not available, the default command interpreter is used. This command must always be terminated by a `newline`, even if the `-n` option is specified.

At any time when output is being sent to the terminal, the user can hit the QUIT key (normally control-\) or the interrupt (BREAK) key. This causes `pg` to stop sending output, and to display the prompt. The user may then enter one of the above commands in the normal manner. Unfortunately, some output is lost when this is done, due to the fact that any characters waiting in the terminal's output queue are flushed when the quit signal occurs.

If the standard output is not a terminal, `pg` acts just like the `cat` command, except that a header is printed before each file (if there is more than one).

FILES

`/usr/lib/terminfo/*/*` *terminfo* terminal information database

USAGE

End-user.

While waiting for terminal input, pg responds to BREAK, DEL, and QUIT by terminating execution. Between prompts, however, these signals interrupt pg's current task and place the user in prompt mode. These signals should be used with caution when input is being read from a pipe, since an interrupt is likely to terminate the other commands in the pipeline.

If terminal tabs are not set every eight positions, undesirable results may occur.

When pg is used as a filter with another command that changes the terminal I/O options, terminal settings may not be restored correctly.

SEE ALSO

ED(BU_CMD), GREP(BU_CMD).

NAME

pr — print files

SYNOPSIS

`pr` [*options*] *files*]

DESCRIPTION

The command `pr` prints the named files on the standard output. If *file* is −, or if no files are specified, the standard input is assumed. By default, the listing is separated into pages, each headed by the page number, a date and time, and the name of the file.

By default, columns are of equal width, separated by at least one space; lines which do not fit are truncated. If the `−s` option is used, lines are not truncated and columns are separated by the separation character.

If the standard output is associated with a terminal, error messages are withheld until `pr` has completed printing.

The below *options* may appear singly, or may be combined in any order:

`+k` Begin printing with page `k` (default is 1).

`−k` Produce `k-column` output (default is 1). This option should not be used with `−m`. The options `−e` and `−i` are assumed for multi-column output.

`−a` Print multi-column output across the page. This option is appropriate only with the `−k` option.

`−m` Merge and print all files simultaneously, one per column (overrides the `−k option)`.

`−d` Double-space the output.

`−eck` Expand `input` tabs to character positions `k`+1, 2*`k`+1, 3*`k`+1, etc. If `k` is 0 or is omitted, default tab settings at every eighth position are assumed. Tab characters in the input are expanded into the appropriate number of spaces. If `c` (any non-digit character) is given, it is treated as the input tab character (default for `c` is the tab character).

`−ick` In `output`, replace white space wherever possible by inserting tabs to character positions `k`+1, 2*`k`+1, 3*`k`+1, etc. If `k` is 0 or is omitted, default tab settings at every eighth position are assumed. If `c` (any non-digit character) is given, it is treated as the output tab character (default for `c` is the tab character).

`−nck` Provide `k-digit` line numbering (default for `k` is 5). The number occupies the first `k`+1 character positions of each column of normal output or each line of `−m` output. If `c` (any non-digit character) is given, it is appended to the line number to separate it from whatever follows (default for `c` is a tab).

`-wk` Set the width of a line to `k` character positions for multi-column output (default is 72).

`-ok` Offset each line by `k` character positions (default is 0). The number of character positions per line is the sum of the width and offset.

`-lk` Set the length of a page to `k` lines (default is 66). If `k` is less than what is needed for the page header and trailer, then the option `-t` is in effect; that is, header and trailer lines are suppressed in order to make room for text.

`-h header`
Use header as the header to be printed instead of the file name.

`-p` Pause before beginning each page if the output is directed to a terminal (`pr` will ring the bell at the terminal and wait for a carriage return).

`-f` Use form-feed character for new pages (default is to use a sequence of line-feeds). Pause before beginning the first page if the standard output is associated with a terminal.

`-r` Print no diagnostic reports on failure to open files.

`-t` Print neither the five-line identifying header nor the five-line trailer normally supplied for each page. Quit printing after the last line of each file without spacing to the end of the page.

`-sc` Separate columns by the single character `c` instead of by the appropriate number of spaces (default for `c` is a tab).

EXAMPLES

- Print `file1` and `file2` as a double-spaced, three-column listing headed by "file list":

```
pr -3dh "file list" file1 file2
```

- Write `file1` on `file2`, expanding tabs to columns 10, 19, 28, ... :

```
pr -e9 -t <file1 >file2
```

USAGE

General.

NAME

ps — report process status

SYNOPSIS

`ps` [*options*]

DESCRIPTION

The command `ps` prints certain information about active processes. Without *options*, information is printed about processes associated with the current terminal. The output consists of a short listing containing only the process-ID, terminal identifier, cumulative execution time, and the command name. Otherwise, the information that is displayed is controlled by the selection of *options*.

The *options* using lists as arguments can have the list specified in one of two forms: a list of identifiers separated from one another by a comma, or a list of identifiers enclosed in double quotes and separated from one another by a comma and/or one or more spaces.

The *options* are:

`-e` Print information about all processes.

`-d` Print information about all processes, except process group leaders.

`-a` Print information about all processes, except process group leaders and processes not associated with a terminal.

`-f` Generate a *full* listing. (See below for meaning of columns in a full listing).

`-l` Generate a *long* listing. See below.

`-n` *namelist*

The argument will be taken as the name of an alternate system *namelist* file in place of the default.

`-t` *termlist*

Restrict listing to data about the processes associated with the terminals given in *termlist*. Terminal identifiers may be specified in one of two forms: the device's file name (e.g., **tty04**) or if the device's file name starts with **tty**, just the digit identifier (e.g., **04**).

`-p` *proclist*

Restrict listing to data about processes whose process-ID numbers are given in *proclist*.

`-u` *uidlist*

Restrict listing to data about processes whose user-ID numbers or login names are given in *uidlist*. In the listing, the numerical-user-ID will be printed unless the `-f` option is used, in which case the login name will be printed.

`-g` *grplist*

Restrict listing to data about processes whose process group leaders are given in *grplist*.

The column headings and the meaning of the columns in a `ps` listing are given below; the letters **f** and **l** indicate the option (`full` or `long`) that causes the corresponding heading to appear; **all** means that the heading always appears. Note that these two options determine only what information is provided for a process; they do *not* determine which processes will be listed.

F	**(l)**	Flags (octal and additive) associated with the process.
S	**(l)**	The state of the process.
UID	**(f,l)**	The user ID number of the process owner; the login name is printed under the **−f** option.
PID	**(all)**	The process ID of the process; it is possible to kill a process if you know this datum.
PPID	**(f,l)**	The process ID of the parent process.
C	**(f,l)**	Processor utilization for scheduling.
PRI	**(l)**	The priority of the process; higher numbers mean lower priority.
NI	**(l)**	Nice value; used in priority computation.
ADDR	**(l)**	The memory address of the process.
SZ	**(l)**	The size in blocks of the core image of the process.
WCHAN		**(l)** The event for which the process is waiting or sleeping; if blank, the process is running.
STIME		**(f)** Starting time of the process.
TTY	**(all)**	The controlling terminal for the process.
TIME	**(all)**	The cumulative execution time for the process.
CMD	**(all)**	The command name; the full command name and its arguments are printed under the **−f** option.

A process that has exited and has a parent, but has not yet been waited for by the parent, is marked **defunct**.

Under the option `-f`, `ps` tries to determine the command name and arguments given when the process was created by examining memory or the swap area. Failing this, the command name, as it would appear without the option `-f`, is printed in square brackets.

FILES

`/etc/passwd` supplies UID information

USAGE

General.

Things can change while `ps` is running; the snap-shot it gives is only true for an instant, and may not be accurate by the time it is displayed.

NAME

pwd — working directory name

SYNOPSIS

`pwd`

DESCRIPTION

The command `pwd` prints the path name of the working (current) directory.

ERRORS

"Cannot open .." and "Read error in .." indicate possible file system trouble.

USAGE

General.

SEE ALSO

CD(BU_CMD).

NAME

rm, rmdir — remove files or directories

SYNOPSIS

`rm` [*-fri*] *file* ...

`rmdir` *dir* ...

DESCRIPTION

The command `rm` removes the entries for one or more files from a directory. If an entry was the last link to the file, the file is destroyed. Removal of a file requires write permission in its directory, but neither read nor write permission on the file itself.

If a file has no write permission and the standard input is a terminal, its permissions are printed and a line is read from the standard input. If that line begins with **y** the file is deleted, otherwise the file remains. No questions are asked when the option `−f` is given or if the standard input is not a terminal.

If a designated file is a directory, an error comment is printed unless the optional argument `−r` has been used. In that case, `rm` recursively deletes the entire contents of the specified directory, and the directory itself.

If the option `−i` (interactive) is in effect, `rm` asks whether to delete each file, and, under `−r`, whether to examine each directory.

The command `rmdir` removes entries for the named directories, which must be empty.

ERRORS

It is forbidden to remove the file .. in order to avoid the consequences of inadvertently doing something like:

```
rm −r .*
```

USAGE

General.

SEE ALSO

UNLINK(BA_SYS).

NAME

sed — stream editor

SYNOPSIS

`sed` [`-n`] [`-e` *script*] [`-f` *sfile*] [*files*]

DESCRIPTION

The command `sed` copies the named *files* (standard input default) to the standard output, edited according to a script of commands. The `-f` option causes the script to be taken from file *sfile*; these options accumulate. If there is just one `-e` option and no `-f` options, the flag `-e` may be omitted. The `-n` option suppresses the default output. A script consists of editing commands, one per line, of the following form:

[address [, address]] function [arguments]

In normal operation, `sed` cyclically copies a line of input into a *pattern space* (unless there is something left after a `D` command), applies in sequence all commands whose addresses select that pattern space, and at the end of the script copies the pattern space to the standard output (except under `-n`) and deletes the pattern space.

Some of the commands use a *hold space* to save all or part of the *pattern space* for subsequent retrieval.

An address is either a decimal number that counts input lines cumulatively across files, a `$` that addresses the last line of input, or a context address, i.e., a `/regular expression/` in the style of the `ed` command modified as follows:

In a context address, the construction `\?regular expression?`, where `?` is any character, is identical to `/regular expression/`. Note that in the context address `\xabc\xdefx`, the second `x` stands for itself, so that the regular expression is `abcxdef`.

The escape sequence `\n` matches a newline embedded in the pattern space.

A period `.` matches any character except the terminal newline of the pattern space.

A command line with no addresses selects every pattern space.

A command line with one address selects each pattern space that matches the address.

A command line with two addresses selects the inclusive range from the first pattern space that matches the first address through the next pattern space that matches the second. (If the second address is a number less than or equal to the line number first selected, only one line is selected.) Thereafter the process is repeated, looking again for the first address.

Editing commands can be applied only to non-selected pattern spaces by use of the negation function `!` (below).

In the following list of functions the maximum number of permissible addresses for each function is indicated in parentheses.

The argument `text` consists of one or more lines, all but the last of which end with \ to hide the newline. Backslashes in text are treated like backslashes in the replacement string of an s command, and may be used to protect initial blanks and tabs against the stripping that is done on every script line. The argument `rfile` or the argument `wfile` must terminate the command line and must be preceded by exactly one blank. Each `wfile` is created before processing begins. There can be at most 10 distinct `wfile` arguments.

(1) `a\`
`text` Append. Place `text` on the output before reading the next input line.

(2) `b label`
Branch to the : command bearing the `label`. If `label` is empty, branch to the end of the script.

(2) `c\`
`text` Change. Delete the pattern space. With 0 or 1 address or at the end of a 2-address range, place `text` on the output. Start the next cycle.

(2) `d` Delete the pattern space. Start the next cycle.

(2) `D` Delete the initial segment of the pattern space through the first newline. Start the next cycle.

(2) `g` Replace the contents of the pattern space by the contents of the hold space.

(2) `G` Append the contents of the hold space to the pattern space.

(2) `h` Replace the contents of the hold space by the contents of the pattern space.

(2) `H` Append the contents of the pattern space to the hold space.

(1) `i\`
`text` Insert. Place `text` on the standard output.

(2) `l` List the pattern space on the standard output in an unambiguous form. Non-printing characters are spelled in two-digit ASCII and long lines are folded.

(2) `n` Copy the pattern space to the standard output. Replace the pattern space with the next line of input.

(2) `N` Append the next line of input to the pattern space with an embedded newline. (The current line number changes.)

(2) `p` Print. Copy the pattern space to the standard output.

(2) `P` Copy the initial segment of the pattern space through the first newline to the standard output.

(1) `q` Quit. Branch to the end of the script. Do not start a new cycle.

(2) `r rfile`
Read the contents of `rfile`. Place them on the output before reading the next input line.

(2) `s/regular expression/replacement/flags`

Substitute the `replacement` string for instances of the `regular expression` in the pattern space. Any character may be used instead of **/**. For a fuller description see ED(BU_CMD). The value of `flags` is zero or more of:

n n= 1 - 512. Substitute for just the n th occurrence of the `regular expression`.

g Global. Substitute for all nonoverlapping instances of the `regular expression` rather than just the first one.

p Print the pattern space if a replacement was made.

w `wfile`
Write. Append the pattern space to `wfile` if a replacement was made.

(2)**t** `label` Test. Branch to the **:** command bearing the `label` if any substitutions have been made since the most recent reading of an input line or execution of a **t**. If `label` is empty, branch to the end of the script.

(2)**w** `wfile` Write. Append the pattern space to `wfile`.

(2)**x** Exchange the contents of the pattern and hold spaces.

(2)**y/**`string1`**/**`string2`**/**
Transform. Replace all occurrences of characters in `string1` with the corresponding character in `string2`. The lengths of `string1` and `string2` must be equal.

(2)**!** `function`
Don't. Apply the `function` (or group, if `function` is **{}**) only to lines *not* selected by the address(es).

(0)**:** `label` This command does nothing; it bears a `label` for **b** and **t** commands to branch to.

(1)**=** Place the current line number on the standard output as a line.

(2)**{** Execute the following commands through a matching **}** only when the pattern space is selected.

(0) An empty command is ignored.

(0)**#** If a **#** appears as the first character on the first line of a script file, then that entire line is treated as a comment, with one exception. If the character after the **#** is an 'n', then the default output will be suppressed. The rest of the line after **#n** is also ignored. A script file must contain at least one non-comment line.

USAGE

General.

SEE ALSO

AWK(BU_CMD), ED(BU_CMD), GREP(BU_CMD).

NAME

sh, rsh — shell, the standard/restricted command interpreter

SYNOPSIS

`sh` [*flags*] [*args*]

`rsh` [*flags*] [*args*]

DESCRIPTION

The command `sh` is a command interpreter that executes commands read from a terminal or a file. The command `rsh` is a restricted version of the standard command interpreter `sh`; it is used to set up login-names and execution environments whose capabilities are more controlled than those of the standard shell. See **Invocation** below for the meaning of flags and other arguments to the shell.

Commands

A *blank* is a tab or a space.

A *name* is a sequence of letters, digits, or underscores beginning with a letter or underscore.

A *parameter* is a name, a digit, or any of the characters `*`, `@`, `#`, `?`, `-`, `$` and `!`.

A *simple-command* is a sequence of non-blank words separated by blanks. The first word specifies the path-name or file-name of the command to be executed. Except as specified below, the remaining words are passed as arguments to the invoked command. The command-name is passed as argument 0 [see EXEC(BA_SYS)]. The *value* of a simple-command is its exit *status* if it terminates normally, or (octal) `200+`*status* if it terminates abnormally [see SIGNAL(BA_SYS) for a list of status values].

A *pipeline* is a sequence of one or more commands separated by the character `|`. The standard output of each command (except the last) is connected by a *pipe* [see PIPE(BA_SYS)] to the standard input of the next command. Each command is run as a separate process; the shell waits for the last command to terminate. The exit status of a pipeline is the exit status of the last command.

Unless otherwise stated, the value returned by a command is that of the last simple-command executed in the command.

A *list* is a command or a pipeline or a sequence of commands and pipelines separated by the characters `;` or `&` or the character-pairs `&&` or `||`. Of these, the characters `;` and `&`, which have equal precedence, have a precedence lower than that of the character-pairs `&&` and `||`, which have equal precedence. A *list* may optionally be terminated by the characters `;` or `&`.

A series of commands and/or pipelines separated by the character `;` are executed sequentially, while commands and pipelines terminated by the character `&` are executed asynchronously. Thus, `/` causes sequential execution5 of the preceding pipeline; `&` causes asynchronous execution of the preceding pipeline (i.e., the shell does *not* wait for that pipeline to finish). The character-pair

&& or || causes the *list* following it to be executed only if the preceding pipeline returns a zero (non-zero) exit status. An arbitrarily long sequence of newlines may appear in a *list*, instead of the character ;, to delimit commands.

A command is either a simple-command or one of the following:

`for` *name* [`in` *word* ...] `do` *list* `done`
: Each time a `for` command is executed, *name* is set to the next *word* taken from the `in` *word* `list`. `If in` *word* ... is omitted, then the `for` command executes the `do` *list* once for each positional parameter set (see **Parameter Substitution** below). Execution ends when there are no more words in the list.

`case` *word* `in` [*pattern* [| *pattern*] ...) *list* ;;] ... `esac`
: A `case` command executes the *list* associated with the first *pattern* that matches *word*. The form of the patterns is the same as that used for file-name generation (see **File Name Generation**) except that a slash, a leading dot, or a dot immediately following a slash need not be matched explicitly.

`if` *list* `then` *list* [`elif` *list* `then` *list*] ... [`else` *list*] `fi`
: The *list* following `if` is executed and, if it returns a zero exit status, the *list* following the first `then` is executed. Otherwise, the *list* following `elif` is executed and, if its value is zero, the *list* following the next `then` is executed. Failing that, the `else` *list* is executed. If no `else` *list* or `then` *list* is executed, then the `if` command returns a zero exit status.

`while` *list* `do` *list* `done`
: A `while` command repeatedly executes the `while` *list* and, if the exit status of the last command in the list is zero, executes the `do` *list*; otherwise the loop terminates. If no commands in the `do` *list* are executed, then the `while` command returns a zero exit status; `until` may be used in place of `while` to negate the loop termination test.

(*list*)
: Execute *list* in a sub-shell.

{ *list* ; }
: Simply execute *list* (the semi-colon may be replaced by a newline).

`name ( )` { *list* ; }
: Define a function which is referenced by `name`. (New in **UNIX** System V Release 2.0) The body of the function is the *list* of commands between { and } (the semi-colon may be replaced by a newline). Execution of functions is described below (see **Execution**).

The following words are only recognized as the first word of a command and when not quoted:

```
if then else elif fi case esac for
esac for while until do done { }
```

Comments
A word beginning with # causes that word and all the following characters up to a newline to be ignored.

Command Substitution
The standard output from a command enclosed in a pair of grave accents (``) may be used as part or all of a word; trailing newlines are removed.

Parameter Substitution
The character $ is used to introduce substitutable parameters. There are two types of parameters, positional and keyword. If the parameter-name is a single digit (0-9), it is a positional parameter; otherwise, the name must be a legal *name* as defined above, and gives a keyword parameter. Positional parameters may be assigned values by `set`. Keyword parameters (also known as variables) may be assigned values by writing:

`name=`*value* [`name=`*value*] ...

Pattern-matching is not performed on *value*. There cannot be a function and a variable with the same `name`.

$ { *parameter* **}**
The value, if any, of the parameter is substituted. The braces are required only when *parameter* is followed by a letter, digit, or underscore that is not to be interpreted as part of its name. If *parameter* is * or @, all the positional parameters, starting with $1, are substituted (separated by spaces). Parameter $0 is set from argument zero when the shell is invoked.

$ { *parameter* **:** *word* **}**
If *parameter* is set and is non-null, substitute its value; otherwise substitute *word*.

$ { *parameter* **:** =*word* **}**
If *parameter* is not set or is null set it to *word*; the value of the parameter is substituted. Positional parameters may not be assigned to in this way.

$ { *parameter* **?** *word* **}**
If *parameter* is set and is non-null, substitute its value; otherwise, print *word* and exit from the shell. If *word* is omitted, the message `parameter null or not set` is printed.

$ { *parameter* **:** +*word* **}**
If *parameter* is set and is non-null, substitute *word*; otherwise substitute nothing.

In the above, *word* is not evaluated unless it is to be used as the substituted string, so that, in the following example, `pwd` is executed only if `d` is not set or is null:

```
echo ${d:-`pwd`}
```

If the character : is omitted from the above expressions, the shell only checks whether *parameter* is set or not.

The following parameters are automatically set by the shell:

- `#` The number of positional parameters in decimal.
- `–` Flags supplied to the shell on invocation or by the `set` command.
- `?` The decimal value returned by the last synchronously executed command.
- `$` The process number of this shell.
- `!` The process number of the last background command invoked.

The following parameters are used by the shell:

`HOME`
: The default argument (home directory) for the `cd` command.

`PATH`
: The search path for commands (see **Execution** below). The user may not change `PATH` if executing under `rsh`.

`CDPATH`
: The search path for the `cd` command. The syntax and usage is similar to that of `PATH`.

`MAIL`
: If this parameter is set to the name of a mail file, then the shell informs the user of the arrival of mail in the specified file. In UNIX System V Release 2.0, the user is informed only if `MAIL` is set and `MAILPATH` is not set.

`MAILCHECK`
: (New in UNIX System V Release 2.0) This parameter specifies how often (in seconds) the shell will check for the arrival of mail in the files specified by the `MAILPATH` or `MAIL` parameters. The default value is 600 seconds (10 minutes). If set to 0, the shell will check before each primary prompt.

`MAILPATH`
: (New in UNIX System V Release 2.0) The character `:` separated list of file-names. If this parameter is set, the shell informs the user of the arrival of mail in any of the specified files. Each file name can be followed by `%` and a message that will be printed when the modification time changes. The default message is "`you have mail`".

`PS1`
: Primary prompt string, by default `$`.

`PS2`
: Secondary prompt string, by default `>`.

`IFS`
: Internal field separators, normally *space*, *tab*, and *newline*.

`SHACCT`
: If this parameter is set to the name of a file writable by the user, the shell will write an accounting record in the file for each shell procedure executed. (New in UNIX System V Release 2.0)

`SHELL`
When the shell is invoked, it scans the environment (see **Environment** below) for this name. (New in UNIX System V Release 2.0) If it is found and there is an `r` in the file-name part of its value, the shell becomes a restricted shell.

The shell gives defaults for `PATH, PS1, PS2, MAILCHECK, IFS.`

Blank Interpretation

After parameter and command substitution, the results of substitution are scanned for internal-field-separator characters (those found in `IFS`) and split into distinct arguments where such characters are found. Explicit null arguments (" " or ′′) are retained. Implicit null arguments (those resulting from parameters that have no values) are removed.

File Name Generation

Following substitution, each command *word* is scanned for the characters `*`, `?`, and `[`. If one of these characters appears the word is regarded as a *pattern*. The word is replaced with alphabetically sorted file names that match the pattern. If no file name is found that matches the pattern, the word is left unchanged. The character `.` at the start of a file-name or immediately following a `/`, as well as the character `/` itself, must be matched explicitly.

- `*` Matches any string, including the null-string.
- `?` Matches any single character.
- `[...]` Matches any one of the enclosed characters. A pair of characters separated by `-` matches any character lexically between the pair, inclusive. If the first character following the opening `[` is a `!` any character *not* enclosed is matched.

Quoting

The following characters have a special meaning to the shell and cause termination of a word unless quoted:

`;` `&` `(` `)` `|` `^` `<` `>` *newline* *space* *tab*

A character may be *quoted* (i.e., made to stand for itself) by preceding it with the character `\`. The pair `\`*newline* is ignored. All characters enclosed between a pair of single quote marks (`' '`), except a single quote, are quoted. Inside double quote marks (`" "`), parameter and command substitution occurs and `\` quotes the characters `\`, `` ` ``, `"`, and `$`. The character-pair `$*` is equivalent to `$1 $2 ...`, whereas `$@` is equivalent to `$1 $2 ....`

Prompting

When used interactively, the shell prompts with the value of `PS1` before reading a command. If at any time a newline is typed and further input is needed to complete a command, the secondary prompt (i.e., the value of `PS2`) is issued.

Input/Output

Before a command is executed, its input and output may be redirected using a special notation interpreted by the shell. The following may appear anywhere in a simple-command, or may precede or follow a command and are *not* passed on to the invoked command; substitution occurs before *word* or *digit* is used:

<*word*	Use file *word* as standard input (file-descriptor `0`).
>*word*	Use file *word* as standard output (file-descriptor `1`). If the file does not exist it is created; otherwise, it is truncated to zero length.
>>*word*	Use file *word* as standard output. If the file exists, output is appended to it (by first seeking to the end-of-file); otherwise, the file is created.
<<[-]*word*	The shell input is read up to a line that is the same as *word* or to an end-of-file. The resulting document becomes the standard input. If any character of *word* is quoted, no interpretation is placed upon the characters of the document; otherwise, parameter and command substitution occurs, (unescaped) *newline* is ignored, and \\ must be used to quote the characters \\, $, \`, and the first character of `word`. If - is appended to <<, all leading tabs are stripped from *word* and from the document.
<&*digit*	Use the file associated with file-descriptor *digit* as standard input. Similarly for the standard output using >&*digit*.
<&-	The standard input is closed. Similarly for the standard output using >&-.

If a digit precedes any of the above, the digit specifies the file-descriptor to be associated with the file (instead of the default `0` or `1`). For example:

```
... 2>&1
```

associates file-descriptor `2` with the file currently associated with file-descriptor `1`.

The order in which redirections are specified is significant. The shell evaluates redirections left-to-right. For example:

```
... 1>xxx 2>&1
```

first associates file-descriptor `1` with file *xxx*. It associates file-descriptor `2` with the file-associated with file descriptor `1` (i.e., *xxx*). If the order of redirections were reversed, file-descriptor `2` would be associated with the terminal (assuming file-descriptor `1` had been) and file-descriptor `1` would be associated with file *xxx*.

If a command is followed by & the default standard input for the command is the empty file `/dev/null`. Otherwise, the environment for the execution of a command contains the file-descriptors of the invoking shell as modified by input/output specifications.

Redirection of output is not allowed in the restricted shell.

Environment

The *environment* is a list of name-value pairs that is passed to an executed program in the same way as a normal argument list. The shell interacts with the environment in several ways. On invocation, the shell scans the environment and creates a parameter for each name found, giving it the corresponding value. If the user modifies the value of any of these parameters or creates new parameters, none of these affects the environment unless the `export` command is used to bind the shell's parameter to the environment (see also `set -a`). A parameter may be removed from the environment with the `unset` command (new in UNIX System V Release 2.0). The environment seen by any executed command is thus composed of any unmodified name-value pairs originally inherited by the shell, minus any pairs removed by `unset`, plus any modifications or additions, all of which must be noted in `export` commands.

The environment for any *simple-command* may be augmented by prefixing it with one or more assignments to parameters. Thus:

```
TERM=123 cmd
(export TERM; TERM=123; cmd)
```

(where `cmd` uses the value of the environmental variable `TERM`) are equivalent as far as the execution of `cmd` is concerned.

If the `-k` flag is set, *all* keyword arguments are placed in the environment, even if they occur after the command-name. The following first prints `a=b c` and `c`:

```
echo a=b c
set -k
echo a=b c
```

Signals

The `INTERRUPT` and `QUIT` signals for an invoked command are ignored if the command is followed by `&`; otherwise signals have the values inherited by the shell from its parent (but see also the `trap` command below).

Execution

Each time a command is executed, the above substitutions are carried out. If the command name matches one of the **Special Commands** listed below, it is executed in the shell process. If the command name does not match a **Special Command**, but matches the name of a defined function (functions are new in UNIX System V Release 2.0), the function is executed in the shell process (note how this differs from the execution of shell procedures). The positional parameters `$1`, `$2`, ... are set to the arguments of the function. If the command name matches neither a **Special Command** nor the name of a defined function, a new process is created and an attempt is made to execute the command via an EXEC(BA_SYS) routine.

The variable `PATH` defines the search path for the directory containing the command. Alternative directory names are separated by a colon (`:`). Note that the current directory is specified by a null path-name, which can appear immediately after the equal sign or between the colon delimiters anywhere else in the path-list. If the command name contains a / the search path is not used; such commands will not be executed by the restricted shell. Otherwise, each directory in the path is searched for an executable file. If the file has execute permission but is not an executable (`a.out`) file, it is assumed to be a file containing shell commands. A sub-shell is spawned to read it. A parenthesized command is also executed in a sub-shell.

The following is new in UNIX System V Release 2.0:

> The location in the search path where a command was found is remembered by the shell (to help avoid unnecessary calls to the EXEC(BA_SYS) routines later). If the command was found in a relative directory, its location must be re-determined whenever the current directory changes. The shell forgets all remembered locations whenever the `PATH` variable is changed or the `hash -r` command is executed (see below).

Special Commands

Except as specified, input/output redirection is not permitted for these commands in UNIX System V Release 1.0. In UNIX System V Release 2.0, such redirection is permitted; file-descriptor 1 is the default output location.

`:`

No effect; the command does nothing. A zero exit code is returned.

`.` *file*

Read and execute commands from *file* and return. The search path specified by `PATH` is used to find the directory containing *file*.

`break` [*n*]

Exit from the enclosing `for` or `while` loop, if any. If *n* is specified break *n* levels.

`continue` [*n*]

Resume the next iteration of the enclosing `for` or `while` loop. If *n* is specified resume at the *n*-th enclosing loop.

`cd` [*arg*]

Change the current directory to *arg*. The variable `HOME` is the default *arg*. The variable `CDPATH` defines the search path for the directory containing *arg*. Alternative directory names are separated by a colon (`:`). The default path is **null** (specifying the current directory). Note that the current directory is specified by a null path name, which can appear immediately after the equal sign or between the colon delimiters anywhere else in the path list. If *arg* begins with a / the search path is not used. Otherwise, each directory in the path is searched for *arg*. The `cd` command may not be executed by `rsh`.

`echo` [*arg* ...]

Echo arguments [see ECHO(BU_CMD)] for usage and description. (Not a Special Command in UNIX System V Release 1.0)

`eval` [*arg* ...]

The arguments are read as input to the shell and the resulting command(s) executed.

`exec` [*arg* ...]

The command specified by the arguments is executed in place of this shell without creating a new process. Input/output arguments may appear and, if no other arguments are given, cause the shell input/output to be modified.

`exit` [*n*]

Causes a shell to exit with the exit status specified by *n*. If *n* is omitted the exit status is that of the last command executed (an end-of-file will also cause the shell to exit).

`export` [*name* ...]

The given *names* are marked for automatic export to the *environment* of subsequently-executed commands. If no arguments are given, a list of all names that are exported in this shell is printed. Function names may *not* be exported.

`hash` [`-r`] [*name* ...]

For each *name*, the location in the search path of the command specified by *name* is determined and remembered by the shell. (New in UNIX System V Release 2.0) The `-r` option causes the shell to forget all remembered locations. If no arguments are given, information about remembered commands is presented.

`pwd`

Print the current-working-directory. (Not a Special Command in UNIX System V Release 1.0) [see PWD(BU_CMD)] for usage and description.

`read` [*name* ...]

One line is read from the standard input and the first word is assigned to the first *name*, the second word to the second *name*, etc., with leftover words assigned to the last *name*. Only the characters in the variable `IFS` are recognized as delimiters. The return code is 0 unless an end-of-file is encountered.

`readonly` [*name* ...]

The given *names* are marked **readonly** and the values of the these *names* may not be changed by subsequent assignment. If no arguments are given, a list of all **readonly** names is printed.

`return [n]`

Causes a function to exit with the return value specified by *n*. (New in UNIX System V Release 2.0) If *n* is omitted, the return status is that of the last command executed.

`set [--aefhkntuvx [arg ...]]`

- `-a` Mark variables which are modified or created for export. (New in UNIX System V Release 2.0)
- `-e` Exit immediately if a command exits with a non-zero exit status.
- `-f` Disable file-name generation. (New in UNIX System V Release 2.0)
- `-h` Locate and remember function commands as functions are defined (function commands are normally located when the function is executed). (New in UNIX System V Release 2.0)
- `-k` All keyword arguments are placed in the environment for a command, not just those that precede the command name.
- `-n` Read commands but do not execute them.
- `-t` Exit after reading and executing one command.
- `-u` Treat unset variables as an error when substituting.
- `-v` Print shell input lines as they are read.
- `-x` Print commands and their arguments as they are executed.
- `--` Do not change any of the flags; useful in setting `$1` to `-`.

Using `+` rather than `-` causes these flags to be turned off. These flags can also be used upon invocation of the shell. The current set of flags may be found in `$-`. The remaining arguments are positional parameters and are assigned, in order, to `$1`, `$2`, ... If no arguments are given the values of all names are printed.

`shift [n]`

The positional parameters from `$`*n+1*... are renamed `$1`.... If *n* is not given, it is assumed to be 1.

`test`

Evaluate conditional expressions [see TEST(BU_CMD)] for usage and description.

`times`

Print the accumulated user and system times for processes run from the shell.

`trap [arg] [n] ...`

The command *arg* is to be read and executed when the shell receives signal(s) *n*. (Note that *arg* is scanned once when the trap is set and once when the trap is taken). Trap commands are executed in order of signal number. Any attempt to set a trap on a signal that was ignored on entry to the current shell is ineffective. If *arg* is absent all trap(s) *n* are reset to their original values. If *arg* is the null-string this signal is ignored by the shell and by the commands it invokes. If *n* is 0 the command *arg* is executed on exit from the shell. The `trap` command with no arguments prints a list of commands associated with each signal number.

`type` [*name* ...]

For each *name*, indicate how it would be interpreted if used as a command name. (New in UNIX System V Release 2.0)

`ulimit` [`-f` *n*]

If the `-f` *n* option is used, then a size-limit of *n* blocks is imposed on files written by the shell and its child-processes (files of any size may be read). If *n* is omitted, the current limit is printed. If no option is given, `-f` is assumed.

`umask` [*nnn*]

The user file-creation-mask is set to *nnn* [see UMASK(BA_SYS)]. If *nnn* is omitted, the current value of the mask is printed.

`unset` [*name* ...]

For each *name*, remove the corresponding variable or function. (New in UNIX System V Release 2.0) The variables `PATH`, `PS1`, `PS2`, `MAILCHECK` and `IFS` cannot be unset.

`wait` [*n*]

Wait for the specified process and report its termination status. If *n* is not given all currently active child-processes are waited for and the return code is zero.

Invocation

If the shell is invoked through an EXEC(BA_SYS) routine and the first character of argument zero is `-`, commands are initially read from `/etc/profile` and from `$HOME/.profile`, if such files exist. Thereafter, commands are read as described below. The flags below are interpreted by the shell on invocation only; note that unless the `-c` or `-s` flag is specified, the first argument is assumed to be the name of a file containing commands, and the remaining arguments are passed as positional parameters to that command file:

`-c` *string* If the `-c` flag is present commands are read from *string*.

`-s` If the `-s` flag is present or if no arguments remain commands are read from the standard input. Any remaining arguments specify the positional parameters. Shell output (except for **Special Commands**) is written to file-descriptor `2`.

`-i` If the `-i` flag is present or if the shell input and output are attached to a terminal, this shell is *interactive*. In this case `TERMINATE` is ignored (so that `kill 0` does not kill an interactive shell) and `INTERRUPT` is caught and ignored (so that `wait` is interruptible). In all cases, `QUIT` is ignored by the shell.

`-r` If the `-r` flag is present the shell is a restricted shell.

The remaining flags and arguments are described under the `set` command.

For rsh Only

The commnad `rsh` is used to set up login names and execution environments whose capabilities are more controlled than those of the standard shell. The actions of `rsh` are similar to those of `sh`, but the following are disallowed:

changing directory [see CD(BU_CMD)],
setting the value of `PATH`,
specifying path or command names containing `/`,
redirecting output (> and >>).

The restrictions above are enforced after `.profile` is interpreted.

When a command to be executed is found to be a shell procedure, `rsh` invokes `sh` to execute it. Thus, it is possible to provide to the end-user shell procedures that have access to the full power of the standard shell, while imposing a limited menu of commands; this scheme assumes that the end-user does not have write and execute permissions in the same directory.

The net effect of these rules is that the writer of the `.profile` has complete control over user actions, by performing guaranteed setup actions and leaving the user in an appropriate directory (probably *not* the login directory).

EXIT STATUS

Errors detected by the shell, such as syntax errors, cause the shell to return a non-zero exit status. If the shell is being used non-interactively execution of the shell file is abandoned. Otherwise, the shell returns the exit status of the last command executed (see also the `exit` command above).

FILES

`/etc/profile`
`$HOME/.profile`
`/dev/null`

USAGE

General.

(Not for UNIX System V Release 1.0) If a command is executed, and a command with the same name is installed in a directory in the search path before the directory where the original command was found, the shell continues to `exec` the original command. Use the `hash` command to correct.

(Not for UNIX System V Release 1.0) If the current directory or the one above it is moved, `pwd` may not give the correct response. Use the command `cd` with a full path-name to correct this situation.

SEE ALSO

CD(BU_CMD), ECHO(BU_CMD), PWD(BU_CMD), TEST(BU_CMD), UMASK(BU_CMD), DUP(BA_SYS), EXEC(BA_SYS), FORK(BA_SYS), PIPE(BA_SYS), SIGNAL(BA_SYS), SYSTEM(BA_SYS), ULIMIT(BA_SYS), UMASK(BA_SYS), WAIT(BA_SYS).

NAME

sleep — suspend execution for an interval

SYNOPSIS

`sleep` *time*

DESCRIPTION

The command `sleep` suspends execution for *time* seconds. It is used to execute a command after a certain amount of time, as in:

```
(sleep 105; command)&
```

or to execute a command every so often, as in:

```
while true
do
        command
        sleep 37
done
```

USAGE

General.

SEE ALSO

ALARM(BA_SYS), SLEEP(BA_SYS).

NAME

sort — sort and/or merge files

SYNOPSIS

sort [**-cmu**] [**-o***output*] [**-y***kmem*] [**-z***recsz*] [**-dfinr**] [**-bt***x*] [**+***pos1* [**-***pos2*]] [*files*]

DESCRIPTION

The command **sort** sorts lines of all the named files together and writes the result on the standard output. The standard input is read if – is used as a file name or no input files are named.

Comparisons are based on one or more sort keys extracted from each line of input. By default, there is one sort key, the entire input line, and ordering is lexicographic by bytes in machine collating sequence.

The following options alter the default behavior:

−c Check that the input file is sorted according to the ordering rules; give no output unless the file is out of sort.

−m Merge only, the input files are already sorted.

−u Unique: suppress all but one in each set of lines having equal keys.

−o*output* The argument given is the name of an output file to use instead of the standard output. This file may be the same as one of the inputs. There may be optional blanks between **−o** and *output*.

−y*kmem* The amount of main memory used by the sort has a large impact on its performance. Sorting a small file in a large amount of memory is a waste. If this option is omitted, **sort** begins using a system default memory size, and continues to use more space as needed. If this option is presented with a value, *kmem*, **sort** will start using that number of kilobytes of memory, unless the administrative minimum or maximum is violated, in which case the corresponding extremum will be used. Thus, **−y0** is guaranteed to start with minimum memory. By convention, **−y** (with no argument) starts with maximum memory.

−z*recsz* The size of the longest line read is recorded in the sort phase so buffers can be allocated during the merge phase. If the sort phase is omitted via the **−c** or **−m** options, a popular system default size will be used. Lines longer than the buffer size will cause **sort** to terminate abnormally. Supplying the actual number of bytes in the longest line to be merged (or some larger value) will prevent abnormal termination.

The following options override the default ordering rules.

- `-d` "Dictionary" order: only letters, digits and blanks (spaces and tabs) are significant in comparisons.
- `-f` Fold lower case letters into upper case.
- `-i` Ignore characters outside the **ASCII** range 040-0176 in non-numeric comparisons.
- `-n` An initial numeric string, consisting of optional blanks, optional minus sign, and zero or more digits with optional decimal point, is sorted by arithmetic value. The `-n` option implies the `-b` option (see below). Note that the `-b` option is only effective when restricted sort key specifications are in effect.
- `-r` Reverse the sense of comparisons.

When ordering options appear before restricted sort key specifications, the requested ordering rules are applied globally to all sort keys. When attached to a specific sort key (described below), the specified ordering options override all global ordering options for that key.

The notation `+pos1 -pos2` restricts a sort key to one beginning at `pos1` and ending at `pos2`. The characters at positions `pos1` and `pos2` are included in the sort key (provided that `pos2` does not precede `pos1`). A missing `-pos2` means the end of the line.

Specifying `pos1` and `pos2` involves the notion of a field, a minimal sequence of characters followed by a field separator or a newline. By default, the first blank (space or tab) of a sequence of blanks acts as the field separator. All blanks in a sequence of blanks are considered to be part of the next field; for example, all blanks at the beginning of a line are considered to be part of the first field. The treatment of field separators can be altered using the options:

- `-tx` Use `x` as the field separator character; `x` is not considered to be part of a field (although it may be included in a sort key). Each occurrence of `x` is significant (e.g., `xx` delimits an empty field).
- `-b` Ignore leading blanks when determining the starting and ending positions of a restricted sort key. If the `-b` option is specified before the first `+pos1` argument, it will be applied to all `+pos1` arguments. Otherwise, the **b** flag may be attached independently to each `+pos1` or `-pos2` argument (see below).

The arguments `pos1` and `pos2` each have the form `m.n` optionally followed by one or more of the flags **bdfinr**. A starting position specified by `+m.n` is interpreted to mean the `n+1`*st* character in the `m+1`*st* field. A missing `.n` means **.0**, indicating the first character of the `m+1`*st* field. If the **b** flag is in effect `n` is counted from the first non-blank in the `m+1`*st* field; `+m.0`**b** refers to the first non-blank character in the `m+1`*st* field.

A last position specified by `-m.n` is interpreted to mean the `n`*th* character (including separators) after the last character of the `m`*th* field. A missing `.n` means **.0**, indicating the last character of the *mth* field. If the **b** flag is in effect n is counted from the last leading blank in the m+1*st* field; **−m.1b** refers to the first non-blank in the m+1*st* field.

When there are multiple sort keys, later keys are compared only after all earlier keys compare equal. Lines that otherwise compare equal are ordered with all bytes significant.

EXAMPLES

Sort the contents of `infile` with the second field as the sort key:

```
sort +1 -2 infile
```

Sort, in reverse order, the contents of `infile1` and `infile2`, placing the output in `outfile` and using the first character of the second field as the sort key:

```
sort -r -o outfile +1.0 -1.2 infile1 infile2
```

Sort, in reverse order, the contents of `infile1` and `infile2` using the first non-blank character of the second field as the sort key:

```
sort -r +1.0b -1.1b infile1 infile2
```

Print the password file sorted by the numeric user ID (the third colon-separated field):

```
sort -t: +2n -3 /etc/passwd
```

Print the lines of the already sorted file `infile`, suppressing all but the first occurrence of lines having the same third field (the options **−um** with just one input file make the choice of a unique representative from a set of equal lines predictable):

```
sort -um +2 -3 infile
```

ERRORS

`Sort` comments and exits with non-zero status for various trouble conditions (e.g., when input lines are too long), and for disorder discovered under the `−c` option.

When the last line of an input file is missing a newline character, `sort` appends one, prints a warning message, and continues.

USAGE

General.

SEE ALSO

COMM(BU_CMD), JOIN(AU_CMD), UNIQ(BU_CMD).

NAME

spell — find spelling errors

SYNOPSIS

`spell [-v] [-b] [-x] [`*+local_file*`] [`*files*`]`

DESCRIPTION

The command `spell` collects words from the named *files* and looks them up in a spelling list. Words that neither occur among nor are derivable (by applying certain inflections, prefixes, and/or suffixes) from words in the spelling list are printed on the standard output. If no *files* are named, words are collected from the standard input.

Under the `-v` option, all words not literally in the spelling list are printed, and plausible derivations from the words in the spelling list are indicated.

Under the `-b` option, British spelling is checked. Besides preferring *centre, colour, programme, speciality, travelled,* etc., this option insists upon *-ise* in words like *standardise.*

Under the `-x` option, every plausible stem is printed with = for each word.

Under the *+local_file* option, words found in *local_file* are removed from `spell's` output. The argument *local_file* is the name of a user-provided file that contains a sorted list of words, one per line. With this option, the user can specify a set of words that are correct spellings (in addition to `spell's` own spelling list) for each job.

USAGE

End-user.

CAVEATS

In order to the command syntax standard, the *+local_file* option will be changed to the form `-f`*local_file.* The old form will continue to be accepted for some time.

NAME

split — split a file into pieces

SYNOPSIS

`split [ -n ]` [*file*[*name*]]

DESCRIPTION

The command `split` reads *file* and writes it in *n-line* pieces (default 1000 lines) onto a set of output files. The name of the first output file is *name* with *aa* appended, and so on lexicographically, up to *zz* (a maximum of 676 files). The argument *name* cannot be longer than {NAME_MAX}-2 characters. If no output name is given, **x** is default.

If no input file is given, or if – is given in its stead, then the standard input file is used.

USAGE

General.

SEE ALSO

CSPLIT(AU_CMD).

NAME

sum – print checksum and block count of a file

SYNOPSIS

`sum [-r] file`

DESCRIPTION

The command `sum` calculates and prints a checksum for the named file, and also prints the space used by the file, in 512-byte units. The option `-r` causes an alternate algorithm to be used in computing the checksum.

The algorithms used are uniform across all UNIX System V implementations, so that the same checksum is obtained for the same file, independent of the hardware and implementation.

USAGE

General.

NAME

tail — deliver the last part of a file

SYNOPSIS

`tail` [+|-[*number*][`lbc`[`f`]]] [*file*]

DESCRIPTION

The command `tail` copies the named file to the standard output beginning at a designated place. If no file is named, the standard input is used.

Copying begins at distance +*number* from the beginning, or −*number* from the end of the input (if *number* is null, the value 10 is assumed). The arguments *number* is counted in units of lines, blocks, or characters, according to the appended option `l`, `b`, or `c`. When no units are specified, counting is by lines.

With the `-f` ("follow") option, if the input file is not a pipe, the program will not terminate after the line of the input file has been copied, but will enter an endless loop: it sleeps for a second and then attempts to read and copy further records from the input file. Thus it may be used to monitor the growth of a file that is being written by some other process. For example, the command:

```
tail -f fred
```

will print the last ten lines of the file `fred`, followed by any lines that are appended to `fred` between the time `tail` is initiated and killed. As another example, the command:

```
tail -15cf fred
```

will print the last 15 characters of the file `fred`, followed by any lines that are appended to `fred` between the time `tail` is initiated and killed.

USAGE

General.

Tails relative to the end of the file are saved in a buffer, and thus are limited in length.

Various kinds of anomalous behavior may happen with character special files.

NAME

tee — join pipes and make copies of input

SYNOPSIS

`tee` [`-i`] [`-a`] [*file*] ...

DESCRIPTION

The command `tee` transcribes the standard input to the standard output and makes copies in the *files*. The `-i` option ignores interrupts; the `-a` option causes the output to be appended to the *files* rather than overwriting them.

USAGE

General.

NAME

test — condition evaluation command

SYNOPSIS

`test` *expr*
[*expr*]

DESCRIPTION

The command `test` evaluates the expression *expr* and, if its value is true, returns a zero (true) exit status; otherwise, a non-zero (false) exit status is returned; `test` also returns a non-zero exit status if there are no arguments. The following primitives are used to construct *expr:*

−r *file*	true if *file* exists and is readable.
−w *file*	true if *file* exists and is writable.
−x *file*	true if *file* exists and is executable.
−f *file*	true if *file* exists and is a regular file.
−d *file*	true if *file* exists and is a directory.
−c *file*	true if *file* exists and is a character special file.
−b *file*	true if *file* exists and is a block special file.
−p *file*	true if *file* exists and is a named pipe (fifo).
−u *file*	true if *file* exists and its set-user-ID bit is set.
−g *file*	true if *file* exists and its set-group-ID bit is set.
−s *file*	true if *file* exists and has a size greater than zero.
−t[*fildes]*	true if the open file whose file descriptor number is *fildes* (1 by default) is associated with a terminal device.
−z *s1*	true if the length of string *s1* is zero.
−n *s1*	true if the length of the string *s1* is non-zero.
s1 **=** *s2*	true if strings *s1* and *s2* are identical.
s1 **!=** *s2*	true if strings *s1* and *s2* are *not* identical.
s1	true if *s1* is *not* the null string.
n1 **−eq** *n2*	true if the integers *n1* and *n2* are algebraically equal. Any of the comparisons `−ne`, `−gt`, `−ge`, `−lt`, and `−le` may be used in place of `−eq`.

These primaries may be combined with the following operators:

!	unary negation operator.
−a	binary *and* operator.

−o	binary *or* operator (**−a** has higher precedence than **−o**).
(*expr*)	parentheses for grouping.

Notice that all the operators and flags are separate arguments to `test`. Notice also that parentheses are meaningful to `sh` and, therefore, must be escaped.

In the second form of the command (i.e., the one that uses **[ ]**, rather than the word `test`), the square brackets must be delimited by blanks.

USAGE

General.

SEE ALSO

FIND(BU_CMD), SH(BU_CMD).

NAME

touch – update access and modification times of a file

SYNOPSIS

`touch [-amc] [`*mmddhhmm*`[`*yy*`] ]` *file* ...

DESCRIPTION

The command `touch` causes the access and modification times of each *file* to be updated. The *file* is created if it does not exist. If no time is specified the current time is used. The `-a` and `-m` options cause `touch` to update only the access or modification times respectively (default is `-am`). The `-c` option silently prevents `touch` from creating the *file* if it did not previously exist.

The return code from `touch` is the number of files for which the times could not be successfully modified (including files that did not exist and were not created).

USAGE

General.

NAME

tr — translate characters

SYNOPSIS

`tr [ -cds ]` [*string1* [*string2*]]

DESCRIPTION

The command `tr` copies the standard input to the standard output with substitution or deletion of selected characters. Input characters found in *string1* are mapped into the corresponding characters of *string2*. Any combination of the options `-cds` may be used:

`-c` Complements the set of characters in *string1* with respect to the universe of characters whose ASCII codes are 001 through 377 octal.

`-d` Deletes all input characters in *string1*.

`-s` Squeezes all strings of repeated output characters that are in *string2* to single characters.

The following abbreviation conventions may be used to introduce ranges of characters or repeated characters into the strings:

`[a-z]` Stands for the string of characters whose ASCII codes run from character `a` to character `z`, inclusive.

`[a*n]` Stands for `n` repetitions of `a`. If the first digit of `n` is `0`, `n` is considered octal; otherwise, `n` is taken to be decimal. A zero or missing `n` is taken to be huge; this facility is useful for padding *string2*.

The escape character \ may be used to remove special meaning from any character in a string. In addition, \ followed by 1, 2, or 3 octal digits stands for the character whose ASCII code is given by those digits.

The following example creates a list of all the words in *file1* one per line in *file2*, where a word is taken to be a maximal string of alphabetics. The strings are quoted to protect the special characters from interpretation by the command interpreter; 012 is the ASCII code for newline.

`tr -cs "[A-Z][a-z]" "[\012*]"` *<file1 >file2*

USAGE

General.

The command `tr` does not handle ASCII NUL in *string1* or *string2*; it always deletes NUL from input.

NAME

true, false — provide truth values

SYNOPSIS

`true`

`false`

DESCRIPTION

The command `true` does nothing, and returns exit code zero. The command `false` does nothing, and returns a non-zero exit code. They are typically used to construct command procedures. For example,

```
while true
do
        command
done
```

USAGE

General.

SEE ALSO

SH(BU_CMD).

NAME

umask — set file-creation mode mask

SYNOPSIS

`umask` [*ooo*]

DESCRIPTION

The user file-creation mode mask is set to *ooo*. The three octal digits refer to read/write/execute permissions for *owner*, *group*, and *others*, respectively [see CHMOD(BU_CMD)]. The value of each specified digit is subtracted from the corresponding "digit" specified by the system for the creation of a file. For example, `umask 022` removes *group* and *others* write permission (files normally created with mode `777` become mode `755`; files created with mode `666` become mode `644`).

If *ooo* is omitted, the current value of the mask is printed.

USAGE

General.

SEE ALSO

CHMOD(BU_CMD).

NAME

uname — print name of current system

SYNOPSIS

`uname [ -snrvma ]`

DESCRIPTION

The command `uname` prints the current system name on the standard output file. The options cause selected information returned by UNAME(BA_SYS) to be printed:

- `-s` print the system name (default). This is a name by which the system is known in the local installation.
- `-n` print the nodename. The nodename may be a name by which the system is known to a communications network.
- `-r` print the operating system release.
- `-v` print the operating system version.
- `-m` print the machine hardware name.
- `-a` print all the above information.

USAGE

General.

SEE ALSO

UNAME(BA_SYS).

NAME

uniq — report repeated lines in a file

SYNOPSIS

`uniq` [`-udc` [+*n*] [-*n*]] [*input* [*output*]]

DESCRIPTION

The command `uniq` reads the input file comparing adjacent lines. In the normal case, the second and succeeding copies of repeated lines are removed; the remainder is written on the output file. The arguments *input* and *output* should always be different. Note that repeated lines must be adjacent in order to be found [see SORT(BU_CMD)]. If the `-u` flag is used, just the lines that are not repeated in the original file are output. The `-d` option specifies that one copy of just the repeated lines is to be written. The normal mode output is the union of the `-u` and `-d` mode outputs.

The `-c` option supersedes `-u` and `-d` and generates an output report in default style but with each line preceded by a count of the number of times it occurred.

The `n` arguments specify skipping an initial portion of each line in the comparison:

`-n` The first `n` fields together with any blanks before each are ignored. A field is defined as a string of non-space, non-tab characters separated by tabs and spaces from its neighbors.

`+n` The first `n` characters are ignored. Fields are skipped before characters.

USAGE

General.

SEE ALSO

COMM(BU_CMD), SORT(BU_CMD).

NAME

wait – await completion of process

SYNOPSIS

`wait` [*pid*]

DESCRIPTION

With no argument, `wait` waits until all processes started with & have completed, and reports on abnormal terminations. If a numeric argument *pid* is given, and is the process id of a background process, then `wait` waits until that process has completed. Otherwise, if *pid* is not a background process, `wait` waits until all background processes have completed.

USAGE

General.

SEE ALSO

SH(BU_CMD), WAIT(BA_SYS).

NAME

wc — word count

SYNOPSIS

`wc [-lwc]` [*files*]

DESCRIPTION

The command `wc` counts lines, words, and characters in the named files, or in the standard input if no *files* appear. It also keeps a total count for all named files. A word is defined as a maximal string of characters delimited by spaces, tabs, or newlines.

The options `l`, `w`, and `c` may be used in any combination to specify that a subset of lines, words, and characters are to be reported. The default is `−lwc`.

When *files* are specified on the command line, their names will be printed along with the counts.

USAGE

General.

Chapter 2

Advanced Utilities

NAME

at, batch — execute commands at a later time

SYNOPSIS

```
at time [date] [+ increment]
at -r job ...
at -l [job] ...

batch
```

DESCRIPTION

The commands `at` and `batch` read commands from standard input to be executed at a later time. The command `at` allows you to specify when the commands should be executed, while jobs queued with `batch` will execute when system load level permits. The option `-r` removes jobs previously scheduled with `at`. The `-l` option reports all jobs scheduled for the invoking user.

Standard output and standard error output are mailed to the user unless they are redirected elsewhere. The environment variables, current directory, umask, and ulimit are retained when the commands are executed. Open file descriptors, traps, and priority are lost.

Users are permitted to use `at` if their name appears in the file `/usr/lib/cron/at.allow`. If that file does not exist, the file `/usr/lib/cron/at.deny` is checked to determine if the user should be denied access to `at`. If neither file exists, only root is allowed to submit a job. If only `at.deny` exists and is empty, global usage is permitted. The allow/deny files consist of one user name per line.

The *time* may be specified as 1, 2, or 4 digits. One and two digit numbers are taken to be hours, four digits to be hours and minutes. The time may alternately be specified as two numbers separated by a colon, meaning `hour:minute`. A suffix `am` or `pm` may be appended; otherwise a 24-hour clock time is understood. The suffix `zulu` may be used to indicate GMT. The special names `noon`, `midnight`, `now`, and `next` are also recognized.

An optional *date* may be specified as either a month name followed by a day number (and possibly year number preceded by a comma) or a day of the week (fully spelled or abbreviated to three characters). Two special "days", `today` and `tomorrow` are recognized. If no *date* is given, `today` is assumed if the given hour is greater than the current hour and `tomorrow` is assumed if it is less. If the given month is less than the current month (and no year is given), next year is assumed.

The optional *increment* is simply a number suffixed by one of the following: `minutes`, `hours`, `days`, `weeks`, `months`, or `years`. (The singular form is also accepted.)

Thus legitimate commands include:

```
at 0815am Jan 24
at 8:15am Jan 24
at now + 1 day
at 5 pm Friday
```

The commands `at` and `batch` write the job number and schedule time to standard error.

The command `batch` submits a batch job. It is almost equivalent to "at now", but not quite. For one, it goes into a different queue. For another, "at now" does not work: it is too late (and results in an error message).

The option `-r` removes jobs previously scheduled by `at` or `batch`. The job number is the number reported at invocation by `at` or `batch`. Job numbers can also be obtained by using the `-l` option. Only the super-user is allowed to remove another user's jobs.

EXAMPLES

The `at` and `batch` commands read from standard input the commands to be executed at a later time. It may be useful to redirect standard output within the specified commands.

This sequence can be used at a terminal:

> `batch`
> `spell` *filename* >*outfile*
> EOT

This sequence, which demonstrates redirecting standard error to a pipe, is useful in a command procedure (the sequence of output redirection specifications is significant):

> `batch <<!`
> `spell` *filename* 2>&1 >outfile | `mail` *loginid*
> !

To have a job reschedule itself, `at` can be invoked from within the procedure.

FILES

`/usr/lib/cron/at.allow` - list of allowed users

`/usr/lib/cron/at.deny` - list of denied users

USAGE

General.

SEE ALSO

CRON(AU_CMD).

NAME

chown, chgrp — change owner or group

SYNOPSIS

`chown` *owner file* ...

`chgrp` *group file* ...

DESCRIPTION

The command `chown` changes the owner of the *files* to *owner*. The owner may be either a decimal user-ID or a login name found in the password file.

The command `chgrp` changes the group- ID of the *files* to *group*. The group may be either a decimal group-ID or a group name found in the group file.

If either command is invoked by other than the super-user, the set-user-ID and set-group-ID bits of the file mode will be cleared.

FILES

`/etc/passwd`
`/etc/group`

USAGE

General.

SEE ALSO

CHMOD(BU_CMD), CHOWN(BA_SYS).

NAME

cron — clock daemon

SYNOPSIS

`/etc/cron`

DESCRIPTION

The command `cron` executes commands at specified dates and times. Regularly scheduled commands can be specified according to instructions found in crontab files; users can submit their own crontab file via the `crontab` command. Commands which are to be executed only once may be submitted via the `at` command.

A history of all actions taken by cron are recorded in a system log file.

USAGE

Administrator.

Since `cron` never exits, it should only be executed once. This is best done by running it from the initialization process.

SEE ALSO

AT(AU_CMD), CRONTAB(AU_CMD), SH(BU_CMD).

NAME

crontab — user crontab file

SYNOPSIS

```
crontab [file]
crontab -r
crontab -l
```

DESCRIPTION

The command `crontab` copies the specified *file*, or standard input if no file is specified, into a directory that holds all users' crontabs. The `-r` option removes a user's crontab from the crontab directory. The option `-l` will list the crontab file of the invoking user.

Users are permitted to use `crontab` if their names appear in the file `/usr/lib/cron/cron.allow`. If that file does not exist, the file `/usr/lib/cron/cron.deny` is checked to determine if the user should be denied access to `crontab`. If neither file exists, only root is allowed to submit a job. If only `cron.deny` exists and is empty, global usage is permitted. The allow/deny files consist of one user name per line.

A crontab file consists of lines of six fields each. The fields are separated by spaces or tabs. The first five are integer patterns that specify the following:

minute (0–59),
hour (0–23),
day of the month (1–31),
month of the year (1–12),
day of the week (0–6 with 0=Sunday).

Each of these patterns may be either an asterisk (meaning all legal values) or a list of elements separated by commas. An element is either a number or two numbers separated by a minus sign (meaning an inclusive range). Note that the specification of days may be made by two fields (day of the month and day of the week). If both are specified as a list of elements, each one is effective independent of the other. For example, 0 0 1,15 * 1 would run a command on the first and fifteenth of each month, as well as on every Monday. To specify days by only one field, the other field should be set to * (for example, 0 0 * * 1 would run a command only on Mondays).

The sixth field of a line in a crontab file is a string that is executed by the command interpreter at the specified times. A percent character in this field (unless escaped by \) is translated to a newline character. Only the first line (up to a % or end of line) of the command field is executed by the command interpreter. The other lines are made available to the command as standard input. The command `cron` supplies a default environment, defining the environmental variables `HOME`, `LOGNAME`, and `PATH`.

NOTE: If standard output and standard error are not redirected, any generated output or errors will be mailed to the user.

FILES

`/usr/lib/cron/cron.allow` list of allowed users

`/usr/lib/cron/cron.deny` list of denied users

USAGE

General.

The new crontab file for a user overwrites an existing one.

SEE ALSO

SH(BU_CMD), CRON(AU_CMD).

NAME

csplit — context split

SYNOPSIS

`csplit` [-s] [-k] [-f*prefix*] *file arg1* [. . . *argn*]

DESCRIPTION

The command `csplit` reads *file* and separates it into *n*+1 sections, defined by the arguments *arg1*... *argn*. By default the sections are placed in xx00 ... xxnn (nn may not be greater than 99). These sections get the following pieces of *file*:

00: From the start of *file* up to (but not including) the line referenced by *arg1*.

01: From the line referenced by *arg1* up to the line referenced by *arg2*.

.

.

.

n+1: From the line referenced by *argn* to the end of *file*.

If the *file* argument is a – then standard input is used.

The options to `csplit` are:

−s `csplit` normally prints the character counts for each file created. If the −s option is present, `csplit` suppresses the printing of all character counts.

−k `csplit` normally removes created files if an error occurs. If the −k option is present, `csplit` leaves previously created files intact.

−f*prefix*
If the −f option is used, the created files are named *prefix*00 ... *prefixn*. The default is xx00 ... xxn.

The arguments (*arg1* ... *argn*) to `csplit` can be a combination of the following:

/rexp/ A file is to be created for the section from the current line up to (but not including) the line containing the regular expression `rexp`. (Regular expressions as in ED(BU_CMD) are accepted.) The current line becomes the line containing `rexp`. This argument may be followed by an optional + or – some number of lines (e.g., /Page/−5).

%rexp% This argument is the same as /rexp/, except that no file is created for the section.

line_no A file is to be created from the current line up to (but not including) the line number `line_no`. The current line becomes `line_no`.

{num} Repeat argument. This argument may follow any of the above arguments. If it follows a `rexp` type argument, that argument is applied `num` more times. If it follows `lnno`, the file will be split every `lnno` lines (`num` times) from that point.

Enclose all `rexp` type arguments that contain blanks or other characters meaningful to the shell in the appropriate quotes. Regular expressions may not contain embedded newlines. The command `csplit` does not affect the original file; it is the user's responsibility to remove it.

EXAMPLES

This example creates four files, `cobol00` ... `cobol08`:

```
csplit -fcobol file '/procedure division/' /par5./
/par16./
```

After editing the split files, they can be recombined as follows:

```
cat cobol0[0-3] > file
```

Note that this example overwrites the original file.

This example would split the file at every 100 lines, up to 10,000 lines:

```
csplit -k file  100  {99}
```

The `-k` option causes the created files to be retained if there are less than 10,000 lines; however, an error message would still be printed.

```
csplit -k prog.c '%main(%' '/^}/+1' {20}
```

Assuming that `prog.c` follows the normal **C** coding convention of ending routines with a } at the beginning of the line, this example will create a file containing each separate **C** routine (up to 21) in `prog.c`.

ERRORS

An error is reported if an argument does not reference a line between the current position and the end of the file.

USAGE

General.

SEE ALSO

ED(BU_CMD), SH(BU_CMD).

NAME

cu — call another system

SYNOPSIS

`cu [-s` *speed*`] [-l` *line*`] [-h] [-t] [-d] [-o | -e] [-n]` *telno*

`cu [-s`*speed*`] [-h] [-d] [-o | -e] -l` *line*

`cu [-h] [-d] [-o | -e]` *systemname*

DESCRIPTION

The command `cu` calls up another system, which usually is a computer system running UNIX System V, but may be a terminal, or a computer system running another operating system. It manages an interactive conversation, with possible transfers of ASCII files. The third form above, using *systemname*, is new in UNIX System V Release 2.0.

The command `cu` accepts the following options and arguments:

`-s`*speed* Specifies the transmission speed. The default value is "Any" speed, depending on line order in the system devices file.

`-l`*line* Specifies a device name to use as the communication line. This can be used to override the search that would otherwise take place for the first available line having the right speed. When the `-l` option is used without the `-s` option, the speed of a line is taken from the devices file. When the `-l` and `-s` options are used together, `cu` searches the devices file to check if the requested speed for the requested line is available. If so, the connection is made at the requested speed; otherwise, an error message is printed and the call is not made. If the specified device is associated with an auto dialer, a telephone number must be provided. Using this option with *systemname* rather than *telno* is not allowed (see *systemname* below).

`-h` Emulates local echo, supporting calls to other computer systems which expect terminals to be set to half-duplex mode.

`-t` Used to dial an ASCII terminal which has been set to auto answer. Appropriate mapping of carriage-return to carriage-return-line-feed pairs is set.

`-d` Causes diagnostic traces to be printed.

`-o` Designates that odd parity is to be generated for data sent to the remote system.

`-e` Designates that even parity is to be generated for data sent to the remote system.

`-n` For added security, will prompt the user to provide the telephone number to be dialed rather than taking it from the command line. (New in UNIX System V Release 2.0.)

telno When using an automatic dialer, the argument is the telephone number with equal signs for secondary dial tone or minus signs placed appropriately for delays of 4 seconds.

systemname A uucp system name may be used rather than a telephone number; in this case, `cu` will obtain an appropriate direct line or telephone number from a system file.

Note: the *systemname* option should not be used in conjunction with the `-l` and `-s` options as `cu` will connect to the first available line for the system name specified ignoring the requested line and speed.

After making the connection, `cu` runs as two processes: the *transmit* process reads data from the standard input and, except for lines beginning with ~, passes it to the remote system; the *receive* process accepts data from the remote system and, except for lines beginning with ~,passes it to the standard output. Normally, an automatic DC3/DC1 protocol is used to control input from the remote so the buffer is not overrun. Lines beginning with ~ have special meanings.

The *transmit* process interprets the following user initiated commands:

`~.` terminate the conversation.

`~!` escape to an interactive command interpreter on the local system.

`~!cmd...` execute `cmd` on the local system

`~$cmd...` run `cmd` locally and send its output to the remote system for execution.

`~%cd` change the directory on the local system. (New in UNIX System V Release 2.0.)

`~%take from [to]` copy file `from` (on the remote system) to file `to` on the local system. If `to` is omitted, the `from` argument is used in both places.

`~%put from [to]` copy file `from` (on local system) to file `to` on remote system. If `to` is omitted, the `from` argument is used in both places.

`~~line` send the line `~line` to the remote system.

`~%break` transmit a BREAK to the remote system (which can also be specified as `~%b`).

`~%nostop` toggles between DC3/DC1 input control protocol and no input control. This is useful in case the remote system is one which does not respond properly to the DC3 and DC1 characters.

The *receive* process normally copies data from the remote system to its standard output.

The use of `~%put` requires STTY(AU_CMD) and CAT(BU_CMD) on the remote side. It also requires that the current erase and kill characters on the remote system be identical to these current control characters on the local system. Backslashes are inserted at appropriate places.

The use of `~%take` requires the existence of `echo` and `cat` on the remote system. Also, `tabs` mode [see STTY(AU_CMD)] should be set on the remote system if tabs are to be copied without expansion to spaces.

When `cu` is used on system `X` to connect to system `Y` and subsequently used on system `Y` to connect to system `Z`, commands on system `Y` can be executed by using ~~. For example, uname can be executed on `Z`, `X`, and `Y` as follows (the response is given in brackets):

```
uname [ Z ]
~[X]!uname [ X ]
~~[Y]!uname [ Y ]
```

In general, ~ causes the command to be executed on the original machine; ~~ causes the command to be executed on the next machine in the chain.

EXAMPLES

To dial a system whose telephone number is 9 1 201 555 1212 using 1200 baud (where dial tone is expected after the 9):

```
cu  -s 1200   9=12015551212
```

If the speed is not specified, "Any" is the default value.

To log in to a system connected by a direct line:

`cu  -l  /dev/ttyXX` or5 `cu -l ttyXX`

To dial a system with the specific line and a specific speed:

```
cu  -s 1200  -l  ttyXX
```

To dial a system using a specific line associated with an auto dialer:

```
cu  -l  culXX  9=12015551212
```

To use a system name:

`cu` *systemname*

ERRORS

Exit code is 0 for normal exit, otherwise, −1.

USAGE

End-user.

SEE ALSO

CAT(BU_CMD), ECHO(BU_CMD), STTY(AU_CMD), UNAME(BU_CMD), UUCP(AU_CMD).

NAME

dd — convert and copy a file

SYNOPSIS

`dd` [*option=value*] ...

DESCRIPTION

The command `dd` copies the specified input file to the specified output with possible conversions. The standard input and output are used by default. The input and output block size may be specified to take advantage of raw physical I/O.

Option	*Values*
`if=file`	input file name; standard input is default
`of=file`	output file name; standard output is default
`ibs=n`	input block size `n` bytes (default 512)
`obs=n`	output block size (default 512)
`bs=n`	set both input and output block size, superseding `ibs` and `obs`; also, if no conversion is specified, it is particularly efficient since no in-core copy need be done
`cbs=n`	conversion buffer size
`skip=n`	skip `n`" input blocks before starting copy
`seek=n`	seek `n` blocks from beginning of output file before copying
`count=n`	copy only `n`" input blocks
`conv=ascii`	convert **EBCDIC** to **ASCII**
`ebcdic`	convert **ASCII** to **EBCDIC**
`ibm`	slightly different map of **ASCII** to **EBCDIC**
`lcase`	map alphabetics to lower case
`ucase`	map alphabetics to upper case
`swab`	swap every pair of bytes
`noerror`	do not stop processing on an error
`sync`	pad every input block to `ibs`
`... , ...`	several comma-separated conversions

Where sizes are specified, a number of bytes is expected. A number may end with **k**, **b**, or **w** to specify multiplication by 1024, 512, or 2, respectively; a pair of numbers may be separated by **x** to indicate a product.

The option `cbs` is used only if `ascii` or `ebcdic` conversion is specified. In the former case `cbs` characters are placed into the conversion buffer, converted to **ASCII**, and trailing blanks trimmed and newline added before sending the line to the output. In the latter case **ASCII** characters are read into the conversion buffer, converted to **EBCDIC**, and blanks added to make up an output block of size `cbs`.

After completion, `dd` reports the number of whole and partial input and output blocks.

EXAMPLE

This command will read an **EBCDIC** tape blocked ten 80-byte **EBCDIC** card images per block into the **ASCII** file `x`:

```
dd if=/dev/rmt/0m of=x ibs=800 cbs=80
conv=ascii,lcase
```

Note the use of raw magtape. The command `dd` is especially suited to I/O on the raw physical devices because it allows reading and writing in arbitrary block sizes.

USAGE

General.

New-lines are inserted only on conversion to **ASCII**; padding is done only on conversion to **EBCDIC**.

NAME

dircmp — directory comparison

SYNOPSIS

`dircmp` [`-d`] [`-s`] *dir1* *dir2*

DESCRIPTION

The command `dircmp` examines *dir1* and *dir2* and generates various tabulated information about the contents of the directories. Listings of files that are unique to each directory are generated for all the options. If no option is specified, a list is output indicating whether the file names common to both directories have the same contents.

`-d` Compare the contents of files with the same name in both directories and output a list telling what must be changed in the two files to bring them into agreement. The list format is described in DIFF(BU_CMD).

`-s` Suppress messages about identical files.

USAGE

General.

SEE ALSO

CMP(BU_CMD), DIFF(BU_CMD).

NAME

egrep, fgrep — search a file for a pattern

SYNOPSIS

`egrep` [*options*] [*expression*] [*files*]

`fgrep` [*options*] [*strings*] [*files*]

DESCRIPTION

The `egrep` and `fgrep` commands search the input *files* (standard input default) for lines matching a pattern. Normally, each line found is copied to the standard output. The patterns used by `egrep` are full regular *expressions*; `fgrep` patterns are fixed *strings*. The following *options* are recognized:

`−v` All lines but those matching are printed.
`−x` (Exact) only lines matched in their entirety are printed (`fgrep` only).
`−c` Only a count of matching lines is printed.
`−i` Ignore upper/lower case distinction during comparisons.
`−l` Only the names of files with matching lines are listed (once), separated by newlines.
`−n` Each line is preceded by its relative line number in the file.
`−e` *expression*
(`egrep` only.) Same as a simple *expression* argument, but useful when the *expression* begins with a −
`−f` *file*
The regular *expression* (`egrep`) or *strings* list (`fgrep`) is taken from the *file*.

In all cases, the file name is output if there is more than one input file. Care should be taken when using characters in *expression* that may also be meaningful to the command interpreter. It is safest to enclose the entire *expression* argument in single quotes '...'.

The command `fgrep` searches for lines that contain one of the *strings* separated by newlines.

The command `egrep` accepts regular expressions as in ED(BU_CMD), except for `\(` and `\)`, with the addition of:

1. A regular expression followed by **+** matches one or more occurrences of the regular expression.
2. A regular expression followed by **?** matches 0 or 1 occurrences of the regular expression.
3. Two regular expressions separated by | or by a newline match strings that are matched by either.
4. A regular expression may be enclosed in parentheses **()** for grouping.

The order of precedence of operators is **[]**, then *** ? +**, then concatenation, then | and newline.

ERRORS

Exit status is 0 if any matches are found, 1 if none, 2 for syntax errors or inaccessible files (even if matches were found).

USAGE

General.

Lines are limited to BUFSIZ characters; longer lines are truncated. (BUFSIZ is defined in `/usr/include/stdio.h`.)

CAVEATS

The functionality of `egrep` and `fgrep` will eventually be provided in GREP(BU_CMD), and these two commands discontinued.

SEE ALSO

ED(BU_CMD), GREP(BU_CMD), SED(BU_CMD).

NAME

ex — text editor

SYNOPSIS

`ex [-] [-v] [-r] [-R] [+command] [-l] [file...]`

DESCRIPTION

The command `ex` is a line oriented text editor, which supports both command and display editing [see VI(AU_CMD)]. The command line options are:

–	Suppress all interactive-user feedback. This is useful in processing editor scripts.
`-v`	Invokes `vi`
`-r`	Recover the named files after an editor or system crash. If no files are named a list of all saved files will be printed.
`-R`	*Readonly* mode set, prevents accidentally overwriting the file.
+*command*	Begin editing by executing the specified editor search or positioning *command*.
`-l`	LISP mode; indents appropriately for *lisp* code; the `( ) { } [[` and `]]` commands in `vi` are modified to have meaning for lisp.

The *file* argument(s) indicates files to be edited, in the order specified.

The name of the file being edited by `ex` is the `current` file. The text of the file is read into a buffer, and all editing changes are performed in this buffer; changes have no effect on the file until the buffer is written out explicitly.

The *alternate* file name is the name of the last file mentioned in an editor command, or the previous current file name if the last file mentioned became the current file. The character `%` in filenames is replaced by the current file name, and the character `#` by the alternate file name.

The named buffers `a` through `z` may be used for saving blocks of text during the edit. If the buffer name is specified in upper case, the buffer is appended to rather than being overwritten.

The read-only mode can be cleared from within the edit by setting the `noreadonly` edit option (see **Edit Options** below). Writing to a different file is allowed in read-only mode; in addition, the write can be forced by using `!` (see the `write` command below).

When an error occurs `ex` sends the BEL character to the terminal (to sound the bell) and prints a message. If an interrupt signal is received, `ex` returns to the command level in addition to the above actions. If the editor input is from a file, `ex` exits at the interrruption. (The bell action may be disabled by the use of an edit option, see below.)

If the system crashes, `ex` attempts to preserve the buffer if any unwrtten changes were made. The command line option `-r` is used to retrieve the saved changes.

At the beginning, `ex` is in the *command* mode, which is indicated by the `:` prompt. The `input` mode is entered by `append`, `insert`, or `change` commands; it is left (and command mode re-entered) by typing a period `.` alone at the beginning of a line.

Command lines beginning with the double quote character `"` are ignored. (this may used for comments in an editor script.)

Addressing

`.` Dot `.` refers to the current line. There is always a current line; the positioning may be the result of an explicit movement by the user, or the result of a command that affected multiple lines (in which case it is usually the last line affected).

`n` The `nth` line in the buffer, with lines numbered sequentially from 1.

`$` The last line in the buffer.

`%` Abbreviation for `1,$`, the entire buffer.

+n
-n An offset relative to the current line. (The forms `.+3`, `+3`, and `+++` are equivalent.)

/pat/
?pat? Line containing the pattern (regular expression) *pat*, scanning forward (`//`) or backward (`??`). The trailing `/` or `?` may be omitted if the line is only to be printed. If the pattern is omitted, the previous pattern specified is used.

\`x* Lines may be marked using single lower case letters (see the `mark` command below); *\`x refers to line marked *x*. In addition, the previous current line is marked before each non-relative motion; this line may be referred to by using \` for *x*.

Addresses to commands consist of a series of line addresses (specified as above), separated by `,` or `;`. Such address lists are evaluated left-to-right. When `;` is the separator, the current line is set to the value of the previous address before the next address is interpreted. If more addresses are given than the command requires, then all but the last one or two are ignored. Where a command requires two addresses, the first line must precede the second one in the buffer. A null address in a list defaults to the current line.

Command names and abbreviations

abbrev	**ab**	next	**n**	unmap	**unm**
append	**a**	number	**# nu**	version	**ve**
args	**ar**	preserve	**pre**	visual	**vi**
change	**c**	print	**p**	write	**w**
copy	**co**	put	**pu**	xit	**x**
delete	**d**	quit	**q**	yank	**ya**
edit	**e**	read	**re**	(window)	**z**
file	**f**	recover	**re**	(escape)	**!**
global	**g v**	rewind	**rew**	(lshift)	**<**
insert	**i**	set	**se**	(rshift)	**>**
join	**j**	shell	**sh**	(resubst)	**& s**
list	**l**	source	**so**	(scroll)	**^D**
map		substitute	**s**	(line no)	**=**
mark	**k ma**	unabbrev	**una**		
move	**m**	undo	**u**		

Command descriptions

In the following, `line` is a single line address, given in any of the forms described in the **Addressing** section above; `range` is a pair of line addresses, separated by a comma or semicolon (see the **Addressing** section for the difference between the two); `count` is a positive integer, specifying the number of lines to be affected by the command; `flags` is one or more of the characters `#`, `p`, and `l`; the corresponding command to print the line is executed after the command completes. Any number of + or - characters may also be given with these flags.

When `count` is used, `range` is not effective; only a line number should be specified instead, to indicate the first line affected by the command. (If a range is given, then the last line of the range is taken as the starting line for the command.)

These modifiers are all optional; the defaults are as follows, unless otherwise stated: the default for `line` is the current line; the default for `range` is the current line only (.,.); the default for `count` is 1; the default for `flags` is null.

When only a `line` or a `range` is specified (with a null command), the implied command is `print`; if a null line is entered, the next line is printed (equivalent to '`.+1p`')

`ab word rhs`

Add the named abbreviation to the current list. In visual mode, if `word` is typed as a complete word during input, it is replaced by the string `rhs`.

`line a`

Enters input mode; the input text is placed after the specified line. If line 0 is specified, the text is placed at the beginning of the buffer. The last input line becomes the current line, or the target line, if no lines are input.

`ar`

The argument list is printed, with the current argument inside [and].

`range c count`

Enters input mode; the input text replaces the specified lines. The last input line becomes the current line; if no lines are input, the effect is the same as a delete.

`range co line flags`

A copy of the specified lines (`range`) is placed after the specified destination line; line 0 specifes that the lines are to be placed at the beginning of the buffer.

`range d buffer count`

The specified lines are deleted from the buffer. If a named buffer is specified, the deleted text is saved in it. The line after the deleted lines becomes the current line, or the last line if the deleted lines were at the end.

`e +line file`

Begin editing a new file. If the current buffer has been modified since the last write, then a warning is printed and the command is aborted. This action may be overridden by appending the character ! to the command ("`e! file`"). The current line is the last line of the buffer; however, if this command is executed from within `visual`, the current line is the first line of the buffer. If the `+line` option is specified, the current line is set to the specified position, where `line` may be a number (or $) or specified as "`/pat`" or "`?pat`".

`f`

Prints the current file name and other information, including the number of lines and the current position.

`range g /pat/ cmds`

First marks the lines within the given range that match the given pattern. Then the given command(s) are executed with . set to each marked line.

`Cmds` may be specified on multiple lines by hiding newlines with a backslash. If `cmds` are omitted, each line is printed. `Append`, `change`, and `insert` commands are omitted; the terminating dot may be omitted if it ends `cmds`. `Visual` commands are also permitted, and take input from the terminal.

The `global` command itself, and the `undo` command are not allowed in `cmds`. The edit options `autoprint`, `autoindent` and `report` are inhibited.

`range v /pat/ cmds`
This is the same as the `global` command, except that `cmds` is run on the lines that **do not** match the pattern.

`line i`
Enters input mode; the input text is placed before the specified line. The last line input becomes the current line, or the line before the target line, if no lines were input.

`range j count flags`
Joins the text from the specified lines together into one line. White space is adjusted to provide at least one blank character, to if there was a period at the end of the line, or none if the first following character is a `)`. Extra white space at the start of a line is discarded.

Appending the command with a `!` causes a simpler join with no white space processing.

`range l count flags`
Prints the specified lines with tabs printed as '^I' and the end of each line marked with a trailing `$`. (The only useful flag is `#`, for line numbers.) The last line printed becomes the current line.

`map x rhs`
The `map` command is used to define macros for use in `visual` mode. The first argument is a single character, or the sequence '#n', where `n` is a digit, to refer to the function key `n`. When this character or function key is typed in `visual` mode, the action is as if the corresponding `rhs` had been typed. If `!` is appended to the command `map`, then the mapping is effective during insert mode rather than command mode. Special characters, white space, and newline must be escaped with a control-V to be entered in the arguments.

`line ma x`
(The letter `k` is an alternative abbreviation for the `mark` command.) The specified line is given the specified mark `x`, which must be a single lower case letter. (The `x` must be preceded by a space or tab.) The current line position is not affected.

`range m line`
Moves the specified lines (`range`) to be after the target line. The first of the moved lines becomes the current line.

`n`
The next file from the command line argument list is edited. Appending a `!` to the command overrides the warning about the buffer having been modifed since the last write (discarding any changes). The argument list may be replaced by specifying a new one on this command line.

`range nu count flags`

(The character # is an alternative abbreviation for the `number` command.) Prints the lines, each preceded by its line number. (The only useful flag is `l`.) The last line printed becomes the current line.

`pre`

The current editor buffer is saved as though the system had just crashed. This command is for use in emergencies, for example when a write does not work, and the buffer cannot be saved in any other way.

`range p count`

Prints the specified lines, with non-printing characters printed as control characters in the form '^**x**'; DEL is represented as '^?'. The last line printed becomes the current line.

`line pu buffer`

Puts back deleted or "yanked" lines. A buffer may be specified; otherwise, the text in the unnamed buffer (where delted or yanked text is placed by default) is restored.

`q`

Causes termination of the edit. If the buffer has been modified since the last write, a warning is printed and the command fails. This warning may be overridden by appending a ! to the command (discarding changes).

`line r file`

Places a copy of the specified file in the buffer after the target line (which may be line 0 to place text at the beginning). If no `file` is named the current file is the default. If there is no current file then `file` becomes the current file. The last line read becomes the current line; in `visual` the first line read becomes the current line.

If `file` is given as "!`string`" then `string` is taken to be a system command, and passed to the command interpreter; the resultant output is read in to the buffer. A blank or tab must precede the !.

`rec file`

Recovers `file` from the save area, after an accidental hangup or a system crash.

`rew`

The argument list is rewound, and the first file in the list is edited. Any warnings may be overridden by appending a !.

`se parameter`

With no arguments, the set command prints those options whose values have been changed from the default settings; with the parameter `all` it prints all of the option values.

Giving an option name followed by a `?` causes the current value of that option to be printed. The `?` is necessary only for Boolean valued options. Boolean options are given values by the form 'se `option`' to turn them on, or 'se `nooption`' to turn them off; string and numeric options are assigned by the form 'se `option`=value'. More than one parameter may be given; they are interpreted left to right.

See **Edit Options** below for further details about options.

`sh`
: The user is put into the command interpreter [usually `sh`; see SH(BU_CMD)]; editing is resumed on exit.

`so file`
: Reads and executes commands from the specified file. Such `so` commands may be nested.

`range s /pat/repl/ options count flags`
: On each specified line, the first instance of the pattern `pat` is replaced by the string `repl`. (See **Regular Expressions** and **Replacement Strings** below.) If `options` includes the letter `g` (global), then all instances of the pattern in the line are substituted. If the option letter `c` (confirm) is included, then before each substitution the line is typed with the pattern to be replaced marked with ^ characters; a response of `y` causes the substitution to be done, while any other input aborts it. The last line substituted becomes the current line.

`una word`
: Delete `word` from the list of abbreviations.

`u`
: Reverses the changes made by the previous editing command. For this purpose, `global` and `visual` are considered single commands. Commands which affect the external environment, such as `write`, `edit` and `next`, cannot be undone. An `undo` can itself be reversed.

`unm x`
: The macro definition for `x` is removed.

`ve`
: Prints the current version of the editor.

`line vi type count`
: Enters visual mode at the specified line. The `type` is optional, and may be `-` or `.`, as in the `z` command, to specify the position of the specified line on the screen window. (The default is to place the line at the top of the screen window.) A `count` specifies an

initial window size; the default is the value of the edit option `window`. The command `Q` exits visual mode. [For more information, see VI(AU_CMD)]

`range w file`

Writes the specified lines (the whole buffer, if no `range` is given) out to `file`, printing the number of lines and characters written. If `file` is not specified, the default is the current file. (The command fails with an error message if there is no current file and no file is specified.)

If an alternate file is specified, and the file exists, then the write will fail; it may be forced by appending a `!` to the command. An existing file may be appended to by appending '>>' to the command. If the file does not exist, an error is reported.

If the file is specified as '`!string`', then `string` is taken as a system command; the command interpreter is invoked, and the specified lines are passed as standard input to the command.

The command `wq` is equivalent to a `w` followed by a `q`; `wq!` is equivalent to `w!` followed by `q`.

`x`

Writes out the buffer if any changes have been made, and then (in any case) quits.

`range ya buffer count`

Places the specified lines in the named buffer. If no buffer is specified, the unnamed buffer is used (where the most recently deleted or yanked text is placed by default).

`line z type count`

If `type` is omitted, then `count` lines following the specified line (default current line) are printed. The default for `count` is the value of the edit option `window`.

If `type` is specified, it must be `-` or `.`; a `-` causes the line to be placed at the bottom of the screen, while a `.` causes the line to be placed in the middle. The last line printed becomes the current line.

`! command`

The remainder of the line after the `!` is passed to the system command interpreter for execution. A warning is issued if the buffer has been changed since the last write. A single `!` is printed when the command completes. The current line position is not affected.

Within the text of `command` `%` and `#` are expanded as filenames, and `!` is replaced with the text of the previous `!` command. (Thus `!!` repeats the previous `!` command.) If any such expansion is done, the expanded line will be echoed.

`range! command`
In this form of the ! command, the specified lines (there is no default; see previous paragraph) are passed to the command interpreter as standard input; the resulting output replaces the specified lines.

`range < count`
Shift the specified lines to the left; the number of spaces to be shifted is determined by the edit option `shiftwidth`. Only white space (blanks and tabs)is lost in shifting; other characters are not affected. The last line changed becomes the current line.

`range > count`
Shift the specified lines to the right, by inserting white space (see previous paragraph for further details).

`range & options count flags`
Repeats the previous substitute command, as if '&' were replaced by the previous '`s/pat/repl/`'. (The same effect is obtained by omitting the '`/pat/repl/`' string in the `substitute` command.)

`^D` (control-D)
Control-D (ASCII EOT) prints the next n lines, where n is the value of the edit option `scroll`.

`line =`
Prints the line number of the specified line (default last line). The current line position is not affected.

Regular Expressions

Regular expressions are interpreted according to the setting of the edit option `magic`; the following assumes the setting `magic`. The differences caused by the setting `nomagic` are described below.

The following constructs are used to construct regular expressions:

`char` An ordinary character matches itself. The following characters are not ordinary, and must be escaped (preceded by '\') to have their ordinary meaning: '^ at the beginning of a pattern; '$ at the end of a pattern; '* anywhere other than the beginning of a pattern; '., \, [, and ~, anywhere in a pattern.

^ When at the beginning of a pattern, matches the beginning of the line.

$ When at the end of a pattern, matches the end of the line.

. matches any single character in the line.

\< Matches the beginning of a "word". That is, the matched string must begin in a letter, digit, or underline, and be preceded by the beginning of the line or a character other than the above.

\> Matches the end of a "word" (see previous paragraph).

[string] Matches any single character in `string`. Within string, the following have special meanings: a pair of characters separated by - defines a range (e.g., '[a-z]' defines any lower case letter); the character ^, if it is the first one in `string`, causes the construct to match characters other than those specified in `string`. These special meaning can be removed by escaping the characters.

* Matches zero or more occurrences of the preceding regular expression.

~ Matches the replacement part of the last `substitute` command.

\(...\) A regular expression may be enclosed in escaped parentheses; this serves only to identify them for substitution actions.

A concatenation of two regular expressions is a regular expression that matches the concatenation of the strings matched by each component.

When `nomagic` is set, the only characters with special meanings are ^ at the beginning of a pattern, $ at the end of a pattern, and '\'. The characters `.`, `*`, `[`, and ~ lose their special meanings, unless escaped by a '\'.

Replacement Strings

The character & ('\& if `nomagic` is set) in the replacement string stands for the text matched by the pattern to be replaced. The character ~ ('\~ if `nomagic` is set) is replaced by the replacement part of the `previous` substitute command. The sequence '`\n`', where `n` is an integer, is replaced by the text matched by the pattern enclosed in the `n`th set of parentheses '`\(`' and '`\)`'. The sequence '`\u`' ('`\l`') causes the immediately following character in the replacement to be converted to upper-case (lower-case), if this character is a letter. The sequence '`\U`' ('`\L`') turns such conversion on, until the sequence '`\E`' or '`\e`' is encountered, or the end of the replacement string is reached.

Edit Options

The command `ex` has a number of options that modify its behavior. These options have default settings, which may be changed using the `set` command (see above). Options may also be set at startup by putting a `set` command string in the environmental variable `EXINIT`, or in the file `.exrc` in the `HOME` directory, or in `.exrc` in the current directory.

Options are Boolean unless otherwise specified.

`autoindent, ai`
If autoindent is set, each line in insert mode is indented (using blanks and tabs) to align with the previous line. (Starting indentation is determined by the line appended after, or the line inserted before, or the first line changed.) Additional indentation can be provided as usual; succeeding lines will automatically be indented to the new alignment. Reducing the indent is achieved by typing control-D one or more times; the cursor is moved back `shiftwidth` spaces for each control-D. (A ^ followed by a control-D removes all indentation temporarily for the current line; a 0 followed by a control-D removes all indentation.)

`autoprint, ap`
The current line is printed after each command that changes buffer text. (Autoprint is suppressed in globals.)

`autowrite, aw`
The buffer is written (to the current file) if it has been modified, and a `next`, `rewind`, or ! command is given.

`beautify, bf`
Causes all control characters other than tab, newline and formfeed to be discarded from the input text.

`directory, dir`
The value of this option specifies the directory in which the editor buffer is to be placed. If this directory is not writeable by the user, the editor quits.

`edcompatible, ed`
Causes the presence of `g` and `c` suffixes on substitute commands to be remembered, and toggled by repeating the suffixes.

`ignorecase, ic`
All upper case characters in the text are mapped to lower case in regular expression matching. Also, all upper case characters in regular expressions are mapped to lower case, except in character class specifications.

`lisp`
`Autoindent` mode, and the `( ) { } [[ ]]` commands in `visual` are suitable modified for *lisp* code.

`list`
All printed lines will be displayed with tabs shown as "^I", and the end of line marked by a `$`.

`magic`
Changes interpretation of characters in regular expressions and substitution replacement strings (see the relevant sections above).

`number, nu`
Causes lines to be printed with line numbers.

`paragraphs, para`
The value of this option is a string, in which successive pairs of characters specify the names of text-processing macros which begin paragraphs. (A macro appears in the text in the form `.XX`, where the `.` is the first character in the line.)

`prompt`
When set, command mode input is prompted for with a `:`; when unset, no prompt is displayed.

`redraw`
The editor simulates an intelligent terminal on a dumb terminal. (Since this is likely to require a large amount of output to the terminal, it is useful only at high transmission speeds.)

`remap`
If set, then macro translation allows for macros defined in terms of other macros; translation continues until the final product is obtained. If unset, then a one-step translation only is done.

`report`
The value of this option gives the number of lines that must be changed by a command before a report is generated on the number of lines affected.

`scroll`
The value of this option determines the number of lines scrolled on a control-D, and the number of lines displayed by the `z` command (twice the value of scroll).

`sections`
The value of this option is a string, in which successive pairs of characters specify the names of text-processing macros which begin sections. (See `paragraphs` option above.)

`shiftwidth, sw`
The value of this option gives the width of a software tab stop, used during `autoindent`, and by the shift commands.

`showmatch, sm`
In `visual` mode, when a) or } is typed, the matching (or { is shown if it is still on the screen.

`slowopen, slow`
In `visual` mode, prevents screen updates during input to improve throughput on unintelligent terminals.

`tabstop, ts`
The value of this options specifies the software tab stops to be used by the editor to expand tabs in the input file.

`terse`
When set, error messages are shorter.

`window`
The number of lines in a text window in `visual` mode.

`wrapscan, ws`
When set, searches (using '//' or '??') wrap around the end of the file; when unset, searches stop at the beginning or the end of the file, as appropriate.

`wrapmargin, wm`
In `visual` mode, if the value of this option is greater than zero (say `n`), then a newline is automatically added to an input line, at a word boundary, so that lines end at least `n` spaces from the right margin of the terminal screen.

`writeany, wa`
Inhibits the checks otherwise made before write commands, allowing a write to any file (provided the system allows it).

FILES

`/usr/lib/terminfo/*/*`	terminfo terminal capability database
`$HOME/.exrc`	editor initialization file
`./.exrc`	editor initialization file

USAGE

End-user.

The `undo` command causes all marks to be lost on lines that were changed and then restored.

The `z` command prints a number of logical rather than physical lines. More than a screen-ful of output may result if long lines are present.

Null characters are discarded in input files and cannot appear in resultant files.

SEE ALSO

VI(AU_CMD).

NAME

id — print user and group IDs and names

SYNOPSIS

`id`

DESCRIPTION

The command `id` writes a message on the standard output giving the user- and group- IDs and the corresponding names of the invoking process. If the effective and real IDs do not match, both are printed.

USAGE

General.

SEE ALSO

LOGNAME(AU_CMD), GETUID(BA_SYS).

NAME

join — join two files on identical-valued field

SYNOPSIS

`join` [*options*] *file1 file2*

DESCRIPTION

The command `join` performs an "equality join" on the files *file1* and *file2*. If *file1* is `-`, the standard input is used in its place.

A field must be specified for each file as the "join field", on which the files are compared. There is one line in the output for each pair of lines in *file1* and *file2* that have identical join fields. The output line normally consists of the common field, then the rest of the line from *file1*, then the rest of the line from *file2*. This format can be changed by using the `-o` option (see below).

The files *file1* and *file2* must be sorted in increasing ASCII collating sequence on the fields on which they are to be joined, normally the first in each line.

The default input field separators are blank, tab, or newline. In this case, multiple separators count as one field-separator, and leading separators are ignored. The default output field-separator is a blank.

Some of the options below use the argument `n`. This argument should be a `1` or a `2` referring to either *file1* or *file2*, respectively. The following options are recognized:

`-a`*n* In addition to the normal output, produce a line for each unpairable line in file *n*, where *n* is `1` or `2`.

`-e`*s* Replace empty output fields by string *s*.

`-j`*nm* Join on the *m*th field of file *n*. If *n* is missing, use the *m*th field in each file. Fields are numbered starting with `1`.

`-o`*list* Each output line comprises the fields specified in *list*, each element of which has the form *n*`.`*m*`,`1 where *n* is a file number and *m* is a field number. The common field is not printed unless specifically requested.

`-t`*c* Use character *c* as a separator, for both input and output. Every appearance of *c* in a line is significant.

USAGE

General.

Filenames that are numeric may cause conflict when the `-o` option is used right before listing filenames.

SEE ALSO

AWK(BU_CMD), COMM(BU_CMD), SORT(BU_CMD), UNIQ(BU_CMD).

NAME

logname — get login name

SYNOPSIS

`logname`

DESCRIPTION

The command `logname` returns the user's login name.

USAGE

General.

NAME

lp, cancel — send/cancel requests to an LP line printer

SYNOPSIS

`lp` [`-c`] [`-d`*dest*] [`-m`] [`-n`*number*] [`-o`*option*] [`-s`] [`-t`*title*] [`-w`] *files*

`cancel` [*ids*] [*printers*]

DESCRIPTION

The command `lp` arranges for the named files and associated information (collectively called a *request*) to be printed by a line printer. If no file names are mentioned, the standard input is assumed. The file name — stands for the standard input and may be supplied on the command line in conjunction with named *files*. The order in which *files* appear is the same order in which they will be printed.

The command `lp` associates a unique ID with each request and prints it on the standard output. This ID can be used later to cancel (see *cancel*) or find the status [see LPSTAT(AU_CMD)] of the request.

The following options to `lp` may appear in any order and may be intermixed with file names:

`-c` Make copies of the *files* to be printed immediately when `lp` is invoked. Normally, *files* will not be copied, but will be linked whenever possible. If the `-c` option is not given, then the user should be careful not to remove any of the *files* before the request has been printed in its entirety. It should also be noted that in the absence of the `-c` option, any changes made to the named *files* after the request is made but before it is printed will be reflected in the printed output.

`-d`*dest* Choose *dest* as the printer or class of printers that is to do the printing. If *dest* is a printer, then the request will be printed only on that specific printer. If *dest* is a class of printers, then the request will be printed on the first available printer that is a member of the class. Under certain conditions (printer unavailability, file space limitation, etc.), requests for specific destinations may not be accepted [see LPSTAT(AU_CMD)]. By default, *dest* is taken from the environmental variable `LPDEST` (if it is set). Otherwise, a default destination (if one exists) for the computer system is used. Destination names vary between systems [see LPSTAT(AU_CMD)].

`-m` Send mail [see MAIL(BU_CMD)] after the files have been printed. By default, no mail is sent upon normal completion of the print request.

`-n`*number* Print *number* copies (default of 1) of the output.

−o*option*	Specify printer-dependent or class-dependent *options*. Several such *options* may be collected by specifying the −o keyletter more than once.
−s	Suppress messages from `lp` such as "request id is ...".
−t*title*	Print *title* on the banner page of the output.
−w	Write a message on the user's terminal after the *files* have been printed. If the user is not logged in, then mail will be sent instead.

The command `cancel` cancels line printer requests that were made by the `lp` command. The command line arguments may be either request *ids* (as returned by `lp`) or *printer* names [for a complete list, use LPSTAT(AU_CMD).] Specifying a request *id* cancels the associated request even if it is currently printing. Specifying a *printer* cancels the request which is currently printing on that printer. In either case, the cancellation of a request that is currently printing frees the printer to print its next available request.

USAGE

General.

SEE ALSO

LPSTAT(AU_CMD), MAIL(BU_CMD),

NAME

lpstat — print LP status information

SYNOPSIS

`lpstat` [*options*]

DESCRIPTION

The command `lpstat` prints information about the current status of the LP line printer system.

If no *options* are given, then `lpstat` prints the status of all requests made to LP(AU_CMD) by the user. Any arguments that are not *options* are assumed to be request *ids* as returned by `lp` [see LP(AU_CMD)]. The command `lpstat` prints the status of such requests. The *options* may appear in any order and may be repeated and intermixed with other arguments. Some of the keyletters below may be followed by an optional *list* that can be in one of two forms: a list of items separated from one another by a comma, or a list of items enclosed in double quotes and separated from one another by a comma and/or one or more spaces. For example:

```
-u"user1, user2, user3"
```

The omission of a *list* following such keyletters causes all information relevant to the keyletter to be printed, for example:

```
lpstat -o
```

prints the status of all output requests.

`-a`[*list*] Print acceptance status of destinations for output requests. *list* is a list of intermixed printer names and class names.

`-c`[*list*] Print class names and their members. *list* is a list of class names.

`-d` Print the system default destination for output requests.

`-o`[*list*] Print the status of output requests. *list* is a list of intermixed printer names, class names, and request *ids*.

`-p`[*list*] Print the status of printers. *list* is a list of printer names.

`-r` Print the status of the LP request scheduler

`-s` Print a status summary, including the status of the line printer scheduler, the system default destination, a list of class names and their members, and a list of printers and their associated devices.

`-t` Print all status information.

`-u`[*list*] Print status of output requests for users. *list* is a list of login names.

`-v`[*list*] Print the names of printers and the path names of the devices associated with them. *list* is a list of printer names.

USAGE

General.

SEE ALSO

LP(AU_CMD).

NAME

mailx — interactive message processing system

SYNOPSIS

`mailx` [*options*] [*name*...]

DESCRIPTION

The command `mailx` provides a comfortable, flexible environment for sending and receiving messages electronically. When reading mail, `mailx` provides commands to facilitate saving, deleting, and responding to messages. When sending mail, `mailx` allows editing, reviewing and other modification of the message as it is entered.

Incoming mail is stored in a standard file for each user, called the system *mailbox* for that user. When `mailx` is called to read messages, the *mailbox* is the default place to find them. As messages are read, they are marked to be moved to a secondary file for storage, unless specific action is taken, so that the messages need not be seen again. This secondary file is called the *mbox* and is normally located in the user's HOME directory (see `MBOX`, in **ENVIRONMENTAL VARIABLES** below for a description of this file). Messages remain in this file until specifically removed.

On the command line, *options* start with a dash (—) and any other arguments are taken to be destinations (recipients). If no recipients are specified, `mailx` will attempt to read messages from the *mailbox*. Command line options are:

`-e` Test for presence of mail. The command `mailx` prints nothing and exits with a successful return code if there is mail to read.

`-f` [*filename*] Read messages from *filename* instead of *mailbox*. If no *filename* is specified, the *mbox* is used.

`-F` Record the message in a file named after the first recipient. Overrides the "record" variable, if set (see **ENVIRONMENTAL VARIABLES**).

`-h`*number* The number of network "hops" made so far. This is provided for network software to avoid infinite delivery loops.

`-H` Print header summary only.

`-i` Ignore interrupts. See also "ignore" (**ENVIRONMENTAL VARIABLES**).

`-n` Do not initialize from the system default *Mailx.rc* file.

`-N` Do not print initial header summary.

`-r`*address* Pass *address* to network delivery software. All tilde commands are disabled.

`-s`*subject*	Set the Subject header field to *subject*.
`-u`*user*	Read *user*'s *mailbox*. This is only effective if *user*'s *mailbox* is not read protected.

When reading mail, `mailx` is in *command mode*. A header summary of the first several messages is displayed, followed by a prompt indicating `mailx` can accept regular commands (see **COMMANDS** below). When sending mail, `mailx` is in *input mode*. If no subject is specified on the command line, a prompt for the subject is printed. As the message is typed, `mailx` will read the message and store it in a temporary file. Commands may be entered by beginning a line with the tilde (`~`) escape character followed by a single command letter and optional arguments. See **TILDE ESCAPES** for a summary of these commands.

At any time, the behavior of `mailx` is governed by a set of *environmental variables*. These are flags and valued parameters which are set and cleared via the `set` and `unset` commands. See **ENVIRONMENTAL VARIABLES** below for a summary of these parameters.

Regular commands are of the form:

[*command*] [*msglist*] [*arguments*]

If no command is specified in *command-mode*, `print` is assumed. In *input mode*, commands are recognized by the escape character, and lines not treated as commands are taken as input for the message.

Each message is assigned a sequential number, and there is at any time the notion of a 'current' message, marked by a '>' in the header summary. Many commands take an optional list of messages (*msglist*) to operate on, which defaults to the current message. A *msglist* is a list of message specifications separated by spaces, which may include:

`n`	Message number `n`.
`.`	The current message.
`^`	The first undeleted message.
`$`	The last message.
`*`	All messages.
`n-m`	An inclusive range of message numbers.
user	All messages from *user*.
`/string`	All messages with `string` in the subject line (case ignored).
`:`*c*	All messages of type *c*, where *c* is one of:
`d`	deleted messages
`n`	new messages
`o`	old messages
`r`	read messages
`u`	unread messages

Note that the context of the command determines whether this type of message specification makes sense.

Other arguments are usually arbitrary strings whose usage depends on the command involved. File names, where expected, can be specified with metacharacters understood by the command interpreter. Special characters are recognized by certain commands and are documented with the commands below.

At start-up time, `mailx` reads commands from a system-wide file to initialize certain parameters, then from a private start-up file (`$HOME/.mailrc`) for personalized variables. Most regular commands are legal inside start-up files, the most common use being to set up initial display options and alias lists. The following commands are not legal in the start-up file: `!`, `Copy`, `edit`, `followup`, `Followup`, `hold`, `mail`, `preserve`, `reply`, `Reply`, `shell`, and `visual`. Any errors in the start-up file cause the remaining lines in the file to be ignored.

COMMANDS

The following is a complete list of `mailx` commands:

! *command*
: Escape to the command interpreter. See "`SHELL`" (**ENVIRONMENTAL VARIABLES**).

`# comment`
: Null command (comment). This may be useful in *.mailrc* files.

=
: Print the current message number.

?
: Prints a summary of commands.

alias *alias name ...*

group *alias name ...*
: Declare an alias for the given names. The names will be substituted when *alias* is used as a recipient. Useful in the *.mailrc* file.

`alternates` *name ...*
: Declares a list of alternate names for the user's login. When responding to a message, these names are removed from the list of recipients for the response. With no arguments, **alt**ernates prints the current list of alternate names. See also "allnet" (**ENVIRONMENTAL VARIABLES**).

`cd` [*directory*]

`chdir` [*directory*]
: Change directory. If *directory* is not specified, `$HOME` is used.

copy [*filename*]

copy [*msglist*] *filename*
: Copy messages to the file without marking the messages as saved. Otherwise equivalent to the `save` command.

`Copy` [*msglist*]
Save the specified messages in a file whose name is derived from the author of the message to be saved, without marking the messages as saved. Otherwise equivalent to the `Save` command.

`delete` [*msglist*]
Delete messages from the *mailbox*. If "autoprint" is set, the next message after the last one deleted is printed (see **ENVIRONMENTAL VARIABLES**).

`discard` [*header-field* ...]
`ignore` [*header-field* ...]
Suppresses printing of the specified header fields when displaying messages on the screen. Examples of header fields to ignore are "status" and "cc." The fields are included when the message is saved. The `Print` and `Type` commands override this command.

`dp` [*msglist*]
`dt` [*msglist*]
Delete the specified messages from the *mailbox* and print the next message after the last one deleted. Roughly equivalent to a `delete` command followed by a `print` command.

`echo` *string* ...
Echo the given strings (like ECHO(BU_CMD).)

`edit` [*msglist*]
Edit the given messages. The messages are placed in a temporary file and the "`EDITOR`" variable is used to get the name of the editor (see **ENVIRONMENTAL VARIABLES**). Default editor is `ed`.

`exit`
`xit`
Exit from `mailx`, without changing the *mailbox*. No messages are saved in the *mbox* (see also `quit`).

`file` [*filename*]
`folder` [*filename*]
Quit from the current file of messages and read in the specified file. Several special characters are recognized when used as file names, with the following substitutions:

%	the current *mailbox*.
%user	the *mailbox* for user.
#	the previous file.
&	the current *mbox*.

Default file is the current *mailbox*.

`folders`
Print the names of the files in the directory set by the "folder" variable (see **ENVIRONMENTAL VARIABLES**).

followup [*message*]

Respond to a message, recording the response in a file whose name is derived from the author of the message. Overrides the "record" variable, if set. See also the Followup, Save, and Copy commands and "outfolder" (**ENVIRONMENTAL VARIABLES**).

Followup [*msglist*]

Respond to the first message in the *msglist*, sending the message to the author of each message in the *msglist*. The subject line is taken from the first message and the response is recorded in a file whose name is derived from the author of the first message. See also the followup, Save, and Copy commands and "outfolder" (**ENVIRONMENTAL VARIABLES**).

from [*msglist*]

Prints the header summary for the specified messages.

group *alias name* ...
alias *alias name* ...

Declare an alias for the given *names*. The names will be substituted when *alias* is used as a recipient. Useful in the *.mailrc* file.

headers [*message*]

Prints the page of headers which includes the message specified. The "screen" variable sets the number of headers per page (see **ENVIRONMENTAL VARIABLES**). See also the z command.

help

Prints a summary of commands.

hold [*msglist*]
preserve [*msglist*]

Holds the specified messages in the *mailbox*.

if s|r
mail-commands
else *mail-commands*
endif

Conditional execution, where s will execute following *mail-commands*, up to an else or endif, if the program is in *send* mode, and r causes the *mail-commands* to be executed only in *receive* mode. Useful in the *.mailrc* file.

ignore *header-field* ...
discard *header-field* ...

Suppresses printing of the specified header fields when displaying messages on the screen. Examples of header fields to ignore are "status" and "cc." All fields are included when the message is saved. The Print and Type commands override this command.

list

Prints all commands available. No explanation is given.

mail *name* ...

Mail a message to the specified users.

mbox [*msglist*]

Arrange for the given messages to end up in the standard *mbox* save file when `mailx` terminates normally. See `MBOX` (**ENVIRONMENTAL VARIABLES**) for a description of this file. See also the `exit` and `quit` commands.

next [*message*]

Go to next message matching *message*. A *msglist* may be specified, but in this case the first valid message in the list is the only one used. This is useful for jumping to the next message from a specific user, since the name would be taken as a command in the absence of a real command. See the discussion of *msglist*s above for a description of possible message specifications.

pipe [*msglist*] [*command*]
| [*msglist*] [*command*]

Pipe the message through the given *command*. The message is treated as if it were read. If no arguments are given, the current message is piped through the command specified by the value of the "cmd" variable. If the "page" variable is set, a form feed character is inserted after each message (see **ENVIRONMENTAL VARIABLES**).

preserve [*msglist*]
hold [*msglist*]

Preserve the specified messages in the *mailbox*.

Print [*msglist*]
Type [*msglist*]

Print the specified messages on the screen, including all header fields. Overrides suppression of fields by the `ignore` command.

print [*msglist*]
type [*msglist*]

Print the specified messages. If "crt" is set, the messages longer than the number of lines specified by the "crt" variable are paged through the command specified by the `PAGER` environment variable. The default command is `pg`. (See **ENVIRONMENTAL VARIABLES**).

quit

Exit from `mailx`, storing messages that were read in *mbox* and unread messages in the *mailbox*. Messages that have been explicitly saved in a file are deleted.

Reply [*msglist*]
Respond [*msglist*]

Send a response to the author of each message in the *msglist*. The subject line is taken from the first message. If "record" is set to a file name, the response is saved (see **ENVIRONMENTAL VARIABLES**).

reply [*message*]
respond [*message*]

Reply to the specified message, including all other recipients of the message. If "record" is set to a file name, the response is saved at the end of that file (see **ENVIRONMENTAL VARIABLES**).

Save [*msglist*]

Save the specified messages in a file whose name is derived from the author of the first message. The name of the file is taken to be the author's name with all network addressing stripped off. See also the Copy, followup, and Followup commands and "outfolder" (**ENVIRONMENTAL VARIABLES**).

save [*filename*]
save [*msglist*] *filename*

Save the specified messages in the given file. The file is created if it does not exist. The message is deleted from the *mailbox* when mailx terminates unless "keepsave" is set (see also **ENVIRONMENTAL VARIABLES** and the exit and quit commands).

set
set *name*
set *name*=*string*
set *name*=*number*

Define a variable called *name*. The variable may be given a null, string, or numeric value. set by itself prints all defined variables and their values. See **ENVIRONMENTAL VARIABLES** for detailed descriptions of the mailx variables.

shell

Invoke an interactive command interpreter (see also SHELL (**ENVIRONMENTAL VARIABLES**)).

size [*msglist*]

Print the size in characters of the specified messages.

source *filename*

Read commands from the given file and return to command mode.

top [*msglist*]

Print the top few lines of the specified messages. If the "toplines" variable is set, it is taken as the number of lines to print (see **ENVIRONMENTAL VARIABLES**). The default is 5.

touch [*msglist*]

Touch the specified messages. If any message in *msglist* is not specifically saved in a file, it will be placed in the *mbox* upon normal termination. See exit and quit.

Type [*msglist*]
Print [*msglist*]

Print the specified messages on the screen, including all header fields.

Overrides suppression of fields by the `ignore` command.

`type` [*msglist*]
`print` [*msglist*]
Print the specified messages. If "crt" is set, the messages longer than the number of lines specified by the "crt" variable are paged through the command specified by the `PAGER` variable. The default command is `pg`. (See **ENVIRONMENTAL VARIABLES**).

`undelete` [*msglist*]
Restore the specified deleted messages. Will only restore messages deleted in the current mail session. If "autoprint" is set, the last message of those restored is printed (see **ENVIRONMENTAL VARIABLES**).

`unset` *name* ...
Causes the specified variables to be erased. If the variable was imported from the execution environment (i.e., an environment variable) then it cannot be erased.

`version`
Prints the current version and release date.

`visual` [*msglist*]
Edit the given messages with a screen editor. The messages are placed in a temporary file and the `VISUAL` variable is used to get the name of the editor (see **ENVIRONMENTAL VARIABLES**).

`write` [*msglist*] *filename*
Write the given messages on the specified file, minus the header and trailing blank line. Otherwise equivalent to the `save` command.

`xit`
`exit`
Exit from `mailx`, without changing the *mailbox*. No messages are saved in the *mbox* (see also `quit`).

`z[+|-]`
Scroll the header display forward or backward one screen—full. The number of headers displayed is set by the "screen" variable (see **ENVIRONMENTAL VARIABLES**).

TILDE ESCAPES

The following commands may be entered only from *input mode*, by beginning a line with the tilde escape character (`~`). See "escape" (**ENVIRONMENTAL VARIABLES**) for changing this special character.

`~!` *command*
Escape to the command interpreter.

`~.` Simulate end of file (terminate message input).

`~:` *mail-command*
`~_` *mail-command*

Perform the command-level request. Valid only when sending a message while reading mail.

~? Print a summary of tilde escapes.

~A Insert the autograph string "Sign" into the message (see **ENVIRONMENTAL VARIABLES**).

~a Insert the autograph string "sign" into the message (see **ENVIRONMENTAL VARIABLES**).

~b *name* ...
Add the *names* to the blind carbon copy (Bcc) list.

~c *name* ...
Add the *names* to the carbon copy (Cc) list.

~d Read in the *dead.letter* file. See "DEAD" (**ENVIRONMENTAL VARIABLES**) for a description of this file.

~e Invoke the editor on the partial message. See also EDITOR (**ENVIRONMENTAL VARIABLES**).

~f [*msglist*]
Forward the specified messages. The messages are inserted into the message, without alteration.

~h Prompt for Subject line and To, Cc, and Bcc lists. If the field is displayed with an initial value, it may be edited.

~i *string*
Insert the value of the named variable into the text of the message. For example, ~A is equivalent to ~i **Sign**.

~m [*msglist*]
Insert the specified messages into the letter, shifting the new text to the right one tab stop. Valid only when sending a message while reading mail.

~p Print the message being entered.

~q Quit from input mode by simulating an interrupt. If the body of the message is not null, the partial message is saved in *dead.letter*. See DEAD (**ENVIRONMENTAL VARIABLES**) for a description of this file.

~r *filename*
~< *filename*
~< ! *command*
Read in the specified file. If the argument begins with an exclamation point (!), the rest of the string is taken as an arbitrary system command and is executed, with the standard output inserted into the message.

~s *string* ...
Set the subject line to *string*.

~t *name* ...
: Add the given *names* to the To list.

~v
: Invoke a preferred screen editor on the partial message. See also VISUAL" (**ENVIRONMENTAL VARIABLES**).

~w *filename*
: Write the partial message onto the given file, without the header.

~x
: Exit as with ~q except the message is not saved in *dead.letter*.

~| *command*
: Pipe the body of the message through the given *command*. If the *command* returns a successful exit status, the output of the command replaces the message.

ENVIRONMENTAL VARIABLES

The following are environment variables taken from the execution environment and are not alterable within mailx.

HOME=*directory*
: The user's base of operations.

MAILRC=*filename*
: The name of the start-up file. Default is $HOME/.mailrc.

The following variables are internal mailx variables. They may be imported from the execution environment or set via the set command at any time. The unset command may be used to erase variables.

allnet All network names whose last component (login name) match are treated as identical. This causes the *msglist* message specifications to behave similarly. Default is noallnet. See also the alternates command and the "metoo" variable.

append
: Upon termination, append messages to the end of the *mbox* file instead of prepending them. Default is noappend.

askcc
: Prompt for the Cc list after message is entered. Default is noaskcc.

asksub
: Prompt for subject if it is not specified on the command line with the −s option. Enabled by default.

autoprint
: Enable automatic printing of messages after delete and undelete commands. Default is noautoprint.

bang
: Enable the special-case treatment of exclamation points (!) in escape command lines as in VI(AU_CMD). Default is nobang.

`cmd=`*command*
Set the default command for the `pipe` command. No default value.

`conv=conversion`
Convert uucp addresses to the specified address style. Conversion is disabled by default. See also "sendmail" and the `-U` command line option.

`crt=`*number*
Pipe messages having more than `number` lines through the command specified by the value of the "PAGER" variable (PG(BU_CMD) by default). Disabled by default.

`DEAD=`*filename*
The name of the file in which to save partial letters in case of untimely interrupt or delivery errors. Default is $HOME/dead.letter.

`debug`
Enable verbose diagnostics for debugging. Messages are not delivered. Default is `nodebug`.

`dot`
Take a period on a line by itself during input from a terminal as end-of-file. Default is `nodot`.

`EDITOR=`*command*
The command to run when the `edit` or `~e` command is used. Default is ED(BU_CMD).

`escape=c`
Substitute `c` for the `~` escape character.

`folder=`*directory*
The directory for saving standard mail files. User-specified file names beginning with a plus (+) are expanded by preceding the file name with this directory name to obtain the real file name. If *directory* does not start with a slash (/), $HOME is prepended to it. In order to use the plus (+) construct on a `mailx` command line, "folder" must be an exported environment variable. There is no default for the "folder" variable. See also "outfolder" below.

`header`
Enable printing of the header summary when entering `mailx`. Enabled by default.

`hold`
Preserve all messages that are read in the *mailbox* instead of putting them in the standard *mbox* save file. Default is `nohold`.

`ignore`
Ignore interrupts while entering messages. Handy for noisy dial-up lines. Default is `noignore`.

`ignoreeof`
Ignore end-of-file during message input. Input must be terminated by a period (.) on a line by itself or by the `~.` command. Default is `noignoreeof`. See also "dot" above.

`keep`
When the *mailbox* is empty, truncate it to zero length instead of removing it. Disabled by default.

`keepsave`
Keep messages that have been saved in other files in the *mailbox* instead of deleting them. Default is `nokeepsave`.

`MBOX`=*filename*
The name of the file to save messages which have been read. The `xit` command overrides this function, as does saving the message explicitly in another file. Default is `$HOME/mbox`.

`metoo`
If the user's login appears as a recipient, do not delete it from the list. Default is `nometoo`.

`LISTER`=*command*
The command (and options) to use when listing the contents of the "folder" directory. The default is `ls`.

`onehop`
When responding to a message that was originally sent to several recipients, the other recipient addresses are normally forced to be relative to the originating author's machine for the response. This flag disables alteration of the recipients' addresses, improving efficiency in a network where all machines can send directly to all other machines.

`outfolder`
Causes the files used to record outgoing messages to be located in the directory specified by the "folder" variable unless the path name is absolute. Default is `nooutfolder`. See "folder" above and the `Save`, `Copy`, `followup`, and `Followup` commands.

`page`
Used with the `pipe` command to insert a form feed after each message sent through the pipe. Default is `nopage`.

`PAGER`=*command*
The command to use as a filter for paginating output. This can also be used to specify the options to be used. Default is `pg`.

`prompt`=*string*
Set the `command mode` prompt to *string*. Default is "? ".

`quiet`
Refrain from printing the opening message and version when entering `mailx`. Default is `noquiet`.

`record=`*filename*
Record all outgoing mail in *filename*. Disabled by default. See also "outfolder" above.

`save`
Enable saving of messages in *dead.letter* on interrupt or delivery error. See "DEAD" for a description of this file. Enabled by default.

`screen=`*number*
Sets the number of lines in a screen-full of headers for the headers command.

`sendmail=`*command*
Alternate command for delivering messages. Default is `mail`.

`sendwait`
Wait for background mailer to finish before returning. Default is `nosendwait`.

`SHELL=`*command*
The name of a preferred command interpreter. Default is `sh`.

`showto`
When displaying the header summary and the message is from the user, print the recipient's name instead of the author's name.

`sign=`*string*
The variable inserted into the text of a message when the `~a` (autograph) command is given. No default (see also `~i` (TILDE ESCAPES)).

`Sign=`*string*
The variable inserted into the text of a message when the `~A` command is given. No default (see also `~i` (TILDE ESCAPES)).

`toplines=`*number*
The number of lines of header to print with the `top` command. Default is 5.

`VISUAL=`*command*
The name of a preferred screen editor. Default is `vi`.

FILES

`$HOME/.mailrc`	users's start-up file
`$HOME/mbox`	secondary storage file

USAGE

End-user.

SEE ALSO

MAIL(BU_CMD), PG(BU_CMD), LS(BU_CMD), VI(AU_CMD).

NAME

mesg — permit or deny messages

SYNOPSIS

`mesg [y | n]`

DESCRIPTION

The command `mesg` with argument `n` prevents another user from writing to the invoking user's terminal, (e.g., by using `write` [see WRITE(AU_CMD)]). The command `mesg` with argument `y` reinstates write permission. With no arguments, `mesg` reports the current state without changing it.

ERRORS

Exit status is 0 if messages are receivable, 1 if not, 2 on error.

FILES

`/dev/tty*`

USAGE

General.

SEE ALSO

WRITE(AU_CMD).

NAME

newgrp — change to a new group

SYNOPSIS

`newgrp` [−] [*group*]

DESCRIPTION

The command `newgrp` changes a user's group identification. The user remains logged in and the current directory is unchanged, but calculations of access permissions to files are performed with respect to the new real and effective group IDs.

Exported environmental variables retain their values after invoking `newgrp`; however, all unexported variables are either reset to their default value or set to null. Environmental variables (such as `PS1`, `PS2`, `PATH`, `MAIL`, and `HOME`), unless exported, are reset to default values.

With no arguments, `newgrp` changes the group identification back to the group specified in the user's password file entry.

If the first argument to `newgrp` is a −, the environment is changed to what would be expected if the user actually logged in again.

FILES

`/etc/group`	system's group file
`/etc/passwd`	system's password file

USAGE

End-user.

SEE ALSO

SH(BU_CMD).

NAME

news — print news items

SYNOPSIS

`news [-a] [-n] [-s] [`*items*`]`

DESCRIPTION

The command `news` prints files from the system news directory.

When invoked without arguments, `news` prints the contents of all current files in the news directory, most recent first, with each preceded by an appropriate header. `news` stores the "currency" time as the modification date of a file named `.news_time` in the user's home directory (the identity of this directory is determined by the environmental variable `HOME`); only files more recent than this currency time are considered "current."

The `-a` option causes `news` to print all items, regardless of currency. In this case, the stored time is not changed.

The `-n` option causes `news` to report the names of the current items without printing their contents, and without changing the stored time.

The `-s` option causes `news` to report how many current items exist, without printing their names or contents, and without changing the stored time.

All other arguments are assumed to be specific news items that are to be printed.

If an interrupt (DEL or BREAK) is typed during the printing of a news item, printing stops and the next item is started. Another `interrupt` within one second of the first causes the program to terminate.

FILES

`/etc/profile`
`$HOME/.news_time`

USAGE

End-user.

NAME

od — octal dump

SYNOPSIS

od [−bcdosx] [*file*] [[+]*offset*[.][b]]

DESCRIPTION

The command od prints *file* in one or more formats as selected by the options. If no file is specified, the standard input is used. If no option is specified, −o is the default.

For the purposes of this description, *word* refers to a 16-bit unit, independent of the word size of the machine.

The meanings of the options are:

−b Interpret bytes in octal.

−c Interpret bytes in ASCII. Certain non-graphic characters appear as C escapes: NUL=\0, BS=\b, FF=\f, NL=\n, CR=\r, HT=\t; others appear as 3-digit octal numbers.

−d Interpret *words* in unsigned decimal.

−o Interpret *words* in octal.

−s Interpret *words* in signed decimal.

−x Interpret *words* in hex.

The offset argument specifies the offset in the file where dumping is to commence. This argument is normally interpreted as octal bytes. If . is appended, the offset is interpreted in decimal. If b is appended, the offset is interpreted in units of 512 bytes. If the file argument is omitted, the offset argument must be preceded by +.

USAGE

General.

NAME

passwd — change login password

SYNOPSIS

`passwd` [*name*]

DESCRIPTION

The command `passwd` changes or installs a password associated with the login *name*.

Ordinary users may change only the password which corresponds to their login *name*.

The command `passwd` prompts ordinary users for their old password, if any. It then prompts for the new password twice. If password aging is in effect, then the first time the new password is entered, `passwd` checks to see if the old password has "aged" sufficiently. If "aging" is insufficient the new password is rejected and `passwd` terminates.

If "aging" is sufficient, a check is made to insure that the new password meets construction requirements. When the new password is entered a second time, the two copies of the new password are compared. If the two copies are not identical the cycle of prompting for the new password is repeated for at most two more times.

The super-user may change any password; hence, `passwd` does not prompt the super-user for the old password. The super-user is not forced to comply with password aging and password construction requirements. The super-user can create a null password by entering a carriage return in response to the prompt for a new password.

FILES

`/etc/passwd`

USAGE

End-user.

NAME

shl – shell layer manager

SYNOPSIS

`shl`

DESCRIPTION

The command `shl` allows a user to interact with more than one shell from a single terminal. The user controls these shells, known as *layers*, using the commands described below.

The *current layer* is the layer which can receive input from the keyboard. Other layers attempting to read from the keyboard are blocked. Output from multiple layers is multiplexed onto the terminal. To have the output of a layer blocked when it is not current, the `stty` option `loblk` may be set within the layer.

The `stty` character `swtch` (set to control-Z if NUL) is used to switch control to `shl` from a layer. The command `shl` has its own prompt, `>>>`, to help distinguish it from a layer.

A *layer* is a shell which has been bound to a virtual tty device (`/dev/sxt/*`). The virtual device can be manipulated like a real tty device using `stty` and `ioctl()`. [See STTY(AU_CMD) and IOCTL(BA_SYS) respectively.] Each layer has its own process group ID.

Definitions

A *name* is a sequence of characters delimited by a blank, tab or newline. Only the first eight characters are significant. The *names* (1) through (7) cannot be used when creating a layer. They are used by `shl` when no name is supplied. They may be abbreviated to just the digit.

Commands

The following commands may be issued from the `shl` prompt level. Any unique prefix is accepted.

`create` [*name*]

Create a layer called *name* and make it the current layer. If no argument is given, a layer will be created with a name of the form `(#)` where `#` is the last digit of the virtual device bound to the layer. The shell prompt variable `PS1` is set to the name of the layer followed by a space. A maximum of seven layers can be created.

`block` *name* [*name* ...]

For each *name*, block the output of the corresponding layer when it is not the current layer. This is equivalent to setting the `stty` option `loblk` within the layer.

`delete` *name* [*name* ...]

For each *name*, delete the corresponding layer. All processes in the process group of the layer are sent the SIGHUP signal.

`help` (or ?)

Print the syntax of the `shl` commands.

`layers` [`-l`] [*name* ...]

For each *name*, list the layer name and its process group. The `-l` option produces a long listing. If no arguments are given, information is presented for all existing layers.

`resume` [*name*]

Make the layer referenced by *name* the current layer. If no argument is given, the last existing current layer will be resumed.

`toggle`

Resume the layer that was current before the last current layer.

`unblock` *name* [*name* ...]

For each *name*, do not block the output of the corresponding layer when it is not the current layer. This is equivalent to setting the `stty` option `-loblk` within the layer.

`quit`

Exit `shl`. All layers are sent the SIGHUP signal.

name

Make the layer referenced by *name* the current layer.

FILES

`/dev/sxt/*` Virtual tty devices

USAGE

General.

SEE ALSO

SH(BU_CMD), STTY(AU_CMD), IOCTL(BA_SYS), SIGNAL(BA_SYS).

NAME

stty — set the options for a terminal

SYNOPSIS

`stty [-a] [-g]` [*options*]

DESCRIPTION

The command `stty` sets certain terminal I/O options for the device that is its standard input; without arguments, it reports the settings of certain options; with the `-a` option, it reports all of the option settings; with the `-g` option, it reports current settings in a form that can be used as an argument to another `stty` command. Detailed information about the modes listed in the first five groups below may be found in IOCTL(BA_SYS). Options in the last group are implemented using options in the previous groups. Note that many combinations of options make no sense, but no sanity checking is performed. The options are selected from the following:

Control Modes

`parenb (-parenb)`
enable (disable) parity generation and detection.

`parodd (-parodd)`
select odd (even) parity.

`cs5 cs6 cs7 cs8`
select character size.

`0`
hang up phone line immediately.

`number`
Set terminal baud rate to the number given, if possible. (All speeds are not supported by all hardware interfaces.)

`hupcl (-hupcl)`
hang up (do not hang up) modem connection on last close.

`hup (-hup)`
same as `hupcl (-hupcl)`.

`cstopb (-cstopb)`
use two (one) stop bits per character.

`cread (-cread)`
enable (disable) the receiver.

`clocal (-clocal)`
assume a line without (with) modem control.

`loblk (-loblk)`
block (do not block) output from a non-current layer.

Input Modes

`ignbrk` (`-ignbrk`)
: ignore (do not ignore) break on input.

`brkint` (`-brkint`)
: signal (do not signal) INTR on break.

`ignpar` (`-ignpar`)
: ignore (do not ignore) parity errors.

`parmrk` (`-parmrk`)
: mark (do not mark) parity errors.

`inpck` (`-inpck`)
: enable (disable) input parity checking.

`istrip` (`-istrip`)
: strip (do not strip) input characters to seven bits.

`inlcr` (`-inlcr`)
: map (do not map) NL to CR on input.

`igncr` (`-igncr`)
: ignore (do not ignore) CR on input.

`icrnl` (`-icrnl`)
: map (do not map) CR to NL on input.

`iuclc` (`-iuclc`)
: map (do not map) upper-case alphabetics to lower case on input.

`ixon` (`-ixon`)
: enable (disable) START/STOP output control. Output is stopped by sending an ASCII DC3 and started by sending an ASCII DC1.

`ixany` (`-ixany`)
: allow any character (only DC1) to restart output.

`ixoff` (`-ixoff`)
: request that the system send (not send) START/STOP characters when the input queue is nearly empty/full.

Output Modes

`opost` (`-opost`)
: post-process output (do not post-process output; ignore all other output modes).

`olcuc` (`-olcuc`)
: map (do not map) lower-case alphabetics to upper case on output.

`onlcr` (`-onlcr`)
: map (do not map) NL to CR-NL on output.

`ocrnl (-ocrnl)`
map (do not map) CR to NL on output.

`onocr (-onocr)`
do not (do) output CRs at column zero.

`onlret (-onlret)`
on the terminal NL performs (does not perform) the CR function.

`ofill (-ofill)`
use fill characters (use timing) for delays.

`ofdel (-ofdel)`
fill characters are DELs (NULs).

`cr0 cr1 cr2 cr3`
select style of delay for carriage returns.

`nl0 nl1`
select style of delay for line-feeds.

`tab0 tab1 tab2 tab3`
select style of delay for horizontal tabs.

`bs0 bs1`
select style of delay for backspaces.

`ff0 ff1`
select style of delay for form-feeds.

`vt0 vt1`
select style of delay for vertical tabs.

Local Modes

`isig (-isig)`
enable (disable) the checking of characters against the special control characters INTR, QUIT, and SWTCH.

`icanon (-icanon)`
enable (disable) canonical input (ERASE and KILL processing).

`xcase (-xcase)`
canonical (unprocessed) upper/lower-case presentation.

`echo (-echo)`
echo back (do not echo back) every character typed.

`echoe (-echoe)`
echo (do not echo) ERASE character as a backspace-space-backspace string. Note: this mode will erase the ERASEed character on many CRT terminals; however, it does *not* keep track of column position and, as a result, may be confusing on escaped characters, tabs, and backspaces.

`echok` (`-echok`)
echo (do not echo) NL after KILL character.

`lfkc` (`-lfkc`)
the same as `echok` (`-echok`); obsolete.

`echonl` (`-echonl`)
echo (do not echo) NL.

`noflsh` (`-noflsh`)
disable (enable) flush after INTR, QUIT, or SWTCH.

Control Assignments

`control-character c`
set `control-character` to `c`, where `control-character` is `erase`, `kill`, `intr`, `quit`, `swtch`, `eof`, `eol`, `min`, or `time` (`min` and `time` are used with `-icanon`). If `c` is preceded by a caret (^), then the value used is the corresponding CTRL character (e.g., "`^d`" is a **CTRL-d**); "^?" is interpreted as DEL and "^-" is interpreted as undefined.

`line i`
set line discipline to `i` (0 < `i` < 127).

Combination Modes

`evenp` or `parity`
enable `parenb` and `cs7`.

`oddp`
enable `parenb`, `cs7`, and `parodd`.

`-parity`, `-evenp`, or `-oddp`
disable `parenb`, and set `cs8`.

`raw` (`-raw` or `cooked`)
enable (disable) raw input and output (no ERASE, KILL, INTR, QUIT, SWTCH, EOT, or output post processing).

`nl` (`-nl`)
unset (set) `icrnl`, `onlcr`. In addition `-nl` unsets `inlcr`, `igncr`, `ocrnl`, and `onlret`.

`lcase` (`-lcase`)
set (unset) `xcase`, `iuclc`, and `olcuc`.

`LCASE` (`-LCASE`)
same as `lcase` (`-lcase`).

`tabs` (`-tabs` or `tab8`)
preserve (expand to spaces) tabs when printing.

`ek`
reset ERASE and KILL characters back to normal # and @.

sane
resets all modes to some reasonable values.

USAGE
End-user.

SEE ALSO
IOCTL(BA_SYS).

NAME

su — become super-user or another user

SYNOPSIS

`su` [−] [*name* [*arg* ...]]

DESCRIPTION

The command `su` allows one to become another user without logging off. The default user *name* is `root` (i.e., super-user).

To use `su`, the appropriate password must be supplied (unless one is already `root`). If the password is correct, `su` will execute a new environment with the real and effective user ID set to that of the specified user. The new command interpreter will be the optional program named in the specified user's password file entry, or the default if none is specified. Normal user ID privileges can be restored by entering EOT (control-D).

Any additional arguments given on the command line are passed to the command interpreter.

The following statements are true only if the command interpreter named in the specified user's password file entry is `sh` [see SH(BU_CMD)]. If the first argument to `su` is a −, the environment will be changed to what would be expected if the user actually logged in as the specified user. Otherwise, the environment is passed along with the possible exception of `PATH`.

All attempts to become another user using `su` are logged.

FILES

`/etc/passwd`	system's password file
`/etc/profile`	system's profile
`$HOME/.profile`	user's profile

USAGE

General.

SEE ALSO

SH(BU_CMD).

NAME

tabs — set tabs on a terminal

SYNOPSIS

`tabs` [*tabspec*] [`+m`*n*] [`-T`*type*]

DESCRIPTION

The command `tabs` sets the tab stops on the user's terminal according to the tab specification *tabspec*, after clearing any previous settings.

Three types of tab specification are accepted for *tabspec*: "canned," repetitive, arbitrary. If no *tabspec* is given, the default value is `-8`, i.e., "standard" tabs. The lowest column number is 1. Note that for `tabs`, column 1 always refers to the leftmost column on a terminal, even one whose column markers begin at 0.

`-code` Gives the name of one of a set of "canned" tabs. The legal codes and their meanings are as follows:

`-a` 1,10,16,36,72
Assembler, IBM System/370, first format

`-a2` 1,10,16,40,72
Assembler, IBM System/370, second format

`-c` 1,8,12,16,20,55
COBOL, normal format

`-c2` 1,6,10,14,49
COBOL compact format (columns 1-6 omitted).

`-c3` 1,6,10,14,18,22,26,30,34,38,42,46,50,54,58,62,67
COBOL compact format (columns 1-6 omitted), with more tabs than `-c2`. This is the recommended format for COBOL.

`-f` 1,7,11,15,19,23
FORTRAN

`-p` 1,5,9,13,17,21,25,29,33,37,41,45,49,53,57,61
PL/I

`-s` 1,10,55
SNOBOL

`-u` 1,12,20,44
UNIVAC 1100 Assembler

In addition to these "canned" formats, three other types exist:

`-n` A repetitive specification requests tabs at columns 1+n, 1+2*n, etc. Of particular importance is the value `-8`: this represents the "standard" tab setting, and is the most likely tab setting to be found at a terminal. Another special case is the value `-0`, implying no tabs at all.

`n1,n2,...` The arbitrary format permits the user to type any chosen set of numbers, separated by commas, in ascending order. Up to 40 numbers are allowed. If any number (except the first one) is preceded by a plus sign, it is taken as an increment to be added to the previous value. Thus, the tab lists 1,10,20,30 and 1,10,+10,+10 are considered identical.

Any of the following may be used also; if a given flag occurs more than once, the last value given takes effect:

−T*type* The command `tabs` usually needs to know the type of terminal in order to set tabs and always needs to know the type to set margins. The argument *type* is a terminal name. If no `−T` flag is supplied, `tabs` searches for the environmental variable `TERM`. If no *type* can be found, `tabs` tries a sequence that will work for many terminals.

+m*n* The margin argument may be used for some terminals. It causes all tabs to be moved over *n* columns by making column *n+1* the left margin. If `+m` is given without a value of *n*, the value assumed is 10. For a TermiNet, the first value in the tab list should be 1, or the margin will move even further to the right. The normal (leftmost) margin on most terminals is obtained by `+m0`. The margin for most terminals is reset only when the `+m` flag is given explicitly.

Tab and margin setting is performed via the standard output.

USAGE

End-user.

NAME

tar — file archiver

SYNOPSIS

`tar` [*option*] [*file* ...]

DESCRIPTION

The command `tar` creates archives of files; it is often used to save files on (and restore from) magnetic tape. Its actions are controlled by the *option* argument. The *option* is a string of characters containing at most one function letter and possibly one or more modifiers. Other arguments to the command are *files* (or directory names) specifying which files are to be archived or restored. In all cases, appearance of a directory name refers to the files and (recursively) subdirectories of that directory.

The function portion of the option is specified by one of the following letters:

`r` The named *files* are written on the end of the archive.

`x` The named *files* are extracted from the archive. If a named file matches a directory whose contents had been written onto the archive, this directory is (recursively) extracted. If a named file in the archive does not exist on the system, the file is created with the same mode as the one in the archive, except that the set-user-ID and set-group-ID modes are not set unless the user is super-user. If the files exist, their modes are not changed except as described above. The owner, group, and modification time are restored (if possible). If no *files* argument is given, the entire content of the archive is extracted. Note that if several files with the same name are in the archive, the last one overwrites all earlier ones.

`t` The names of all the files in the archive are listed.

`u` The named *files* are added to the archive if they are not already there, or have been modified since last written into the archive. This option implies option `r`.

`c` Create a new archive; writing begins at the beginning of the archive, instead of after the last file. This option implies the `r` option.

The following characters may be used in addition to the letter that selects the desired function:

`v` Normally, `tar` does its work silently. The `v` (verbose) modifier causes it to type the name of each file it treats, preceded by the option letter. With the `t` option, `v` gives more information about the archive entries than just the name.

`w` Causes `tar` to print the action to be taken, followed by the name of the file, and then wait for the user's confirmation. If a word beginning with `y` is given, the action is performed. Any other input means "no". This modifier is invalid with the `t` option.

`f` Causes `tar` to use the next argument as the name of the archive instead of the default, which is usually a tape drive. If the name of the file is –, `tar` writes to the standard output or reads from the standard input, whichever is appropriate. Thus, `tar` can be used as the head or tail of a pipeline. The command `tar` can also be used to move directory hierarchies with the command:

`(cd fromdir; tar cf – .) | (cd todir; tar xf –)`

`b` Causes tar to use the next argument as the blocking factor for tape records. The default is 1, the maximum is 20. This option should only be used with (raw) magnetic tape archives (see `f` above). The block size is determined automatically when reading tapes (options `x` and `t`).

`l` Tells `tar` to report if it cannot resolve all of the links to the files being archived. If `l` is not specified, no error messages are printed. This modifier is valid only with the options `c`, `r`, and `u`.

`m` Tells `tar` not to restore the modification times. The modification time of the file will be the time of extraction. This modifier is invalid with the `t` option.

`o` Causes extracted files to take on the user and group identifier of the user running the program rather than those on the archive. This modifier is valid only with the `x` option.

ERRORS

The command `tar` reports bad option characters and read/write errors.

It also reports an error if enough memory is not available to hold the link tables.

USAGE

General.

NAME

tty – get the name of the terminal

SYNOPSIS

`tty [-s]`

DESCRIPTION

The command `tty` prints the path name of the user's terminal. The `-s` option inhibits printing of the terminal path name, allowing one to test just the exit code.

ERRORS

Exit codes:

2	if invalid options were specified,
0	if standard input is a terminal,
1	otherwise.

An error is reported if the standard input is not a terminal and `-s` is not specified.

USAGE

General.

NAME

uucp, uulog, uuname — system-to-system copy

SYNOPSIS

`uucp` [*options*] *source-files destination-file*

`uulog` [`-s` *system*]

`uuname` [`-l`]

DESCRIPTION

uucp

The command `uucp` copies files named by the *source-file* arguments to the *destination-file* argument. (Note that some `uucp` options are new to UNIX System V Release 2.0; see the options paragraph below for details.) A file name may be a path name on your machine, or may have the form:

system-name ! *path-name*

where *system-name* is taken from a list of system names that `uucp` knows about. The destination *system-name* may also be a list of names such as:

system-name ! *system-name* ! ... ! *system-name* ! *path-name*

in which case, an attempt is made to send the file via the specified route to the destination. Care should be taken to ensure that intermediate nodes in the route are willing to forward information.

The shell metacharacters `?`, `*`, and `[...]` appearing in *path-name* will be expanded on the appropriate system. Path-names may be one of:

(1) a full path-name.

(2) a path-name preceded by ~*name* where *name* is a login name on the specified system and is replaced by that user's login directory. Note that if an invalid login is specified, the default will be to the public directory (`PUBDIR`).

(3) a path-name specified as ~/*dest*, where the destination *dest* is appended to `PUBDIR`.

NOTE: This destination will be treated as a file name unless more than one file is being transferred by this request or the destination is already a directory. To ensure that it is a directory, follow the destination with a `/`. For example, `~/dan/` as the destination will make the directory `PUBDIR/dan` if it does not exist and put the requested file(s) in that directory.

(4) anything else is prefixed by the current directory.

If the result is an erroneous path-name for the remote system, the copy will fail. If the *destination-file* is a directory, the last part of the *source-file* name is used.

The command `uucp` gives universal read and write permissions and preserves execute permissions across the transmission.

The following options are interpreted by `uucp`:

- `-c` Do not copy local file to the spool directory for transfer to the remote machine (default).
- `-C` Force the copy of local files to the spool directory for transfer.
- `-d` Make all necessary directories for the file copy (default).
- `-f` Do not make intermediate directories for the file copy.
- `-j` Output the job identification ASCII string on the standard output. This job identification can be used by `uustat` to obtain the status or terminate a job. (This option is new to UNIX System V Release 2.0.)
- `-m` Send mail to the requester when the copy is completed.
- `-n`*user* Notify *user* on the remote system that a file was sent.
- `-r` Do not start the file transfer; just queue the job. (This option is new to UNIX System V Release 2.0.)

uulog

The command `uulog` queries a log file of `uucp` or `uuxqt` transactions.

If the `-s` option is specified, then `uulog` prints information about file transfer work involving system *system*.

uuname

The command `uuname` lists the `uucp` names of known systems. The `-l` option returns the local system name.

USAGE

General.

The domain of remotely accessible files can (and for obvious security reasons, usually should) be severely restricted.

SEE ALSO

MAIL(BU_CMD), UUSTAT(AU_CMD), UUX(AU_CMD).

NAME

uustat — uucp status inquiry and job control

SYNOPSIS

`uustat` [*options*]

DESCRIPTION

The command `uustat` will display the status of, or cancel, previously specified `uucp` commands, or provide general status on `uucp` connections to other systems.

Not all combinations of options are valid. Only one of the following options can be specified with `uustat`:

`-q` List the jobs queued for each machine.

`-k` *jobid* Kill the `uucp` request whose job identification is *jobid*. The killed `uucp` request must belong to the person issuing the `uustat` command unless that user is the superuser.

`-r` *jobid* Rejuvenate *jobid*. The files associated with *jobid* are touched so that their modification time is set to the current time. This prevents the cleanup daemon from deleting the job until the jobs modification time reaches the limit imposed by the daemon.

The options below may not be used with the ones listed above; however, these options may be used singly or together:

`-s` *sys* Report the status of all `uucp` requests for remote system *sys*.

`-u` *user* Report the status of all `uucp` requests issued by *user*.

When no options are given, `uustat` outputs the status of all `uucp` requests issued by the current user.

USAGE

General.

SEE ALSO

UUCP(AU_CMD).

NAME

uuto, uupick — public system-to-system file copy

SYNOPSIS

`uuto` [`-p`] [`-m`] *source-files destination*

`uupick` [`-s` *system*]

DESCRIPTION

uuto

The command `uuto` sends *source-files* to *destination.* The command `uuto` uses the UUCP(AU_CMD) facility to send files, while it allows the local system to control the file access. A source-file name is a path name on the user's machine. Destination has the form: "*system!user*" where *system* is taken from a list of system names that `uucp` knows about [see `uuname` in UUCP(AU_CMD).] The argument *user* is the login name of someone on the specified system.

Two options are available:

- `-p` Copy the source file into the spool directory before transmission.
- `-m` Send mail to the sender when the copy is complete.

The files (or subtrees if directories are specified) are sent to a public directory (PUBDIR) on *system*. Specifically, the files are sent to the directory

`PUBDIR/receive/`*user/fsystem*,

where *user* is the recipient, and *fsystem* is the sending system.

The recipient is notified by `mail` of the arrival of files.

uupick

The command `uupick` may be used by a user to accept or reject the files transmitted to the user. Specifically, `uupick` searches PUBDIR on the user's system for files sent to the user. For each entry (file or directory) found, one of the following messages is printed on the standard output:

`from system:` *dir* `dirname ?`

`from system:` *file* `file-name ?`

The command `uupick` then reads a line from the standard input to determine the disposition of the file. The user's possible responses are:

<newline>	Go on to next entry.
`d`	Delete the entry.
`m [` *dir* `]`	Move the entry to named directory *dir*. If *dir* is not specified as a complete path name a destination relative to the current directory is assumed. If no destination is given, the default is the current directory.

`a` [*dir*]	Same as `m` except moving all the files sent from *system*.
`p`	Print the content of the file to standard output.
`q`	Stop and exit.
EOT	(control-D.) Same as `q`.
`!`*command*	Escape to the command interpreter to execute *command*.
`*`	Print a usage summary for `uuto`.

The command `uupick` invoked with the `-s` *system* option will only search for files (and list any found) sent from *system*.

USAGE

General.

SEE ALSO

MAIL(BU_CMD), UUCP(AU_CMD), UUSTAT(AU_CMD), UUX(AU_CMD),

NAME

uux — remote command execution

SYNOPSIS

`uux` [*options*] *command-string*

DESCRIPTION

The command `uux` will gather zero or more files from various systems, execute a command on a specified system, and then send the standard output of the command to a file on a specified system.

The *command-string* is made up of one or more arguments that are similar to normal command arguments, except that the command and any file names may be prefixed by *system-name*!. A null *system-name* is interpreted as the local system.

The following statements are relevant if SH(BU_CMD) is the command interpreter.

> The metacharacter * will not give the desired result.
>
> The redirection tokens `>>` and `<<` are not implemented.

A file name may be specified as for `uucp`: it may be a full path name, a path name preceded by *~name* (which is replaced by the corresponding login directory), a path name specified as *~/dest* (*dest* is prefixed by PUBDIR), or a simple file name (which is prefixed by the current directory). See UUCP(AU_CMD) for the details.

As an example, the command

```
uux "!diff usg!/usr/dan/file1
pwba!/a4/dan/file2 >!~/dan/file.diff"
```

will get the `file1` and `file2` files from the "usg" and "pwba" machines, execute `diff`, and put the results in `file.diff` in the local PUBDIR/dan directory. (PUBDIR is the `uucp` public directory on the local system.)

The execution of commands on remote systems takes place in an execution directory known to the `uucp` system. All files required for the execution will be put into this directory unless they already reside on that machine. Therefore, the non-local file names (without path or machine reference) must be unique within the `uux` request. The following command will **not** work:

```
uux "a!diff b!/usr/dan/xyz c!/usr/dan/xyz
>!xyz.diff"
```

because the file `xyz` will be copied from the `b` system as well as the `c` system, causing a name conflict. The command

```
uux "a!diff a!/usr/dan/xyz c!/usr/dan/xyz
>!xyz.diff"
```

will work (provided `diff` is a permitted command), because the local file `xyz` (which is not copied) does not conflict with the copied file `xyz` from the `c` system.

Any characters special to the command interpreter should be quoted either by quoting the entire *command-string* or quoting the special characters as individual arguments.

The command `uux` will attempt to get all files to the execution system. For files that are output files, the file name must be escaped using parentheses. For example, the command

```
uux a!cut -f1 b!/usr/file \(c!/usr/file\)
```

gets `/usr/file` from system "b", sends it to system "a", performs a `cut` command on that file, and sends the result of the `cut` command to system "c".

The command `uux` will notify the user (by mail) if the requested command on the remote system was disallowed. This notification can be turned off by the `-n` option. The response comes by mail from the remote machine.

The following options are interpreted by `uux`:

- `-` The standard input to `uux` is made the standard input to the *command-string*.
- `-j` Output the job identification ASCII string on the standard output. This job identification can be used by `uustat` to obtain the status or terminate a job. (This option is new to UNIX System V Release 2.0.)
- `-n` Do not notify the user if the command fails.

USAGE

General.

Note that, for security reasons, many installations will limit the list of commands executable on behalf of an incoming request from `uux`. Many sites will permit little more than the receipt of mail via `uux`.

Only the first command of a pipeline [see SH(BU_CMD)] may have a *system-name*!. All other commands are executed on the system of the first command.

SEE ALSO

UUCP(AU_CMD), UUSTAT(AU_CMD).

NAME

vi — screen-oriented (visual) display editor

SYNOPSIS

`vi` [−r *file*] [−*l*] [−*wn*] [−*R*] [+*command*] *file* ...

DESCRIPTION

`vi` (visual) is a display-oriented text editor. It is based on the underlying line editor EX(AU_CMD): it is possible to switch back and forth between the two, and to execute `ex` commands from within `vi`.

When using `vi`, the terminal screen acts as window into the file being edited. Changes made to the file are reflected in the screen display; the position of the cursor on the screen indicates the position within the file.

The environmental variable `TERM` must give the terminal type; the terminal must be defined in the *terminfo* database. As for `ex`, editor initialization scripts can be placed in the environmental variable `EXINIT`, or the file `.exrc` in the current or home directory.

Options

The following options are interpreted by `vi`:

−r*file* — Recover *file* after an editor or system crash. If *file* is not specified a list of all saved files will be printed.

−l — set **LISP** mode (see **Edit Options** below).

−w*n* — Set the default window size to *n*.

−R — Read only mode; the **readonly** flag is set, preventing accidental overwriting of the file.

+*command* — The specified `ex` command is interpreted before editing begins.

VI COMMANDS

General Remarks

See EX(AU_CMD) for the complete description of `ex`. Only the `visual` mode of the editor is described here.

At the beginning, `vi` is in the *command* mode; the *input* mode is entered by several commands used to insert or change text. In input mode, ESC (escape) is used to leave input mode; in command mode, it is used to cancel a partial command; the terminal bell is sounded if the editor is not in input mode and there is no partially entered command.

The last (bottom) line of the screen is used to echo the input for search commands (/ and ?), for `ex` commands (:), and system commands (!). It is also used to report errors or print other messages.

An interrupt (BREAK or DEL) typed during text input, or during the input of a command on the bottom line, terminates the input (or cancels the command) and returns the editor to command mode. During command mode an interrupt causes the bell to be sounded; in general the bell indicates an error (such as unrecognized key).

Lines displayed on the screen containing only a '~' indicate that the last line above them is the last line of the file (the '~' lines are past the end of the file). On a terminal with limited local intelligence, there may be lines on the screen marked with an '@': these indicate space on the screen not corresponding to lines in the file. (These lines may be removed by entering a 'control-R', forcing the editor to retype the screen without these holes.)

Command Summary

Most commands accept a preceding number as an argument, either to give a size or position (for display or movement commands), or as a repeat count (for commands that change text). For simplicity, this optional argument will be referred to as `count` when its effect is described.

The following operators can be followed by a movement command, in order to specify an extent of text to be affected: `c`, `d`, `y`, `<`, `>`, `!`, and `=`. The region specified is from the current cursor position to just before the cursor position indicated by the move. If the command operates on lines only, then all the lines which fall partly or wholly within this region are affected. Otherwise the exact marked region is affected.

In the following, control characters are indicated in the form '^X', which stands for 'control-X'. The intended ASCII character name is also given.

Unless otherwise specified, the commands are interpreted in command mode and have no special effect in input mode.

^B (STX) Scrolls backward to display the window above the current one. A count specifies the number of windows to go back. Two lines of overlap are kept if possible.

^D (EOT) Scrolls forward a half-window of text. A count gives the number of (logical) lines to scroll, and is remembered for future **^D** and **^U** commands.

In input mode, backs `shiftwidth` spaces over the indentation provided by `autoindent` or **^T**.

^E (ENQ) Scrolls forward one line, leaving the cursor where it is if possible.

^F (ACK) Scrolls forward to display the window below the current one. A count specifies the number of windows to go forward. Two lines of overlap are kept if possible.

^G (BEL) Prints the current file name and other information, including the number of lines and the current position. (Equivalent to the ex command **f**.)

^H (BS) Moves one space to the left (stops at the left margin). A count specifies the number of spaces to back up. (Same as **h**.)

In input mode, backs over the last input character without erasing it.

^J (LF) Moves the cursor down one line in the same column. A count specifies the number of lines to move down. (Same as **^N** and **j**.)

^L (FF) Clears and redraws the screen. (Used when the screen is scrambled for any reason.)

^M (CR) Moves to the first non-white character in the next line. A count specifies the number of lines to go forward.

^N (SO) Same as **^J** and **j**.

^P (DLE) Moves the cursor up one line in the same column. A count specifies the number of lines to move up. (Same as **k**.)

^R (DC2) Redraws the current screen, eliminating the false lines marked with '@' (which do not correspond to actual lines in the file).

^T (DC4) In input mode, if at the beginning of the line or preceded only by white space, inserts `shiftwidth` white space. This inserted space can only be backed over using **^D**.

^U (NAK) Scrolls up a half-window of text. A count gives the number of (logical) lines to scroll, and is remembered for future **^D** and **^U** commands.

^V (SYN) In input mode, quotes the next character to make it possible to insert special characters (including ESC) into the file.

^W (ETB) In input mode, backs up one word; the deleted characters remain on the display.

^Y (EM) Scrolls backward one line, leaving the cursor where it is if possible.

^[(ESC) Cancels a partially formed command; sounds the bell if there is none.

In input mode, terminates input mode.

When entering a command on the bottom line of the screen (ex command line or search pattern with \ or **?**), terminates input and executes command.

SPACE — Moves one space to the right (stops at the end of the line). A count specifies the number of spaces to go forward. (Same as **l**.)

! — An operator which passes specified lines from the buffer as standard input to the specified system command, and replaces those lines with the standard output from the command. The **!** is followed by a movement command specifying the lines to be passed (lines from the current position to the end of the movement) and then the command (terminated as usual by a return). A count preceding the **!** is passed on to the movement command after **!**.

Doubling ! and preceding it by a count causes that many lines, starting with the current line, to be passed.

" — Precedes a named buffer specification. There are named buffers **1-9** in which the editor places deleted text. The named buffers **a-z** are available to the user for saving deleted or yanked text.

$** — Moves to the end of the current line. A count specifies the number of lines to go forward. (e.g., **2$ goes to the end of the next line.)

% — Moves to the parenthesis or curly brace which matches the parenthesis or brace at the current cursor position.

& — Same as the **ex** command **&** (repeats previous substitute command).

When followed by a ′, returns to the previous context, placing the cursor at the beginning of the line. (The previous context is set whenever a non-relative move is made.) When followed by a letter **a-z**, returns to the line marked with that letter (see the **m** command), at the first non-white character in the line.

When used with an operator such as **d** to specify an extent of text, the operation takes place over complete lines. (See also **`**.)

When followed by a **`**, returns to the previous context, placing the cursor at the character position marked. (The previous context is set whenever a non-relative move is made.) When followed by a letter **a-z**, returns to the line marked with that letter (see the **m** command), at the character position marked.

When used with an operator such as **d** to specify an extent of text, the operation takes place from the exact marked place to the current position within the line. (See also ′.)

[[Backs up to the previous section boundary. A section is defined by the value of the `sections` option. Lines which start with a formfeed (^L character) or { also stop [[.

If the option *lisp* is set, stops at each (at the beginning of a line.

]] Moves forward to a section boundary (see [[).

^ Moves to the first non-white position on the current line.

(Moves backward to the beginning of a sentence. A sentence ends at a . ! or ? which is followed by either the end of a line or by two spaces. Any number of closing)] " and ` characters may appear between the . ! or ? and the spaces or end of line. A count moves back that many sentences.

If the *lisp* option is set. moves to the beginning of a LISP s-expression. Sentences also begin at paragraph and section boundaries (see { and [[below).

) Moves forward to the beginning of a sentence. A count moves forward that many sentences. (See (.)

{ Moves back to the beginning of the preceding paragraph. A paragraph is defined by the value of the `paragraphs` option. A completely empty line, and a section boundary (see [[above), are also taken to begin paragraphs. A count specifies the number of paragraphs to move backward.

} Moves forward to the beginning of the next paragraph. A count specifies the number of paragraphs to move forward. (See {.)

| Requires a count; the cursor is placed in that column (if possible).

\+ Moves to the first non-white character in the next line. A count specifies the number of lines to go forward. (Same as ^M.)

, Reverse of the last **f F t** or **T** command, looking the other way in the current line. A count is equivalent to repeating the search that many times.

\- Moves to the first non-white character in the previous line. A count specifies how many lines to move back.

. Repeats the last command which changed the buffer. A count is passed on to the command being repeated.

/ Reads a string from the last line on the screen, interprets it as a regular expression, and scans forward for the next occurrence of a matching string. The search begins when return is entered to terminate the pattern; it may be terminated with an interrupt (or DEL).

When used with an operator to specify an extent of text, the defined region is from the current cursor position to the beginning of the matched string. Whole lines may be specified by giving an offset from the matched line (using a closing / followed by a +n or -n).

Regular expressions are described in EX(AU_CMD).

0 Moves to the first character on the current line. (Is not interpreted as a command when preceded by a non-zero digit.)

: Begins an `ex` command. The :, as well as the entered command, is echoed on the bottom line; It is executed when the input is terminated by entering a return.

; Repeats the last single character find using **f F t** or **T**. A count is equivalent to repeating the search that many times.

< An operator which shifts lines left one `shiftwidth`. May be followed by a move to specify lines. A count is passed through to the move command.

When repeated (<<), shifts the current line (or count lines starting at the current one).

> An operator which shifts lines right one `shiftwidth`. (See <.)

= If the `lisp` option is set, then reindents the specified lines, as though they were typed in with *lisp* and *autoindent* set. May be preceded by a count to indicate how many lines to process, or followed by a move command for the same purpose.

? Scans backwards, the reverse of /. (See /.)

A Appends at the end of line. (Same as **$a**.)

B Backs up a word, where a word is any non-blank sequence, placing the cursor at the beginning of the word. A count gives the number of words to go back.

C Changes the rest of the text on the current line. (Same as **c$**.)

D Deletes the rest of the text on the current line. (same as **d$**.)

E Moves forward to the end of a word, where a word is any non-blank sequence. A count gives the number of words to go forward.

F Must be followed by a single character; scans backwards in the current line for that character, moving the cursor to it if found. A count is equivalent to repeating the search that many times.

G Goes to the line number given as preceding argument, or the end of the file if no preceding count is given.

H Moves the cursor to the top line on the screen. If a count is given, then the cursor is moved to that line on the screen, counting from the top. The cursor is placed on the first non-white character on the line. If used as the target of an operator, full lines are affected.

I Inserts at the beginning of a line. (Same as **↑i**.)

J Joins the current line with the next one, supplying appropriate white space: one space between words, two spaces after a period, and no spaces at all if the first character of the next line is). A count causes that many lines to be joined rather than two.

L Moves the cursor to the first non-white character of the last line on the screen. A count moves to that line counting form the bottom. When used with an operator, whole lines are affected.

M Moves the cursor to the middle line on the screen, at the first non-white position on the line.

N Scans for the next match of the last pattern given to / or ?, but in the reverse direction; this is the reverse of **n**.

O Opens a new line above the current line and enters input mode.

P Puts the last deleted text back before/above the cursor. The text goes back as whole lines above the cursor if it was deleted as whole lines. Otherwise the text is inserted just before the cursor.

May be preceded by a named buffer specification ("*x*), to retrieve the contents of the buffer.

Q Quits from *vi* and enters *ex* command mode.

R Replaces characters on the screen with characters entered, until the input is terminated with ESC.

S Changes whole lines (same as **cc**). A count changes that many lines.

T Must be followed by a single character; scans backwards in the current line for that character, and if found, places the cursor just after that character. A count is equivalent to repeating the search that many times.

U Restores the current line to its state before the cursor was last moved to it.

W Moves forward to the beginning of a word in the current line, where a word is a sequence of non-blank characters. A count specifies the number of words to move forward.

X Deletes the character before the cursor. A count repeats the effect, but only characters on the current line are deleted.

Y Places (yanks) a copy of the current line into the unnamed buffer (same as **yy**). A count copies that many lines. May be preceded by a buffer name to put the copied line(s) in that buffer.

ZZ Exits the editor, writing out the buffer if it was changed since the last write. (Same as the **ex** command **x**.)

a Enters input mode, appending the entered text after the current cursor position; A count causes the inserted text to be replicated that many times, but only if the inserted text is all on one line.

b Backs up to the beginning of a word in the current line. A word is a sequence of alphanumerics, or a sequence of special characters. A count repeats the effect.

c Deletes the specified region of text, and enters input mode to replace it with the entered text. If more than part of a single line is affected, the deleted text is saved in the numeric buffers. If only part of the current line is affected, then the last character to be deleted is marked with a **$**. A count is passed through to the move command.

d Deletes the specified region of text. If more than part of a line is affected, the text is saved in the numeric buffers. A count is passed through to the move command.

e Moves forward to the end of the next word, defined as for **b**. A count repeats the effect.

f Must be followed by a single character; scans the rest of the current line for that character, and moves the cursor to it if found. A count repeats the find that many times.

h Moves the cursor one character to the left. (Same as **^H**.) A count repeats the effect.

i Enters input mode, inserting the entered text before the cursor. (See **a**.)

j Moves the cursor one line down in the same column. (Same as **^J** and **^N**.)

k Moves the cursor one line up. (Same as **^P**.)

l Moves the cursor one character to the right. (Same as SPACE.)

m Must be followed by a single lower case letter **x**; marks the current position of the cursor with that letter. The exact position is referred to by **`x**; the line is referred to by **'x**.

n Repeats the last / or ? scanning commands.

o Opens a line below the current line and enters input mode; otherwise like **O**.

p Puts text after/below the cursor; otherwise like **P**.

r Must be followed by a single character; the character under the cursor is replaced by the specified one. (The new character may be a newline.) A count replaces each of the following count characters with the single character given.

s Deletes the single character under the cursor, and enters input mode; the entered text replaces the deleted character. A count specifies how many characters from the current line are changed. The last character to be changed is marked with a $, as for **c**.

t Must be followed by a single character; scans the rest of the line for that character. The cursor is moved to just before the character, if it is found. A count is equivalent to repeating the search that many times.

u Reverses the last change made to the current buffer. If repeated, will alternate between these two states, thus is its own inverse. When used after an insert which inserted text on more than one line, the lines are saved in the numeric named buffers.

w Moves forward to the beginning of the next word, where word is the same as in **b**. A count specifies how many words to go forward.

x Deletes the single character under the cursor. With a count deletes that many characters forward from the cursor position, but only on the current line.

y Must be followed by a movement command; the specifed text is copied (yanked) into the unnamed temporary buffer. If preceded by a named buffer specification, "*x*, the text is placed in that buffer also.

z Redraws the screen with the current line placed as specified by the following character: return specifies the top of the screen, . the center of the screen, and - the bottom of the screen. A count may be given after the z and before the following character to specify the new screen size for the redraw. A count before the z gives the number of the line to place in the center of the screen instead of the default current line.

USAGE

General.

SEE ALSO

EX(AU_CMD).

NAME

wall — write to all users

SYNOPSIS

`/etc/wall`

DESCRIPTION

The command `wall` reads its standard input until an end-of-file. It then prints this message on the terminals of all users currently logged-in, preceded by:

Broadcast Message from *login-id*

The sender must be super-user to override any protections the users may have invoked [see MESG(AU_CMD)].

USAGE

Administrator.

The command `wall` is used to warn all users, typically prior to shutting down the system.

SEE ALSO

MESG(AU_CMD), WRITE(AU_CMD).

NAME

who — who is on the system

SYNOPSIS

`who` [*options*] [*file*]

`who am i`

`who am I`

DESCRIPTION

The command `who` can list the user's name, terminal line, login time, elapsed time since activity occurred on the line, and the process-ID of the command interpreter for each current system user. It examines the `/etc/utmp` file to obtain its information. If *file* is given, that file is examined instead.

The command `who` with the `am i` or `am I` option identifies the invoking user.

Except for the default `-s` option, the general format for output entries is:

name **[state]** *line time activity pid* **[comment] [exit]**

With options, `who` can list logins, logoffs, reboots, and changes to the system clock, as well as other processes spawned by the `init` process. These options are:

`-u` This option lists only those users who are currently logged in. The *name* is the user's login name. The *line* is the name of the line as found in the directory `/dev`. The *time* is the time that the user logged in. The *activity* is the number of hours and minutes since activity last occurred on that particular line. A dot `(.)` indicates that the terminal has seen activity in the last minute and is therefore "current". If more than twenty-four hours have elapsed or the line has not been used since boot time, the entry is marked `old`. This field is useful when trying to determine whether a person is working at the terminal or not. The *pid* is the process-ID of the user's login process.

`-T` This option is the same as the `-u` option, except that the *state* of the terminal line is printed. The *state* describes whether someone else can write to that terminal. A `+` appears if the terminal is writable by anyone; a `-` appears if it is not. The super-user can write to all lines having a `+` or a `-` in the *state* field. If a bad line is encountered, a `?` is printed.

`-l` This option lists only those lines on which the system is waiting for someone to login. The *name* field is LOGIN in such cases. Other fields are the same as for user entries except that the *state* field does not exist.

`-H` This option will print column headings above the regular output. (This option is new in UNIX System V Release 2.0.)

`-q` This is a quick `who`, displaying only the names and the number of users currently logged on. When this option is used, all other options are ignored. (This option is new in UNIX System V Release 2.0.)

`-p` This option lists any other process which is currently active and has been previously spawned by `init`.

`-d` This option displays all processes that have expired and not been respawned by `init`. The `exit` field appears for dead processes and contains the termination and exit values of the dead process. This can be useful in determining why a process terminated.

`-b` This option indicates the time and date of the last reboot.

`-r` This option indicates the current *run-level* of the `init` process.

`-t` This option indicates the last change to the system clock.

`-a` This option processes `/etc/utmp` or the named *file* with all options turned on.

`-s` This option is the default and lists only the *name*, *line*, and *time* fields.

FILES

`/etc/utmp`
`/dev/tty*`

USAGE

General.

NAME

write — write to another user

SYNOPSIS

`write` *user* [*terminal*]

DESCRIPTION

The command `write` copies lines from the user's terminal to that of another user. When first called, it sends the message:

`Message from` *sender-login-id* (*ttynn*) [*date*]. . .

to the user addressed. When it has successfully completed the connection, it also sends two bells to the sender's terminal to indicate that what the sender is typing is being sent.

The recipient of the message should write back, by typing `write` *sender-login-id*, on receipt of the initial message. Whatever each user types (except for command escapes, see below) is printed on the other user's terminal, until an end-of-file or an interrupt is sent. At that point `write` writes "EOT" on the other terminal and exits. The recipient can also stop further messages from coming in by executing "mesg n".

To write to a user who is logged in more than once, the *terminal* argument may be used to indicate which terminal to send to (e.g., `tty00`); otherwise, the first writable instance of the user found in `/etc/utmp` is assumed and an informational message is written.

A user may deny or grant write permission by use of the `mesg` command. Certain commands disallow messages in order to prevent interference with their output. However, if the sender has super-user permissions, messages can be forced onto a write-inhibited terminal.

If the character `!` is found at the beginning of a line, `write` calls the command interpreter to execute the rest of the line as a command.

ERRORS

The following errors are reported:

- the user addressed is not logged on.
- the user addressed denies write permission [see MESG(AU_CMD)].
- the user's terminal is set to `mesg n`; recipient cannot respond.
- the recipient changes permission after `write` had begun.

FILES

`/etc/utmp`

USAGE

End-user.

SEE ALSO

MESG(AU_CMD), WHO(AU_CMD).

Chapter 3

Administered Systems Utilities

NAME

accton, acctwtmp, chargefee, ckpacct, dodisk, lastlogin, monacct, prdaily, prtacct, shutacct, startup, turnacct – miscellaneous accounting and support commands

SYNOPSIS

`/usr/lib/acct/accton` [*file*]

`/usr/lib/acct/acctwtmp` *reason*

`/usr/lib/acct/chargefee` *login-name number*

`/usr/lib/acct/ckpacct` [*blocks*]

`/usr/lib/acct/dodisk` [*files*]

`/usr/lib/acct/lastlogin`

`/usr/lib/acct/monacct` *number*

`/usr/lib/acct/prdaily` [`-l`] [`-c`] [*mmdd*]

`/usr/lib/acct/prtacct file` [*heading*]

`/usr/lib/acct/shutacct` [*reason*]

`/usr/lib/acct/startup`

`/usr/lib/acct/turnacct on | off | switch`

DESCRIPTION

The accounting software provides utilities to collect data on: process accounting, connect accounting, disk usage, command usage, summary command usage, and users' last login.

The `runnacct` [see RUNACCT(AS_CMD)] and `monacct` commands use the utilities listed here to produce daily and monthly summary files and reports that can be printed using `prdaily`; they use a number of intermediate files and support utilities that can also be used to tailor make new accounting systems. Many of these utilities produce or manipulate "total accounting" (**tacct**) records which can be summarized by `acctmerg` [see ACCTMERG(AS_CMD)] and printed using `prtacct`.

The command `accton` without parameters turns process accounting off. If *file* is given, `accton` will turn accounting on. The argument *file* must be the name of an existing file (normally `/usr/adm/pacct`), to which the system appends process accounting records [see ACCT(KE_SYS)].

The command `acctwtmp` writes a *utmp* structure in record to its standard output. The record contains the current time and a string of characters that describe the *reason*. A record type of ACCOUNTING is assigned. The argument *reason* must be a string of (11 or less) characters, numbers, **$**, or spaces. For example, the following are suggestions for use in startup and shutdown procedures, respectively:

```
acctwtmp "acctg on" >> /etc/wtmp
acctwtmp "acctg off" >> /etc/wtmp
```

The command `chargefee` is invoked to charge a *number* of units to *login-name*. An ASCII **tacct** record is written to `/usr/adm/fee`, to be merged with other accounting records by `acctmerg`.

The command `ckpacct` is typically initiated via `cron` It periodically checks the size of `/usr/adm/pacct`. If the size exceeds *blocks*, 1000 by default, `turnacct` will be invoked with argument `switch`. If the number of free disk blocks in the `/usr` file system falls below 500, `ckpacct` will automatically turn off the collection of process accounting records via the `off` argument to `turnacct`. The accounting will be activated again on the next invocation of `ckpacct` when at least this number of blocks is restored.

The command `dodisk` is typically invoked by `cron` to perform the disk accounting functions. By default, it will do disk accounting on the special files in `/etc/checklist`. If *files* are used, they should be the special file names of mountable filesystems; disk accounting will be done on these filesystems only.

The command `lastlogin` is invoked (typically by `runacct`) to update `/usr/adm/acct/sum/loginlog`, which shows the last date on which each person logged in.

The command `monacct` is typically invoked once each month. The argument *number* indicates which month or period it is. If *number* is not given, it defaults to the current month (01–12). This default is useful if `monacct` is to executed via `cron` on the first day of each month. The command `monacct` creates summary files in `/usr/adm/acct/fiscal`, restarts summary files in `/usr/adm/acct/sum`, and deletes the previous days' accounting reports (see `prdaily` below).

The command `prdaily` is invoked (typically by `runacct`) to format a report of the previous day's accounting data. The report resides in `/usr/adm/acct/sum/rprt`*mmdd* where *mmdd* is the month and day of the report. The current daily accounting reports may be printed by typing `prdaily`. Previous days' accounting reports can be printed by using the *mmdd* option and specifying the report date desired. The `-l` option prints a report of exceptional usage by login id for the specifed date. Previous daily reports are removed and therefore inaccessible after each invocation of `monacct`. The `-c` option prints a report of exceptional resource usage by command, and may be used on current day's accounting data only.

The command `prtacct` can be used to format and print any total accounting (**tacct**) file.

The command `shutacct` is typically invoked during a system shutdown (usually in `/etc/shutdown`) to turn process accounting off and append a "reason" record to `/etc/wtmp`.

The command `startup` is typically called by the system initialization routine to turn on process accounting whenever the system is brought up.

The command `turnacct` is an interface to `accton` to turn process accounting **on** or **off**. The `switch` argument turns accounting off, moves the current `/usr/adm/pacct` to the next free name in `/usr/adm/pacctincr` (where `incr` is a number starting with 1 and incrementing by one for each additional `pacct` file), then turns accounting back on again.

FILES

`/etc/wtmp`	login/logoff summary
`/etc/passwd`	used for login name to user ID conversions
`/usr/lib/acct`	directory for accounting commands
`/usr/adm/fee`	accumulator for fees
`/usr/adm/pacct`	current file for process accounting
`/usr/adm/acct/sum`	summary directory

USAGE

Administrator.

SEE ALSO

ACCTCMS(AS_CMD), ACCTCOM(AS_CMD), ACCTCON(AS_CMD), ACCTMERG(AS_CMD), ACCTPRC(AS_CMD), CRON(AU_CMD), DISKUSG(AS_CMD), FWTMP(AS_CMD), RUNACCT(AS_CMD), ACCT(KE_SYS).

NAME

acctcms — command summary from per-process accounting records

SYNOPSIS

`/usr/lib/acct/acctcms` [*options*] *files*

DESCRIPTION

The command `acctcms` reads one or more *files*, normally in the form produced by ACCT(KE_SYS). It adds all records for processes that executed identically-named commands, sorts them, and writes them to the standard output, normally using an internal summary format. The *options* are:

- `−a` Print output in **ASCII** rather than in the internal summary format. The output includes command name, number of times executed, total kcore-minutes, total CPU minutes, total real minutes, mean size (in K), mean CPU minutes per invocation, "hog factor", characters transferred, and blocks read and written, as in ACCTCOM(AS_CMD). Output is normally sorted by total kcore-minutes.
- `−c` Sort by total CPU time, rather than total kcore-minutes.
- `−j` Combine all commands invoked only once under "***other".
- `−n` Sort by number of command invocations.
- `−s` Any file names encountered hereafter are already in internal summary format.

The following options may be used only with the `-a` option.

- `−p` Output a prime-time-only command summary.
- `−o` Output a non-prime (offshift) time only command summary.

When `−p` and `−o` are used together, a combination prime and non-prime time report is produced. All the output summaries will be total usage except number of times executed, CPU minutes, and real minutes which will be split into prime and non-prime.

A typical sequence for performing daily command accounting and for maintaining a running total is:

```
acctcms file ... >today
cp total previoustotal
acctcms −s today previoustotal >total
acctcms −a −s today
```

USAGE

Administrator.

SEE ALSO

ACCT(AS_CMD), ACCTCON(AS_CMD), ACCTMERG(AS_CMD), ACCTPRC(AS_CMD), FWTMP(AS_CMD), RUNACCT(AS_CMD), ACCTCOM(AS_CMD), ACCT(KE_SYS).

NAME

acctcom — search and print process accounting file(s)

SYNOPSIS

`acctcom` [[*options*] [*file*]] ...

DESCRIPTION

The command `acctcom` reads *file*, the standard input, or `/usr/adm/pacct`, in the form produced by ACCT(KE_SYS) and writes selected records to the standard output. Each record represents the execution of one process and shows the **COMMAND NAME, USER, TTYNAME, START TIME, END TIME, REAL (SEC), CPU (SEC), MEAN SIZE(K)**, and optionally, **F** (the `fork/exec` flag: **1** for `fork` without `exec`), **STAT** (the system exit status), **HOG FACTOR, KCORE MIN, CPU FACTOR, CHARS TRNSFD**, and **BLOCKS R/W** (total blocks read and written).

The command name is prepended with a # if it was executed with `super-user` privileges. If a process is not associated with a known terminal, a **?** is printed in the **TTYNAME** field.

If no *files* are specified, and if the standard input is associated with a terminal or `/dev/null`, `/usr/adm/pacct` is read; otherwise, the standard input is read.

If any *file* arguments are given, they are read in their respective order. Each file is normally read forward, i.e., in chronological order by process completion time. The *options* are:

- `-a` Show average statistics about the processes selected. The statistics will be printed after the output records.
- `-b` Read backwards, showing latest commands first. This *option* has no effect when the standard input is read.
- `-f` Print the `fork/exec` flag and system exit status columns in the output.
- `-h` Instead of mean memory size, show the fraction of total available CPU time consumed by the process during its execution (the "hog factor").
- `-i` Print columns containing total blocks read and written.
- `-k` Instead of memory size, show total kcore-minutes.
- `-m` Show mean core size (the default).
- `-r` Show CPU factor (user time/(system-time + user-time).
- `-t` Show separate system and user CPU times.
- `-v` Exclude column headings from the output.
- `-l`*line* Show only processes belonging to terminal `/dev/`*line*.
- `-u`*user* Show only processes belonging to *user* that may be specified by: a user ID, a login name that is then converted to a user ID, a **#** which designates only those processes executed with super-user privileges, or **?** which designates only those processes associated with unknown user IDs.
- `-g`*group* Show only processes belonging to *group*. The *group* may be

designated by either the group ID or group name.

- `-s`*time* Select processes existing at or after *time*, given in the format `hr[:min[:sec]]`.
- `-e`*time* Select processes existing at or before *time*.
- `-S`*time* Select processes starting at or after *time*.
- `-E`*time* Select processes ending at or before *time*. Using the same `time` for both `-S` and `-E` shows the processes that existed at *time*.
- `-n`*pattern* Show only commands matching *pattern* that may be a regular expression as in ED(BU_CMD) except that + means one or more occurrences.
- `-q` Do not print any output records, just print the average statistics as with the `-a` option.
- `-o`*ofile* Copy selected process records in the input data format to *ofile;* suppress standard output printing.
- `-H`*factor* Show only processes that exceed *factor*, where factor is the "hog factor" as explained in option `-h` above.
- `-O`*sec* Show only processes with CPU system time exceeding *sec* seconds.
- `-C`*sec* Show only processes with total CPU time, system plus user, exceeding *sec* seconds.
- `-I`*chars* Show only processes transferring more characters than the cut-off number given by *chars*.

FILES

/etc/passwd
/etc/group
/usr/adm/pacct

USAGE

Administrator.

SEE ALSO

ACCT(KE_SYS), ACCT(AS_CMD), ACCTCMS(AS_CMD), ACCTCON(AS_CMD), ACCTMERG(AS_CMD), ACCTPRC(AS_CMD), FWTMP(AS_CMD), RUNACCT(AS_CMD).

NAME

acctcon1, acctcon2, prctmp — connect-time accounting

SYNOPSIS

`/usr/lib/acct/acctcon1` [*options*]

`/usr/lib/acct/acctcon2`

`/usr/lib/acct/prctmp`

DESCRIPTION

The command `acctcon1` converts a sequence of login/logoff records read from its standard input to a sequence of session records, one per login session. Its input should normally be redirected from `/etc/wtmp`. The record format is ASCII, giving device, user ID, login name, prime connect time (seconds), non-prime connect time (seconds), session starting time (numeric), and starting date and time. The *options* are:

`-p` Print input only, showing line name, login name, and time (in both numeric and date/time formats).

`-t` The command `acctcon1` maintains a list of lines on which users are logged in. When it reaches the end of its input, it emits a session record for each line that still appears to be active. It normally assumes that its input is a current file, so that it uses the current time as the ending time for each session still in progress. The `-t` flag causes it to use, instead, the last time found in its input, thus assuring reasonable and repeatable numbers for non-current files.

`-l` *file* *File* is created to contain a summary of line usage showing line name, number of minutes used, percentage of total elapsed time used, number of sessions charged, number of logins, and number of logoffs. This file helps track line usage, identify bad lines, and find software and hardware oddities. Various events during logoff each generate logoff records, so that the number of logoffs is often three to four times the number of sessions.

`-o` *file* *File* is filled with an overall record for the accounting period, giving starting time, ending time, and the count and type of various accounting records produced by `acctwtmp` [see ACCT(AS_CMD)].

The command `acctcon2` expects as input a sequence of login session records (as produced by `acctcon1`), and converts them into total accounting records.

The argument `prctmp` can be used to print the session record file as produced by `acctcon1`.

EXAMPLES

These commands are typically used as shown below. The file `ctmp` can be used by `acctprc1` [see ACCTPRC(AS_CMD)]:

```
acctcon1 -t -l lineuse -o reboots <wtmp | sort +1n
+2 >ctmp

acctcon2 <ctmp | acctmerg >ctacct
```

FILES

`/etc/wtmp`

USAGE

Administrator.

The command `wtmpfix` [see FWTMP(AS_CMD)] can be used to correct for the confusion caused by date changes.

SEE ALSO

ACCT(AS_CMD), ACCTCMS(AS_CMD), ACCTCOM(AS_CMD), ACCTMERG(AS_CMD), ACCTPRC(AS_CMD), FWTMP(AS_CMD), RUNACCT(AS_CMD), ACCT(KE_SYS).

NAME

acctmerg — merge or add total accounting files

SYNOPSIS

`/usr/lib/acct/acctmerg` [*options*] [*file* ...]

DESCRIPTION

The command `acctmerg` reads its standard input and up to nine additional files, all in the total accounting (**tacct**) format or an ASCII version thereof. It merges these inputs by adding records whose keys (normally user ID and name) are identical, and expects the inputs to be sorted on those keys. *Options* are:

- `-a` Produce output in ASCII version of **tacct**.
- `-i` Input files are in ASCII version of **tacct**.
- `-p` Print input with no processing.
- `-t` Produce a single record that totals all input.
- `-u` Summarize by user ID, rather than user ID and name.
- `-v` Produce output in verbose ASCII format, using more precise notation for floating point numbers.

EXAMPLES

The following sequence is useful for making "repairs" to any file kept in this format:

`acctmerg -v` <*file1* >*file2*
(edit *file2* as desired)
`acctmerg -i` <*file2* >*file1*

USAGE

Administrator.

SEE ALSO

ACCT(AS_CMD), ACCTCMS(AS_CMD), ACCTCOM(AS_CMD), ACCTCON(AS_CMD), ACCTPRC(AS_CMD), FWTMP(AS_CMD), RUNACCT(AS_CMD), ACCT(KE_SYS).

NAME

acctprc1, acctprc2 — process accounting

SYNOPSIS

`/usr/lib/acct/acctprc1` [*ctmp*]

`/usr/lib/acct/acctprc2`

DESCRIPTION

The command `acctprc1` reads input in the form produced by ACCT(KE_SYS), supplies login names corresponding to user IDs, then writes for each process an ASCII line giving user ID, login name, prime CPU time (tics), non-prime CPU time (tics), and mean memory size (in memory segment units). A memory segment of the mean memory size is a unit of measure for the number of bytes in a logical memory segment on a particular processor. For example, this measure could be in 64-byte units on one machine and in 512-byte units on another. If *ctmp* is given, it is expected to contain a list of login sessions, in the form described in ACCTCON(AS_CMD), sorted by user ID and login name. If this file is not supplied, it obtains login names from the password file. The information in *ctmp* is used to distinguish among different login names that share the same user ID.

The command `acctprc2` reads records in the form written by `acctprc1`, merges and sorts them by user ID and name, then writes them to the standard output as total accounting records.

These commands are typically used as shown below:

```
acctprc1 ctmp </usr/adm/pacct | acctprc2
>ptacct
```

FILES

`/etc/passwd`

USAGE

Administrator.

SEE ALSO

ACCT(AS_CMD), ACCTCMS(AS_CMD), ACCTCOM(AS_CMD), ACCTCON(AS_CMD), ACCTMERG(AS_CMD), FWTMP(AS_CMD), RUNACCT(AS_CMD), ACCT(KE_SYS).

NAME

clri — clear i-node

SYNOPSIS

`/etc/clri` *file-system i-number* ...

DESCRIPTION

The command `clri` writes zeros on the 64 bytes occupied by the i-node(s) numbered *i-number*. The argument *file-system* must be a special file name referring to a device containing a file system. After `clri` is executed, any blocks in the affected file will show up as "missing" in an `fsck` [see FSCK(AS_CMD)] of the *file-system*. This command should only be used in emergencies and extreme care should be exercised.

Read and write permission is required on the specified *file-system* device. The i-node becomes allocatable.

The primary purpose of this routine is to remove a file which for some reason appears in no directory. If it is used to clear an i-node which does appear in a directory, care should be taken to track down the entry and remove it. Otherwise, when the i-node is reallocated to some new file, the old entry will still point to that file. At that point removing the old entry will destroy the new file. The new entry will again point to an unallocated i-node, so the whole cycle is likely to be repeated again and again.

USAGE

Administrator.

SEE ALSO

FSCK(AS_CMD), FSDB(AS_CMD), NCHECK(AS_CMD).

NAME

devnm — device name

SYNOPSIS

`/etc/devnm` [*pathname*]

DESCRIPTION

The command `devnm` identifies the special file associated with the mounted file system where the named file or directory resides. The full *pathname* must be given.

EXAMPLE

The command:

```
/etc/devnm /usr
```

produces

```
/dev/dsk/0s1 /usr
```

if

`/usr` is mounted on

`/dev/dsk/0s1`.

FILES

`/dev/dsk/*`
`/etc/mnttab`

USAGE

Administrator.

SEE ALSO

SETMNT(AS_CMD).

NAME

diskusg, acctdisk — generate disk accounting data by user-ID

SYNOPSIS

`/usr/lib/acct/diskusg` [*options*] [*special-file* ...]

`/usr/lib/acct/acctdisk`

DESCRIPTION

The command `diskusg` generates disk accounting information for the file-system identified by the *special-files*. The command `diskusg` prints lines on the standard output, one per user, in the following format:

uid login #blocks

where *uid* is the numerical user-ID of the user, *login* is the login-name of the user, and *#blocks* is the total number of disk blocks allocated to this user.

The command `diskusg` recognizes the following options:

`-s` The input data is already in `diskusg` output format; all lines combined into a single line per user.

`-v` Verbose; print a list on standard error of all files that are charged to no one.

`-i` *fnmlist* Ignore the data on those file systems whose file system name is in *fnmlist*. The argument *fnmlist* is a list of file system names separated by commas or enclosed within quotes. The command `diskusg` compares each name in this list with the file system name stored in the volume-ID [see `labelit` in VOLCOPY(AS_CMD)].

`-p` *file* Use *file* as the name of the password file to generate login-names. `/etc/passwd` is used by default.

`-u` *file* Write records to *file* of files that are charged to no one. Records consist of special file-name, i-node number, and user-ID.

The argument `acctdisk` expects a sequence of disk accounting information, as produced by `diskusg` (sorted by user-ID and login-name), and generates total accounting records that can be merged with other accounting records. The command `diskusg` is normally run in `dodisk` [see ACCT(AS_CMD)].

FILES

`/etc/passwd` used for user-ID to login-name conversions

USAGE

Administrator.

SEE ALSO

ACCT(AS_CMD), VOLCOPY(AS_CMD), ACCT(KE_SYS).

NAME

fsck — file system consistency check and interactive repair

SYNOPSIS

`/etc/fsck` [*options*] [*file-systems*]

DESCRIPTION

The command `fsck` audits and interactively repairs inconsistent conditions for files. If the file system is consistent then the number of files, number of blocks used, and number of blocks free are reported. If the file system is inconsistent the user is prompted for concurrence before each correction is attempted. It should be noted that most corrective actions will result in some loss of data. The amount of data lost and its severity may be determined from the diagnostic output. The default action for each consistency correction is to wait for the user to respond `yes` or `no`. If the user does not have write permission `fsck` will default to a `-n` action.

The file system should be unmounted while `fsck` is used. If this is not possible, care should be taken that the system is quiescent and that it is rebooted immediately afterwards.

The following options are interpreted by `fsck`.

`-y` Assume a yes response to all questions asked by `fsck`.

`-n` Assume a no response to all questions asked by `fsck`; do not open the file system for writing.

`-sX` Ignore the actual free list and (unconditionally) reconstruct a new one. `X` is a hardware dependent option, which specifes how the free list is to be created; if it is not given, the values used when the file system was created, or other default values, are used.

`-SX` Conditionally reconstruct the free list. This option is like `-sX` above except that the free list is rebuilt only if there were no discrepancies discovered in the file system. Using `-S` will force a no response to all questions asked by `fsck`. This option is useful for forcing free list reorganization on uncontaminated file systems.

`-t` *file* If `fsck` cannot obtain enough memory to keep its tables, it uses a scratch file. If the `-t` option is specified, the file named in the next argument is used as the scratch file, if needed. Without the `-t` flag, `fsck` will prompt the user for the name of the scratch file. The file chosen should not be on the file system being checked, and if it is not a special file or did not already exist, it is removed when `fsck` completes.

`-q` Quiet `fsck`. Do not print size-check messages in Phase 1. Unreferenced FIFOs will silently be removed. If `fsck` requires it, counts in the superblock will be automatically fixed and the free list salvaged.

`-D` Directories are checked for bad blocks. Useful after system crashes.

`-f` Fast check of block and sizes (Phase 1) and free list (Phase 5). Free list will be reconstructed (Phase 6) if necessary.

If no *file-systems* are specified, `fsck` will read a list of default file systems from the file `/etc/checklist`.

Inconsistencies checked are as follows:

1. Blocks claimed by more than one i-node or the free list.
2. Blocks claimed by i-node or free list outside range of file system.
3. Incorrect link counts.
4. Size checks:
   Incorrect number of blocks.
   Directory size not 16-byte aligned.
5. Bad i-node format.
6. Blocks not accounted for anywhere.
7. Directory checks:
   File pointing to unallocated i-node.
   I-node number out of range.
8. Super Block checks:
   More than {INODE_MAX} inodes.
   More blocks for i-nodes than there are in the file system.
9. Bad free block list format.
10. Total free block and/or free i-node count incorrect.

Orphaned files and directories (allocated but unreferenced) are, with the user's concurrence, reconnected by placing them in the `lost+found` directory, if the files are nonempty. The user will be notified if the file or directory is empty or not. If it is empty, `fsck` will silently remove them. The command `fsck` will force the reconnection of nonempty directories. The name assigned is the i-node number. The only restriction is that the directory `lost+found` must preexist in the root of the file system being checked and must have empty slots in which entries can be made. This is accomplished by making `lost+found`, copying a number of files to the directory, and then removing them (before `fsck` is executed).

Checking the raw device is almost always faster and should be used with everything but the `root` file system.

FILES

`/etc/checklist`

USAGE

Administrator.

I-node numbers for . and .. in each directory should be checked for validity.

NAME

fsdb — file system debugger

SYNOPSIS

`/etc/fsdb special` [−]

DESCRIPTION

The command `fsdb` can be used to patch up a damaged file system after a crash. It has conversions to translate block and i-numbers into their corresponding disk addresses. Also included are mnemonic offsets to access different parts of an i-node. These greatly simplify the process of correcting control block entries or descending the file system tree.

The command `fsdb` contains several error-checking routines to verify i-node and block addresses. These can be disabled if necessary by invoking `fsdb` with the optional − argument or by the use of the `O` symbol. (from the superblock of the file system as the basis for these checks.)

Numbers are considered decimal by default. Octal numbers must be prefixed with a zero. During any assignment operation, numbers are checked for a possible truncation error due to a size mismatch between source and destination.

The command `fsdb` reads a block at a time and will therefore work with raw as well as block I/O. A buffer management routine is used to retain commonly used blocks of data in order to reduce the number of read system calls. All assignment operations result in an immediate write-through of the corresponding block.

The symbols recognized by `fsdb` are:

#	absolute address
`i`	convert from i-number to i-node address
`b`	convert to block address
`d`	directory slot offset
`+,−`	address arithmetic
`q`	quit
`>,<`	save, restore an address
`=`	numerical assignment
`=+`	incremental assignment
`=−`	decremental assignment
`=`	character string assignment
`O`	error checking flip flop
`p`	general print facilities
`f`	file print facility
`B`	byte mode
`W`	word mode
`D`	double word mode
`!`	escape to the command interpreter

The print facilities generate a formatted output in various styles. The current address is normalized to an appropriate boundary before printing begins. It advances with the printing and is left at the address of the last item printed. The output can be terminated at any time by typing the delete character. If a number follows the `p` symbol, that many entries are printed. A check is made to detect block boundary overflows since logically sequential blocks are generally not physically sequential. If a count of zero is used, all entries to the end of the current block are printed. The print options available are:

`i`	print as i-nodes
`d`	print as directories
`o`	print as octal words
`e`	print as decimal words
`c`	print as characters
`b`	print as octal bytes

The `f` symbol is used to print data blocks associated with the current i-node. If followed by a number, that block of the file is printed. (Blocks are numbered from zero.) The desired print option letter follows the block number, if present, or the `f` symbol. This print facility works for small as well as large files. It checks for special devices and that the block pointers used to find the data are not zero.

Dots, tabs, and spaces may be used as function delimiters but are not necessary. A line with just a new-line character will increment the current address by the size of the data type last printed. That is, the address is set to the next byte, word, double word, directory entry or i-node, allowing the user to step through a region of a file system. Information is printed in a format appropriate to the data type. Bytes, words and double words are displayed with the octal address followed by the value in octal and decimal. A `.B` or `.D` is appended to the address for byte and double word values, respectively. Directories are printed as a directory slot offset followed by the decimal i-number and the character representation of the entry name. I-nodes are printed with labeled fields describing each element.

The following mnemonics are used for i-node examination and refer to the current working i-node:

`md`	mode
`ln`	link count
`uid`	user ID number
`gid`	group ID number
`sz`	file size
`a#`	data block numbers (0 − 12)
`at`	access time
`mt`	modification time
`maj`	major device number
`min`	minor device number

EXAMPLES

`386i`	prints i-number 386 in an i-node format. This now becomes the current working i-node.

`ln=4`	changes the link count for the working i-node to 4.
`ln=+1`	increments the link count by 1.
`fc`	prints, in **ASCII**, block zero of the file associated with the working i-node.
`2i.fd`	prints the first 32 directory entries for the root i-node of this file system.
`d5i.fc`	changes the current i-node to that associated with the 5th directory entry (numbered from zero) found from the above command. The first logical block of the file is then printed in **ASCII**.
`512B.p0o`	prints the superblock of this file system in octal.
`2i.a0b.d7=3`	changes the i-number for the seventh directory slot in the root directory to 3. This example also shows how several operations can be combined on one command line.
`d7.nm=`	changes the name field in the directory slot to the given string. Quotes are optional when used with `nm` if the first character is alphabetic.
`a2b.p0d`	prints the third block of the current i-node as directory entries.

USAGE

Administrator.

SEE ALSO

FSCK(AS_CMD).

NAME

fuser — identify processes using a file or file structure

SYNOPSIS

`/etc/fuser [-ku] `*files* `[-] [[-ku] `*files*`]`

DESCRIPTION

The command `fuser` lists the process IDs of the processes using the *files* specified as arguments. For block special devices, all processes using any file on that device are listed. The process ID is followed by `c`, `p` or `r` if the process is using the file as its current directory, the parent of its current directory (only when in use by the system), or its `root` directory, respectively. If the `-u` option is specified, the login name, in parentheses, also follows the process ID. In addition, if the `-k` option is specified, the SIGKILL signal is sent to each process. Only the super-user can terminate another user's process [see KILL(BA_SYS))] Options may be respecified between groups of files. The new set of options replaces the old set, with a lone dash canceling any options currently in force.

The process IDs are printed as a single line on the standard output, separated by spaces and terminated with a single new line. All other output is written on standard error.

EXAMPLES

`fuser -ku /dev/dsk/1s?`
will terminate all processes that are preventing disk drive one from being unmounted if typed by the super-user, listing the process ID and login name of each as it is killed.

`fuser -u /etc/passwd`
will list process IDs and login names of processes that have the password file open.

`fuser -ku /dev/dsk/1s? -u /etc/passwd`
will do both of the above examples in a single command line.

USAGE

Administrator.

The command `fuser` works with a snapshot of the system tables, which is true only for an instant. It is possible that other processes begin accessing the specified file(s) after this snapshot is taken.

SEE ALSO

KILL(BA_SYS).

NAME

fwtmp, wtmpfix — manipulate connect accounting records

SYNOPSIS

`/usr/lib/acct/fwtmp` **[-ic]**

`/usr/lib/acct/wtmpfix` [*files*]

DESCRIPTION

fwtmp

The command `fwtmp` reads from the standard input and writes to the standard output, converting binary records of the type found in `/etc/wtmp` to formatted **ASCII** records. The **ASCII** version is useful to enable editing bad records or general purpose maintenance of the file.

The argument *−ic* is used to denote that input is in **ASCII** form, and output is to be written in binary form.

wtmpfix

The command `wtmpfix` examines the standard input or named files in `wtmp` format, corrects the time/date stamps to make the entries consistent, and writes to the standard output. A − can be used in place of *files* to indicate the standard input. If time/date corrections are not performed, `acctcon1` will fault when it encounters certain date-change records.

Each time the date is set, a pair of date change records are written to `/etc/wtmp`. The first record is the old date denoted by the string `old time` placed in the line field and the flag `OLD_TIME` placed in the type field of the `<utmp.h>` structure. The second record specifies the new date and is denoted by the string `new time` placed in the line field and the flag `NEW_TIME` placed in the type field. The command `wtmpfix` uses these records to synchronize all time stamps in the file.

In addition to correcting time/date stamps, `wtmpfix` will check the validity of the name field to ensure that it consists solely of alphanumeric characters or spaces. If it encounters a name that is considered invalid, it will change the login name to **INVALID** and write a diagnostic to the standard error. In this way, `wtmpfix` reduces the chance that `acctcon1` will fail when processing connect accounting records.

FILES

`/etc/wtmp`

USAGE

Administrator.

SEE ALSO

ACCT(AS_CMD), ACCTCMS(AS_CMD), ACCTCOM(AS_CMD), ACCTCON(AS_CMD), ACCTMERG(AS_CMD), ACCTPRC(AS_CMD), RUNACCT(AS_CMD), ACCT(KE_SYS).

NAME

init — change system run level

SYNOPSIS

`/etc/init[0123456sq]`

DESCRIPTION

The command `init` is used to direct the actions of the `init` process, which is the system process spawner. (The `init` command provides the `init` process with certain directives; it is important to keep in mind the distinction between the two.)

The system is in a particular *run-level* at any given time. The processes spawned by the `init` process for each of these *run-levels* is defined in the `/etc/inittab` file. The system can be in one of eight *run-levels*, `0-6` and `s` (or `S`). The *run-level* is changed when the System Administrator runs the `init` command.

If the *run-level* `s` (`S`) is specified, the `init` process goes into the SINGLE-USER level. This is the only *run-level* that does not require the existence of a properly formatted `/etc/inittab` file. (If that file does not exist, then by default the SINGLE USER level is entered.)

If a *run-level* of `0` through `6` is specified, the `init` process enters the corresponding *run-level*.

The following arguments are accepted by `init`:

`0-6` tells `init` to place the system in one of the *run-levels* `0-6`.

`q` (or `Q`) tells `init` to re-examine the `/etc/inittab` file. It is often used after that file has been changed, in order to check its correctness.

`s` (or `S`) tells `init` to enter the SINGLE-USER level. When this level change is effected, the virtual system terminal, `/dev/console`, is changed to the terminal from which the command was executed

FILES

`/etc/inittab`

USAGE

Administrator.

NAME

ipcrm — remove a message queue, semaphore set or shared memory id

SYNOPSIS

`ipcrm` [*options*]

DESCRIPTION

The command `ipcrm` will remove one or more specified message, semaphore or shared memory identifiers. The identifiers are specified by the following *options*:

`-q` *msqid* removes the message queue identifier *msqid* from the system and destroys the message queue and data structure associated with it.

`-m` *shmid* removes the shared memory identifier *shmid* from the system. The shared memory segment and data structure associated with it are destroyed after the last detach operation.

`-s` *semid* removes the semaphore identifier *semid* from the system and destroys the set of semaphores and data structure associated with it.

`-Q` *msgkey* removes the message queue identifier, created with key *msgkey*, from the system and destroys the message queue and data structure associated with it.

`-M` *shmkey* removes the shared memory identifier, created with key *shmkey*, from the system. The shared memory segment and data structure associated with it are destroyed after the last detach.

`-S` *semkey* removes the semaphore identifier, created with key *semkey*, from the system and destroys the set of semaphores and data structure associated with it.

The details of the removes are described in MSGCTL(KE_SYS), SHMCTL(KE_SYS), and SEMCTL(KE_SYS). The identifiers and keys may be found by using IPCS(AS_CMD).

SEE ALSO

IPCS(AS_CMD), MSGCTL(KE_SYS), MSGGET(KE_SYS), MSGOP(KE_SYS), SEMCTL(KE_SYS), SEMGET(KE_SYS), SEMOP(KE_SYS), SHMCTL(KE_SYS), SHMGET(KE_SYS), SHMOP(KE_SYS).

NAME

ipcs — report inter-process communication facilities status

SYNOPSIS

`ipcs` [*options*]

DESCRIPTION

The command `ipcs` prints certain information about active inter-process communication facilities. Without *options*, information is printed in short format for message queues, shared memory, and semaphores that are currently active in the system. Otherwise, the information that is displayed is controlled by the following *options*:

`-q` Print information about active message queues.

`-m` Print information about active shared memory segments.

`-s` Print information about active semaphores.

If any of the options `-q`, `-m`, or `-s` are specified, information about only those indicated will be printed. If none of these three are specified, information about all three will be printed.

`-b` Print biggest allowable size information. (Maximum number of bytes in messages on queue for message queues, size of segments for shared memory, and number of semaphores in each set for semaphores.) See below for meaning of columns in a listing.

`-c` Print creator's login name and group name. See below.

`-o` Print information on outstanding usage. (Number of messages on queue and total bytes in messages on queue for message queues and number of processes attached to shared memory segments.)

`-p` Print process number information. (Process ID of last process to send a message, process ID of last process to receive a message on message queues, process ID of creating process, process ID of last process to attach or detach on shared memory segments) See below.

`-t` Print time information. (Time of the last control operation that changed the access permissions for all facilities. Time of last `msgsnd` and last `msgrcv` operations on message queues, last `shmat` and last `shmdt` operations on shared memory, last `semop` operation on semaphores.) See below.

`-a` Use all print *options*. (This is a shorthand notation for `-b`, `-c`, `-o`, `-p`, and `-t`.)

`-C` *corefile*

Use the file *corefile* in place of `/dev/kmem`.

`-N` *namelist*

The argument will be taken as the name of an alternate *namelist* file, instead of the default.

The column headings and the meaning of the columns in an `ipcs` listing are given below; the letters in parentheses indicate the *options* that cause the corresponding heading to appear; **all** means that the heading always appears. Note that these *options* only determine what information is provided for each facility; they do *not* determine which facilities will be listed.

`T` (all)
Type of the facility:

- `q` message queue;
- `m` shared memory segment;
- `s` semaphore.

ID (all)
The identifier for the facility entry.

KEY (all)
The key used as an argument in calls to `msgget`, `semget`, or `shmget` to create the facility entry. (Note: The key of a shared memory segment is changed to **IPC_PRIVATE** when the segment has been removed until all processes attached to the segment detach it.)

MODE (all)
The facility access modes and flags: The mode consists of 11 characters, interpreted as follows.

The first character is:

- `S` if a process is waiting on a `msgsnd` operation;
- `D` if the associated shared memory segment has been removed. It will disappear when the last process attached to the segment detaches it;
- `–` if the corresponding condition is not true.

The second character is:

- `R` if a process is waiting on a `msgrcv` operation;
- `C` if the associated shared memory segment is to be cleared when the first attach operation is executed;
- `–` if the corresponding condition is not true.

The next nine characters are interpreted as three sets of three bits each. The first set refers to the owner's permissions; the next to permissions of others in the user-group of the facility entry; and the last to all others. Within each set, the first character indicates permission to read, the second indicates permission to write or alter the facility entry, and the last is currently unused.

The permissions are indicated as follows:

- `r` if read permission is granted;
- `w` if write permission is granted;
- `a` if alter permission is granted;
- `–` if the indicated permission is *not* granted.

(Thus the first character in a set of three can either be `r` or `-`; the second character can be either `w`, `a`, or `-`; the last character can only be `-`.)

OWNER (all)
The login name of the owner of the facility entry.

GROUP (all)
The group name of the group of the owner of the facility entry.

CREATOR (a,c)
The login name of the creator of the facility entry.

CGROUP (a,c)
The group name of the group of the creator of the facility entry.

CBYTES (a,o)
The number of bytes in messages currently outstanding on the associated message queue.

QNUM (a,o)
The number of messages currently outstanding on the associated message queue.

QBYTES (a,b)
The maximum number of bytes allowed in messages outstanding on the associated message queue.

LSPID (a,p)
The process ID of the last process to send a message to the associated queue.

LRPID (a,p)
The process ID of the last process to receive a message from the associated queue.

STIME (a,t)
The time the last message was sent to the associated queue.

RTIME (a,t)
The time the last message was received from the associated queue.

CTIME (a,t)
The time when the associated entry was created or changed.

NATTCH (a,o)
The number of processes attached to the associated shared memory segment.

SEGSZ (a,b)
The size of the associated shared memory segment.

CPID (a,p)
The process ID of the creator of the shared memory entry.

LPID (a,p)
The process ID of the last process to attach or detach the shared memory segment.

ATIME (a,t)
The time the last attach was completed to the associated shared memory segment.

DTIME (a,t)
The time the last detach was completed on the associated shared memory segment.

NSEMS (a,b)
The number of semaphores in the set associated with the semaphore entry.

OTIME (a,t)
The time the last semaphore operation was completed on the set associated with the semaphore entry.

SEE ALSO

MSGOP(KE_SYS), SEMOP(KE_SYS), SHMOP(KE_SYS).

USAGE

Things can change while `ipcs` is running; therefore the status it reports may no longer be accurate at the time it is seen.

NAME

killall — kill all active processes

SYNOPSIS

`/etc/killall` [*signal*]

DESCRIPTION

The command `killall` is a procedure used to kill all active processes not directly related to the calling procedure.

The command `killall` is chiefly used to terminate all processes with open files so that the mounted file systems will be unbusied and can be unmounted.

The command `killall` sends *signal* to all remaining processes not belonging to the above group of exclusions. If no *signal* is specified, SIGKILL is used.

USAGE

Administrator.

NAME

link, unlink — exercise link and unlink system calls

SYNOPSIS

`/etc/link` *file1 file2*

`/etc/unlink` *file*

DESCRIPTION

The commands `link` and `unlink` perform their respective system calls on their arguments, without any error checking.

These commands may only be executed by the super-user.

USAGE

Administrator.

SEE ALSO

LINK(BA_SYS), UNLINK(BA_SYS).

NAME

mkfs — construct a file system

SYNOPSIS

`/etc/mkfs` *special blocks*[*:i-nodes*] [*gap blocks/cyl*]

`/etc/mkfs` *special proto* [*gap blocks/cyl*]

DESCRIPTION

The command `mkfs` constructs a file system by writing on the special file according to the directions found in the remainder of the command line. The command waits 10 seconds before starting to construct the file system. If the second argument is given as a string of digits, `mkfs` builds a file system with a single empty directory on it. The size of the file system is the value of *blocks* interpreted as a decimal number. This is the number of 512-byte units the file system will occupy. The boot program is left uninitialized.

If the second argument is a file name that can be opened, `mkfs` assumes it to be a prototype file *proto*, and will take its directions from that file. The prototype file contains tokens separated by spaces or new-lines. The first token is the name of a file to be copied onto block zero as the bootstrap program. The second token is a number specifying the size of the created file system in physical disk blocks. Typically it will be the number of blocks on the device, perhaps diminished by space for swapping. The next token is the number of i-nodes in the file system. The next set of tokens comprise the specification for the root file. File specifications consist of tokens giving the mode, the user ID, the group ID, and the initial contents of the file. The syntax of the contents field depends on the mode.

The mode token for a file is a 6-character string. The first character specifies the type of the file. (The characters **−bcd** specify regular, block special, character special and directory files respectively.) The second character of the type is either **u** or **−** to specify set-user-ID mode or not. The third is **g** or **−** for the set-group-ID mode. The rest of the mode is a 3 digit octal number giving the owner, group, and other read, write, execute permissions.

Two decimal number tokens come after the mode; they specify the user and group IDs of the owner of the file.

If the file is a regular file, the next token is a path name whence the contents and size are copied. If the file is a block or character special file, two decimal number tokens follow which give the major and minor device numbers. If the file is a directory, `mkfs` makes the entries and then reads a list of names and (recursively) files specifications for the entries in the directory. The scan is terminated with the token **$**.

If a prototype is used, there is an upper limit on the size of a file that can be initialized. This limit is implementation dependent, but is at least 64K bytes.

A sample prototype specification follows:

```
/stand/diskboot
4872 110
d--755 3 1
usr   d--755 3 1
      sh                    ---755 3 1 /bin/sh
      ken                   d--755 6 1
                            $
      b0                    b--644 3 1 0 0
      c0                    c--644 3 1 0 0
      $
$
```

USAGE

Administrator.

NAME

mknod — build special file

SYNOPSIS

`/etc/mknod` *name* `c` | `b` *major minor*

`/etc/mknod` *name* `p`

DESCRIPTION

The command `mknod` makes a directory entry and corresponding i-node for a special file.

The command `mknod` can also be used to create FIFOs (named pipes) (second case in **SYNOPSIS** above).

The first argument is the *name* of the entry. In the first case above, the second argument is `b` if the special file is block-type (disks, tape) or `c` if it is character-type (other devices). The last two arguments are numbers specifying the *major* device type and the *minor* device (e.g., unit, drive, or line number), which may be either decimal or octal (any number with a leading zero).

The assignment of major device numbers is specific to each system.

The command `mknod` may only be used by the superuser, to make special files.

USAGE

Administrator.

SEE ALSO

MKNOD(BA_SYS).

NAME

mount, umount — mount and dismount file system

SYNOPSIS

`/etc/mount` [*special directory* [`-r`]]

`/etc/umount` *special*

DESCRIPTION

The command `mount` announces to the system that a removable file system is present on the device *special*. The *directory* must exist already; it becomes the name of the root of the newly mounted file system.

These commands maintain a table of mounted devices. If invoked with no arguments, `mount` prints the table.

The option `−r` indicates that the file is to be mounted read-only. Physically write-protected and magnetic tape file systems must be mounted in this way or errors will occur when access times are updated, whether or not any explicit write is attempted.

The command `umount` announces to the system that the removable file system previously mounted on device *special* is to be removed.

ERRORS

The command `mount` issues a warning if the file system to be mounted is currently mounted under another name.

The command `umount` reports an error if the special file is not mounted or if it is busy. The file system is busy if it contains an open file, a user's working directory, or another mounted file system.

FILES

`/etc/mnttab`	mount table

USAGE

Administrator.

Some degree of validation is done on the file system; however, it is generally unwise to mount garbage file systems.

SEE ALSO

SETMNT(AS_CMD), MOUNT(BA_SYS), UMOUNT(BA_SYS).

NAME

mvdir — move a directory

SYNOPSIS

`/etc/mvdir` *dirname name*

DESCRIPTION

The command `mvdir` moves directories within a file system. The argument *dirname* must be a directory; *name* must not be an existing file. If *name* is a directory, then *dirname* is moved to *name/dirname* provided no such file or directory already exists. Neither name may be a sub-set of the other (`/x/y` cannot be moved to `/x/y/z`, nor vice versa).

Only the super-user can use `mvdir`.

USAGE

Administrator.

NAME

ncheck — generate names from i-numbers

SYNOPSIS

`/etc/ncheck` [`−i` *i-numbers*] [`-a`] [`-s`] [*file-system*]

DESCRIPTION

The command `ncheck` with no argument generates a path-name vs. i-number list of all files on a set of default file systems. Names of directory files are followed by `/..` The `−i` option reduces the report to only those files whose i-numbers follow. The `−a` option allows printing of the names `/.` and `/..`, which are ordinarily suppressed. The `−s` option reduces the report to special files and files with set-user-ID mode; it is intended to discover concealed violations of security policy.

A file system may be specified.

ERRORS

When the file system structure is improper, `??` denotes the "parent" of a parentless file and a path-name beginning with `...` denotes a loop.

USAGE

Administrator.

SEE ALSO

FSCK(AS_CMD).

NAME

nice — run a command at low priority

SYNOPSIS

`nice` [*−increment*] *command*

DESCRIPTION

The command `nice` executes *command* with a lower CPU scheduling priority.

The *increment* is a positive integer less than {NZERO}; if it is not given, the default is half of that (rounded up).

The super-user may run commands with priority higher than normal by using a negative increment, e.g., `nice −−2`.

An *increment* larger than the maximum is equivalent to the maximum.

The command `nice` returns the exit status of the subject command.

USAGE

General, except for super-user restriction stated above.

SEE ALSO

NICE(KE_SYS).

NAME

pwck, grpck — password/group file checkers

SYNOPSIS

`/etc/pwck` [*file*]

`/etc/grpck` [*file*]

DESCRIPTION

The command `pwck` scans the password file and notes any inconsistencies. The checks include validation of the number of fields, login name, user ID, group ID, and whether the login directory and optional program name exist. The default password file is `/etc/passwd`.

The command `grpck` verifies all entries in the group file. This verification includes a check of the number of fields, group name, group ID, and whether all login names appear in the password file. In addition, group entries in `/etc/group` with no login names are flagged. The default group file is `/etc/group`.

FILES

`/etc/group`
`/etc/passwd`

USAGE

Administrator.

NAME

runacct — run daily accounting

SYNOPSIS

`/usr/lib/acct/runacct` [*mmdd* [*state*]]

DESCRIPTION

The command `runacct` is the main daily accounting procedure. It is normally initiated via `cron`. The command `runacct` processes connect, fee, disk, and process accounting files. It also prepares summary files for `prdaily` or billing purposes. Unless otherwise specified, files named here reside in the directory `/usr/adm/acct/nite`.

The command `runacct` takes care not to damage active accounting files or summary files in the event of errors. It records its progress by writing descriptive diagnostic messages into the file `active`. When an error is detected, a message is written to `/dev/console`, mail is sent to the users `root` and `adm`, and `runacct` terminates. The command `runacct` uses a series of lock files to protect against re-invocation. The files `lock` and `lock1` are used to prevent simultaneous invocation, and the file `lastdate` is used to prevent more than one invocation per day.

The command `runacct` breaks its processing into separate, restartable *states* using *statefile* to remember the last *state* completed. It accomplishes this by writing the *state* name into *statefile*. The command `runacct` then looks in *statefile* to see what it has done and to determine what to process next. The *states* are executed in the following order:

SETUP
: Move active accounting files into working files.

WTMPFIX
: Verify integrity of `/etc/wtmp` file; correct date changes if needed.

CONNECT1
: Produce connect session records [see ACCTCON(AS_CMD)].

CONNECT2
: Convert session records into total accounting records.

PROCESS
: Convert process accounting records into total accounting records.

MERGE
: Merge the total connect and process accounting records.

FEES
: Convert output of `chargefee` into total accounting records and merge with the above (connect and process) total accounting records.

DISK
: Merge disk total accounting records with the above (connect, process, and fee) total accounting records. This merge forms the daily total

accounting records.

MERGETACCT
Merge the daily total accounting records with the summary total accounting records in `/usr/adm/acct/sum/tacct`.

CMS
Produce command summaries in internal format.

USEREXIT
Any installation-dependent accounting programs can be included here.

CLEANUP
Write **ASCII** command summaries into the file `/usr/adm/acct/sum/rprtxxxx` [see `prdaily` in ACCT(AS_CMD)]. Remove temporary files and exit.

To restart `runacct` after a failure, first check the `active` file for diagnostics, then fix up any corrupted data files such as `pacct\f5or\f5wtmp`. The `lock` files and `lastdate` file must be removed before `runacct` can be restarted. The argument `mmdd` is necessary if `runacct` is being restarted, and specifies the month and day for which `runacct` will rerun the accounting. Entry point for processing is based on the contents of *statefile*; to override this, include the desired *state* on the command line to designate where processing should begin.

FILES

```
/usr/src/cmd/acct/nite/active
/usr/src/cmd/acct/nite/lock
/usr/src/cmd/acct/nite/lock1
/usr/src/cmd/acct/nite/lastdate
/usr/src/cmd/acct/nite/statefile
/usr/adm/acct/sum/rprtxxxx
/usr/adm/acct/sum/tacct
/usr/adm/pacct
/etc/wtmp
```

USAGE

Administrator.
Normally `runacct` should not be restarted in the **SETUP** state. **SETUP** should be run manually and restart should be done by:

`runacct` *mmdd* **WTMPFIX**

SEE ALSO

ACCT(AS_CMD), ACCTCMS(AS_CMD), ACCTCOM(AS_CMD), ACCTCON(AS_CMD), ACCTMERG(AS_CMD), ACCTPRC(AS_CMD), CRON(AU_CMD), FWTMP(AS_CMD), ACCT(KE_SYS).

NAME

sa1, sa2, sadc — system activity report package

SYNOPSIS

`/usr/lib/sa/sadc` [*t n*] [*ofile*]

`/usr/lib/sa/sa1` [*t n*]

`/usr/lib/sa/sa2` [*options*] [`-s` *time*] [`-e` *time*] [`-i` *sec*]

DESCRIPTION

System activity data can be accessed at the special request of a user [see SAR(AS_CMD)] and automatically on a routine basis as described here. The operating system contains a number of counters that are incremented as various system actions occur. These include CPU utilization counters, buffer usage counters, disk and tape I/O activity counters, TTY device activity counters, switching and system-call counters, file-access counters, queue activity counters, and counters for interprocess communications.

The commands `sadc`, `sa1`, and `sa2`, are used to sample, save, and process this data.

The command `sadc`, the data collector, samples system data *n* times every *t* seconds and writes in binary format to *ofile* or to standard output. If *t* and *n* are omitted, a special record is written. This facility is typically used at system boot time to mark the time at which the counters restart from zero.

The utility `sa1`, a variant of `sadc`, is used to collect and store data in the binary file `/usr/adm/sa/sadd` where `dd` is the current day. The options *t* and *n* cause records to be written *n* times at an interval of *t* seconds, (once if the options are omitted).

The utility `sa2`, a variant of `sar`, writes the day's system activity report in the file `/usr/adm/sa/sardd`. The options are explained in SAR(AS_CMD).

FILES

`/usr/adm/sa/sadd` daily data file
`/usr/adm/sa/sardd` daily report file

USAGE

Administrator.

SEE ALSO

SAR(AS_CMD).

NAME

sadp — disk access profiler

SYNOPSIS

`sadp [-th] [-d` *device*[*-drive*]] *s* [*n*]

DESCRIPTION

The command `sadp` reports disk access location and seek distance, in tabular or histogram form. It samples disk activity once every second during an interval of *s* seconds. This is done repeatedly if *n* is specified.

The argument *drive* specifies the disk drives and it may be:

a drive number in the range supported by *device*,

or

two numbers separated by a minus (indicating an inclusive range),

or

a list of drive numbers separated by commas.

The `-d` option may be omitted, if only one *device* is present.

The `-t` option (default) causes the data to be reported in tabular form. The `-h` option produces a histogram of the data on the printer. Default is `-t`.

USAGE

Administrator.

NAME

sar — system activity reporter

SYNOPSIS

`sar` [*options*] [−*ofile*] *t* [*n*]

sar [*options*] [`-s` *time*] [`-e` *time*] [`-i` *sec*] [`-f` *file*]

DESCRIPTION

In the first form above, the `sar` command, in the first instance, samples cumulative activity counters in the operating system at *n* intervals of *t* seconds. If the −`o` option is specified, it saves the samples in *file* in binary format. The default value of *n* is 1. In the second form, with no sampling interval specified, `sar` extracts data from a previously recorded *file*, either the one specified by the −`f` option or, by default, the standard system activity daily data file `/usr/adm/sa/sadd` for the current day `dd`. The starting and ending times of the report can be bounded via the −`s` and −`e` *time* arguments of the form `hh`[:`mm`[:`ss`]]. The −`i` option selects records at *sec* second intervals. Otherwise, all intervals found in the data file are reported.

In either case, subsets of data to be printed are specified by option:

−`u` Report CPU utilization (the default):
%usr, %sys, %wio, %idle — portion of time running in user mode, running in system mode, idle with some process waiting for block I/O, and otherwise idle.

−`b` Report buffer activity:
bread/s, bwrit/s — transfers per second of data between system buffers and disk or other block devices;
lread/s, lwrit/s — accesses of system buffers;
%rcache, %wcache — cache hit ratios, e. g., 1 — bread/lread;
pread/s, pwrit/s — transfers via raw (physical) device mechanism.

−`d` Report activity for each block device, e. g., disk or tape drive. When data is displayed, the device specification `dsk-` is generally used to represent a disk drive. The device specification used to represent a tape drive is machine dependent. The activity data reported is:
%busy, avque — portion of time device was busy servicing a transfer request, average number of requests outstanding during that time;
r+w/s, blks/s — number of data transfers from or to device, number of bytes transferred in 512-byte units;
avwait, avserv — average time in ms. that transfer requests wait idly on queue, and average time to be serviced (which for disks includes seek, rotational latency and data transfer times).

−`y` Report TTY device activity:
rawch/s, canch/s, outch/s — input character rate, input character rate processed by canon, output character rate;
rcvin/s, xmtin/s, mdmin/s — receive, transmit and modem interrupt rates.

- `-c` Report system calls:
  scall/s — system calls of all types;
  sread/s, swrit/s, fork/s, exec/s — specific system calls;
  rchar/s, wchar/s — characters transferred by read and write system calls.
- `-w` Report system swapping and switching activity:
  swpin/s, swpot/s, bswin/s, bswot/s — number of transfers and number of 512-byte units transferred for swapins and swapouts (including initial loading of some programs);
  pswch/s — process switches.
- `-a` Report use of file access system routines:
  iget/s, namei/s, dirblk/s.
- `-q` Report average queue length while occupied, and % of time occupied:
  runq-sz, %runocc — run queue of processes in memory and runnable;
  swpq-sz, %swpocc — swap queue of processes swapped out but ready to run.
- `-v` Report status of process, i-node, file, record lock and file header tables:
  proc-sz, inod-sz, file-sz, lock-sz, fhdr-sz — entries/size for each table, evaluated once at sampling point;
  ov — overflows that occur between sampling points for each table.
- `-m` Report message and semaphore activities:
  msg/s, sema/s — primitives per second.
- `-A` Report all data (all options effective).

EXAMPLES

To see today's CPU activity so far:

```
sar
```

To watch CPU activity evolve for 10 minutes and save data:

```
sar -o temp 60 10
```

To later review disk and tape activity from that period:

```
sar -d -f temp
```

FILES

`/usr/adm/sa/sadd` daily data file, where `dd` are digits representing the day of the month.

USAGE

Administrator.

SEE ALSO

SA1(AS_CMD).

NAME

setmnt — establish mount table

SYNOPSIS

`/etc/setmnt`

DESCRIPTION

The command `setmnt` creates the `/etc/mnttab` table, which is needed for both the `mount` and `umount` [see MOUNT(AS_CMD)] commands. The command `setmnt` reads standard input and creates a `mnttab` entry for each line. Input lines have the format:

filesys node

where *filesys* is the name of the file system's *special file* and *node* is the root name of that file system. Thus *filesys* and *node* become the first two strings in the `/etc/mnttab` entry.

FILES

`/etc/mnttab`

USAGE

Administrator.

SEE ALSO

MOUNT(AS_CMD).

NAME

sync — flush system buffers

SYNOPSIS

`sync`

DESCRIPTION

The command `sync` executes the `sync` system source routine. If the system is to be stopped, `sync` must be executed to ensure file system integrity. It will flush all previously unwritten system buffers out to disk, thus assuring that all file modifications up to that point will be saved.

USAGE

Administrator.

SEE ALSO

SYNC(BA_SYS).

NAME

sysdef — system definition

SYNOPSIS

`/etc/sysdef` [*opsys* [*master*]]

DESCRIPTION

The command `sysdef` analyzes the named operating system file (or the default one if none is specified) and extracts configuration information. The master file contains the hardware and software specifications. (The default master file is used if one is not specified.) This includes all hardware devices as well as system devices and all tunable parameters.

USAGE

Administrator.

NAME

timex — time a command; report process data and system activity

SYNOPSIS

`timex` [*options*] *command*

DESCRIPTION

The given *command* is executed; the elapsed time, user time and system time spent in execution are reported in seconds. Optionally, process accounting data for the *command* and all its children can be listed or summarized, and total system activity during the execution interval can be reported.

The output of `timex` is written on standard error.

The options are:

`-p` List process accounting records for *command* and all its children. Suboptions `f`, `h`, `k`, `m`, `r`, and `t` modify the data items reported, as defined in ACCTCOM(AS_CMD). The number of blocks read or written and the number of characters transferred are always reported.

`-o` Report the total number of blocks read or written and total characters transferred by *command* and all its children.

`-s` Report total system activity (not just that due to *command*) that occurred during the execution interval of *command*. All the data items listed in SAR(AS_CMD) are reported.

USAGE

General.

SEE ALSO

ACCTCOM(AS_CMD), SAR(AS_CMD).

NAME

volcopy, labelit — copy file systems with label checking

SYNOPSIS

`/etc/volcopy` [*options*] *fsname special1 volname1 special2 volname2*

`/etc/labelit` *special* [*fsname volume* [−*n*]]

DESCRIPTION

volcopy

The command `volcopy` makes a literal copy of the file system using a blocksize matched to the device. The options are:

`−a` invoke a verification sequence requiring a positive operator response instead of the standard delay before the copy is made

`−s` (default) invoke the DEL if wrong verification sequence.

Other options are used only with tapes:

`−bpi`*density*	bits-per-inch
`−feet`*size*	size of reel in feet
`−reel`*num*	beginning reel number for a restarted copy,
`−buf`	use double buffered I/O.

The program requests length and density information if it is not given on the command line or is not recorded on an input tape label. If the file system is too large to fit on one reel, `volcopy` will prompt for additional reels. Labels of all reels are checked. Tapes may be mounted alternately on two or more drives. If `volcopy` is interrupted, it will ask if the user wants to quit or wants to escape to the command interpreter. In the latter case, the user can perform other operations (e.g.: `labelit`) and return to `volcopy` by exiting the command interpreter.

The *fsname* argument represents the file system name on the device (e.g.: `root, u1`) being copied.

The *special* should be the physical disk section or tape (e.g.: `/dev/rdsk/1s5`, `/dev/rmt/0m`, etc.).

The *volname* is the physical volume name and should match the external label sticker. Such label names are limited to six or fewer characters. The argument *volname* may be − to use the existing volume name.

The arguments *special1* and *volname1* are the device and volume from which the copy of the file system is being extracted. The arguments *special2* and *volname2* are the target device and volume.

labelit

The command `labelit` can be used to provide initial labels for unmounted disk or tape file systems. With the optional arguments omitted, `labelit` prints current label values. The −n option provides for initial labeling of new tapes only (this destroys previous contents).

USAGE

Administrator.

NAME

whodo — who is doing what

SYNOPSIS

`/etc/whodo`

DESCRIPTION

The command `whodo` produces merged, reformatted, and dated output from the WHO(AU_CMD) and PS(BU_CMD) commands.

FILES

`/etc/passwd`

USAGE

General.

SEE ALSO

PS(BU_CMD), WHO(AU_CMD).

Chapter 4

Software Development Utilities

NAME

admin — create and administer SCCS files

SYNOPSIS

admin [-n] [-i[*name*]] [-r*rel*] [-t[*name*]] [-f*flag*[*flag-val*]] [-d*flag*[*flag-val*]] [-a*login*] [-e*login*] [-m[*mrlist*]] [-%[*comment*]] [-h] [-z] *file* ...

DESCRIPTION

The command admin is used to create new SCCS files and change parameters of existing ones. Arguments to admin, which may appear in any order, consist of options, which begin with –, and named files (note that SCCS file names must begin with s.). If a named file does not exist, it is created, and its parameters are initialized according to the specified options. Parameters not initialized by an option are assigned a default value. If a named file does exist, parameters corresponding to specified options are changed, and other parameters are left as is.

If a directory is named, admin behaves as though each file in the directory were specified as a named file, except that non-SCCS files (last component of the path name does not begin with s.) and unreadable files are silently ignored. If a name of — is given, the standard input is read; each line of the standard input is taken to be the name of an SCCS file to be processed. Again, non-SCCS files and unreadable files are silently ignored.

The options are as follows. Each is explained as though only one named file is to be processed since the effects of the options apply independently to each named file.

-n This option indicates that a new SCCS file is to be created.

-i[*name*] The *name* of a file from which the text for a new SCCS file is to be taken. The text constitutes the first delta of the file (see –r option for delta numbering scheme). If the i option is used, but the file name is omitted, the text is obtained by reading the standard input until an end-of-file is encountered. If this option is omitted, then the SCCS file is created empty. Only one SCCS file may be created by an admin command on which the i option is supplied. Using a single admin to create two or more SCCS files requires that they be created empty (no –i option). Note that the –i option implies the –n option.

-r*rel* The *rel*ease into which the initial delta is inserted. This option may be used only if the –i option is also used. If the –r option is not used, the initial delta is inserted into release 1. The level of the initial delta is always 1 (by default initial deltas are named 1.1).

-t[*name*] The *name* of a file from which descriptive text for the SCCS file is to be taken. If the –t option is used and admin is creating a new SCCS file (the `-n` and/or `-i` options also used), the descriptive text file name must also be supplied. In the case of existing SCCS files: (1) a `-t` option without a file name causes removal of descriptive text (if any) currently in the SCCS file, and (2) a `-t` option with a file name causes text (if any) in the named file to replace the descriptive text (if any) currently in the SCCS file. This option specifies a *flag*, and, possibly, a value for the *flag*, to be placed in the SCCS file. Several `f` options may be supplied on a single `admin` command line. The allowable *flags* and their values are:

b Allows use of the `-b` option on a `get` command to create branch deltas.

c*ceil* The highest release (i.e., "ceiling"), a number less than or equal to 9999, which may be retrieved by a `get` command for editing. The default value for an unspecified **c** flag is 9999.

f*floor* The lowest release (i.e., "floor"), a number greater than 0 but less than 9999, which may be retrieved by a `get` command for editing. The default value for an unspecified **f** flag is 1.

d*SID* The default delta number (SID) to be used by a `get` command.

i[*str*] Causes the "No id keywords" message issued by `get` or `delta` to be treated as a fatal error. In the absence of this flag, the message is only a warning. The message is issued if no SCCS identification keywords (see `get`) are found in the text retrieved or stored in the SCCS file.

j Allows concurrent `get` commands for editing on the same SID of an SCCS file. This allows multiple concurrent updates to the same version of the SCCS file.

l*list* A *list* of releases to which deltas can no longer be made (**get -e** against one of these "locked" releases fails). The *list* has the following syntax:

<list> ::= <range> | <list> , <range>
<range> ::= *RELEASE NUMBER* | **a**

The character **a** in the *list* is equivalent to specifying all releases for the named SCCS file.

n Causes `delta` to create a "null" delta in each of those releases (if any) being skipped when a delta is made in a *new* release (e.g., in making delta 5.1 after delta 2.7, releases 3 and 4 are skipped). These null deltas serve as "anchor points" so that branch deltas may later be created from them. The absence of this flag causes skipped releases to be non-existent in the SCCS file, preventing branch deltas from being created from them in the future.

q*text* User definable text substituted for all occurrences of the %Q% keyword in SCCS file text retrieved by `get`.

m*mod* *Mod*ule name of the SCCS file substituted for all occurrences of the %M% keyword in SCCS file text retrieved by `get`. If the **m** flag is not specified, the value assigned is the name of the SCCS file with the leading **s.** removed.

t*type* *Type* of module in the SCCS file substituted for all occurrences of %Y% keyword in SCCS file text retrieved by `get`.

v[*pgm*] Causes `delta` to prompt for Modification Request (*MR*) numbers as the reason for creating a delta. The optional value specifies the name of an *MR* number validity checking program. (If this flag is set when creating an SCCS file, the `m` option must also be used even if its value is null).

-d*flag* Causes removal (deletion) of the specified *flag* from an SCCS file. The `-d` option may be specified only when processing existing SCCS files. Several `-d` options may be supplied on a single `admin` command. See the `-f` option for allowable *flag* names. (The **l***list* flag gives a *list* of releases to be "unlocked". See the `-f` option for further description of the **l** flag and the syntax of a *list*.)

-a*login* A *login* name, or numerical group ID, to be added to the list of users which may make deltas (changes) to the SCCS file. A group ID is equivalent to specifying all *login* names common to that group ID. Several `a` options may be used on a single `admin` command line. As many *login*s, or numerical group IDs, as desired may be on the list simultaneously. If the list of users is empty, then anyone may add deltas. If *login* or group ID is preceded by a `!` they are to be denied permission to make deltas.

-e*login* A *login* name, or numerical group ID, to be erased from the list of users allowed to make deltas (changes) to the SCCS file. Specifying a group ID is equivalent to specifying all *login* names common to that group ID. Several `e` options may be used on a single `admin` command line.

-y[*comment*] The *comment* text is inserted into the SCCS file as a comment for the initial delta in a manner identical to that of `delta`. Omission of the `-y` option results in a default comment line being inserted in the form:
date and time created *YY/MM/DD HH:MM:SS* by *login*
The `-y` option is valid only if the `-i` and/or `-n` options are specified (i.e., a new SCCS file is being created).

-m[*mrlist*] The list of Modification Requests (*MR*) numbers is inserted into the SCCS file as the reason for creating the initial delta in a manner identical to `delta`. The **v** flag must be set and the *MR* numbers are validated if the **v** flag has a value (the name of an *MR* number validation program). Diagnostics will occur if the **v** flag is not set or *MR* validation fails.

-h Causes `admin` to check the structure of the SCCS file, and to compare a newly computed check-sum (the sum of all the characters in the SCCS file except those in the first line) with the check-sum that is stored in the first line of the SCCS file. Appropriate error diagnostics are produced.

This option inhibits writing on the file, so that it nullifies the effect of any other options supplied. It is only meaningful when processing existing files.

-z The SCCS file check-sum is recomputed and stored in the first line of the SCCS file (see **-h**, above).

Note that use of this option on a truly corrupted file may prevent future detection of the corruption.

FILES

All SCCS file names must be of the form `s.`*file-name*. New SCCS files are given read-only permission mode (see `chmod`). Write permission in the pertinent directory is, of course, required to create a file. All writing done by `admin` is to a temporary x-file, called `x.`*file-name*, [see GET(SD_CMD)], created with read-only mode if the `admin` command is creating a new SCCS file, or with the same mode as the SCCS file if it exists. After successful execution of `admin`, the SCCS file is removed (if it exists), and the x-file is renamed with the name of the SCCS file. This ensures that changes are made to the SCCS file only if no errors occurred.

The command `admin` also makes use of a transient lock file (called `z.`*file-name*), which is used to prevent simultaneous updates to the SCCS file by different users. See GET(SD_CMD) for further information.

SEE ALSO

DELTA(SD_CMD), GET(SD_CMD), PRS(SD_CMD), WHAT(SD_CMD).

USAGE

General.

It is recommended that directories containing SCCS files be writeable by the owner only, and that SCCS files themselves be read-only. The mode of the directories allows only the owner to modify SCCS files contained in the directories. The mode of the SCCS files prevents any modification at all except by SCCS commands.

NAME

as — common assembler

SYNOPSIS

`as [-o` *objfile*`] [-m] [-V]` *file-name*

DESCRIPTION

The `as` command assembles the named file. The following options may be specified in any order:

−o *objfile*
: Put the output of the assembly in *objfile*. By default, the output file name is formed by removing the suffix, if there is one, from the input file name and appending a suffix.

−m
: Run the `m4` macro pre-processor on the input to the assembler.

−V
: Write the version number of the assembler being run on the standard error output.

SEE ALSO

CC(SD_CMD), LD(SD_CMD), M4(SD_CMD).

USAGE

General.

The command `cc` is the recommended interface to the assembler. The `as` command may not be present on all implementations of UNIX System V.

If the −m option (`m4` macro pre-processor invocation) is used, keywords for `m4` [see M4(SD_CMD)] cannot be used as symbols (variables, functions, labels) in the input file since `m4` cannot determine which are assembler symbols and which are real `m4` macros.

CAVEATS

The −Y option is reserved for future use. It will be used to allow the user to specify the directories where the `m4` preprocessor, and the file of predefined macros are located.

Users will also be able to specify, by means of the `TMPDIR` environmental variable, the directory in which any temporary files are to be created.

These additions are part of the effort to eliminate hard-coded pathnames from the compilation system.

NAME

cc — C compiler

SYNOPSIS

cc [*options*] *file* ...

DESCRIPTION

The cc command is the interface to the C compilation system. The system conceptually consists of a preprocessor, compiler, optimizer, assembler, and link-editor. The cc command processes the supplied options and then executes the various tools with the appropriate arguments.

The suffix of a file-name argument indicates how the file is to be treated. Files whose names end with .c are taken to be C source programs, and may be preprocessed, compiled, optimized, and link-edited. The compilation process may be stopped after the completion of any pass if the appropriate options are supplied. If the compilation process is allowed to complete the assembly phase, then an object program is produced; the object program for a source file called xyz.c is created in a file called xyz.o. However, the .o file is normally deleted if a single C program is compiled and loaded all at one go.

In the same way, arguments whose names end with .s are taken to be assembly source programs, and may be assembled and link-edited. Files with names ending in .i are taken to be preprocessed C source programs and may be compiled, optimized, assembled, and link-edited. Files whose names do not end in .c, .s, or .i are handed to the link-editor.

By default, if an executable file is produced (i.e., the link-edit phase is allowed to complete), the file is called a.out. This default name can be changed with the -o option (see below).

The following options are interpreted by cc:

-c Suppress the link edit phase of the compilation, and do not remove any object files that are produced.

-f Include floating-point support for systems without an automatically included floating-point implementation. This option is ignored on systems that do not need it.

-g Cause the compiler to generate additional information needed for the use of sdb.

-o *outfile*
Use the name outfile, instead of the default a.out, for the executable file produced. This is a link-editor option.

-p Arrange for the compiler to produce code that counts the number of times each routine is called; also, if link editing takes place, a profiled version of the standard C library is linked, and monitor [see MONITOR(SD_LIB)] is automatically called. A mon.out file will then be produce at normal termination of execution of the program. An execution profile can then be generated by use of prof.

-q This option is reserved for specification of implementation specific profiling directives.

-E Run only cpp on the named C programs and send the result to the standard output.

-F This option is reserved for implementation specific optimization directives.

-O Do compilation phase optimization. This option will not affect files.

-P Run only cpp on the named C programs and leave the result on corresponding files suffixed .i. This option is passed to cpp.

-S Compile and do not assemble the named C programs, and leave the assembler-language output on corresponding files suffixed .s.

-W*c*,*arg1*[,*arg2* ...]
Hand off the argument[s] *argi* to phase *c* where *c* is one of [p02al] indicating preprocessor, compiler, optimizer, assembler, or link editor, respectively. For example, -Wa,-m passes -m to the assembler phase.

The cc command also recognizes the options -C, -D, -I, and -U, and passes them (and their associated arguments) directly to the preprocessor without using the -W option. Similarly, the loader options -a, -l, -o, -r, -s, -u, -L, and -V are recognized and passed directly to the loader. See CPP(SD_CMD) and LD(SD_CMD) for descriptions of these options.

Other arguments are taken to be C-compatible object programs, typically produced by an earlier cc or pcc run, or perhaps libraries of C-compatible routines, and are passed directly to the link-editor. These programs, together with the results of any compilations specified, are linked (in the order given) to produce an executable program with the name a.out (unless the -o link-editor option is used).

The standard C library is automatically available to the C program. Other libraries (including the math library) must be specified explicitly using the -l option with cc; see LD(SD_CMD) for details.

FILES

file.c	input file
file.i	preprocessed C source file
file.o	object file
file.s	assembly language file
a.out	link-edited (executable) output

SEE ALSO

CPP(SD_CMD), LD(SD_CMD), PROF(SD_CMD), SDB(SD_CMD), EXIT(BA_SYS), MONITOR(SD_LIB).

USAGE

General.

Arbitrary length variable names are allowed in the C language, starting with UNIX System V Release 2.0.

Since the `cc` command usually creates files in the current directory during the compilation process, it is typically necessary to run the `cc` command in a directory in which a file can be created.

CAVEATS

The `-Y` option is reserved for future use. It will be used to allow the user to specify the directories searched by the various components of `cc`.

Users will also be able to specify, by means of the `TMPDIR` environmental variable, the directory in which any temporary files are to be created.

These additions are part of the effort to eliminate hard-coded pathnames from the compilation system.

NAME

cflow — generate C flowgraph

SYNOPSIS

`cflow` [−r] [−ix] [−i_] [−d*num*] *files*

DESCRIPTION

The command `cflow` analyzes a collection of C, YACC, LEX, assembler, and object files and attempts to build a graph charting the external references. Files suffixed in `.y`, `.l`, `.c`, and `.i` are YACC'd, LEX'd, and C-preprocessed (bypassed for `.i` files) as appropriate, and then run through the first pass of `lint`. (The **−I**, **−D**, and **−U** options of the C-preprocessor are also understood by `cflow`.) Files suffixed with `.s` are assembled and information is extracted (as in `.o` files) from the symbol table. The output of all this processing is collected and turned into a graph of external references which is displayed upon the standard output.

Each line of output begins with a reference (i.e., line) number, followed by a suitable amount of indentation indicating the level. Then the name of the global (normally only a function not defined as an external or beginning with an underscore; see below for the `−i` inclusion option) a colon and its definition. For information extracted from C source, the definition consists of an abstract type declaration (e.g., `char *`), and, delimited by angle brackets, the name of the source file and the line number where the definition was found. Definitions extracted from object files indicate the file name and location counter under which the symbol appeared (e.g., `text`).

Once a definition of a name has been printed, subsequent references to that name contain only the reference number of the line where the definition may be found. For undefined references, only **< >** is printed.

The following options are interpreted by `cflow`:

`−r` Reverse the "caller:callee" relationship producing an inverted listing showing the callers of each function. The listing is also sorted in lexicographical order by callee.

`−ix` Include external and static data symbols. The default is to include only functions in the flowgraph.

`−i_` Include names that begin with an underscore. The default is to exclude these functions (and data if `−ix` is used).

`−d`*num* The *num* decimal integer indicates the depth at which the flowgraph is cut off. By default this is a very large number. Attempts to set the cutoff depth to a non-positive integer will be ignored.

SEE ALSO

CC(SD_CMD), LEX(SD_CMD), LINT(SD_CMD), YACC(SD_CMD).

USAGE

General.

Files produced by `lex` and `yacc` cause the reordering of line number declarations which can confuse `cflow`. To get proper results, feed `cflow` the `yacc` or `lex` input.

NAME

chroot — change root directory for a command

SYNOPSIS

`/etc/chroot` *newroot command*

DESCRIPTION

The command `chroot` executes the given *command*, **relative to the new root**. The meaning of any initial slashes (/) in path names is changed for a command and any of its children to *newroot*. Furthermore, the initial working directory is *newroot*.

This command is restricted to the super-user.

Notice that:

`chroot` *newroot command* >*x*

will create the file *x* relative to the original root, not the new one.

The new root path name is always relative to the current root: even if a `chroot` is currently in effect, the *newroot* argument is relative to the current root of the running process.

SEE ALSO

CHDIR(BA_SYS)

USAGE

General.

The user should exercise caution when referencing special files in the new root file system.

NAME

cpp — the C language preprocessor

SYNOPSIS

`LIBDIR/cpp` [*option* ...] [*ifile* [*ofile*]]

DESCRIPTION

The command `cpp` is the C language preprocessor, which is invoked as the first pass of any C compilation using the `cc` command. Thus the output of `cpp` is designed to be in a form acceptable as input to the next pass of the C compiler.

`LIBDIR` is usually `/lib`.

The `cpp` command optionally accepts two file names as arguments; *ifile* and *ofile* are respectively the input and output for the preprocessor. They default to standard input and standard output if not supplied.

The following options to `cpp` are recognized:

`-P` Preprocess the input without producing the line control information used by the next pass of the C compiler.

`-C` By default, `cpp` strips C-style comments. If the `-C` option is specified, all comments (except those found on `cpp` directive lines) are passed along.

`-U`*name* Remove any initial definition of *name*, where *name* is a reserved symbol that is predefined by the particular preprocessor.

`-D`*name*
`-D`*name*`=`*def*
Define *name* as if by a `#define` directive. If no `=def` is given, *name* is defined as 1. The `-D` option has lower precedence than the `-U` option. That is, if the same name is used in both a `-U` option and a `-D` option, the name will be undefined regardless of the order of the options.

`-I`*dir* Change the algorithm for searching for `#include` files whose names do not begin with / to look in `dir` before looking in the directories on the standard list. Thus, `#include` files whose names are enclosed in "" will be searched for first in the directory of the file with the `#include` line, then in directories named in `-I` options, and last in directories on a standard list. For `#include` files whose names are enclosed in <>, the directory of the file with the `#include` line is not searched.

Two special names are understood by `cpp`. The name __LINE__ is defined as the current line number (as a decimal integer) as known by `cpp`, and __FILE__ is defined as the current file name (as a C string) as known by `cpp`. They can be used anywhere (including in macros) just as any other defined name.

All `cpp` directives start with lines begun by #. Any number of blanks and tabs are allowed between the # and the directive. The directives are:

#define *name token-string*
Replace subsequent instances of *name* with *token-string*.

#define *name*(*arg*, ..., *arg*) *token-string*
Notice that there can be no space between *name* and the (. Replace subsequent instances of *name* followed by a (, a list of comma-separated set of tokens, and a) by *token-string*, where each occurrence of an *arg* in the *token-string* is replaced by the corresponding set of tokens in the comma-separated list. When a macro with arguments is expanded, the arguments are placed into the expanded *token-string* unchanged. After the entire *token-string* has been expanded, `cpp` re-starts its scan for names to expand at the beginning of the newly created *token-string*.

#undef *name*
Cause the definition of *name* (if any) to be forgotten from now on. No additional tokens are permitted on the line after *name*.

#include "*filename*"
#include <*filename*>
Include at this point the contents of *filename* (which will then be run through `cpp`). When the <*filename*> notation is used, *filename* is only searched for in the standard places. See the `-I` option above for more detail. No additional tokens are permitted on the line after the final " or >.

#line *integer-constant* "*filename*"
Causes `cpp` to generate line control information for the next pass of the C compiler. *Integer-constant* is the line number of the next line and *filename* is the file where it comes from. If "*filename*" is not given, the current file name is unchanged. No additional tokens are permitted on the line after the final ".

#endif
Ends a section of lines begun by a test directive (`#if`, `#ifdef`, or `#ifndef`). Each test directive must have a matching `#endif`. No additional tokens are permitted on the line.

#ifdef *name*
The lines following will appear in the output if and only if *name* has been the subject of a previous `#define` without being the subject of an intervening `#undef`. No additional tokens are permitted on the line after *name*.

#ifndef *name*
The lines following will not appear in the output if and only if *name* has been the subject of a previous `#define` without being the subject of an intervening `#undef`. No additional tokens are permitted on the

line after *name*.

`#if` *constant-expression*
Lines following will appear in the output if and only if the *constant-expression* evaluates to non-zero. All binary non-assignment C operators, the `?:` operator, the unary −, `!`, and `@` operators are all legal in *constant-expression*. The precedence of the operators is the same as defined by the C language. There is also a unary operator `defined`, which can be used in *constant-expression* in these two forms: `defined(`*name*`)` or `defined` *name*. This allows the utility of `#ifdef` and `#ifndef` in a `#if` directive. Only these operators, integer constants, and names which are known by `cpp` should be used in *constant-expression*. In particular, the `sizeof` operator is not available.

`#else`
The else part of an `#ifdef`, `#ifndef`, or `#if`. The lines preceding are ignored, and the lines following (upto the `#endif`) are included in the output if the test is false.

The test directives and the optional `#else` directives can be nested.

SEE ALSO

CC(SD CMD).

USAGE

General.

The recommended way to invoke `cpp` is through the `cc` command. See M4(SD_CMD) for a general macro processor.

Include directives should avoid using explicit path-names: for example,

```
#include <file.h>
```

should be used, rather than

```
#include "/usr/include/file.h"
```

CAVEATS

The option `-Y` is reserved for future use. It will be used to specify a directory to be used instead of the standard list, when searching for `#include` files.

Users will also be able to specify, by means of the `TMPDIR` environmental variable, the directory in which any temporary files are to be created.

NAME

cxref — generate C program cross-reference

SYNOPSIS

`cxref` [*options*] *files*

DESCRIPTION

The command `cxref` analyzes a collection of C files and attempts to build a cross-reference table. Information from `#define` lines is included in the symbol table. A listing is produced on standard output of all symbols (auto, static, and global) in each file separately, or with the `-c` option, in combination. Each symbol contains an asterisk (*) before the declaring reference.

In addition to the `-D`, `-I`, and `-U` options (which are identical to their interpretation by `cc`) the following options are interpreted by `cxref`:

`-c` Print a combined cross-reference of all input files.

`-w`*num* Width option which formats output no wider than *num* (decimal) columns. This option will default to 80 if *num* is not specified or is less than 51.

`-o` *file* Direct output to named *file*.

`-s` Operate silently; does not print input file names.

SEE ALSO

CC(SD_CMD).

USAGE

General.

NAME

delta — make a delta (change) to an SCCS file

SYNOPSIS

`delta` [`-r`*SID*] [-s] [-n] [-g*list*] [-*m*[*mrlist*]] [-y[*comment*]] [**-p**] *file* ...

DESCRIPTION

The command `delta` is used to permanently introduce into the named SCCS file changes that were made to the file retrieved by `get` (called the *g-file*, or generated file).

The `delta` command makes a delta to each named SCCS file. If a directory is named, `delta` behaves as though each file in the directory were specified as a named file, except that non-SCCS files (last component of the path name does not begin with **s.**) and unreadable files are silently ignored. If a name of – is given, the standard input is read; in this case the −y option (see below) is required on the command line; if the −m option (see below) would normally be required, then it too is required on the command line. Each line of the standard input is taken to be the name of an SCCS file to be processed.

The `delta` command may issue prompts on the standard output depending upon certain keyletters specified and flags [see ADMIN(SD_CMD)] that may be present in the SCCS file (see −m and −y keyletters below).

Lines beginning with an SOH ASCII character (binary 001) cannot be placed in the SCCS file unless the SOH is escaped. This character has special meaning to SCCS and will cause an error.

Keyletter arguments apply independently to each named file.

`-r`*SID* Uniquely identifies which delta is to be made to the SCCS file. The use of this keyletter is necessary only if two or more outstanding `get`s for editing (`get −e`) on the same SCCS file were done by the same person (login name). The *SID* value specified with the `−r` keyletter can be either the *SID* specified on the `get` command line or the *SID* to be made as reported by the `get` command [see GET(SD_CMD)]. A diagnostic results if the specified *SID* is ambiguous, or, if necessary and omitted on the command line.

`-s` Suppresses the issue, on the standard output, of the created delta's *SID*, as well as the number of lines inserted, deleted and unchanged in the SCCS file.

`-n` Specifies retention of the edited *g-file* (normally removed at completion of delta processing).

`-g`*list* Specifies a *list* [see GET(SD_CMD) for the definition of *list*] of deltas which are to be ignored when the file is accessed at the change level (*SID*) created by this delta.

`-m`[*mrlist*] If the SCCS file has the **v** flag set [see ADMIN(SD_CMD)] then a Modification Request (**MR**) number *must* be supplied as the reason for creating the new delta.

If −m is not used and the standard input is a terminal, the prompt **MRs?** is issued on the standard output before the standard input is read; if the standard input is not a terminal, no prompt is issued. The **MRs?** prompt always precedes the **comments?** prompt (see −y keyletter).

MRs in a list are separated by blanks and/or tab characters. An unescaped new-line character terminates the **MR** list.

Note that if the v flag has a value, it is taken to be the name of a program which will validate the correctness of the **MR** numbers. If a non-zero exit status is returned from **MR** number validation program, `delta` terminates. (It is assumed that the **MR** numbers were not all valid.)

-y[*comment*] Arbitrary text used to describe the reason for making the delta. A null string is considered a valid *comment*.

If −y is not specified and the standard input is a terminal, the prompt **comments?** is issued on the standard output before the standard input is read; if the standard input is not a terminal, no prompt is issued. An unescaped new-line character terminates the comment text.

-p Causes `delta` to print (on the standard output) the SCCS file differences before and after the delta is applied in `diff` format [see DIFF(BU_CMD)].

SEE ALSO

ADMIN(SD_CMD), GET(SD_CMD), PRS(SD_CMD), RMDEL(SD_CMD).

USAGE

General.

NAME

dis — disassembler

SYNOPSIS

dis [−o] [−V] [−L] [−F *function*] [−l *string*] *files*

DESCRIPTION

The dis command produces an assembly language listing of each of its *file* arguments, each of which may be an object file or an archive of object files. The listing includes assembly statements and an octal or hexadecimal representation of the binary that produced those statements.

The following options are interpreted by the disassembler and may be specified in any order.

−o Will print numbers in octal. Default is hexadecimal.

−V Version number of the disassembler will be written to standard error.

−L Invokes a lookup of C source labels in the symbol table for subsequent printing.

−F *function* Disassembles only the named *function* in each object file specified on the command line. This option may be specified a number of times on the command line.

−l *string* Will disassemble the library file specified as *string*. For example, the command `dis -lm` will disassemble the math library.

SEE ALSO

AS(SD_CMD), CC(SD_CMD).

USAGE

General.

CAVEATS

The −s option is reserved for future use. It will be used to specify symbolic disassembly.

NAME

env — set environment for command execution

SYNOPSIS

`env` [-] [*name*=*value*] ... [*command*]

DESCRIPTION

The command `env` obtains the current environment, modifies it according to its arguments, then executes the command with the modified environment. Arguments of the form *name=value* modify the execution environment: they are merged into the inherited environment before the command is executed. The – option causes the inherited environment to be ignored completely, so that the command is executed with exactly the environment specified by the arguments.

If no command is specified, the resulting environment is printed, one name-value pair per line.

SEE ALSO

SH(BU_CMD).

USAGE

General.

NAME

get — get a version of an SCCS file

SYNOPSIS

`get` [`-r` *SID*] [`-c` *cutoff*] [`-e`] [`-b`] [`-i` *list*] [`-x` *list*] [`-k`] [`-l` [`p`]] [`-p`] [`-s`] [`-m`] [`-n`] [`-g`] [`-t`] *file* ...

DESCRIPTION

The command `get` generates an **ASCII** text file from each named SCCS file according to the specifications given by its keyletter arguments, which begin with `-`. The arguments may be specified in any order, but all keyletter arguments apply to all named SCCS files. If a directory is named, `get` behaves as if each file in the directory were specified as a named file, except that non-SCCS files (last component of the path name does not begin with **s.**) and unreadable files are silently ignored. If — is given, the standard input is read; each line of the standard input is taken to be the name of an SCCS file to be processed. Non-SCCS files and unreadable files are silently ignored.

The generated text is normally written into a file called the `g-file` whose name is derived from the SCCS file name by simply removing the leading **s.**; (see also **FILES**, below).

Each of the keyletter arguments is explained below as though only one SCCS file is to be processed, but the effects of any keyletter argument applies independently to each named file.

`-r`*SID* The SCCS Identification string (*SID*) of the version (delta) of an SCCS file to be retrieved. Table 1 below shows, for the most useful cases, what version of an SCCS file is retrieved (as well as the *SID* of the version to be eventually created by `delta` if the `-e` keyletter is also used), as a function of the *SID* specified.

`-c`*cutoff* *Cutoff* date-time, in the form:

YY[MM[DD[HH[MM[SS]]]]]

No changes (deltas) to the SCCS file which were created after the specified *cutoff* date-time are included in the generated **ASCII** text file. Units omitted from the date-time default to their maximum possible values; that is, `-c7502` is equivalent to `-c750228235959`. Any number of non-numeric characters may separate the various 2-digit pieces of the *cutoff* date-time. This feature allows one to specify a *cutoff* date in the form: "`-c77/2/2 9:22:25`".

`-e` Indicates that the `get` is to edit or make a change (delta) to the SCCS file via a subsequent use of `delta`. The `-e` keyletter used in a `get` for a specific version (*SID*) of the SCCS file prevents further `gets` from editing on the same *SID* until `delta` is executed or the **j** (joint edit) flag is set in the SCCS file. Concurrent use of `get -e` for different *SID*s is always allowed.

If the `g-file` generated by `get` with an `-e` keyletter is accidentally ruined in the process of editing it, it may be regenerated by re-executing the `get` command with the `-k` keyletter in place of the `-e` keyletter.

SCCS file protection specified via the ceiling, floor, and authorized user list stored in the SCCS file are enforced when the `-e` keyletter is used.

`-b` Used with the `-e` keyletter to indicate that the new delta should have an *SID* in a new branch as shown in Table 1. This keyletter is ignored if the **b** flag is not present in the file or if the retrieved `delta` is not a leaf `delta`. (A leaf `delta` is one that has no successors on the SCCS file tree.)
Note: A branch `delta` may always be created from a non-leaf `delta`.

`-i`*list* A *list* of deltas to be included (forced to be applied) in the creation of the generated file. The *list* has the following syntax:

<list> ::= <range> | <list> , <range>
<range> ::= *SID* | *SID* − *SID*

SID, the SCCS Identification of a delta, may be in any form shown in the "*SID* Specified" column of Table 1. Partial *SID*s are interpreted as shown in the "*SID* Retrieved" column of Table 1.

`-x`*list* A *list* of deltas to be excluded (forced not to be applied) in the creation of the generated file. See the `-i` keyletter for the *list* format.

`-k` Suppresses replacement of identification keywords (see below) in the retrieved text by their value. The `-k` keyletter is implied by the `-e` keyletter.

`-l[p]` Causes a delta summary to be written into an `l-file`. If `-lp` is used then an `l-file` is not created; the delta summary is written on the standard output instead. See **FILES** for the format of the `l-file`.

`-p` Causes the text retrieved from the SCCS file to be written on the standard output. No `g-file` is created. All output which normally goes to the standard output goes to standard error instead, unless the `-s` keyletter is used, in which case it disappears.

`-s` Suppresses all output normally written on the standard output. However, fatal error messages (which always go to standard error) remain unaffected.

`-m` Causes each text line retrieved from the SCCS file to be preceded by the *SID* of the delta that inserted the text line in the

SCCS file. The format is: *SID*, followed by a horizontal tab, followed by the text line.

−n Causes each generated text line to be preceded with the %M% identification keyword value (see below). The format is: %M% value, followed by a horizontal tab, followed by the text line. When both the −m and −n keyletters are used, the format is: %M% value, followed by a horizontal tab, followed by the −m keyletter generated format.

−g Suppresses the actual retrieval of text from the SCCS file. It is primarily used to generate an `l-file`, or to verify the existence of a particular *SID*.

−t Used to access the most recently created ("top") delta in a given release (e.g., −r 1), or release and level (e.g., −r 1.2).

For each file processed, `get` responds (on the standard output) with the *SID* being accessed and with the number of lines retrieved from the SCCS file.

If the −e keyletter is used, the *SID* of the delta to be made appears after the *SID* accessed and before the number of lines generated. If there is more than one named file or if a directory or standard input is named, each file name is printed (preceded by a new-line) before it is processed. If the −i keyletter is used included deltas are listed following the notation "Included"; if the −x keyletter is used, excluded deltas are listed following the notation "Excluded".

Determination of SCCS Identification String

SID* Specified	−b Keyletter Used†	Other Conditions	SID Retrieved	SID of Delta to be Created
none‡	no	R defaults to mR	mR.mL	mR.(mL+1)
none‡	yes	R defaults to mR	mR.mL	mR.mL.(mB+1).1
R	no	R > mR	mR.mL	R.1***
R	no	R = mR	mR.mL	mR.(mL+1)
R	yes	R > mR	mR.mL	mR.mL.(mB+1).1
R	yes	R = mR	mR.mL	mR.mL.(mB+1).1
R	−	R < mR and R does *not* exist	hR.mL**	hR.mL.(mB+1).1
R	−	Trunk succ.# in release > R and R exists	R.mL	R.mL.(mB+1).1
R.L	no	No trunk succ.	R.L	R.(L+1)
R.L	yes	No trunk succ.	R.L	R.L.(mB+1).1
R.L	−	Trunk succ. in release ≥ R	R.L	R.L.(mB+1).1
R.L.B	no	No branch succ.	R.L.B.mS	R.L.B.(mS+1)
R.L.B	yes	No branch succ.	R.L.B.mS	R.L.(mB+1).1

R.L.B.S	no	No branch succ.	R.L.B.S	R.L.B.(S+1)
R.L.B.S	yes	No branch succ.	R.L.B.S	R.L.(mB+1).1
R.L.B.S	–	Branch succ.	R.L.B.S	R.L.(mB+1).1

* "R", "L", "B", and "S" are the "release", "level", "branch", and "sequence" components of the SID, respectively; "m" means "maximum". Thus, for example, "R.mL" means "the maximum level number within release R"; "R.L.(mB+1).1" means "the first sequence number on the *new* branch (i.e., maximum branch number plus one) of level L within release R". Note that if the SID specified is of the form "R.L", "R.L.B", or "R.L.B.S", each of the specified components *must* exist.

** "hR" is the highest *existing* release that is lower than the specified, *nonexistent*, release R.

*** This is used to force creation of the *first* delta in a *new* release.

\# Successor.

† The **−b** keyletter is effective only if the **b** flag is present in the file. An entry of − means "irrelevant".

‡ This case applies if the **d** (default SID) flag is *not* present in the file. If the **d** flag *is* present in the file, then the SID obtained from the **d** flag is interpreted as if it had been specified on the command line. Thus, one of the other cases in this table applies.

IDENTIFICATION KEYWORDS

Identifying information is inserted into the text retrieved from the SCCS file by replacing *identification keywords* with their value wherever they occur. The following keywords may be used in the text stored in an SCCS file:

Keyword	*Value*
`%M%`	Module name: either the value of the **m** flag in the file, or if absent, the name of the SCCS file with the leading **s.** removed.
`%I%`	SCCS identification (*SID*) (%R%.%L%.%B%.%S%) of the retrieved text.
`%R%`	Release.
`%L%`	Level.
`%B%`	Branch.
`%S%`	Sequence.
`%D%`	Current date (YY/MM/DD).
`%H%`	Current date (MM/DD/YY).
`%T%`	Current time (HH:MM:SS).
`%E%`	Date newest applied delta was created (YY/MM/DD).
`%G%`	Date newest applied delta was created (MM/DD/YY).
`%U%`	Time newest applied delta was created (HH:MM:SS).
`%Y%`	Module type: value of the **t** flag in the SCCS file.
`%F%`	SCCS file name.
`%P%`	Fully qualified SCCS file name.
`%Q%`	The value of the **q** flag in the file.
`%C%`	Current line number. This keyword is intended for identifying

messages output by the program such as "this should not have happened" type errors. It is *not* intended to be used on every line to provide sequence numbers.

`%Z%` The 4-character string @(#) recognizable by `what`.

`%W%` A shorthand notation for constructing `what` strings.
%W% = %Z%%M%<horizontal-tab>%I%

`%A%` Another shorthand notation for constructing *what*(SD_CMD) strings.
%A% = %Z%%Y% %M% %I%%Z%

FILES

Several auxiliary files may be created by `get`. These files are known generically as the `g-file`, `l-file`, `p-file`, and `z-file`. The letter before the hyphen is called the tag. An auxiliary file name is formed from the SCCS file name: the last component of all SCCS file names must be of the form **s.***module-name*, the auxiliary files are named by replacing the leading **s** with the tag. The `g-file` is an exception to this scheme: the `g-file` is named by removing the **s.** prefix. For example, `s.xyz.c`, the auxiliary file names would be `xyz.c`, `l.xyz.c`, `p.xyz.c`, and `z.xyz.c`, respectively.

The `g-file`, which contains the generated text, is created in the current directory (unless the **−p** keyletter is used). A `g-file` is created in all cases, whether or not any lines of text were generated by the `get`. It is owned by the real user. If the **−k** keyletter is used or implied it is writeable by the owner only (read-only for everyone else); otherwise it is read-only. Only the real user need have write permission in the current directory.

The `l-file` contains a table showing which deltas were applied in generating the retrieved text. The `l-file` is created in the current directory if the **−l** keyletter is used; it is read-only and it is owned by the real user. Only the real user need have write permission in the current directory.

Lines in the `l-file` have the following format:

a. A blank character if the delta was applied;
* otherwise.
b. A blank character if the delta was applied or was not applied and ignored;
* if the delta was not applied and was not ignored.
c. A code indicating a "special" reason why the delta was or was not applied:
"I": Included.
"X": Excluded.
"C": Cut off (by a **−c** keyletter).
d. Blank.
e. SCCS identification (*SID*).
f. Tab character.
g. Date and time (in the form YY/MM/DD HH:MM:SS) of creation.
h. Blank.

i. Login name of person who created *delta*.

The comments and **MR** data follow on subsequent lines, indented one horizontal tab character. A blank line terminates each entry.

The `p-file` is used to pass information resulting from a `get` with an **−e** keyletter along to `delta`. Its contents are also used to prevent a subsequent execution of `get` with an **−e** keyletter for the same *SID* until `delta` is executed or the joint edit flag, **j**, is set in the SCCS file. The `p-file` is created in the directory containing the SCCS file and the effective user must have write permission in that directory. It is writeable by owner only, and it is owned by the effective user. The format of the `p-file` is: the gotten *SID*, followed by a blank, followed by the *SID* that the new delta will have when it is made, followed by a blank, followed by the login name of the real user, followed by a blank, followed by the date-time the `get` was executed, followed by a blank and the **−i** keyletter argument if it was present, followed by a blank and the **−x** keyletter argument if it was present, followed by a new-line. There can be an arbitrary number of lines in the `p-file` at any time; no two lines can have the same new delta *SID*.

The `z-file` serves as a *lock-out* mechanism against simultaneous updates. Its contents are the binary process ID of the command (i.e., `get`) that created it. The `z-file` is created in the directory containing the SCCS file for the duration of `get`. The same protection restrictions as those for the `p-file` apply for the `z-file`. The `z-file` is created read-only.

SEE ALSO

ADMIN(SD_CMD), DELTA(SD_CMD), PRS(SD_CMD), WHAT(SD_CMD).

USAGE

General.

NAME

ld — link editor for object files

SYNOPSIS

`ld` [*options*] *file* ...

DESCRIPTION

The `ld` command combines several object files into one, performs relocation, resolves external symbols, and supports symbol table information for symbolic debugging. In the simplest case, the names of several object programs are given, and `ld` combines them, producing an object module that can either be executed or, if the `-r` option is specified, used as input for a subsequent `ld` run. The output of `ld` is left in `a.out`. By default this file is executable if no errors occurred during the load. If any input file *filename*, is not an object file, `ld` assumes it is an archive library.

If any argument is a library, it is searched at the point it is encountered in the argument list. Only those routines defining an unresolved external reference are loaded. The library (archive) symbol table is searched to resolve external references which can be satisfied by library members. The ordering of library members is unimportant, unless there exist multiple library members defining the same external symbol.

The following options are recognized by `ld`:

`-e` *epsym*
Set the default entry point address for the output file to be that of the symbol *epsym*.

`-l`*x*
Search the library which has the abbreviation *x* (e.g., *-lm* to search the math library). A library is searched when its name is encountered, so the placement of a `-l` option is significant.

`-o` *outfile*
Produce an output object file by the name *outfile*. The name of the default object file is `a.out`.

`-r` Retain relocation entries in the output object file. Relocation entries must be saved if the output file is to become an input file in a subsequent `ld` run. The link editor will not complain about unresolved references, and the output file will not be made executable.

`-s` Strip all symbolic information from the output object file.

`-u` *symname*
Enter *symname* as an undefined symbol in the symbol table. This is useful for loading entirely from a library, since initially the symbol table is empty and an unresolved reference is needed to force the loading of the first routine.

`-L` *dir*
Change the algorithm of searching for the library *x* to look in *dir* before

looking in the default library directories. This option is effective only if it precedes the `-l` option on the command line.

`-V` Output a message giving information about the version of `ld` being used.

FILES

`a.out` output file

SEE ALSO

AR(BU_CMD), CC(SD_CMD), STRIP(SD_CMD).

USAGE

General.

When the link editor is called through `cc`, a startup routine is linked with the user's program. This routine calls `exit()` after execution of the main program. If the user calls the link editor directly, then the user must ensure that the program always calls `exit()` rather than falling through the end of the entry routine.

The symbols `etext`, `edata`, and `end` are reserved and are defined by the link editor. It is erroneous for a user program to redefine them.

CAVEATS

The option `-Y` is reserved for future use. It will be used to specify a directory to be used instead of the standard list, when searching for libraries.

Users will also be able to specify, by means of the `TMPDIR` environment variable, the directory in which any temporary files are to be created.

NAME

lex – generate programs for simple lexical analysis of text

SYNOPSIS

`lex` [`-ctvn`] [*file*] ...

DESCRIPTION

The command `lex` generates programs to be used in lexical processing of character input and may be used as an interface to `yacc`.

The input *file*(s), which contain `lex` source code, contain a table of regular expressions each with a corresponding action in the form of a C program fragment. Multiple input *files* are treated as a single file. When `lex` processes *file*(s), this source is translated into a C program. Normally `lex` writes the program it generates to the file `lex.yy.c`. If the `-t` option is used, the resulting program is written instead to the standard output. When the program generated by `lex` is compiled and executed, it will read character input from the standard input and partition it into strings that match the given expressions. When an expression is matched, the input string was matched is left in an external character array `yylex` and the expressions corresponding program fragment, or action, is executed. During pattern matching the set of patterns will be searched for a match in the order in which they appeared in the `lex` source and the single longest possible matchwill be chosen at any point in time. Among rules that match the same number of characters, the rule given first will be matched.

The program generated by `lex`, e.g., `lex.yy.c`, should be compiled and loaded with the `lex` library (using the `-ll` option with `cc`.

The option `-c` indicates C language actions and is the default, `-t` causes the program generated to be written instead to standard output, `-v` provides a one-line summary of statistics of the finite state machine generated, `-n` will not print out the – summary.

Certain table sizes for the resulting finite state machine can be set in the definitions section:

%**p** *n*	number of positions is *n*
%**n** *n*	number of states is *n*
%**e** *n*	number of parse tree nodes is *n*
%**a** *n*	number of transitions is *n*
%**k** *n*	number of packed character classes is *n*
%**o** *n*	size of the output array is *n*

The use of one or more of the above automatically implies the `-v` option, unless the `-n` option is used.

The general format of `lex` source is:

```
{definitions}
%%
{rules}
%%
```

{user subroutines}

The definitions and the user subroutines may be omitted. The first %% is required to mark the beginning of the rules (regular expressions and actions); the second %% is required only if user subroutines follow.

Any line in the source beginning with a blank is assumed to contain only C text and is copied to `lex.yy.c`; if it precedes %% it is copied into the external definition area of the `lex.yy.c` file. Anything included between lines containing only %{ **and** %} is copied unchanged to `lex.yy.c` and the delimiter lines are discarded. Anything after the third %% delimiter is copied to `lex.yy.c`.

Definitions

Definitions must appear before the first %% delimiter. Any line in this section not contained between %{ **and** %} lines and beginning in column 1 is assumed to define a `lex` substitution string. The format of these lines is

name substitute

The *name* must begin with a letter and be followed by at least one blank or tab. The substitute will replace the string {*name*} when it is used in a rule. The curly braces do not imply parentheses; only string substitution is done.

Rules

The rules in `lex` source files are a table in which the left column contains regular expressions and the right column contains actions and program fragments to be executed when the expressions are recognized.

```
re whitespace action
re whitespace action
     ...
```

Because the regular expression, (*re*), portion of a rule is terminated by the first blank or tab, any blank or tab used within a regular expression must be quoted (its special meaning escaped). That is, it must appear within double quotes, square brackets or must be preceded by a backslash character.

The program fragment which is the action associated with a particular *re* may extend across several lines if it is enclosed in curly braces:

```
re whitespace { program statement
                program statement }
```

Regular Expressions

The `lex` command supports the sets of regular expressions recognized by `ed` and `awk`, and some additional expressions. Some characters have special meanings when used in an *re* and are called regular expression operators. Below is a table of expressions supported by `lex`.

Regular Expression	Pattern Matched
c	the character *c* where *c* is not a special character.
\c	the character *c* where *c* is any character.
"c"	the character *c* where *c* is any character except \.
^	the beginning of the line being compared.
$	the end of the line being compared.
.	any character in the input but newline
[s]	any character in the set *s* where *s* is a sequence of characters and/or a range of characters, *c-c*.
[^s]	any character not in the set *s*, where *s* is defined as above.
r*	zero or more successive occurrences of the regular expression *r*.
r+	one or more successive occurrences of the regular expression *r*.
r?	zero or one occurrence of the regular expression *r*.
(r)	the regular expression *r*. (Grouping)
rx	the occurrence of regular expression *r* followed by the occurrence of regular expression *x*. (Concatenation)
r|x	the occurrence of regular expression *r* or the occurrence of regular expression *x*.
<s>r	the occurrence of regular expression *r* only when the program is in start condition (state) *s*.
r/x	the occurrence of regular expression *r* only if it is followed by the occurence of regular expression *x*. (Note this is *r* in the context of *x* and only *r* is matched.)
{S}	the substitution of *S* from the *Definitions* section.
r{m,n}	*m* through *n* successive occurrences of the regular expression *r*.

The notation *r{m,n}* in a rule indicates between *m* and *n* instances of regular expression *r*. It has higher precedence than |, but lower than *, ?, +, and concatenation.

The character ^ at the beginning of an expression permits a successful match only immediately after a new-line, and the character **$** at the end of an expression requires a trailing new-line.

The character **/** in an expression indicates trailing context; only the part of the expression up to the slash is returned in **yytext**, but the remainder of the expression must follow in the input stream. An operator character may be used as an ordinary symbol if it is within double quotes, "c"; preceded by \, \c; or is within square brackets, [c]. Two operators have special meaning when used within square brackets. A - denotes a range, [c-c], unless it is just after the open bracket or before the closing bracket, [-c] or [c-] in which case it has no special meaning. When used within brackets, ^ has the meaning "complement of" if it immediately follows the open bracket, [^c], elsewhere between brackets, [c^], it stands for the ordinary character ^. The special meaning of the \ operator can be escaped *only* by preceding it with another \.

Actions

The default action when a string in the input to a **lex.yy.c** program is *not matched* by any expression is to copy the string to the output. Because the default behavior of a program generated by `lex` is to read the input and copy it to the output, a minimal `lex` source program that has just %% will generate a **C** program that simply copies the input to the output unchanged. A null **C** statement, the statement ';', may be specified as an action in a rule. Any string in the *lex.yy.c* input that matches the pattern portion of such a rule, will be effectively ignored or skipped.

Three special actions are available, **|**, **REJECT,** and **ECHO.** The action | means that the action for the next rule is the action for this rule. **ECHO** prints the string *yytext* on the output. Normally only a single expression is matched by a given string in the input. REJECT means "continue to the next expression that matches the current input" and causes whatever rule was second choice after the current rule to be executed for the same input. Thus, it allows multiple rules to be matched and executed for one input string or overlapping input strings. For example, given the expressions xyz and yz and the input xyz, normally only one pattern, xyz would match and the next attempted match would start at z. If the last action in the xyz rule is REJECT, both this rule and the yz rule would be executed.

The `lex` command provides several routines that can be used in the lex source program: **yymore()**, **yyless(n)**, **input()**, **output(c)**, and **unput(c)**.

The function **yymore()** may be called to indicate that the next input string recognized is to be concatenated onto the end of the current string in **yytext** rather than overwriting it in **yytext**.

yyless(n) returns to the input some of the characters matched by the currently successful expression. The argument "n" indicates the number of initial characters in **yytext** to be retained; the remaining trailing characters in **yytext** are returned to the input.

input() returns the next character from the input. **input** returns 0 on end of file.

unput(c) pushes the character c back onto the input stream to be read later by **input()**.

output(c) writes the character **c** on the output.

To perform custom processing when the end of input is reached, a user may supply their own **yywrap()** function. **yywrap()** is called whenever **lex.yy.c** reaches an end-of-file. If **yywrap()** returns a one, **lex.yy.c** continues with the normal wrap-up on end of input. The default **yywrap()** always returns a one. If the user wants **lex.yy.c** to continue processing with another source of input, then a **yywrap()** must be supplied that arranges for the new input and returns a zero. These routines may be redefined by the user.

The external names generated by `lex` all begin with the prefix **yy** or **YY.**

The program generated by *lex* is named **yylex()**; if the user does not supply a main routine, the default **main()** routine calls **yylex()**. If the user supplies a **main()** routine, it should call **yylex()**.

EXAMPLE

```
D      [0-9]
%%
if     printf("IF statement\n");
[a-z]+     printf("tag, value %s\n",yytext);
0{D}+  printf("octal number %s\n",yytext);
{D}+   printf("decimal number %s\n",yytext);
"++"   printf("unary op\n");
"+"    printf("binary op\n");
"/*"   {   loop:
           while (input() != '*');
           switch (input())
               {
               case '/': break;
               case '*': unput('*');
               default: go to loop;
               }
           }
```

FILES

`lex.yy.c.`

SEE ALSO

CC(SD_CMD), YACC(SD_CMD).

USAGE

General.

NAME

lint — a C program checker

SYNOPSIS

`lint` [*options*] *file* ...

DESCRIPTION

The command `lint` attempts to detect features of the C program files that are likely to be bugs, non-portable, or wasteful. It also checks type usage more strictly than the compilers. Among the things that are currently detected are unreachable statements, loops not entered at the top, automatic variables declared and not used, and logical expressions whose value is constant. Moreover, the usage of functions is checked to find functions that return values in some places and not in others, functions called with varying numbers or types of arguments, and functions whose values are not used or whose values are used but none returned.

The options are described below. Note, however, that the options `-o` and `-o` are new to UNIX System V Release 2.0.

Arguments whose names end with `.c` are taken to be C source files. The following behavior is new in UNIX System V Release 2.0.

Arguments whose names end with `.ln` are taken to be the result of an earlier invocation of `lint` with either the `-c` or the `-o` option used. The `.ln` files are analogous to `.o` (object) files that are produced by the `cc` command when given a `.c` file as input.

Files with other suffixes are warned about and ignored.

The command `lint` will take all the `.c`, `.ln`, files, and `llib-l`*x*(specifed by `-l`*x*), and process them in their command line order. By default, `lint` appends the standard C lint library to the end of the list of files. However, if the `-p` option is used, the portable C lint library (`llib-port.ln`) is appended instead. When the `-c` option is not used, the second pass of `lint` checks this list of files for mutual compatibility. When the `-c` option is used, the `.ln` files and the lint libraries are ignored.

Any number of `lint` options may be used, in any order, intermixed with file-name arguments. The following options are used to suppress certain kinds of complaints:

`-a` Suppress complaints about assignments of long values to variables that are not long.

`-b` Suppress complaints about `break` statements that cannot be reached. (Programs produced by `lex` or `yacc` will often result in many such complaints).

`-h` Do not apply heuristic tests that attempt to intuit bugs, improve style, and reduce waste.

`-u` Suppress complaints about functions and external variables used and not defined, or defined and not used. (This option is suitable for running `lint` on a subset of files of a larger program).

`-v` Suppress complaints about unused arguments in functions.

`-x` Do not report variables referred to by external declarations but never used.

The following arguments alter `lint`'s behavior:

`-l`*x* Include additional lint library `x` (e.g., `-lm` for the math library).

`-n` Do not check compatibility against either the standard or the portable lint library.

`-p` Attempt to check portability.

`-c` Cause `lint` to produce a `.ln` file for every `.c` file on the command line. These `.ln` files are the product of `lint`'s first pass only, and are not checked for inter-function compatibility.

`-o` *lib* Cause `lint` to create a lint library with the name `lib`. The `-c` option nullifies any use of the `-o` option. The lint library produced is the input that is given to `lint`'s second pass. The `-o` option simply causes this file to be saved in the named lint library. To produce the lint library without extraneous messages, use of the `-x` option is suggested. The `-v` option is useful if the source file(s) for the lint library are just external interfaces. These option settings are also available through the use of "lint comments" (see below).

The `-D`, `-U`, and `-I` options of `cpp` [see CPP(SD_CMD)] are also recognized as separate arguments.

(The following is new to UNIX System V Release 2.0.) The `-g` and `-O` options of `cc` are also recognized as separate arguments. These options are ignored, but, by recognizing these options, `lint`'s behavior is closer to that of the `cc` command. Other options are warned about and ignored. The preprocessor symbol "lint" is defined to allow certain questionable code to be altered or removed for `lint`. Therefore, the symbol "lint" should be thought of as a reserved word for all code that is planned to be checked by `lint`.

Certain conventional comments in the C source will change the behavior of `lint`:

/*NOTREACHED*/
: at appropriate points stops comments about unreachable code. (This comment is typically placed just after calls to functions like `exit`.

/*VARARGS*n**/
: suppresses the usual checking for variable numbers of arguments in the following function declaration. The data types of the first *n*

arguments are checked; a missing *n* is taken to be 0.

/*ARGSUSED*/
: turns on the `-v` option for the next function.

/*LINTLIBRARY*/
: at the beginning of a file shuts off complaints about unused functions and function arguments in this file. This is equivalent to using the `-v` and `-x` options.

The command `lint` produces its first output on a per-source-file basis. Complaints regarding included files are collected and printed after all source files have been processed. Finally, if the `-c` option is not used, information gathered from all input files is collected and checked for consistency. At this point, if it is not clear whether a complaint stems from a given source file or from one of its included files, the source file name will be printed followed by a question mark.

The behavior of the `-c` and the `-o` options allows for incremental use of `lint` on a set of C source files. Generally, `lint` is invoked once for each source file with the `-c` option. Each of these invocations produces a `.ln` file which corresponds to the `.c` file, and prints all messages that are about just that source file. After all the source files have been separately run through `lint`, it is invoked once more (without the `-c` option), listing all the `.ln` files with the needed `-l`*x* options. This will print all the inter-file inconsistencies. This scheme works well with `make`; it allows `make` to be used to `lint` only the source files that have been modified since the last time the set of source files were checked by `lint`.

SEE ALSO

CC(SD_CMD), CPP(SD_CMD), MAKE(SD_CMD).

USAGE

General.

NAME

lorder — find ordering relation for an object library

SYNOPSIS

`lorder` *file* ...

DESCRIPTION

The input is one or more object or library archive *files* [see AR(BU_CMD)]. The standard output is a list of pairs of object file names, meaning that the first file of the pair refers to external identifiers defined in the second. The output may be processed by `tsort` to find an ordering of a library suitable for one-pass access by the link editor `ld` Note that `ld` is capable of multiple passes over an archive in the portable archive format and does not require that `lorder` be used when building an archive. The usage of the `lorder` command may, however, allow for a slightly more efficient access of the archive during the link edit process.

EXAMPLE

The following example builds a new library from existing `.o` files.

```
ar -cr library `lorder *.o | tsort`
```

SEE ALSO

AR(BU_CMD), LD(SD_CMD), TSORT(SD_CMD).

USAGE

General.

NAME

m4 — macro processor

SYNOPSIS

`m4` [*options*] [*file* ...]

DESCRIPTION

The command `m4` is a macro processor intended as a front end for Ratfor, C, and other languages. Each of the argument files is processed in order; if there are no files, or if a file name is `-`, the standard input is read. The processed text is written on the standard output.

The options and their effects are as follows:

`-s` Enable line sync output for the C preprocessor (i.e., `#line` directives).

This option must appear before any file names and before the following options.

`-D`*name*[`=`*val*]
Defines *name* to *val* or to null in *val*'s absence.

`-U`*name* undefines *name*.

Macro calls have the form:

```
name(arg1,arg2, ..., argn)
```

The `(` must immediately follow the name of the macro. If the name of a defined macro is not followed by a `(`, it is deemed to be a call of that macro with no arguments. Potential macro names consist of alphabetic letters, digits, and underscore `_`, where the first character is not a digit.

Leading unquoted blanks, tabs, and new-lines are ignored while collecting arguments. Left and right single quotes are used to quote strings. The value of a quoted string is the string stripped of the quotes.

When a macro name is recognized, its arguments are collected by searching for a matching right parenthesis. If fewer arguments are supplied than are in the macro definition, the trailing arguments are taken to be null. Macro evaluation proceeds normally during the collection of the arguments, and any commas or right parentheses which happen to turn up within the value of a nested call are as effective as those in the original input text. After argument collection, the value of the macro is pushed back onto the input stream and rescanned.

The command `m4` makes available the following built-in macros. They may be redefined, but once this is done the original meaning is lost. Their values are null unless otherwise stated.

`define` the second argument is installed as the value of the macro whose name is the first argument. Each occurrence of `$`*n* in the replacement text, where *n* is a digit, is replaced by the *n*-th argument. Argument 0 is the name of the macro; missing arguments are replaced by the null string; **$#** is replaced by the number of arguments; **$*** is replaced by a list of all the arguments separated by commas; **$@** is like **$***, but each argument is quoted (with the current quotes).

`undefine` removes the definition of the macro named in its argument.

`defn` returns the quoted definition of its argument(s). It is useful for renaming macros, especially built-ins.

`pushdef` like *define,* but saves any previous definition.

`popdef` removes current definition of its argument(s), exposing the previous one, if any.

`ifdef` if the first argument is defined, the value is the second argument, otherwise the third. If there is no third argument, the value is null.

`shift` returns all but its first argument. The other arguments are quoted and pushed back with commas in between. The quoting nullifies the effect of the extra scan that will subsequently be performed.

`changequote` change quote symbols to the first and second arguments. The symbols may be up to five characters long. the command `changequote` without arguments restores the original values (i.e., `').

`changecom` change left and right comment markers from the default # and new-line. With no arguments, the comment mechanism is effectively disabled. With one argument, the left marker becomes the argument and the right marker becomes new-line. With two arguments, both markers are affected. Comment markers may be up to five characters long.

`divert` The command `m4` maintains 10 output streams, numbered 0-9. The final output is the concatenation of the streams in numerical order; initially stream 0 is the current stream. The `divert` macro changes the current output stream to its (digit-string) argument. Output diverted to a stream other than 0 through 9 is discarded.

`undivert` causes immediate output of text from diversions named as arguments, or all diversions if no argument. Text may be undiverted into another diversion. Undiverting discards the diverted text.

`divnum` returns the value of the current output stream.

`dnl` reads and discards characters up to and including the next new-line.

`ifelse` has three or more arguments. If the first argument is the same string as the second, then the value is the third argument. If not, and if there are more than four arguments, the process is repeated with arguments 4, 5, 6 and 7. Otherwise, the value is either the fourth string, or, if it is not present, null.

`incr` returns the value of its argument incremented by 1. The value of the argument is calculated by interpreting an initial digit-string as a decimal number.

`decr` returns the value of its argument decremented by 1.

`eval` evaluates its argument as an arithmetic expression, using 32-bit arithmetic. Operators include +, −, *, /, %, ^ (exponentiation), bitwise &, |, ^, and ; relationals; parentheses. Octal and hex numbers may be specified as in C. The second argument specifies the radix for the result; the default is 10. The third argument may be used to specify the minimum number of digits in the result.

`len` returns the number of characters in its argument.

`index` returns the position in its first argument where the second argument begins (zero origin), or −1 if the second argument does not occur.

`substr` returns a substring of its first argument. The second argument is a zero origin number selecting the first character; the third argument indicates the length of the substring. A missing third argument is taken to be large enough to extend to the end of the first string.

`translit` transliterates the characters in its first argument from the set given by the second argument to the set given by the third. No abbreviations are permitted.

`include` returns the contents of the file named in the argument.

`sinclude` is identical to `include`, except that it says nothing if the file is inaccessible.

`syscmd` executes the system command given in the first argument. No value is returned.

`sysval` is the return code from the last call to `syscmd`.

`maketemp` fills in a string of XXXXX in its argument with the current process ID.

`m4exit` causes immediate exit from `m4`. Argument 1, if given, is the exit code; the default is 0.

`m4wrap` argument 1 will be pushed back at final EOF; example: m4wrap(`cleanup()')

`errprint` prints its argument on the diagnostic output file.

`dumpdef` prints current names and definitions, for the named items, or for all if no arguments are given.

`traceon` with no arguments, turns on tracing for all macros (including built-ins). Otherwise, turns on tracing for named macros.

`traceoff` turns off trace globally and for any macros specified. Macros specifically traced by `traceon` can be untraced only by specific calls to `traceoff`.

SEE ALSO

CC(SD_CMD), CPP(SD_CMD).

USAGE

General.

NAME

make — maintain, update, and regenerate groups of programs

SYNOPSIS

`make` **[**`-f` *makefile***] [-p] [-i] [-k] [-s] [-r] [-n] [-e] [-t] [-q]** **[***name* ...**]**

DESCRIPTION

The options are interpreted as follows:

`-f` *makefile* — Description file name. The argument *makefile* is assumed to be the name of a description file. A file name of - denotes the standard input.

`-p` — Print out the complete set of macro definitions and target descriptions.

`-i` — Ignore error codes returned by invoked commands. This mode is entered if the fake target name **.IGNORE** appears in the description file.

`-k` — Abandon work on the current entry if it fails, but continue on other branches that do not depend on that entry.

`-s` — Silent mode. Do not print command lines before executing. This mode is also entered if the fake target name **.SILENT** appears in the description file.

`-r` — Do not use the built-in rules.

`-n` — No execute mode. Print commands, but do not execute them. Even lines beginning with an `@` are printed.

`-e` — Environmental variables override assignments within makefiles.

`-t` — Touch the target files (causing them to be up-to-date) rather than issue the usual commands.

`-q` — Question. The `make` command returns a zero or non-zero status code depending on whether the target file is or is not up-to-date.

The following target names may be defined in the *makefile*, and are interpreted as follows:

.DEFAULT — If a file must be made but there are no explicit commands or relevant built-in rules, the commands associated with the name **.DEFAULT** are used if it exists.

.PRECIOUS — Dependents of this target will not be removed when quit or interrupt are hit.

.SILENT — Same effect as the `-s` option.

.IGNORE — Same effect as the `-i` option.

The command m executes commands in *makefile* to update one or more target names. The argument *name* is typically a program. If no `-f` option is present, *makefile*, *Makefile*, and the SCCS files `s.makefile`, and `s.Makefile` are tried in order. If *makefile* is `-`, the standard input is used. More than one `-f`*makefile* argument pair may appear.

The command `make` updates a target only if its dependents are newer than the target. All prerequisite files of a target are added recursively to the list of targets. Missing files are deemed to be out-of-date.

The argument *makefile* contains a sequence of entries that specify dependencies. The first line of an entry is a blank-separated, non-null list of targets, then a `:`, then a (possibly null) list of prerequisite files or dependencies. Text following a `;` and all following lines that begin with a tab are commands to be executed to update the target. The first line that does not begin with a tab or # begins a new dependency or macro definition. Commands may be continued across lines with the <backslash><new-line> sequence. Everything printed by make (except the initial tab) is passed directly to the command interpreter as is.

The symbols # and new-line surround comments.

The following *makefile* says that `pgm` depends on two files `a.o` and `b.o`, and that they in turn depend on their corresponding source files (`a.c` and `b.c`) and a common file `incl.h`:

```
pgm:  a.o  b.o  cc  a.o  b.o  -o  pgm
a.o:  incl.h  a.c  cc  -c  a.c
b.o:  incl.h  b.c  cc  -c  b.c
```

Command lines are executed one at a time. The first one or two characters in a command can be the following: `-`, `@`, `-@`, or `@-`. If `@` is present, printing of the command is suppressed. If `-` is present, `make` ignores an error. A line is printed when it is executed unless the `-s` option is present, or the entry **.SILENT:** is in *makefile,* or unless the initial character sequence contains a `@`. The `-n` option specifies printing without execution; however, if the command line has the string `$(MAKE)` in it, the line is always executed (see discussion of the `MAKEFLAGS` macro under **Environment**). The `-t` (touch) option updates the modified date of a file without executing any commands.

Commands returning non-zero status normally terminate `make`. If the `-i` option is present, or the entry **.IGNORE:** appears in *makefile,* or the initial character sequence of the command contains `-`, the error is ignored. If the `-k` option is present, work is abandoned on the current entry, but continues on other branches that do not depend on that entry.

Interrupt and quit cause the target to be deleted unless the target is a dependent of the special name **.PRECIOUS**.

Environment

The environment is read by `make`. All variables are assumed to be macro definitions and processed as such. The environmental variables are processed before any makefile and after the internal rules; thus, macro assignments in a makefile override environmental variables. The `-e` option causes the environment to override the macro assignments in a makefile.

The environmental variable `MAKEFLAGS` is processed by `make` as containing any legal input option (except `-f` and `-p`) defined for the command line. Further, upon invocation, `make` "invents" the variable if it is not in the environment, puts the current options into it, and passes it on to invocations of commands. Thus, `MAKEFLAGS` always contains the current input options. This proves very useful for "super-makes". In fact, as noted above, when the `-n` option is used, the command `$(MAKE)` is executed anyway; hence, one can perform a `make -n` recursively on a whole software system to see what would have been executed. This is because the `-n` is put in `MAKEFLAGS` and passed to further invocations of `$(MAKE)`. This is one way of debugging all of the makefiles for a software project without actually doing anything.

Macros

Entries of the form `string1 = string2` are macro definitions. The macro `string2` is defined as all characters up to a comment character or an unescaped new-line. Subsequent appearances of `$(string1`[:*subst1*=[*subst2*]]) are replaced by `string2`. The parentheses are optional if a single character macro name is used and there is no substitute sequence. The optional `:subst1=`*subst2* is a substitute sequence. If it is specified, all non-overlapping occurrences of `subst1` in the named macro are replaced by `subst2`. Strings (for the purposes of this type of substitution) are delimited by blanks, tabs, new-line characters, and beginnings of lines. An example of the use of the substitute sequence is shown under **Libraries.**

Internal Macros

There are five internally maintained macros which are useful for writing rules for building targets.

$*** The macro **$* stands for the file name part of the current dependent with the suffix deleted. It is evaluated only for inference rules.

$@** The **$@ macro stands for the full target name of the current target. It is evaluated only for explicitly named dependencies.

$<** The **$< macro is only evaluated for inference rules or the **.DEFAULT** rule. It is the module which is out-of-date with respect to the target (i.e., the "manufactured" dependent file name). Thus, in the **.c.o** rule, the **$<** macro would evaluate to the `.c` file. An example for making optimized `.o` files from `.c` files is:

```
.c.o:
        cc -c -O $*.c
```

or:

```
.c.o:
        cc -c -O $<
```

$? The `$?` macro is evaluated when explicit rules from the makefile are evaluated. It is the list of prerequisites that are out-of-date with respect to the target; essentially, those modules which must be rebuilt.

$% The `$%` macro is only evaluated when the target is an archive library member of the form `lib(file.o)`. In this case, `$@` evaluates to `lib` and `$%` evaluates to the library member, `file.o`.

Four of the five macros can have alternative forms. When an upper case `D` or **F** is appended to any of the four macros, the meaning is changed to "directory part" for `D` and "file part" for `F`. Thus, `$(@D)` refers to the directory part of the string `$@`. If there is no directory part, `./` is generated. The only macro excluded from this alternative form is `$?`.

Suffixes

Certain names (for instance, those ending with `.o`) have inferable prerequisites such as `.c`, `.s`, etc. If no update commands for such a file appear in *makefile,* and if an inferable prerequisite exists, that prerequisite is compiled to make the target. In this case, `make` has inference rules which allow building files from other files by examining the suffixes and determining an appropriate inference rule to use. Inference rules in the makefile override the default rules.

The internal rules for `make` are compiled into the `make` program. To print out the rules compiled into the `make` program, the following command is used:

```
make -fp - 2>/dev/null </dev/null
```

A tilde in the above rules refers to an SCCS file. Thus, the rule **.c .o** would transform an SCCS C source file into an object file (**.o**). Because the **s.** of the SCCS files is a prefix, it is incompatible with `make`'s suffix point of view. Hence, the tilde is a way of changing any file reference into an SCCS file reference.

A rule with only one suffix (i.e., **.c:**) is the definition of how to build *x* from *x***.c**. In effect, the other suffix is null. This is useful for building targets from only one source file (e.g., command scripts, simple C programs).

Additional suffixes are given as the dependency list for **.SUFFIXES**. Order is significant; the first possible name for which both a file and a rule exist is inferred as a prerequisite.

Here again, the above command for printing the internal rules will display the list of suffixes implemented on the current machine. Multiple suffix lists accumulate; **.SUFFIXES:** with no dependencies clears the list of suffixes.

Inference Rules

The first example can be done more briefly.

```
pgm: a.o b.o
        cc a.o b.o -o pgm
a.o b.o: incl.h
```

This is because `make` has a set of internal rules for building files. The user may add rules to this list by simply putting them in the *makefile*.

Certain macros are used by the default inference rules to permit the inclusion of optional matter in any resulting commands. For example, `BCFLAGS`, `BLFLAGS`, and `BYFLAGS` are used for compiler options to `cc`, `lex`, and `yacc`, respectively. Again, the previous method for examining the current rules is recommended.

The inference of prerequisites can be controlled. The rule to create a file with suffix `.o` from a file with suffix `.c` is specified as an entry with **.c.o:** as the target and no dependents. Commands associated with the target define the rule for making a **.o** file from a **.c** file. Any target that has no slashes in it and starts with a dot is identified as a rule and not a true target.

Libraries

If a target or dependency name contains parentheses, it is assumed to be an archive library, the string within parentheses referring to a member within the library. Thus `lib(file.o)` and **$(LIB)(file.o)** both refer to an archive library which contains **file.o**. (This assumes the `LIB` macro has been previously defined.) The expression **$(LIB)(file1.o file2.o)** is not legal. Rules pertaining to archive libraries have the form **.*XX*.a** where the *XX* is the suffix from which the archive member is to be made. The most common use of the archive interface follows. Here, we assume the source files are all C type source:

```
lib:  lib(file1.o) lib(file2.o) lib(file3.o)
      @echo lib is now up-to-date
.c.a:
      $(CC) -c $(CFLAGS) $<
      ar rv $@ $*.o
      rm -f $*.o
```

In fact, the **.c.a** rule listed above is built into `make` and is unnecessary in this example. A more interesting, but more limited example of an archive library maintenance construction follows:

```
lib:  lib(file1.o) lib(file2.o) lib(file3.o)
      $(CC) -c $(CFLAGS) $(?:.o=.c)
      ar rv lib $?
      rm $?  @echo lib is now up-to-date
.c.a:;
```

Here the substitution mode of the macro expansions is used. The **$?** list is defined to be the set of object file names (inside **lib**) whose C source files are out-of-date. The substitution mode translates the **.o** to **.c**. Note also, the disabling of the **.c.a:** rule, which would have created each object file, one by one. This particular construct speeds up archive library maintenance considerably. This type of construct becomes very cumbersome if the archive library contains a mix of assembly programs and C programs.

FILES

`[Mm]akefile and s.[Mm]akefile`

SEE ALSO

CC(SD_CMD), LEX(SD_CMD), SH(BU_CMD), YACC(SD_CMD).

USAGE

General.

The characters **=** : @ in file names may give trouble.

NAME

nm – print name list of common object file

SYNOPSIS

`nm` [*options*] *file* ...

DESCRIPTION

The `nm` command displays the symbol table of each common object file *file*. The argument *file* may be a relocatable or absolute common object file; or it may be an archive of relocatable or absolute common object files. For each symbol, at least the following information will be printed:

Name The name of the symbol.

Value Its value expressed as an offset or an address depending on its storage class.

Size Its size in bytes, if available.

The output of `nm` may be controlled using the following options:

`-o` Print the value and size of a symbol in octal instead of decimal.

`-x` Print the value and size of a symbol in hexadecimal instead of decimal.

`-e` Print only external and static symbols.

`-f` Produce full output. Print redundant symbols (.text, .data and .bss), normally suppressed.

`-u` Print undefined symbols only.

`-V` Print the version of the nm command executing on the standard error output.

SEE ALSO

CC(SD_CMD), LD(SD_CMD).

USAGE

General.

NAME

prof — display profile data

SYNOPSIS

`prof` [`−tcan`] [**−ox**] [**−g**] [**−z**] [**−m** *mdata*] [*prog*]

DESCRIPTION

The command `prof` interprets a profile file produced by the `monitor` routine. The symbol table in the object file *prog* (`a.out` by default) is read and correlated with a profile file (`mon.out` by default). For each external text symbol the percentage of time spent executing between the address of that symbol and the address of the next is printed, together with the number of times that function was called and the average number of milliseconds per call.

The mutually exclusive options `t`, `c`, `a`, and `n` determine the type of sorting of the output lines:

`−t` Sort by decreasing percentage of total time (default).

`−c` Sort by decreasing number of calls.

`−a` Sort by increasing symbol address.

`−n` Sort lexically by symbol name.

The mutually exclusive options `o` and `x` specify the printing of the address of each symbol monitored:

`−o` Print each symbol address (in octal) along with the symbol name.

`−x` Print each symbol address (in hexadecimal) along with the symbol name.

The following options may be used in any combination:

`−g` Include non-global symbols (static functions).

`−z` Include all symbols in the profile range, even if associated with zero number of calls and zero time.

`−m` *mdata*
Use file *mdata* instead of `mon.out` as the input profile file.

A program creates a profile file if it has been loaded with the `−p` option of `cc` This option to the `cc` command arranges for calls to `monitor` at the beginning and end of execution. It is the call to `monitor` at the end of execution that causes a profile file to be written. The number of calls to a function is tallied if the `−p` option was used when the file containing the function was compiled.

The name of the file created by a profiled program is controlled by the environmental variable `PROFDIR`. If `PROFDIR` is not set, "mon.out" is produced in the directory current when the program terminates. If *PROFDIR*=`string`, "*string/pid.progname*" is produced, where *progname* consists of argv[0] with any path prefix removed, and *pid* is the program's process ID. If PROFDIR is set, but null, no profiling output is produced.

A single function may be split into subfunctions for profiling by means of the MARK macro [see MARK(SD_LIB)].

FILES

mon.out for profile
a.out for namelist

SEE ALSO

CC(SD_CMD), EXIT(BA_SYS), PROFIL(KE_SYS), MONITOR(SD_LIB), MARK(SD_LIB).

USAGE

General.

The times reported in successive identical runs may show variances, because of varying cache-hit ratios due to sharing of the cache with other processes. Even if a program seems to be the only one using the machine, hidden background or asynchronous processes may blur the data.

In rare cases, the clock ticks initiating recording of the program counter may "beat" with loops in a program, grossly distorting measurements. Call counts are always recorded precisely, however.

Only programs that call exit or return from main are guaranteed to produce a profile file, unless a final call to monitor is explicitly coded.

NAME

prs — print an SCCS file

SYNOPSIS

`prs` [*options*] *files*

DESCRIPTION

The command `prs` prints, on the standard output, parts or all of an SCCS file in a user-supplied format. If a directory is named, `prs` behaves as though each file in the directory were specified as a named file, except that non-SCCS files (last component of the path name does not begin with **s.**), and unreadable files are silently ignored. If a name of `-` is given, the standard input is read; each line of the standard input is taken to be the name of an SCCS file or directory to be processed; non-SCCS files and unreadable files are silently ignored.

Arguments to `prs`, which may appear in any order, consist of options, and file names.

All the described options apply independently to each named file. (Note that the `-c` option is new to **UNIX** System V Release 2.0.)

`-d`[*dataspec*] Used to specify the output data specification. The *dataspec* is a string consisting of SCCS file *data keywords* (see **DATA KEYWORDS**) interspersed with optional user supplied text. to specify the SCCS identification string of a delta for which information is desired. If no *SID* is specified, the *SID* of the most recently created delta is assumed.

`-r`*SID* Requests information for all deltas created *earlier* than and including the delta designated via the `-r` keyletter or the date given by the `-c` option.

`-l` Requests information for all deltas created *later* than and including the delta designated via the `-r` keyletter or the date given by the `-c` option.

`-c`[*date-time*] The cutoff *date-time* is in the form:

YY[MM[DD[HH[MM[SS]]]]]

Units omitted from the date-time default to their maximum possible values; for example, `-c7502` is equivalent to `-c750228235959`. Any number of non-numeric characters may separate the various 2-digit pieces of the *cutoff* date in the form: `"-c77/2/2 9:22:25"`.

`-a` Requests printing of information for both removed, i.e., delta type = *R*, [see **RMDEL(SD_CMD)**] and existing, i.e., delta type = *D*, deltas. If the `-a` keyletter is not specified, information for existing deltas only is provided.

DATA KEYWORDS

Data keywords specify which parts of an SCCS file are to be retrieved and output. All parts of an SCCS file have an associated data keyword. There is no limit on the number of times a data keyword may appear in a *dataspec*.

The information printed by `prs` consists of: (1) the user-supplied text; and (2) appropriate values (extracted from the SCCS file) substituted for the recognized data keywords in the order of appearance in the *dataspec*. The format of a data keyword value is either *Simple* (S), in which keyword substitution is direct, or *Multi-line* (M), in which keyword substitution is followed by a carriage return.

User-supplied text is any text other than recognized data keywords. A tab is specified by **\t** and carriage return/new-line is specified by **\n**. The default data keywords are:

":Dt:\t:DL:**\nMRs:**\n:MR:COMMENTS:\n:C:"

SCCS Files Data Keywords

Keyword	*Data Item*	*File Section*	*Value*	*Format*
:Dt:	Delta information	Delta Table	See below*	S
:DL:	Delta line statistics	"	:Li:/:Ld:/:Lu:	S
:Li:	Lines inserted by Delta	"	nnnnn	S
:Ld:	Lines deleted by Delta	"	nnnnn	S
:Lu:	Lines unchanged by Delta	"	nnnnn	S
:DT:	Delta type	"	*D* or *R*	S
:I:	SCCS ID string (SID)	"	:R:.:L:.:B:.:S:	S
:R:	Release number	"	nnnn	S
:L:	Level number	"	nnnn	S
:B:	Branch number	"	nnnn	S
:S:	Sequence number	"	nnnn	S
:D:	Date Delta created	"	:Dy:/:Dm:/:Dd:	S
:Dy:	Year Delta created	"	nn	S
:Dm:	Month Delta created	"	nn	S
:Dd:	Day Delta created	"	nn	S
:T:	Time Delta created	"	:Th:::Tm:::Ts:	S
:Th:	Hour Delta created	"	nn	S
:Tm:	Minutes Delta created	"	nn	S
:Ts:	Seconds Delta created	"	nn	S
:P:	Programmer who created Delta	"	logname	S
:DS:	Delta sequence number	"	nnnn	S
:DP:	Predecessor Delta seq-no.	"	nnnn	S
:DI:	Seq-no. of deltas incl., excl., ignored	"	:Dn:/:Dx:/:Dg:	S
:Dn:	Deltas included (seq #)	"	:DS: :DS:...	S
:Dx:	Deltas excluded (seq #)	"	:DS: :DS:...	S
:Dg:	Deltas ignored (seq #)	"	:DS: :DS:...	S

:MR:	MR numbers for delta	"	text	M
:C:	Comments for delta	"	text	M
:UN:	User names	User Names	text	M
:FL:	Flag list	Flags	text	M
:Y:	Module type flag	"	text	S
:MF:	MR validation flag	"	*yes* or *no*	S
:MP:	MR validation pgm name	"	text	S
:KF:	Keyword error/warning flag	"	*yes* or *no*	S
:KV:	Keyword validation string	"	text	S
:BF:	Branch flag	"	*yes* or *no*	S
:J:	Joint edit flag	"	*yes* or *no*	S
:LK:	Locked releases	"	:R:...	S
:Q:	User-defined keyword	"	text	S
:M:	Module name	"	text	S
:FB:	Floor boundary	"	:R:	S
:CB:	Ceiling boundary	"	:R:	S
:Ds:	Default SID	"	:I:	S
:ND:	Null delta flag	"	*yes* or *no*	S
:FD:	File descriptive text	Comments	text	M
:BD:	Body	Body	text	M
:GB:	Gotten body	"	text	M
:W:	A form of *what*(SD_CMD) string	N/A	:Z::M:\t:I:	S
:A:	A form of *what*(SD_CMD) string	N/A	:Z::Y: :M: :I::Z:	S
:Z:	*what*(SD_CMD) string delimiter	N/A	@(#)	S
:F:	SCCS file name	N/A	text	S
:PN:	SCCS file path name	N/A	text	S

* :Dt: = :DT: :I: :D: :T: :P: :DS: :DP:

EXAMPLES

```
prs -d"Users and/or user IDs for :F: are:\n:UN:" s.file
```

may produce on the standard output:

```
Users and/or user IDs for s.file are:
xyz
131
abc
```

```
prs -d"Newest delta for pgm :M: : :I: Created :D: By :P:" -r
s.file
```

may produce on the standard output:

```
Newest delta for pgm main.c: 3.7 Created 77/12/1 By cas
```

As a *special case:*

```
prs s.file
```

may produce on the standard output:

```
D 1.1 77/12/1 00:00:00 cas 1 000000/00000/00000
MRs:
bl78-12345
bl79-54321
COMMENTS:
this is the comment line for s.file initial delta
```

for each delta table entry of the "D" type. The only keyletter argument allowed to be used with the *special case* is the **-a** keyletter.

SEE ALSO

ADMIN(SD_CMD), DELTA(SD_CMD), GET(SD_CMD), WHAT(SD_CMD).

USAGE

General.

NAME

rmdel — remove a delta from an SCCS file

SYNOPSIS

`rmdel -r`

DESCRIPTION

The command `rmdel` removes the delta specified by the *SID* from each named SCCS file. The delta to be removed must be the newest (most recent) delta in its branch in the delta chain of each named SCCS file. In addition, the *SID* specified must **not** be that of a version being edited for the purpose of making a delta (i.e., if a *p-file* [see GET(SD_CMD)] exists for the named SCCS file, the *SID* specified must **not** appear in any entry of the *p-file*).

If a directory is named, `rmdel` behaves as though each file in the directory were specified as a named file, except that non-SCCS files (last component of the path name does not begin with **s.**) and unreadable files are silently ignored. If a name of — is given, the standard input is read; each line of the standard input is taken to be the name of an SCCS file to be processed; non-SCCS files and unreadable files are silently ignored.

The restrictions on removal of a delta are: (1) the user who made a delta can remove it; (2) the owner of the file and directory can remove a delta.

SEE ALSO

DELTA(SD_CMD), GET(SD_CMD), PRS(SD_CMD).

USAGE

General.

NAME

sact — print current SCCS file editing activity

SYNOPSIS

`sact` *files*

DESCRIPTION

The command `sact` informs the user of any impending deltas to a named SCCS file. This situation occurs when `get -e` has been previously executed without a subsequent execution of `delta`. If a directory is named on the command line, `sact` behaves as though each file in the directory were specified as a named file, except that non-SCCS files and unreadable files are silently ignored. If a name of — is given, the standard input is read with each line being taken as the name of an SCCS file to be processed.

The output for each named file consists of five fields separated by spaces.

Field 1 specifies the SID of a delta that currently exists in the SCCS file to which changes will be made to make the new delta.

Field 2 specifies the SID for the new delta to be created.

Field 3 contains the logname of the user who will make the delta (i.e., executed a `get` for editing).

Field 4 contains the date that `get -e` was executed.

Field 5 contains the time that `get -e` was executed.

SEE ALSO

DELTA(SD_CMD), GET(SD_CMD), UNGET(SD_CMD).

USAGE

General.

NAME

sdb — symbolic debugger

SYNOPSIS

`sdb` [*objfile* [*corfile* [*directory-list*]]]

DESCRIPTION

The command `sdb` is a symbolic debugger that can be used with C and Fortran77 (F77) programs. It may be used to examine their object files and core files and to provide a controlled environment for their execution.

The argument *objfile* is an executable program file which has been compiled with the `-g` (debug) option; if it has not been compiled with the `-g` option, or if it is not an executable file, the symbolic capabilities of `sdb` will be limited, but the file can still be examined and the program debugged. The default for *objfile* is `a.out`. The argument *corfile* is assumed to be a core image file produced after executing *objfile;* the default for *corfile* is *core*. The core file need not be present. A − in place of *corfile* will force `sdb` to ignore any core image file. The colon-separated list of directories (*directory-list*) is used to locate the source files used to build *objfile*.

It is useful to know that at any time there is a *current line* and *current file*. If *corfile* exists then they are initially set to the line and file containing the source statement at which the process terminated. Otherwise, they are set to the first line in `main()`. The current line and file may be changed with the source file examination commands.

By default, warnings are provided if the source files used in producing *objfile* cannot be found, or are newer than *objfile*.

Names of variables are written just as they are in C or F77. (The command `sdb` does not truncate names.) Variables local to a procedure may be accessed using the form *procedure:variable*. If no procedure name is given, the procedure containing the current line is used by default.

It is also possible to refer to structure members as *variable.member,* pointers to structure members as *variable−>member* and array elements as *variable*[*number*]. Pointers may be dereferenced by using the form *pointer*[0]. Combinations of these forms may also be used. F77 common variables may be referenced by using the name of the common block instead of the structure name. Blank common variables may be named by the form *.variable*. A number may be used in place of a structure variable name, in which case the number is viewed as the address of the structure, and the template used for the structure is that of the last structure referenced by `sdb`. An unqualified structure variable may also be used with various commands. Generally, `sdb` will interpret a structure as a set of variables. Thus, `sdb` will display the values of all the elements of a structure when it is requested to display a structure. An exception to this interpretation occurs when displaying variable addresses. An entire structure does have an address, and it is this value `sdb` displays, not the addresses of individual elements.

Elements of a multidimensional array may be referenced as *variable*[*number*][*number*]..., or as *variable*[*number,number,...*]. In place of *number*, the form *number;number* may be used to indicate a range of values, * may be used to indicate all legitimate values for that subscript, or subscripts may be omitted entirely if they are the last subscripts and the full range of values is desired. As with structures, `sdb` displays all the values of an array or of the section of an array if trailing subscripts are omitted. It displays only the address of the array itself or of the section specified by the user if subscripts are omitted. A multidimensional parameter in an F77 program cannot be displayed as an array, but it is actually a pointer, whose value is the location of the array. The array itself can be accessed symbolically from the calling function.

A particular instance of a variable on the stack may be referenced by using the form *procedure:variable,number*. All the variations mentioned in naming variables may be used. *Number* is the occurrence of the specified procedure on the stack, counting the top, or most current, as the first. If no procedure is specified, the procedure currently executing is used by default.

It is also possible to specify a variable by its address. All forms of integer constants which are valid in C may be used, so that addresses may be input in decimal, octal or hexadecimal.

Line numbers in the source program are referred to as *file-name:number* or *procedure:number*. In either case the number is relative to the beginning of the file. If no procedure or file name is given, the current file is used by default. If no number is given, the first line of the named procedure or file is used.

While a process is running under `sdb`, all addresses refer to the executing program.

Commands

The commands for examining data in the program are:

`t` Print a stack trace of the terminated or halted program.

`T` Print the top line of the stack trace.

variable/clm
Print the value of *variable* according to length *l* and format *m*. A numeric count *c* indicates that a region of memory, beginning at the address implied by *variable*, is to be displayed. The length specifiers are:

`b` one byte

`h` two bytes (half word)

`l` four bytes (long word)

Legal values for *m* are:

- `c` character
- `d` decimal
- `u` decimal, unsigned
- `o` octal
- `x` hexadecimal
- `s` Assume *variable* is a string pointer and print characters starting at the address pointed to by the variable.
- `a` Print characters starting at the variable's address. This format may not be used with register variables.
- `p` pointer to procedure
- `i` disassemble machine-language instruction with addresses printed numerically and symbolically.

The length specifiers are only effective with the formats `c`, `d`, `u`, `o` and `x`. Any of the specifiers, `c`, `l`, and `m`, may be omitted. If all are omitted, `sdb` choses a length and a format suitable for the variable's type as declared in the program. If `m` is specified, then this format is used for displaying the variable. A length specifier determines the output length of the value to be displayed, sometimes resulting in truncation. A count specifier `c` tells `sdb` to display that many units of memory, beginning at the address of *variable*. The number of bytes in one such unit of memory is determined by the length specifier `l`, or if no length is given, by the size associated with the *variable*. If a count specifier is used for the `s` or `a` command, then that many characters are printed. Otherwise successive characters are printed until either a null byte is reached or 128 characters are printed. The last variable may be redisplayed with the command **./**.

*linenumber***?***lm*
variable:**?***lm*

Print the value at the address from **a.out** or I space given by *linenumber* or *variable* (procedure name), according to the format *lm*. The default format is 'i'.

*variable***=***lm*
*linenumber***=***lm*
*number***=***lm*

Print the address of *variable* or *linenumber*, or the value of *number*, in the format specified by *lm*. If no format is given, then **lx** is used. The last variant of this command provides a convenient way to convert between decimal, octal and hexadecimal.

*variable***!***value*

Set *variable* to the given *value*. The value may be a number, a character constant or a variable. The value must be well defined; expressions which produce more than one value, such as structures, are not allowed. Character constants are denoted **'***character*. Numbers are viewed as integers unless a decimal point or exponent is used. In this case, they are treated as having the type double. Registers are viewed as integers. The *variable* may be an expression which indicates more than one variable, such as an array or structure name. If the address of a variable is given, it is regarded as the address of a variable of type *int*. C conventions are used in any type conversions necessary to perform the indicated assignment.

x
: Print the machine registers and the current machine-language instruction.

The commands for examining source files are:

e *procedure*
e *file-name*
e *directory/*
e *directory file-name*
: The first two forms set the current file to the file containing *procedure* or to *file-name*. The current line is set to the first line in the named procedure or file. Source files are assumed to be in *directory*. The default is the current working directory. The latter two forms change the value of *directory*. If no procedure, file name, or directory is given, the current procedure name and file name are reported.

/regular expression/
: Search forward from the current line for a line containing a string matching *regular expression* as in ED(BU_CMD). The trailing / may be deleted.

?regular expression?
: Search backward from the current line for a line containing a string matching *regular expression* as in ED(BU_CMD). The trailing ? may be deleted.

p
: Print the current line.

z
: Print the current line followed by the next 9 lines. Set the current line to the last line printed.

w
: Window. Print the 10 lines around the current line.

number
: Set the current line to the given line number. Print the new current line.

The commands for controlling the execution of the source program are:

count r *args*
count R
: Run the program with the given arguments. The r command with no arguments reuses the previous arguments to the program while the R command runs the program with no arguments. An argument beginning with < or > causes redirection for the

standard input or output, respectively. If *count* is given, it specifies the number of breakpoints to be ignored.

linenumber `c` *count*
linenumber `C` *count*

Continue after a breakpoint or interrupt. If *count* is given, the program will stop when *count* breakpoints have been encountered. With the `C` command, the signal which caused the program to stop is reactivated; with the `c` command, it is ignored. If a line number is specified then a temporary breakpoint is placed at the line and execution is continued. The breakpoint is deleted when the command finishes. (It may not be possible to set breakpoints in some places, e.g., with shared libraries.)

`s` *count*
`S` *count*

Single step the program through *count* lines. If no count is given then the program is run for one line. `S` is equivalent to `s` except it steps through procedure calls.

`i`
`I`

Single step by one machine-language instruction. With the `I` command, the signal which caused the program to stop is reactivated; with the `i` command, it is ignored.

`k` Kill the program being debugged.

procedure(arg1,arg2,...)
procedure(arg1,arg2,...)/*m*

Execute the named procedure with the given arguments. Arguments can be integer, character or string constants or names of variables accessible from the current procedure. The second form causes the value returned by the procedure to be printed according to format `m`. If no format is given, it defaults to `d`.

linenumber `b` *commands*

Set a breakpoint at the given line. If a procedure name without a line number is given (e.g., "proc:"), a breakpoint is placed at the first line in the procedure even if it was not compiled with the `-g` option. If no *linenumber* is given, a breakpoint is placed at the current line. (It may not be possible to set breakpoints in some places, e.g., with shared libraries.)
If no *commands* are given, execution stops just before the breakpoint and control is returned to `sdb`. Otherwise the *commands* are executed when the breakpoint is encountered and execution continues. Multiple commands are specified by separating them with semicolons. If `k` is used as a command to execute at a breakpoint, control returns to `sdb`, instead of continuing execution.

`B` Print a list of the currently active breakpoints.

linenumber d
Delete a breakpoint at the given line. If no *linenumber* is given then the breakpoints are deleted interactively. Each breakpoint location is printed and a line is read from the standard input. If the line begins with a y or d then the breakpoint is deleted.

D Delete all breakpoints.

l Print the last executed line.

Miscellaneous commands:

!*command*
The command is interpreted by the command interpreter.

new-line
If the previous command printed a source line, then advance the current line by one line and print the new current line. If the previous command displayed a memory location, then display the next memory location.

end-of-file
Scroll. Print the next 10 lines of instructions, source or data depending on which was printed last. (The end-of-file character is usually control-D.)

< *filename*
Read commands from *filename* until the end of file is reached, and then continue to accept commands from standard input. When sdb is told to display a variable by a command in such a file, the variable name is displayed along with the value. This command may not be nested; < may not appear as a command in a file.

" *string*
Print the given string. The C escape sequences of the form *character* are recognized, where *character* is a nonnumeric character.

q Exit the debugger.

FILES

a.out
core

SEE ALSO

CC(SD_CMD), ED(BU_CMD).

USAGE

General.

NAME

size — print section sizes of object files

SYNOPSIS

`size` [−o] [−x] [−V] *files*

DESCRIPTION

The `size` command produces section size information for each section in the loaded object files. The sizes of the loaded sections are printed along with the sum of these sizes. If an archive file is input to the `size` command, the information for all archive members is displayed.

Numbers will be printed in decimal unless either the `−o` or the `−x` option is used, in which case they will be printed in octal or in hexadecimal, respectively.

The `−V` flag will supply the version information on the `size` command.

SEE ALSO

CC(SD_CMD), LD(SD_CMD).

USAGE

General.

NAME

strip — strip symbolic information from an object file

SYNOPSIS

`strip` [−x] [−r] [−V] *file* ...

DESCRIPTION

The `strip` command strips the symbolic information from object files or archives of object files.

The amount of information stripped from the symbol table can be controlled by using any of the following options:

`−x` Do not strip static or external symbol information.

`−r` Do not strip static or external symbol information, or relocation information.

`−V` Print the version of the strip command, on the standard error output.

If there is any relocation information in the object file and any symbol table information is to be stripped, `strip` will report an error and terminate without stripping *file* unless the `−r` flag is used.

SEE ALSO

AR(BU_CMD), CC(SD_CMD), LD(SD_CMD).

USAGE

General.

The purpose of this command is to reduce the file storage overhead taken by the object file.

NAME

time — time a command

SYNOPSIS

`time` *command*

DESCRIPTION

The *command* is executed; after it is complete, `time` prints the elapsed time during the command, the time spent executing system code, and the time spent in execution of the user code. Times are reported in seconds.

The times are printed on standard error.

USAGE

General.

When `time` is used on a multi-processor system the sum of system and user time could be greater than real time.

NAME

tsort — topological sort

SYNOPSIS

`tsort` [*file*]

DESCRIPTION

The command `tsort` produces on the standard output a totally ordered list of items consistent with a partial ordering of items mentioned in the input *file*. If no *file* is specified, the standard input is understood.

The input consists of pairs of items (nonempty strings) separated by blanks. Pairs of different items indicate ordering. Pairs of identical items indicate presence, but not ordering.

SEE ALSO

LORDER(SD_CMD).

USAGE

General.

NAME

unget — undo a previous get of an SCCS file

SYNOPSIS

`unget` **[−r***SID***] [−s] [−n]** *files*

DESCRIPTION

The command `unget` undoes the effect of a `get −e` done prior to creating the intended new delta. If a directory is named, `unget` behaves as though each file in the directory were specified as a named file, except that non-SCCS files and unreadable files are silently ignored. If a name of − is given, the standard input is read with each line being taken as the name of an SCCS file to be processed.

Keyletter arguments apply independently to each named file.

`−r`*SID* Uniquely identifies which delta is no longer intended. (This would have been specified by `get` as the new delta). The use of this keyletter is necessary only if two or more outstanding `get`s for editing on the same SCCS file were done by the same person (login name). An error is reported if the specified *SID* is ambiguous, or if it is necessary and omitted on the command line.

`−s` Suppresses the printout, on the standard output, of the intended delta's *SID*.

`−n` Causes the retention of the file that was obtained by `get`, which would normally be removed from the current directory.

SEE ALSO

DELTA(SD_CMD), GET(SD_CMD), SACT(SD_CMD).

USAGE

General.

NAME

val — validate SCCS file

SYNOPSIS

`val -`

`val [-s] [-rSID] [-mname] [-ytype] file ...`

DESCRIPTION

The command `val` determines if the specified *file* is an SCCS file meeting the characteristics specified by the options. The arguments may appear in any order.

The command `val` has a special argument, –, which causes reading of the standard input until an end-of-file condition is detected. Each line read is independently processed as if it were a command line argument list.

The command `val` generates diagnostic messages on the standard output for each command line and file processed, and also returns a single 8-bit code upon exit as described below

The options are defined as follows. The effects of any option apply independently to each named file on the command line.

`-s` Silences the diagnostic message normally generated on the standard output for any error that is detected while processing each named file on a given command line.

`-r`*SID* *SID* (SCCS Identification String) is an SCCS delta number. A check is made to determine if the *SID* is ambiguous (e. g., `-r1` is ambiguous because it physically does not exist but implies 1.1, 1.2, etc., which may exist) or invalid (e. g., `-r1.0` or `-r1.1.0` are invalid because neither case can exist as a valid delta number). If the *SID* is valid and not ambiguous, a check is made to determine if it actually exists.

`-m`*name* The argument *name* is compared with the SCCS %M% keyword in *file*.

`-y`*type* The argument*type* is compared with the SCCS %Y% keyword in *file*.

The 8-bit code returned by `val` is a disjunction of the possible errors, i. e., can be interpreted as a bit string where (moving from left to right) set bits are interpreted as follows:

bit 0 = missing file argument;
bit 1 = unknown or duplicate keyletter argument;
bit 2 = corrupted SCCS file;
bit 3 = cannot open file or file not SCCS;
bit 4 = *SID* is invalid or ambiguous;
bit 5 = *SID* does not exist;
bit 6 = %Y%, –y mismatch;

bit 7 = %M%, −m mismatch;

Note that `val` can process two or more files on a given command line and in turn can process multiple command lines (when reading the standard input). In these cases an aggregate code is returned — a logical **OR** of the codes generated for each command line and file processed.

SEE ALSO

ADMIN(SD_CMD), DELTA(SD_CMD), GET(SD_CMD), PRS(SD_CMD).

USAGE

General.

NAME

what — identify SCCS files

SYNOPSIS

`what [-s]` *files*

DESCRIPTION

The command `what` searches the given files for all occurrences of the pattern that the `get` command substitutes for %Z% (@(#)) and prints out what follows until the first ", >, new-line, \, or null character. For example, if the C program in file **f.c** contains

```
char ident[] = "@(#)identification informa-
tion";
```

and **f.c** is compiled to yield **f.o** and **a.out**, then the command

```
what f.c f.o a.out
```

will print

f.c:	identification information
f.o:	identification information
a.out:	identification information

The command `what` is intended to be used in conjunction with the SCCS `get` command, which automatically inserts identifying information, but it can also be used where the information is inserted manually.

There is only one option (new in UNIX System V Release 2.0):

`-s` Quit after finding the first occurrence of pattern in each file.

ERRORS

Exit status is 0 if any matches are found, otherwise 1.

SEE ALSO

GET(SD_CMD).

USAGE

General.

NAME

xargs — construct argument list(s) and execute command

SYNOPSIS

`xargs` [*options*] [*command*[*initial-arguments*]]

DESCRIPTION

The command `xargs` combines the fixed *initial-arguments* with arguments read from standard input to execute the specified *command* one or more times. The number of arguments read for each *command* invocation and the manner in which they are combined are determined by the options specified.

If *command* is omitted, `echo` is used.

Arguments read in from standard input are defined to be contiguous strings of characters delimited by one or more blanks, tabs, or new-lines; empty lines are always discarded. Blanks and tabs may be embedded as part of an argument if escaped or quoted. Characters enclosed in quotes (single or double) are taken literally, and the delimiting quotes are removed. Outside of quoted strings a backslash (\) quotes the next character.

Each argument list is constructed starting with the *initial-arguments,* followed by some number of arguments read from standard input (Exception: see `−i`). Options `−i`, `−l`, and `−n` determine how arguments are selected for each command invocation. When none of these options are coded, the *initial-arguments* are followed by arguments read continuously from standard input until an internal buffer is full, and then *command* is executed with the accumulated args. This process is repeated until there are no more args. When there are conflicts (e.g., `−l` vs. `−n`), the last option has precedence. The recognized options are:

`−l`*number* The argument *command* is executed for each non-empty *number* lines of arguments from standard input. The last invocation of *command* will be with fewer lines of arguments if fewer than *number* remain. A line is considered to end with the first new-line *unless* the last character of the line is a blank or a tab; a trailing blank/tab signals continuation through the next non-empty line. If *number* is omitted, 1 is assumed. Option `−x` is forced.

`−i`*replstr* Insert mode: *command* is executed for each line from standard input, taking the entire line as a single arg, inserting it in *initial-arguments* for each occurrence of *replstr.* A maximum of 5 arguments in *initial-arguments* may each contain one or more instances of *replstr.* Blanks and tabs at the beginning of each line are thrown away. Constructed arguments may not grow larger than 255 characters, and option `−x` is also forced. {} is assumed for *replstr* if not specified.

`−n`*number* Execute *command* using as many standard input arguments as possible, up to *number* arguments maximum. Fewer arguments will be used if their total size is greater than *size* characters, and for the last invocation if there are fewer than *number* arguments remaining. If option `-x` is also invoked, each *number* arguments must fit in the *size* limitation, else `xargs` terminates execution.

`-t` Trace mode: The *command* and each constructed argument list are echoed to standard error just prior to their execution.

`-p` Prompt mode: The user is asked whether to execute *command* each invocation. Trace mode (`-t`) is turned on to print the command instance to be executed, followed by a **?...** prompt. A reply of `y` (optionally followed by anything) will execute the command; anything else, including just a carriage return, skips that particular invocation of *command*.

`-x` Causes `xargs` to terminate if any argument list would be greater than *size* characters; `-x` is forced by the options `-i` and `-l`. When neither of the options `-i`, `-l`, or `-n` are coded, the total length of all arguments must be within the *size* limit.

`-s`*size* The maximum total size of each argument list is set to *size* characters; *size* must be a positive integer less than or equal to 470. If `-s` is not coded, 470 is taken as the default. Note that the character count for *size* includes one extra character for each argument and the count of characters in the command name.

`-e`*eofstr* The argument *eofstr* is taken as the logical end-of-file string. Underscore (_) is assumed for the logical **EOF** string if `-e` is not invoked. The option `-e` with no *eofstr* coded turns off the logical **EOF** string capability (underbar is taken literally). The command `xargs` reads standard input until either end-of-file or the logical **EOF** string is encountered.

The command `xargs` will terminate if either it receives a return code of −1 from, or if it cannot execute, *command*. (Thus *command* should explicitly *exit* with an appropriate value to avoid accidentally returning with −1.)

EXAMPLES

The following will move all files from directory $1 to directory $2, and echo each move command just before doing it:

```
ls $1 | xargs -i -t mv $1/{} $2/{}
```

The following will combine the output of the parenthesized commands onto one line, which is then echoed to the end of file `log`:

```
(logname; date; echo $0 $*) | xargs >>log
```

The user is asked which files in the current directory are to be archived and archives them into `arch` (1.) one at a time, or (2.) many at a time.

```
1.  ls | xargs -p -l ar r arch
2.  ls | xargs -p -l | xargs ar r arch
```

The following will execute with successive pairs of arguments originally typed as command line arguments:

```
echo $* | xargs -n2 diff
```

SEE ALSO

ECHO(BU_CMD).

USAGE

General.

NAME

yacc — a compiler-compiler

SYNOPSIS

`yacc [−vdlt]` *grammar*

DESCRIPTION

The `yacc` command provides a general tool for describing the input to a program. More precisely, `yacc` converts a context-free grammar into a set of tables for a simple automaton which executes an LR(1) parsing algorithm. The grammar may be ambiguous; built-in precedence rules are used to break ambiguities.

The output file, `y.tab.c`, must be compiled by the C compiler to produce a program `yyparse`. This program must be loaded with the lexical analyzer function, `yylex`, as well as `main` and `yyerror`, an error handling routine. These routines must be supplied by the user (however, see the description of the `yacc` library below); `lex` is useful for creating lexical analyzers usable by `yacc`.

If the `−v` option is used, the file `y.output` is prepared, which contains a description of the parsing tables and a report on conflicts generated by ambiguities in the grammar.

If the `−d` option is used, the file `y.tab.h` is generated with the **#define** statements that associate the `yacc`-assigned "token codes" with the user-declared "token names". This allows source files other than `y.tab.c` to access the token codes.

If the `−l` option is used, the code produced in `y.tab.c` will *not* contain any **#line** constructs. This should only be used after the grammar and the associated actions are fully debugged.

Runtime debugging code is always generated in `y.tab.c` under conditional compilation control. By default, this code is not included when `y.tab.c` is compiled. However, when `yacc`'s `−t` option is used, this debugging code will be compiled by default. Independent of whether the `−t` option was used, the runtime debugging code is under the control of **YYDEBUG**, a pre-processor symbol. If **YYDEBUG** has a non-zero value, then the debugging code is included. If its value is zero, then the code will not be included. The size and execution time of a program produced without the runtime debugging code will be smaller and slightly faster.

Yacc Library

The `yacc` library `liby.a` facilitates the initial use of `yacc` by providing the routines:

```
main()

yyerror(s)
    char *s;
```

These routines may be loaded by using the `−ly` option with `cc`. `main()` just calls `yyparse()`. `yyerror()` simply prints the string (error message) s when a syntax error is detected.

YACC SPECIFICATIONS

The `yacc` user constructs a specification of the input process; this includes rules describing the input structure, code to be invoked when these rules are recognized, and a low-level routine to do the basic input. The command `yacc` then generates the (integer-valued) function `yyparse`; it in turn calls `yylex`, the lexical analyzer, to obtain input tokens.

A structure recognized (and returned) by the lexical analyzer is called a *terminal symbol*, here referred to as a *token* (literal characters must also be passed through the lexical analyzer, and are also considered tokens). A structure recognized by the parser is called a *nonterminal symbol*. The argument *name* refers to either tokens or nonterminal symbols.

Every specification file consists of three sections: *declarations*, *grammar rules*, and *programs*, separated by double percent marks ("%%"). The declarations and programs sections may be empty. If the latter is empty, then the preceding %% mark separating it from the rules section may be omitted.

Blanks, tabs and newlines are ignored, except that they may not appear in names or multi-character reserved symbols. Comments are enclosed in /* ... */, and may appear wherever a name is legal.

Names may be of arbitrary length, made up of letters, dot ".", underscore "_", and non-initial digits. Upper and lower case letters are distinct. Names beginning in "yy" should be avoided, since the `yacc` parser uses such names.

A literal consists of a character enclosed in single quotes. The C escape sequences (e.g., '\n') are recognized.

Declarations

The following declarators may be used in the declarations section:

%token

Names representing tokens must be declared; this is done by writing

%token *name1 name2* ...

in the declarations section. Every name not defined in this section is assumed to represent a nonterminal symbol. Every nonterminal symbol must appear on the left side of at least one grammar rule.

%start

The *start symbol* represents the largest, most general structure described by the grammar rules. By default, it is the left hand side of the first grammar rule; this default may be overridden by declaring:

%start symbol

%left

%right

%nonassoc

Precedence and associativity rules attached to tokens are declared using these keywords. This is done by a series of lines, each beginning with one of the keywords %left, %right, or %nonassoc, followed by a list of tokens. All tokens on the same line have the same precedence level and associativity; the lines are in order of increasing precedence or binding strength. %left denotes that the operators on that line are left associative, and %right similary denotes right associative operators. %nonassoc denotes operators that may not associate with themselves. (A token declared using one of these keywords need not be declared by %token as well.)

%prec

Unary operators must, in general, be given a precedence. In cases where a unary and binary operator have the same symbolic representation, but need to be given different precedences, the keyword %prec is used to change the precedence level associated with a particular grammar rule. %prec appears immediately after the body of the grammar rule, before the action or closing semicolon (see Grammar Rules below), and is followed by a token name or a literal. It causes the precedence of the grammar rule to become that of the following token name or literal.

%union

By default, the values returned by actions and the lexical analyzer are integers. Other types, including structures, are supported: the `yacc` value stack is declared to be a union of the various types of values desired. The command `yacc` keeps track of types, and inserts appropriate union member names so that the resulting parser will be strictly type-checked. The declaration is done by including a statement of the form:

```
%union {
        body of union
}
```

Alternatively, the union may be declared in a header file, and a typedef used to define the variable YYSTYPE to represent this union. The header file must be included in the declarations section, by using a "#include" construct within %{ and %} (see below). Union members must be associated with the various names. The construction <*name*> is used to indicate a union member name; if this follows one of the keywords %token %left, %right, and %nonassoc, the union member name is associated with the tokens listed.

%type

This key word is used to associate union member names with nonterminals, in the form:

```
%type <ntype> a b ...
```

Other declarations and definitions can appear in the declarations section, enclosed by the marks "%{" and "%}". These have global scope within the file, so that they may be used in the rules and programs sections.

Grammar Rules

The rules section is comprised of one or more grammar rules. A grammar rule has the form:

A : BODY ;

A represents a nonterminal name, and BODY represents a sequence of zero or more names and literals. The colon and the semicolon are `yacc` punctuation. If there are several successive grammar rules with the same left hand side, the vertical bar '|' can be used to avoid rewriting the left hand side; in this case the semicolon must occur only after the last rule. The BODY part may be empty to indicate that the nonterminal symbol matches the empty string.

The ASCII NUL character (0 or '\0') should not be used in grammar rules.

With each grammar rule, the user may associate actions to be performed each time the rule is recognized in the input process. These actions may return values, and may obtain the values returned by previous actions. In addition, the lexical anlayzer can return values for tokens, if desired.

An action is an arbitrary C statement, and as such can do input or output, call subprograms, and alter external variables. An action is one or more statements enclosed in curly braces "{" and "}". Certain pseudo-variables can be used in the action: a value can be returned by assigning it to $$; the variables $1, $2, ..., refer to the values returned by the components of the right side of a rule, reading from left to right. By default, the value of a rule is the value of the first element in it. Actions may occur in the middle of a rule as well as at the end; an action may access the values returned by symbols (and actions) to its left, and in turn the value it returns may be accessed by actions to its right.

Internal rules to resolve ambiguities are:

1. In a shift/reduce conflict, the default is to do the shift.

2. In a reduce/reduce conflict, the default is to reduce by the grammar rule that occurs *earlier* in the input sequence.

In addition, the declared precedences and associativities (see Declarations Section above) are used to resolve parsing conflicts as follows:

1. A precedence and associativity is associated with each grammar rule; it is the precedence and associativity of the last token or literal in the body of the rule. If the %prec keyword is used, it overrides this default. Some grammar rules may have no precedence and associativity.

2. When there is a reduce/reduce conflict, or there is a shift/reduce conflict and either the input symbol or the grammar rule has no precedence and associativity, then the two rules given above are used.

3. If there is a shift/reduce conflict, and both the grammar rule and the input symbol have precedence and associativity associated with them, then the conflict is resolved in favor of the action (shift or reduce) associated with the higher precedence. If the precedences are the same, then the associativity is used; left associative implies reduce, right associative implies shift, and nonassociative implies error.

Conflicts resolved by precedence are not counted in the shift/reduce and reduce/reduce conflicts reported by `yacc`.

The token name "error" is reserved for error handling. This name can be used in grammar rules; in effect, it suggests places where errors are expected, and recovery might take place. When an error is encountered, the parser behaves as if the token "error" were the current lookahead token, and performs the action encountered. The lookahead token is then reset to the token that caused the error. If no special error rules have been specified, the processing halts when an error is detected.

In order to prevent a series of error messages, the parser, after detecting an error, remains in error state until three tokens have been successfully read and shifted. If an error is detected when the parser is already in error state, no message is given, and the input token is quietly deleted.

The statement

yyerrok;

in an action resets the parser back to its normal mode; it may be used if it is desired to force the parser to believe that an error has been fully recovered from.

The statement

yyclearin;

in an action is used to clear the previous lookahead token; it may be used if a user-supplied routine is to be used to find the correct place to resume input.

Programs

The programs section may include the definition of the lexical analyzer `yylex`, and any other functions, for example those used in the actions specified in the grammar rules.

`yylex` is an integer-valued function, which returns the *token number*, representing the kind of token read. If there is a value associated with that token, it should be assigned to the external variable `yylval`. The parser and `yylex` must agree on these token numbers in order for communication between them to take place. The numbers may be chosen by `yacc`, or chosen by the user. In either case, the "#define" construct of C is used to allow `yylex` to return these numbers symbolically. If the token numbers are chosen by `yacc`, then literals are given the numerical value of the character in the local character set, and other names are assigned token numbers starting at 257.

A token may be assigned a number by following its first appearance in the declarations section with a nonnegative integer. Names and literals not defined this way retain their default definition. All token numbers must be distinct.

The end of the input is marked by a special token called the *endmarker.* The endmarker must have token number 0 or negative. (these values are not legal for any other token.) All lexical analyzers should return 0 or negative as a token number upon reaching the end of their input. If the token upto, but excluding, the endmarker form a structure which matches the start symbol, the parser *accepts* the input. If the endmarker is seen in any other context, it is an error.

ERRORS

The number of reduce-reduce and shift-reduce conflicts is reported on the standard error output; a more detailed report is found in the **y.output** file. Similarly, if some rules are not reachable from the start symbol, this is also reported.

FILES

`y.output`
`y.tab.c`
`y.tab.h`

SEE ALSO

LEX(SD_CMD).

USAGE

General.

Part II

System Routines

Chapter 5

Base System Routines

NAME

abort — generate an abnormal process termination

SYNOPSIS

```
int abort()
```

DESCRIPTION

The function `abort` first closes all open files if possible, then causes a signal to be sent to the process. This invokes abnormal process termination routines, such as a core dump, which are implementation dependent.

APPLICATION USAGE

The signal sent by `abort` should not be caught or ignored by applications.

SEE ALSO

EXIT(BA_SYS), SIGNAL(BA_SYS).

CAVEATS

The function `abort` will send the `SIGABRT` signal rather than the `SIGIOT` signal.

NAME

access — determine accessibility of a file

SYNOPSIS

```
int access(path, amode)
char *path;
int amode;
```

DESCRIPTION

The function `access` checks the file named by the path-name pointed to by `path` for accessibility according to the bit-pattern contained in `amode`, using the real-user-ID instead of the effective-user-ID, and the real-group-ID instead of the effective-group-ID.

The bit-pattern contained in `amode` is constructed as follows:

- `04` read
- `02` write
- `01` execute (search)
- `00` check existence of file

Thus, `amode` is the sum of the values of the access modes to be checked.

The owner of a file has permission checked with respect to the *owner* read, write, and execute mode-bits. Members of the file's group other than the owner have permissions checked with respect to the *group* mode-bits, and all others have permissions checked with respect to the *other* mode-bits.

RETURN VALUE

If the requested access is permitted, `access` returns 0; otherwise, it returns -1 and `errno` indicates the error.

ERRORS

The function `access` fails and `errno` equals:

`ENOTDIR`	if a component of the path-prefix is not a directory.
`ENOENT`	if the named file does not exist.
`EACCES`	if a component of the path-prefix denies search permission, or if the permission-bits of the file-mode forbid the requested access.
`EROFS`	if write access is requested for a file on a read-only file system.
`ETXTBSY`	if write access is requested for a pure procedure (shared text) file being executed.
`EINVAL`	if `amode` is invalid.

SEE ALSO

CHMOD(BA_SYS), STAT(BA_SYS).

CAVEATS

The `<unistd.h>` header file will define these symbolic constants for `amode`:

Name	*Description*
R_OK	test for *read* permission.
W_OK	test for *write* permission.
X_OK	test for *execute* permission.
F_OK	test for existence of file.

NAME

alarm — set a process alarm clock

SYNOPSIS

```
unsigned alarm(sec)
unsigned sec;
```

DESCRIPTION

The function `alarm` instructs the alarm clock of the calling-process to send the signal `SIGALRM` to the calling-process after the number of real time seconds specified by `sec` have elapsed [see SIGNAL(BA_SYS)].

Alarm requests are not stacked; successive calls reset the alarm clock of the calling-process.

If `sec` is `0`, any previously made alarm request is canceled.

The FORK(BA_SYS) routine sets the alarm clock of a new process to `0`. A process created by the EXEC(BA_SYS) family of routines inherits the time left on the old process's alarm clock.

RETURN VALUE

If successful, `alarm` returns the amount of time previously remaining in the alarm clock of the calling-process.

SEE ALSO

EXEC(BA_SYS), FORK(BA_SYS), PAUSE(BA_SYS), SIGNAL(BA_SYS).

NAME

chdir — change working directory

SYNOPSIS

```
int chdir(path)
char *path;
```

DESCRIPTION

The function `chdir` causes the named directory to become the current working directory and the starting point for path-searches for path-names not beginning with `/`.

The argument `path` points to the path-name of a directory.

RETURN VALUE

If successful, `chdir` returns `0`; otherwise, it returns `-1`, it does *not* change the current-working-directory, and `errno` indicates the error.

ERRORS

The function `chdir` fails and `errno` equals:

`ENOTDIR` if a component of the path-name is not a directory.

`ENOENT` if the named directory does not exist.

`EACCES` if any component of the path-name denies search permission.

NAME

chmod — change mode of file

SYNOPSIS

```
int chmod(path, mode)
char *path;
int mode;
```

DESCRIPTION

The function `chmod` sets the access-permission-bits of the mode of the named file according to the bit-pattern contained in `mode`.

The argument `path` points to a path-name naming a file.

The access-permission-bits are interpreted as follows; the value of `mode` should be the sum of the values of the desired permissions:

04000 Set user-ID on execution.
02000 Set group-ID on execution.
01000 Reserved.
00400 Read by owner.
00200 Write by owner.
00100 Execute (search if a directory) by owner.
00040 Read by group.
00020 Write by group.
00010 Execute (search) by group.
00004 Read by others (i.e., anyone else).
00002 Write by others.
00001 Execute (search) by others.

The effective-user-ID of the process must match the owner of the file or be super-user to change the mode of a file.

If the effective-user-ID of the process is not super-user and the effective-group-ID of the process does not match the group-ID of the file, mode-bit 02000 (set group-ID on execution) is cleared. This prevents an ordinary user from making itself an effective member of a group to which it does not belong. Similarly, the CHOWN(BA_SYS) routine clears the set-user-ID and set-group-ID-bits when invoked by other than the super-user.

RETURN VALUE

If successful, `chmod` returns 0; otherwise, it returns -1, it does *not* change the file-mode, and `errno` indicates the error.

ERRORS

The function `chmod` fails and `errno` equals:

`ENOTDIR` if a component of the path-prefix is not a directory.

`ENOENT` if the named file does not exist.

`EACCES` if a component of the path-prefix denies search permission.

EPERM if the effective-user-ID does not match the owner of the file and the effective-user-ID is not super-user.

EROFS if the named file resides on a read-only file system.

SEE ALSO

CHOWN(BA_SYS), MKNOD(BA_SYS).

CAVEATS

Symbolic constants defining the access-permission-bits will be added to the `<sys/stat.h>` header file and should be used to construct `mode`.

Enforcement-mode file and record-locking will be added:

> If the mode-bit `02000` (set group-ID on execution) is set and the mode-bit `01000` (execute or search by group) is not set, enforcement-mode file and record-locking will exist on an ordinary-file. This may affect future calls to OPEN(BA_SYS), CREAT(BA_SYS), READ(BA_SYS) and WRITE(BA SYS) routines on this file.

NAME

chown — change owner and group of a file

SYNOPSIS

```
int chown(path, owner, group)
char *path;
int owner, group;
```

DESCRIPTION

The function `chown` sets the owner-ID and group-ID of the named file to the numeric values contained in `owner` and `group`, respectively.

The argument `path` points to a path-name naming a file.

Only processes with effective-user-ID equal to the file-owner or super-user may change the ownership of a file.

If `chown` is invoked successfully by other than the super-user, it clears the set-user-ID and set-group-ID-bits of the file-mode, `04000` and `02000` respectively. (This prevents ordinary users from making themselves effectively other users or members of a group to which they don't belong.)

RETURN VALUE

If successful, `chown` returns 0; otherwise, it returns -1, it does *not* change the owner and group of the named file, and `errno` indicates the error.

ERRORS

The function `chown` fails and `errno` equals:

`ENOTDIR`	if a component of the path-prefix is not a directory.
`ENOENT`	if the named file does not exist.
`EACCES`	if a component of the path-prefix denies search permission.
`EPERM`	if the effective-user-ID does not match the owner of the file and the effective-user-ID is not super-user.
`EROFS`	if the named file resides on a read-only file system.

SEE ALSO

CHMOD(BA_SYS).

NAME

close — close a file-descriptor

SYNOPSIS

```
int close(fildes)
int fildes;
```

DESCRIPTION

The function `close` closes the file-descriptor indicated by `fildes`.

The argument `fildes` is an open file-descriptor [see **file-descriptor** in **Definitions**].

All outstanding record-locks on the file indicated by `fildes` that are owned by the calling-process are removed.

RETURN VALUE

If successful, `close` returns 0; otherwise, it returns -1 and `errno` indicates the error.

ERRORS

The function `close` fails and `errno` equals:

`EBADF` if `fildes` is not a valid open file-descriptor.

APPLICATION USAGE

Normally, applications should use the *stdio* routines to open, close, read and write files. Thus, an application that had used the FOPEN(BA_SYS) *stdio* routine to open a file would use the corresponding FCLOSE(BA_SYS) *stdio* routine rather than the CLOSE(BA_SYS) routine.

The record and file locking features are an update that followed UNIX System V Release 1.0 and UNIX System V Release 2.0.

SEE ALSO

CREAT(BA_SYS), DUP(BA_SYS), EXEC(BA_SYS), FCNTL(BA_SYS), OPEN(BA_SYS), PIPE(BA_SYS).

NAME

creat — create a new file or rewrite an existing one

SYNOPSIS

```
int creat(path, mode)
char *path;
int mode;
```

DESCRIPTION

The function `creat` creates a new ordinary file or prepares to rewrite an existing file named by the path-name pointed to by `path`.

If the file exists, the length is truncated to zero, the mode and owner are unchanged, and the file is open for writing [see `O_WRONLY` in OPEN(BA_SYS)]. If the file does not exist, the file's owner-ID is set to the effective-user-ID of the process; the group-ID of the file is set to the effective-group-ID of the process; and the access permission bits [see CHMOD(BA_SYS)] of the file-mode are set to the value of `mode` modified as follows:

> The file-mode bits are ANDed with the complement of the process' file-mode-creation-mask [see UMASK(BA_SYS)]. Thus, `creat` clears each bit in the file-mode whose corresponding bit in the file-mode-creation-mask is set.

If successful, `creat` returns the file-descriptor and the file is open for writing. A new file may be created with a `mode` that forbids writing, but eventhough `mode` forbids writing, `creat` opens the file for writing.

The call `creat(path, mode)` is the same as the following [see OPEN(BA_SYS)]:

```
open(path, O_WRONLY | O_CREAT | O_TRUNC, mode)
```

The file-pointer is set to the beginning of the file. The file-descriptor is set to remain open across calls to the EXEC(BA_SYS) routines [see FCNTL(BA_SYS)]. No process may have more than {OPEN_MAX} files open simultaneously.

RETURN VALUE

If successful, `creat` returns the file-descriptor (a non-negative integer); otherwise, it returns -1 and `errno` indicates the error.

ERRORS

The function `creat` fails and `errno` equals:

`ENOTDIR` if a component of the path-prefix is not a directory.

`ENOENT` if a component of the path-name should exist but does not.

`EACCES` if a component of the path-prefix denies search permission, or if the file does not exist and the directory in which the file is to be created does not permit writing, or if the file exists and write permission is denied.

EROFS	if the named file does or would reside on a read-only file-system.
ETXTBSY	if the file is a pure procedure (shared text) file being executed.
EISDIR	if the named file is an existing directory.
EMFILE	if {OPEN_MAX} file-descriptors are currently open in the calling-process.
ENOSPC	if the directory to contain the file cannot be extended.
ENFILE	if the system file table is full.

APPLICATION USAGE

Normally, applications should use the *stdio* routines to open, close, read and write files. In this case, the FOPEN(BA_SYS) *stdio* routine should be used rather than the CREAT(BA_SYS) routine.

SEE ALSO

CHMOD(BA_SYS), CLOSE(BA_SYS), DUP(BA_SYS), FCNTL(BA_SYS), LSEEK(BA_SYS), OPEN(BA_SYS), READ(BA_SYS), UMASK(BA_SYS), WRITE(BA_SYS).

CAVEATS

Symbolic constants defining the access permission bits will be defined by the `<sys/stat.h>` header file and should be used to construct `mode`.

Enforcement-mode file and record locking features will be added:

> The function `creat` will set `errno` to `EAGAIN` if the file exists, enforcement-mode file and record-locking is set and there are outstanding record-locks on the file [see CHMOD(BA_SYS)].

NAME

dup — duplicate an open file-descriptor

SYNOPSIS

```
int dup(fildes)
int fildes;
```

DESCRIPTION

The function `dup` returns a new file-descriptor having the following in common with the original:

Same open file (or pipe).

Same file-pointer (i.e., both file-descriptors share one file-pointer).

Same access mode (read, write or read/write).

The argument `fildes` is an open file-descriptor [see **file-descriptor** in **Definitions**].

The new file-descriptor is set to remain open across calls to the EXEC(BA_SYS) routines [see FCNTL(BA_SYS)].

The file-descriptor returned is the lowest one available.

RETURN VALUE

If successful, `dup` returns the file-descriptor (a non-negative integer); otherwise, it returns -1 and `errno` indicates the error.

ERRORS

The function `dup` fails and `errno` equals:

`EBADF`	if `fildes` is not a valid open file-descriptor.
`EMFILE`	if {OPEN_MAX} file-descriptors are currently open in the calling-process.

SEE ALSO

CREAT(BA_SYS), CLOSE(BA_SYS), EXEC(BA_SYS), FCNTL(BA_SYS), OPEN(BA_SYS), PIPE(BA_SYS).

NAME

execl, execv, execle, execve, execlp, execvp — execute a file

SYNOPSIS

```
int execl(path, arg0, arg1, ... argn, (char *)0)
char *path, *arg0, *arg1, ... *argn;

int execv(path, argv)
char *path, *argv[];

int execle(path, arg0, arg1, ... argn, (char *)0, envp)
char *path, *arg0, *arg1, ... *argn, *envp[];

int execve(path, argv, envp)
char *path, *argv[], *envp[];

int execlp(file, arg0, arg1, ... argn, (char *)0)
char *file, *arg0, *arg1, ... *argn;

int execvp(file, argv)
char *file, *argv[];
```

DESCRIPTION

All forms of the function `exec` transform the calling-process into a new process. The new process is constructed from an ordinary, executable file called the *new-process-file*. This file consists of a header, a text segment, and a data segment. There can be no return from a successful `exec` because the calling-process image is overlaid by the new process image.

When a C program is executed, it is called as follows:

```
main(argc, argv, envp)
int argc;
char **argv, **envp;
```

where `argc` is the argument count, `argv` is an array of character pointers to the arguments themselves and `envp` is an array of character pointers to null-terminated strings that constitute the environment for the new process. The argument `argc` is conventionally at least one and the initial member of the array points to a string containing the name of the file.

The argument `path` points to a path-name that identifies the new-process-file. For `execlp` and `execvp`, the argument `file` points to the new-process-file. The path-prefix for this file is obtained by a search of the directories passed as the *environment* line `PATH=` [see ENVVAR(BA_ENV) and SYSTEM(BA_SYS)].

The arguments `arg0, arg1, ... argn` are pointers to null-terminated character strings. These strings constitute the argument list available to the new process. By convention, at least `arg0` must be present and point to a string that is the same as `file` or `path` (or its last component).

The argument `argv` is an array of character pointers to null-terminated strings. These strings constitute the argument list available to the new process. By convention, `argv[0]` must point to a string that is the same as `file` or `path` (or its last component), and `argv` is terminated by a null pointer.

The argument `envp` is an array of character pointers to null-terminated strings. These strings constitute the environment for the new process, and `envp` is terminated by a null-pointer. For `execl` and `execv`, a pointer to the environment of the calling-process is made available in the global cell:

```
extern char **environ;
```

and is used to pass the environment of the calling-process to the new process.

The file-descriptors open in the calling-process remain open in the new process, except for those whose *close-on-exec* flag is set [see FCNTL(BA_SYS)]. For those file-descriptors that remain open, the file-pointer is unchanged.

Signals set to the default action (`SIG_DFL`) in the calling-process will be set to the default action in the new process. Signals set to be ignored (`SIG_IGN`) by the calling-process will be ignored by the new process. Signals set to be caught by the calling-process will be set to the default action in the new process [see SIGNAL(BA_SYS)].

If the set-user-ID-on-execution mode bit of the new-process-file is set, the `exec` sets the effective-user-ID of the new process to the owner-ID of the new-process-file [see CHMOD(BA_SYS)]. Similarly, if the set-group-ID mode bit of the new-process-file is set, the effective-group-ID of the new process is set to the group-ID of the new-process-file. The real-user-ID and real-group-ID of the new process remain the same as those of the calling-process. The effective-user-ID and group-ID of the new process are saved for use by the SETUID(BA_SYS) routine.

The new process also inherits at least the following attributes from the calling-process:

process-ID
parent-process-ID
process-group-ID
tty-group-ID [see EXIT(BA_SYS) and SIGNAL(BA_SYS)]
time left until an alarm clock signal [see ALARM(BA_SYS)]
current-working-directory
root-directory
file mode creation mask [see UMASK(BA_SYS)]
file size limit [see ULIMIT(BA_SYS)]
`utime`, `stime`, `cutime`, and `cstime` [see TIMES(BA_SYS)]
(file-locks [see FCNTL(BA_SYS) and LOCKF(BA_SYS)])

RETURN VALUE

If the `exec` returns to the calling-process, an error has occurred; the `exec` returns -1 and `errno` indicates the error.

ERRORS

An `exec` returns to the calling-process and `errno` equals:

`ENOENT` if one or more components of the path-name of the new-process-file do not exist.

`ENOTDIR` if a component of the path-prefix of the new-process-file is not a directory.

`EACCES` if a directory in the new-process-file's path-prefix denies search permission, or if the new-process-file is not an ordinary file [see MKNOD(BA_SYS)], or if the new-process-file's mode denies execution permission.

`ENOEXEC` if the `exec` is not an `execlp` or `execvp`, and the new-process-file has the appropriate access permission but is not a valid executable object.

`ETXTBSY` if the new-process-file is a pure procedure (shared text) file that is currently open for writing by some process.

`ENOMEM` if the new process image requires more memory than is allowed by the hardware or system-imposed maximum.

`E2BIG` if the number of bytes in the new process image's argument list exceeds the system-imposed limit of {ARG_MAX} bytes.

`EFAULT` if the new-process-file image is corrupted.

APPLICATION USAGE

Two interfaces for these functions are available. The list (`l`) versions: `execl`, `execle` and `execlp`, are useful when a known file with known arguments is being called. The arguments are the character-strings that are the file-name and the arguments. The variable (`v`) versions: `execv`, `execve` and `execvp`, are useful when the number of arguments is unknown in advance. The arguments are a file-name and a vector of strings containing the arguments.

If possible, applications should use the SYSTEM(BA_SYS) routine, which is easier to use and supplies more functions, rather than the FORK(BA_SYS) and EXEC(BA_SYS) routines.

SEE ALSO

ALARM(BA_SYS), EXIT(BA_SYS), FORK(BA_SYS), SIGNAL(BA_SYS), TIMES(BA_SYS), ULIMIT(BA_SYS), UMASK(BA_SYS).

NAME

exit, _exit — terminate process

SYNOPSIS

```
void exit(status)
int status;

void _exit(status)
int status;
```

DESCRIPTION

The function `exit` may cause cleanup actions before the process exits [see FCLOSE(BA_SYS)]. The function `_exit` does not.

The functions `exit` and `_exit` terminate the calling-process with the following consequences:

All of the file-descriptors open in the calling-process are closed.

If the parent-process of the calling-process is executing a WAIT(BA_SYS) routine, it is notified of the calling-process's termination and the low-order eight bits (i.e., bits `0377`) of `status` are made available to it. If the parent is not waiting, the child's status will be made available to it when the parent subsequently executes the WAIT(BA_SYS) routine.

If the parent-process of the calling-process is not executing a WAIT(BA_SYS) routine, the calling-process is transformed into a zombie-process. A zombie-process is an inactive process that has no process space allocated to it, and it will be deleted at some later time when its parent executes the WAIT(BA_SYS) routine.

Terminating a process by exiting does not terminate its children. The parent-process-ID of all of the calling-process's existing child-processes and zombie-processes is set to the process-ID of a special system-process. That is, these processes are inherited by a special system-process.

If the calling-process is a process-group-leader, and is associated with a controlling-terminal [see TERMIO(BA_ENV)], the `SIGHUP` signal is sent to each process that has a process-group-ID and tty-group-ID equal to that of the calling-process.

RETURN VALUE

Neither `exit` nor `_exit` return a value.

APPLICATION USAGE

Normally applications should use `exit` rather than `_exit`.

SEE ALSO

SIGNAL(BA_SYS), WAIT(BA_SYS).

NAME

fclose, fflush — close or flush a stream

SYNOPSIS

```
#include <stdio.h>

int fclose(stream)
FILE *stream;

int fflush(stream)
FILE *stream;
```

DESCRIPTION

The function `fclose` causes any buffered data for the named `stream` to be written out, and the `stream` to be closed.

The function `fclose` is performed automatically for all open files upon calling the EXIT(BA_SYS) routine.

The function `fflush` causes any buffered data for the named `stream` to be written to that file. The `stream` remains open.

RETURN VALUE

The functions `fclose` and `fflush` will return 0 for success, and `EOF` if any error (such as trying to write to a file that has not been opened for writing) was detected.

SEE ALSO

CLOSE(BA_SYS), EXIT(BA_SYS), FOPEN(BA_SYS), SETBUF(BA_LIB).

NAME

fcntl — file control

SYNOPSIS

```
#include <fcntl.h>

int fcntl(fildes, cmd, arg)
int fildes, cmd;
```

DESCRIPTION

The function `fcntl` provides for control over open files.

The argument `fildes` is an open file-descriptor [see **file-descriptor** in **Definitions**].

The data type and value of `arg` are specific to the type of command specified by `cmd`. The symbolic names for commands and file status flags are defined by the `<fcntl.h>` header file.

The commands available are:

`F_DUPFD` Return a new file-descriptor as follows:

Lowest numbered available file-descriptor greater than or equal to the argument `arg`.

Same open file (or pipe) as the original file.

Same file-pointer as the original file (i.e., both file-descriptors share one file-pointer).

Same access-mode (*read*, *write* or *read/write*) [see ACCESS(BA_SYS)].

Same file status flags [see OPEN(BA_SYS)].

Set the close-on-exec flag associated with the new file-descriptor to remain open across calls to any EXEC(BA_SYS) routines.

`F_GETFD` Get the close-on-exec flag associated with the file-descriptor `fildes`. If the low-order bit is 0 the file will remain open across calls to any EXEC(BA_SYS) routines; otherwise, the file will be closed upon execution of any EXEC(BA_SYS) routines.

`F_SETFD` Set the close-on-exec flag associated with `fildes` to the low-order bit of `arg` (0 or 1 as above).

`F_GETFL` Get `file` status flags:

`O_RDONLY, O_WRONLY, O_RDWR, O_NDELAY, O_APPEND.`

[see OPEN(BA_SYS)].

`F_SETFL` Set file status flags to `arg`. Only the flags `O_NDELAY` and `O_APPEND` may be set with `fcntl`.

The following commands are used for file-locking and record-locking (see also **APPLICATION USAGE** below). Locks may be placed on an entire file or segments of a file.

`F_GETLK` Get the first lock which blocks the lock description given by the variable of type `struct flock` (see below) pointed to by `arg`. The information retrieved overwrites the information passed to `fcntl` in the structure `flock`. If no lock is found that would prevent this lock from being created, then the structure is passed back unchanged except for the lock type which will be set to `F_UNLCK`.

NOTE: This command was added to `fcntl` following UNIX System V Release 1.0 and UNIX System V Release 2.0, and cannot be expected to be available in those releases.

`F_SETLK` Set or clear a file segment lock according to the variable of type `struct flock` (see below) pointed to by `arg`. `F_SETLK` is used to establish read (`F_RDLCK`) and write (`F_WRLCK`) locks, as well as remove either type of lock (`F_UNLCK`). `F_RDLCK`, `F_WRLCK`, and `F_UNLCK` are defined by the `<fcntl.h>` header file. If a read or write lock cannot be set, `fcntl` will return immediately with an error value of −1.

NOTE: This command was added to `fcntl` following UNIX System V Release 1.0 and UNIX System V Release 2.0, and cannot be expected to be available in those releases.

`F_SETLKW` This command is the same as `F_SETLK` except that if a read or write lock is blocked by other locks, the process will sleep until the segment is free to be locked.

NOTE: This command was added to `fcntl` following UNIX System V Release 1.0 and UNIX System V Release 2.0, and cannot be expected to be available in those releases.

The structure `flock` defined by the `<fcntl.h>` header file describes a lock. It describes the type (`l_type`), starting offset (`l_whence`), relative offset (`l_start`), size (`l_len`), and process-ID (`l_pid`):

```
short l_type;   /* F_RDLCK, F_WRLCK, F_UNLCK */
short l_whence; /* flag for starting offset */
long  l_start;  /* relative offset in bytes */
long  l_len;    /* if 0 then until EOF */
short l_pid;    /* returned with F_GETLK */
```

When a read-lock has been set on a segment of a file, other processes may also set read-locks on that segment or a portion of it. A read-lock prevents any other process from setting a write-lock on any portion of the protected area. The file-descriptor on which a read-lock is being placed must have been opened with read-access.

A write-lock prevents any other process from setting a read-lock or a write-lock on any portion of the protected area. Only one write-lock and no read-locks may be set on a given segment of a file at a given time. The file-descriptor on which a write-lock is being set must be open with write-access.

The value of `l_whence` is `0`, `1` or `2` to indicate that the relative offset, `l_start` bytes, will be measured from the start of the file, current position or end of the file, respectively. The value of `l_len` is the number of consecutive bytes to be locked. The process-ID field `l_pid` is used only with `F_GETLK` to return the value for a blocking-lock.

Locks may start and extend beyond the current end of a file, but may not be negative relative to the beginning of the file. A lock may be set to always extend to the end of file by setting `l_len` to zero (0). If such a lock also has `l_start` set to zero (0), the whole file will be locked.

Changing or unlocking a segment from the middle of a larger locked segment leaves two smaller segments locked at each end of the originally locked segment. Locking a segment already locked by the calling-process causes the old lock type to be removed and the new lock type to take effect. All locks placed by a process on a file are removed when the process closes the file-descriptor for the file or the process with the file-descriptor terminates. Child-processes do not inherit locks after the FORK(BA_SYS) routine is executed.

RETURN VALUE

If successful, `fcntl` returns a value that depends on `cmd` as follows:

- `F_DUPFD` a new file-descriptor.
- `F_GETFD` a value of flag (only the low-order bit is defined).
- `F_SETFD` a value other than -1.
- `F_GETFL` a value of file flags.
- `F_SETFL` a value other than -1.
- `F_GETLK` a value other than -1.
- `F_SETLK` a value other than -1.
- `F_SETLKW` a value other than -1.

If unsuccessful, `fcntl` returns -1 and `errno` indicates the error.

ERRORS

The function `fcntl` fails and `errno` equals:

- `EBADF` if `fildes` is not a valid open file-descriptor.
- `EMFILE` if `cmd` is `F_DUPFD` and {OPEN_MAX} file-descriptors are currently open in the calling-process.
- `EINVAL` if `cmd` is `F_DUPFD` and `arg` is negative or greater than or equal to {OPEN_MAX}; or if `cmd` is `F_GETLK`, `F_SETLK` or `F_SETLKW` and `arg` or the data it points to is invalid.

`EACCES` if `cmd` is `F_SETLK` the type of lock (`l_type`) is a read-lock (`F_RDLCK`) or write-lock (`F_WRLCK`) and the segment of a file to be locked is already write-locked by another process or the type is a write-lock and the segment of a file to be locked is already read-locked or write-locked by another process.

`ENOLCK` if `cmd` is `F_SETLK` or `F_SETLKW`, the type of lock is a read-lock or write-lock and there are no more file-locks available (too many segments are locked).

`EDEADLK` if `cmd` is `F_SETLKW`, the lock is blocked by some lock from another process and putting the calling-process to sleep, waiting for that lock to become free, would cause a deadlock.

APPLICATION USAGE

Because in the future the variable `errno` will be set to `EAGAIN` rather than `EACCES` when a section of a file is already locked by another process, portable application programs should expect and test for either value, for example:

```
flk->l_type = F_RDLCK;
if (fcntl(fd, F_SETLK, flk) == -1)
    if ((errno == EACCES) || (errno == EAGAIN))
        /*
         * section locked by another process,
         * check for either EAGAIN or EACCES
         * due to different implementations
         */
    else if ...
        /*
         * check for other errors
         */
```

The features of `fcntl` that deal with file and record locking are an update that followed UNIX System V Release 1.0 and UNIX System V Release 2.0.

SEE ALSO

CLOSE(BA_SYS), EXEC(BA_SYS), OPEN(BA_SYS), LOCKF(BA_SYS).

CAVEATS

The error condition which currently sets `errno` to `EACCES` will instead set `errno` to `EAGAIN` [see also **APPLICATION USAGE** above].

Enforcement-mode file-locking and record locking will be added:

If enforcement-mode file and record-locking is set and there are outstanding record-locks on the file, this may affect future calls to READ(BA_SYS) and WRITE(BA_SYS) routines on the file [see CHMOD(BA_SYS)].

NAME

ferror, feof, clearerr, fileno — stream status inquiries

SYNOPSIS

```
#include <stdio.h>

int ferror(stream)
FILE *stream;

int feof(stream)
FILE *stream;

void clearerr(stream)
FILE *stream;

int fileno(stream)
FILE *stream;
```

DESCRIPTION

The function `ferror` determines if an I/O error occurred when reading from or writing onto the named `stream`.

The function `feof` determines if `EOF` occurred when reading from the named `stream`.

The function `clearerr` resets both the error and `EOF` indicator to false on the named `stream`. The `EOF` indicator is reset when the file-pointer associated with `stream` is repositioned (e.g., by the FSEEK(BA_SYS) or REWIND(BA_SYS) routines) or can be reset with `clearerr`.

The function `fileno` gets the integer file-descriptor associated with the named `stream` [see OPEN(BA_SYS)].

RETURN VALUE

The function `ferror` returns non-zero when an I/O error occurred reading from or writing onto the named `stream`; otherwise, it returns zero.

The function `feof` returns non-zero when `EOF` occurred reading from the named `stream`; otherwise, it returns zero.

The function `fileno` returns the integer file-descriptor number associated with the named `stream`.

APPLICATION USAGE

All of these functions are macros; thus, they cannot be declared or redeclared.

The function `fileno` returns a file-descriptor that non-*stdio* routines, such as WRITE(BA_SYS) and LSEEK(BA_SYS) routines, can use to manipulate the associated file, but these routines are not recommended for use by application-programs.

SEE ALSO

OPEN(BA_SYS), FOPEN(BA_SYS).

NAME

fopen, freopen, fdopen — open a stream

SYNOPSIS

```
#include <stdio.h>

FILE *fopen(path, type)
char *path, *type;

FILE *freopen(path, type, stream)
char *path, *type;
FILE *stream;

FILE *fdopen(fildes, type)
int fildes;
char *type;
```

DESCRIPTION

The function `fopen` opens the file named by `path` and associates a stream with it [see **stream in Definitions**]. The function `fopen` returns a pointer to the `FILE` structure associated with the stream.

The function `freopen` substitutes the named file in place of the open `stream`. The original `stream` is closed, regardless of whether the open ultimately succeeds. The function `freopen` returns a pointer to the `FILE` structure associated with `stream`.

The function `freopen` is typically used to attach the preopened streams associated with `stdin`, `stdout` and `stderr` to other files. The standard error output stream, `stderr`, is by default unbuffered but use of `freopen` causes it to be buffered or line-buffered.

The argument `path` points to a character-string that names the file to be opened.

The argument `type` is a character-string having one of the following values:

`r` open for reading.

`w` truncate or create for writing.

`a` append; open for writing at the end of the file, or create for writing.

`r+` open for update (reading and writing).

`w+` truncate or create for update.

`a+` append; open or create for update (appending) to the end of the file.

When a file is opened for update, both input and output may be done on the resulting `stream`. However, output may not be directly followed by input without an intervening call to the FSEEK(BA_SYS) or REWIND(BA_SYS) routine, and input may not be directly followed by output without an intervening call to the FSEEK(BA_SYS) or REWIND(BA_SYS) routine or an input operation which encounters end-of-file.

When a file is opened for append (i.e., when `type` is `a` or `a+`) it is impossible to overwrite information already in the file. The FSEEK(BA_SYS) routine may be used to reposition the file-pointer to any position in the file, but when output is written to the file, the current file-pointer is disregarded. All output is written at the end of the file. For example, if two separate processes open the same file for append, each process may write to the file without overwriting output being written by the other, and the output from the two processes would be interleaved in the file.

The function `fdopen` associates a `stream` with a file-descriptor, `fildes`. The `type` of `stream` given to `fdopen` must agree with the mode of the already open file. File-descriptors are obtained from the routines which open files but do not return pointers to a `FILE` structure `stream`. Streams are necessary input for many of the *stdio* routines.

RETURN VALUE

The functions `fopen` and `freopen` return a `NULL` pointer if `path` cannot be accessed or if `type` is invalid or if the file cannot be opened.

The function `fdopen` returns a `NULL` pointer if `fildes` is not an open file-descriptor or if `type` is invalid or if the file cannot be opened.

The function `fopen` or `fdopen` may also fail if no *stdio* streams are free.

ERRORS

When the file cannot be opened, `fopen` or `freopen` fails and `errno` equals:

`ENOTDIR`	if a component of the path-prefix in `path` is not a directory.
`ENOENT`	if the named file does not exist or a component of the path-name should exist but does not.
`EACCES`	if search permission is denied for a component of the path-prefix or `type` permission is denied for the named file.
`EISDIR`	if the named file is a directory and `type` permission is write or read/write.
`EROFS`	if the named file resides on a read-only file system and `type` permission is write or read/write.
`ETXTBSY`	if the file is a pure procedure (shared text) file that is being executed and `type` permission is write or read/write.
`EINTR`	if a signal was caught during the open operation.

SEE ALSO

CREAT(BA_SYS), DUP(BA_SYS), OPEN(BA_SYS), PIPE(BA_SYS), FCLOSE(BA_SYS), FSEEK(BA_SYS).

NAME

fork — create a new process

SYNOPSIS

```
int fork()
```

DESCRIPTION

The function `fork` creates a new process (child-process) that is a copy of the calling-process (parent-process). The child-process inherits the following attributes from the parent-process:

environment
close-on-exec flag [see EXEC(BA_SYS)]
signal-handling settings (i.e., `SIG_DFL`, `SIG_IGN`, *address*)
set-user-ID mode bit
set-group-ID mode bit
process-group-ID
tty-group-ID [see EXIT(BA_SYS) and SIGNAL(BA_SYS)]
current-working-directory
root-directory
file mode creation mask [see UMASK(BA_SYS)]
file size limit [see ULIMIT(BA_SYS)]

Additional attributes associated with an Extension to the Base System may be inherited from the parent-process [see, for example, EFFECTS(KE_ENV)].

The child-process differs from the parent-process as follows:

The child-process has a unique process-ID

The child-process has a different parent-process-ID (i.e., the process-ID of the parent-process).

The child-process has its own copy of the parent's file-descriptors. Each of the child-process's file-descriptors shares a common file-pointer with the corresponding file-descriptor of the parent-process.

The child-process's `utime`, `stime`, `cutime`, and `cstime` are set to 0. The time left until an alarm clock signal is reset to 0.

The child-process does not inherit file-locks set by the parent-process [see FCNTL(BA_SYS) or LOCKF(BA_SYS)].

RETURN VALUE

If successful, `fork` returns 0 to the child-process and returns the process-ID of the child-process to the parent-process; otherwise, it returns -1 to the parent-process, it does *not* create any child-process, and `errno` indicates the error.

ERRORS

The function `fork` fails and `errno` equals:

`EAGAIN` if the system-imposed limit on the total number of processes under execution system-wide {PROC_MAX} or by a single user-ID {CHILD_MAX} would be exceeded.

`ENOMEM` if the process requires more space than the system can supply.

APPLICATION USAGE

The function `fork` creates a new process that is a copy of the calling-process and both processes will run as system resources become available. Because the goal is typically to create a new process that is *different* from the parent-process (i.e., the goal is to start a new program running) often the child-process immediately calls an EXEC(BA_SYS) routine to transform itself and start the new program.

If possible, applications should use the SYSTEM(BA_SYS) routine, which is easier to use and supplies more functionality, rather than the FORK(BA_SYS) and EXEC(BA_SYS) routines.

SEE ALSO

ALARM(BA_SYS), EXEC(BA_SYS), FCNTL(BA_SYS), LOCKF(BA_SYS), SIGNAL(BA_SYS), TIMES(BA_SYS), ULIMIT(BA_SYS), UMASK(BA_SYS), WAIT(BA_SYS).

NAME

fread — buffered input

SYNOPSIS

```
#include <stdio.h>

int fread(ptr, size, nitems, stream)
char *ptr;
int size, nitems;
FILE *stream;
```

DESCRIPTION

The function `fread` reads into an array pointed to by `ptr` up to `nitems` items of data from the named input `stream`, where an item of data is a sequence of bytes (not necessarily terminated by a null byte) of length `size`. The function `fread` stops appending bytes if an end-of-file or error condition is encountered while reading `stream`, or if `nitems` items have been read. The function `fread` increments the data-pointer in `stream` to point to the byte following the last byte read if there is one [see FSEEK(BA_SYS)]. The function `fread` does not change the contents of `stream`.

RETURN VALUE

If successful, `fread` returns the number of items read. If `size` or `nitems` is non-positive, `fread` returns 0 and does *not* read any items.

APPLICATION USAGE

The argument `size` is typically `sizeof(*ptr)`, where the C operator `sizeof` gives the length of an item pointed to by `ptr`. If `ptr` points to a data type other than `char` it should be cast into a pointer to `char`.

The FERROR(BA_SYS) or FEOF(BA_SYS) routines must be used to distinguish between an error condition and an end-of-file condition.

SEE ALSO

FERROR(BA_SYS), FOPEN(BA_SYS), FSEEK(BA_SYS), FWRITE(BA_SYS), GETC(BA_LIB), GETS(BA_LIB), PRINTF(BA_LIB), PUTC(BA_LIB), PUTS(BA_LIB), READ(BA_SYS), SCANF(BA_LIB). WRITE(BA_SYS),

CAVEATS

The type of the argument `size` to the functions `fread` and `fwrite` will be declared through the `typedef` facility in a header file as `size_t`.

NAME

fseek, rewind, ftell — reposition a file-pointer in a stream

SYNOPSIS

```
#include <stdio.h>

int fseek(stream, offset, whence)
FILE *stream;
long offset;
int whence;

void rewind(stream)
FILE *stream;

long ftell(stream)
FILE *stream;
```

DESCRIPTION

The function `fseek` sets the position of the next input or output operation on the `stream`. The new position is at the signed distance `offset` bytes from the beginning, from the current position, or from the end of the file, according as `whence` has the value `0`, `1`, or `2`.

The call `rewind(stream)` is equivalent to the following:

```
fseek(stream,0L,0)
```

except that `rewind` returns no value.

The functions `fseek` and `rewind` undo any effects of the UNGETC(BA_LIB) routine. After `fseek` or `rewind`, the next operation on a file opened for update may be either input or output.

The function `ftell` returns the offset of the current byte relative to the beginning of the file associated with the named `stream`. The offset is always measured in bytes.

RETURN VALUE

The function `fseek` returns non-zero for improper seeks; otherwise, it returns zero. An improper seek is, for example, an `fseek` on a file that has not been opened via the FOPEN(BA_SYS) routine; on a device incapable of seeking, such as a terminal; or on a stream opened via the POPEN(BA_SYS) routine.

SEE ALSO

LSEEK(BA_SYS), FOPEN(BA_SYS), POPEN(BA_SYS), UNGETC(BA_LIB).

CAVEATS

The `<unistd.h>` header file will define symbolic constants for the values of `whence` [see LSEEK(BA_SYS)].

NAME

fwrite — buffered output

SYNOPSIS

```
#include <stdio.h>

int fwrite(ptr, size, nitems, stream)
char *ptr;
int size, nitems;
FILE *stream;
```

DESCRIPTION

The function `fwrite` appends to the named output `stream` at most `nitems` items of data from the array pointed to by `ptr`. The function `fwrite` stops appending when it has appended `nitems` items of data or if an error condition is encountered on `stream`. The function `fwrite` does not change the contents of the array pointed to by `ptr`. The function `fwrite` increments the data-pointer in `stream` by the number of bytes written.

RETURN VALUE

If successful, `fwrite` returns the number of items written. If `size` or `nitems` is non-positive, `fwrite` returns 0 and does *not* write any items.

APPLICATION USAGE

The argument `size` is typically `sizeof(*ptr)`, where the C operator `sizeof` gives the length of an item pointed to by `ptr`. If `ptr` points to a data type other than `char` it should be cast into a pointer to `char`.

The FERROR(BA_SYS) or FEOF(BA_SYS) routines must be used to distinguish between an error condition and an end-of-file condition.

SEE ALSO

FERROR(BA_SYS), FOPEN(BA_SYS), FREAD(BA_SYS), FSEEK(BA_SYS), GETC(BA_LIB), GETS(BA_LIB), PRINTF(BA_LIB), PUTC(BA_LIB), PUTS(BA_LIB), READ(BA_SYS), SCANF(BA_LIB). WRITE(BA_SYS),

CAVEATS

The type of the argument `size` to the functions `fread` and `fwrite` will be declared through the `typedef` facility in a header file as `size_t`.

NAME

getcwd — get path-name of current working directory

SYNOPSIS

```
char *getcwd(buf, size)
char *buf;
int size;
```

DESCRIPTION

The function `getcwd` returns a pointer to the current directory path-name. The value of `size` must be at least two greater than the length of the path-name to be returned.

RETURN VALUE

If `size` is not large enough or if an error occurs in a lower-level function, `getcwd` returns `NULL` and `errno` indicates the error.

ERRORS

The function `getcwd` fails and `errno` equals:

`EINVAL` if `size` is zero

`ERANGE` if `size` not large enough to hold the path-name.

NAME

getgid, getegid — get real-group-ID and effective-group-ID.

SYNOPSIS

```
unsigned short getgid()

unsigned short getegid()
```

DESCRIPTION

The function `getgid` returns the real-group-ID of the calling-process.

The function `getegid` returns the effective-group-ID of the calling-process.

SEE ALSO

GETGID(BA_SYS), SETGID(BA_SYS), SETUID(BA_SYS).

NAME

getpid, getpgrp, getppid — get process-ID, process-group-ID, and parent-process-ID

SYNOPSIS

```
int getpid()

int getpgrp()

int getppid()
```

DESCRIPTION

The function `getpid` returns the process-ID of the calling-process.

The function `getpgrp` returns the process-group-ID of the calling-process.

The function `getppid` returns the parent-process-ID of the calling-process.

SEE ALSO

EXEC(BA_SYS), FORK(BA_SYS), SETPGRP(BA_SYS), SIGNAL(BA_SYS).

NAME

getuid, geteuid — get real-user-ID and effective-user-ID.

SYNOPSIS

```
unsigned short getuid()

unsigned short geteuid()
```

DESCRIPTION

The function `getuid` returns the real-user-ID of the calling-process.

The function `geteuid` returns the effective-user-ID of the calling-process.

SEE ALSO

GETGID(BA_SYS), SETGID(BA_SYS), SETUID(BA_SYS).

NAME

ioctl — control device

SYNOPSIS

```
int ioctl(fildes, request, arg)
int fildes, request;
```

DESCRIPTION

The function `ioctl` performs a variety of device control-functions by passing the request to a device-driver to perform *device-specific* control-functions.

NOTE: This control is not frequently used and the basic input/output operations are performed by the READ(BA_SYS) and WRITE(BA_SYS) routines.

The argument `fildes` is an open file-descriptor that refers to a device.

The argument `request` selects the device control-function and depends on the device being addressed.

The argument `arg` represents additional information needed by the specific device to perform the requested function. The data-type of `arg` depends upon the particular control-function, but it is either an integer or a pointer to a device-specific data-structure.

In addition to device-specific functions, many device-drivers provide generic functions, (e.g., the general terminal interface [see TERMIO(BA_ENV)]).

RETURN VALUE

If successful, `ioctl` returns a value that depends upon the device control-function, but must be an integer value; otherwise, it returns -1 and `errno` indicates the error.

ERRORS

The function `ioctl` fails and `errno` equals:

`EBADF` if `fildes` is not a valid open file-descriptor.

`ENOTTY` if `fildes` is not associated with a device-driver that accepts control-functions.

`EINTR` if a signal was caught during the `ioctl` operation.

The function `ioctl` also fails if the device-driver detects an error. In this case, the error is passed through `ioctl` without change to the caller. A particular device-driver might not have all of the following error cases.

Requests to standard device-drivers fail and `errno` equals:

`EINVAL` if `request` or `arg` are not valid for this device.

`EIO` if some physical I/O error has occurred.

`ENXIO` if `request` and `arg` are valid for this device-driver, but the particular sub-device can not perform the service requested.

SEE ALSO

The specific device reference documents and generic devices such as the general terminal interface [see TERMIO(BA_ENV)].

NAME

kill — send a signal to a process or a group of processes

SYNOPSIS

```
#include <signal.h>
int kill(pid, sig)
int pid, sig;
```

DESCRIPTION

The function `kill` sends a signal to a process or a group of processes.

The signal sent is specified by `sig`, and is either `0` or from the list in SIGNAL(BA_SYS). If `sig` is `0` (the null-signal), error checking is done but no signal is sent. This checks the validity of `pid`. The process or group of processes to receive `sig` is specified by `pid` as follows:

If `pid < 0`, send `sig` to the process whose process-ID equals `pid`.

If `pid = 0`, send `sig` to all processes, except special system-processes, whose process-group-ID equals the process-group-ID of the sending-process.

If `pid < 0`, but not `-1`, send `sig` to all processes whose process-group-ID equals the absolute value of `pid`.

If `pid = -1`, send `sig` to all processes, except special system-processes.

Of the processes specified by `pid`, only those where the real-user-ID or effective-user-ID of the sending-process matches the real-user-ID or effective-user-ID of the receiving-process are sent the signal, unless the effective-user-ID of the sending-process is super-user.

RETURN VALUE

If successful, `kill` returns `0`; otherwise, it returns `-1`, it does *not* send any signal, and `errno` indicates the error.

ERRORS

The function `kill` fails and `errno` equals:

`EINVAL`	if `sig` is not a valid signal number.
`EINVAL`	if `sig` is `SIGKILL` and `pid` is a special system-process.
`ESRCH`	if no process corresponding to `pid` can be found.
`EPERM`	if the user-ID of the sending-process is not super-user, and its real-user-ID (or effective-user-ID) does not match either the real-user-ID or effective-user-ID of the receiving-process.

SEE ALSO

GETPID(BA_SYS), SETPGRP(BA_SYS), SIGNAL(BA_SYS).

CAVEATS

The variable `errno` will equal `EPERM` if `sig` is `SIGKILL` and `pid` is a special system-process.

NAME

link — link to a file

SYNOPSIS

```
int link(path1, path2)
char *path1, *path2;
```

DESCRIPTION

The function `link` creates a new link (directory entry) for the existing file.

The argument `path1` points to a path-name naming an existing file.

The argument `path2` points to a path-name naming the new directory entry to be created.

RETURN VALUE

If successful, `link` returns `0`; otherwise, it returns `-1`, it does *not* create any link, and `errno` indicates the error.

ERRORS

The function `link` fails and `errno` equals:

`ENOTDIR`	if a component of either path-prefix is not a directory.
`ENOENT`	if a component of either path-name should exist but does not.
`EACCES`	if a component of either path-prefix denies search permission, or if the requested link requires writing in a directory with a mode that denies write permission.
`EEXIST`	if the link named by `path2` exists.
`EPERM`	if the file named by `path1` is a directory and the effective-user-ID is not super-user.
`EXDEV`	if the link named by `path2` and the file named by `path1` are on different logical devices (file-systems) and the implementation does not permit cross-device links.
`EROFS`	if the requested link requires writing in a directory on a read-only file-system.
`EMLINK`	if the maximum number of links to a single file, {LINK_MAX}, would be exceeded.
`ENOSPC`	if the directory to contain the link cannot be extended.

SEE ALSO

UNLINK(BA_SYS).

NAME

lockf — record locking on files

SYNOPSIS

```
#include <unistd.h>

int lockf(fildes, function, size)
int fildes, function;
long size;
```

DESCRIPTION

NOTE: The function `lockf` first became available following UNIX System V Release 1.0 and UNIX System V Release 2.0.

The function `lockf` will allow sections of a file to be locked. Calls to `lockf` from other processes which try to lock the locked file section either return an error value or go to sleep until the resource becomes unlocked. All the locks for a process are removed when the process terminates [see FCNTL(BA_SYS) for more information about record-locking].

The argument `fildes` is an open file-descriptor. The file-descriptor must have been opened with write-only permission (`O_WRONLY`) or with read/write permission (`O_RDWR`) in order to establish a lock with this function call [see OPEN(BA_SYS)].

The argument `function` is a control value which specifies the action to be taken. The permissible values for `function` are defined by the `<unistd.h>` header file as follows:

```
#define F_ULOCK 0 /* unlock locked sections */
#define F_LOCK  1 /* lock a section */
                  /* for exclusive use */
#define F_TLOCK 2 /* test and lock a section */
                  /* for exclusive use */
#define F_TEST  3 /* test section for locks */
                  /* by other processes */
```

`F_TEST` detects if a lock by another process is present on the specified section; `F_LOCK` and `F_TLOCK` both lock a section of a file if the section is available; `F_ULOCK` removes locks from a section of the file. All other values of `function` are reserved for future extensions and will result in an error return if they are not implemented.

The argument `size` is the number of contiguous bytes to be locked or unlocked. The resource to be locked or unlocked starts at the current offset in the file and extends forward for a positive size or backward for a negative size (the preceding bytes up to but not including the current offset). If `size` is `0`, the section from the current offset through the largest file offset {FCHR_MAX} is locked (i.e., from the current offset through the present or any future end-of-file). An area need not be allocated to the file in order to be locked as such locks may exist past the end-of-file.

The sections locked with `F_LOCK` or `F_TLOCK` may, in whole or in part, contain or be contained by a previously locked section for the same process. When this occurs, or if adjacent locked sections would occur, the sections are combined into a single locked section. If the request requires that a new element be added to the table of active locks and this table is already full, an error is returned, and the new section is not locked.

`F_LOCK` and `F_TLOCK` requests differ only in the action taken if the resource is unavailable. `F_LOCK` causes the calling-process to sleep until the resource is available; `F_TLOCK` causes `lockf` to return -1 and `errno` to equal `EACCES` if the section is already locked by another process.

`F_ULOCK` requests may release (wholly or in part) one or more locked sections controlled by the process. Locked sections will be unlocked starting at the point of the file offset through `size` bytes or to the end of file if `size` is 0. When all of a locked section is not released (i.e., the beginning or end of the area to be unlocked falls within a locked section) the remaining portions of that section are still locked by the process. For example, releasing a center portion of a locked section will leave the portions of the section before and after it locked and requires an additional element in the table of active locks. If this table is full, an `EDEADLK` error is returned in `errno` and the requested section is not released.

A potential for deadlock occurs if a process controlling a locked resource is put to sleep by accessing another process's locked resource. Thus, calls to `lockf` or the FCNTL(BA_SYS) routine scan for a deadlock prior to sleeping on a locked resource. An error return is made if sleeping on the locked resource would cause a deadlock.

Sleeping on a resource is interrupted with any signal. The ALARM(BA_SYS) routine may be used to provide a timeout facility in applications requiring it.

RETURN VALUE

If successful, `lockf` returns 0; otherwise, it returns -1 and `errno` indicates the error.

ERRORS

The function `lockf` fails and `errno` equals:

`EBADF` if `fildes` is not a valid open file-descriptor.

`EACCES` if `function` is `F_TLOCK` or `F_TEST` and the section is already locked by another process.

`EDEADLK` if `function` is `F_LOCK` and a deadlock would occur; also if `function` is `F_LOCK`, `F_TLOCK` or `F_ULOCK` and the system lock table has too few entries to honor the request.

APPLICATION USAGE

Because in the future the variable `errno` will be set to `EAGAIN` rather than `EACCES` when a section of a file is already locked by another process, portable application programs should expect and test for either value, for example:

```
if (lockf(fd, F_TLOCK, siz) == -1)
    if ((errno == EAGAIN) || (errno == EACCES))
        /*
         * section locked by another process
         * check for either EAGAIN or EACCES
         * due to different implementations
         */
    else if ...
        /*
         * check for other errors
         */
```

File-locking and record-locking should not be used in combination with the FOPEN(BA_SYS), FREAD(BA_SYS), FWRITE(BA_SYS), etc. *stdio* routines. Instead, the more primitive, non-buffered routines (e.g., the OPEN(BA_SYS) routine) should be used. Unexpected results may occur in processes that do buffering in the user address space. The process may later read/write data which is/was locked. The *stdio* routines are the most common source of unexpected buffering.

SEE ALSO

CHMOD(BA_SYS), CLOSE(BA_SYS), CREAT(BA_SYS), FCNTL(BA_SYS), OPEN(BA_SYS), READ(BA_SYS), WRITE(BA_SYS).

CAVEATS

The error condition which currently sets `errno` to `EACCES` will instead set `errno` to `EAGAIN` [see also **APPLICATION USAGE** above].

Enforcement-mode file and record locking will be added:

> Sections of a file will be locked with advisory-mode or enforcement-mode locks depending on the mode of the file [see CHMOD(BA_SYS)]

NAME

lseek — move read/write file-pointer

SYNOPSIS

```
long lseek(fildes, offset, whence)
int fildes;
long offset;
int whence;
```

DESCRIPTION

The function `lseek` modifies the file-pointer associated with the file-descriptor, `fildes`, without affecting the physical device, as follows:

If `whence` = 0, `lseek` sets the file-pointer to `offset` bytes.

If `whence` = 1, `lseek` adds `offset` to the file-pointer.

If `whence` = 2, `lseek` sets the file-pointer to the length of the file plus `offset` bytes.

If successful, `lseek` returns the resulting pointer location, as measured in bytes from the beginning of the file.

The argument `fildes` is an open file-descriptor [see **file-descriptor** in **Definitions**].

The function `lseek` allows the file-pointer to be set beyond the existing data in the file. If data are later written at this point, subsequent reads in the gap between the previous end of data and the newly written data will return bytes of value 0 until data are written into the gap.

RETURN VALUE

If successful, `lseek` returns a file-pointer value; otherwise, it returns -1, it does *not* change the file-pointer, and `errno` indicates the error.

ERRORS

The function `lseek` fails and `errno` equals:

`EBADF` if `fildes` is not an open file-descriptor.

`ESPIPE` if `fildes` is associated with a pipe or FIFO.

`EINVAL` if `whence` is not 0, 1, or 2.

The significance of the file-pointer associated with a device incapable of seeking, such as a terminal, is undefined.

APPLICATION USAGE

Normally, applications should use the *stdio* routines to open, close, read, write and manipulate files. Thus, an application that had used the FOPEN(BA_SYS) *stdio* routine to open a file would use the FSEEK(BA_SYS) *stdio* routine rather than `lseek`.

SEE ALSO

CREAT(BA_SYS), DUP(BA_SYS), FCNTL(BA_SYS), OPEN(BA_SYS).

CAVEATS

The `<unistd.h>` header file will define symbolic constants for the argument `whence` to the functions `seek` and `lseek` as follows:

Name	*Description*
SEEK_SET	set file-pointer to `offset`.
SEEK_CUR	set file-pointer to current plus `offset`.
SEEK_END	set file-pointer to EOF plus `offset`.

NAME

malloc, free, realloc, calloc, mallopt, mallinfo — fast main memory allocator

SYNOPSIS

```
#include <malloc.h>

char *malloc(size)
unsigned size;

void free(ptr)
char *ptr;

char *realloc(ptr, size)
char *ptr;
unsigned size;

char *calloc(nelem, elsize)
unsigned nelem, elsize;

int mallopt(cmd, value)
int cmd, value;

struct mallinfo mallinfo()
```

DESCRIPTION

The function `malloc` and the function `free` provide a simple general-purpose memory allocation package.

The function `malloc` returns a pointer to a block of at least `size` bytes suitably aligned for any use.

The argument to the function `free` is a pointer to a block previously allocated by the function `malloc`; after the function `free` is performed this space is made available for further allocation.

Undefined results will occur if the space assigned by the function `malloc` is overrun or if an invalid value for `ptr` is passed to the function `free`.

The function `realloc` changes the size of the block pointed to by `ptr` to `size` bytes and returns a pointer to the (possibly moved) block. The contents will be unchanged up to the lesser of the new and old sizes.

The function `calloc` allocates space for an array of `nelem` elements of size `elsize`. The space is initialized to zeros.

Available in UNIX System V Release 2.0, the function `mallopt` plus the function `mallinfo` allow tuning the allocation algorithm at execution time.

The function `mallopt` initiates a mechanism that can be used to allocate small blocks of memory quickly. Using this scheme, a large-group (called a *holding-block*) of these small-blocks is allocated at one time. Then, each time a program requests a small amount of memory from `malloc` a pointer to one of the *pre-allocated* small-blocks is returned. Different holding-blocks are created for different sizes of small-blocks and are created when needed.

The function `mallopt` allows the programmer to set three parameters to maximize efficient small-block allocation for a particular application. The three parameters are:

The value of `size` below which requests to `malloc` will be filled using the special small-block algorithm. Initially, this value, which will be called *maxfast*, is zero, which means that the small-block option is not normally in use by `malloc`.

The number of small-blocks in a holding-block. If holding-blocks have many more small-blocks than the program is using, space will be wasted. If holding-blocks are too small, have too few small-blocks in each, performance gain is lost.

The *grain* of small-block sizes. This value determines what range of small-block sizes will be considered to be the same size. This influences the number of separate holding-blocks allocated. For example, if *grain* were 16-bytes, all small-blocks of 16-bytes or less would belong to one holding-block and blocks from 17-bytes to 32-bytes would belong to another holding-block. Thus, if *grain* is too small space may be wasted because many holding-blocks may be created.

The values for the argument `cmd` to the function `mallopt` are:

`M_MXFAST` Set *maxfast* to `value`. The algorithm allocates all blocks below the size of *maxfast* in large-groups and then doles them out very quickly. The default value for *maxfast* is `0`.

`M_NLBLKS` Set *numlblks* to `value`. The above mentioned large-groups each contain *numlblks* blocks. The value for *numlblks* must be greater than `1`. The default value for *numlblks* is `100`.

`M_GRAIN` Set *grain* to `value`. The sizes of all blocks smaller than *maxfast* are considered to be rounded up to the nearest multiple of *grain*. The value for *grain* must be greater than `0`. The default value for *grain* is the smallest number of bytes which will allow alignment of any data type. The `value` will be rounded up to a multiple of the default when *grain* is set.

`M_KEEP` Preserve data in a freed-block until the next call to the function `malloc`, `realloc`, or `calloc`. This option is provided only for compatibility with the older version of the function `malloc` and is not recommended.

These `cmd` values are defined by the `<malloc.h>` header file.

The function `mallopt` may be called repeatedly, but the parameters may not be changed after the first small-block is allocated from a holding-block. If `mallopt` is called again after the first small-block is allocated using the small-block algorithm, it will return an error.

The function `mallinfo` can be used during a program development to determine the best settings of these parameters for a particular application. The function `mallinfo` must not be called until after some storage has been allocated using the function `malloc`. The function `mallinfo` provides information describing space usage. It returns the structure `mallinfo`, which includes the following members:

```
int arena;     /* total space in arena */
int ordblks;   /* number of ordinary-blocks */
int smblks;    /* number of small-blocks */
int hblkhd;    /* space in holding-block overhead */
int hblks;     /* number of holding-blocks */
int usmblks;   /* space in small-blocks in use */
int fsmblks;   /* space in free small-blocks */
int uordblks;  /* space in ordinary-blocks in use */
int fordblks;  /* space in free ordinary-blocks */
int keepcost;  /* space penalty for keep option */
```

The structure `mallinfo` is defined by the `<malloc.h>` header file.

RETURN VALUE

Each of the allocation functions `malloc`, `realloc`, and `calloc` returns a pointer to space suitably aligned (after possible pointer coercion) for storage of any type of object.

The functions `malloc`, `realloc`, and `calloc` return a `NULL` pointer if `nbytes` is 0 or if there is not enough available memory. When the function `realloc` returns `NULL`, the block pointed to by `ptr` is left intact.

If the function `mallopt` is called after any allocation from a holding-block or if the arguments `cmd` or `value` are invalid, the function `mallopt` will return a non-zero value; otherwise, it will return 0.

APPLICATION USAGE

The functions `mallopt` and `mallinfo` and the `<malloc.h>` header file first appeared in UNIX System V Release 2.0.

In UNIX System V Release 2.0, the developer can control whether the contents of the freed space are destroyed or left undisturbed (see the function `mallopt` above). In UNIX System V Release 1.0, the contents are left undisturbed.

Allocation time increases when many objects have been allocated and not freed. The additional UNIX System V Release 2.0 routines provide some flexibility in dealing with this.

NAME

mknod — make a directory, or a special or ordinary-file

SYNOPSIS

```
int mknod(path, mode, dev)
char *path;
int mode, dev;
```

DESCRIPTION

The function `mknod` creates a new file named by the path-name pointed to by `path`.

The mode of the new file is initialized from `mode`. Where the value of `mode` is interpreted as follows:

`0170000` file type; one of the following:

> `0010000` FIFO-special
> `0020000` character-special
> `0040000` directory
> `0060000` block-special
> `0100000` or `0000000` ordinary-file

`0004000` set user-ID on execution

`0002000` set group-ID on execution

`0001000` (reserved)

`0000777` access permissions; constructed from the following:

> `0000400` read by owner
> `0000200` write by owner
> `0000100` execute (search on directory) by owner
> `0000070` read, write, execute (search) by group
> `0000007` read, write, execute (search) by others

The owner-ID of the file is set to the effective-user-ID of the process. The group-ID of the file is set to the effective-group-ID of the process.

Values of `mode` other than those above are undefined and should not be used. The *owner*, *group* and *other* permission-bits of `mode` are modified by the process's file-mode-creation-mask: `mknod` clears each bit whose corresponding bit in the process's file-mode-creation-mask is set [see UMASK(BA_SYS)].

If `mode` indicates a block-special or character-special file, `dev` is a configuration-dependent specification of a character or block I/O device. If `mode` does not indicate a block-special or character-special device, `dev` is ignored. The value of `dev` comes from the `st_dev` field of the `stat` structure [see STAT(BA_SYS)].

The function `mknod` may be invoked only by the super-user for file types other than FIFO-special.

RETURN VALUE

If successful, `mknod` returns 0; otherwise, it returns -1, it does *not* create a new file, and `errno` indicates the error.

ERRORS

The function `mknod` fails and `errno` equals:

`EPERM`	if the effective-user-ID of the process is not super-user and the file type is not FIFO-special.
`ENOTDIR`	if a component of the path-prefix is not a directory.
`ENOENT`	if a component of the path-prefix does not exist.
`EACCES`	if a component of the path-prefix denies search permission and the effective-user-ID of the process is not super-user.
`EROFS`	if the directory in which the file is to be created is located on a read-only file system.
`EEXIST`	if the named file exists.
`ENOSPC`	if the directory to contain the new file cannot be extended.

SEE ALSO

CHMOD(BA_SYS), EXEC(BA_SYS), STAT(BA_SYS), UMASK(BA_SYS).

NAME

mount — mount a file system

SYNOPSIS

```
int mount(spec, dir, rwflag)
char *spec, *dir;
int rwflag;
```

DESCRIPTION

The function `mount` requests that a removable file system contained on the block-special file identified by the argument `spec` be mounted on the directory identified by the argument `dir`.

The arguments `spec` and `dir` are pointers to path-names.

When `mount` succeeds, references to the file named by `dir` will refer to the root-directory on the mounted file system.

The low-order bit of the argument `rwflag` is used to control write permission on the mounted file system; if the bit is set to 1, writing is forbidden; otherwise, writing is permitted according to individual file accessibility.

The function `mount` may be invoked only by the super-user.

RETURN VALUE

If successful, `mount` returns 0; otherwise, it returns -1 and `errno` indicates the error.

ERRORS

The function `mount` fails and `errno` equals:

`EPERM`	if the effective-user-ID is not super-user.
`ENOENT`	if any of the named files does not exist.
`ENOTDIR`	if a component of a path-prefix is not a directory.
`ENOTBLK`	if the device identified by `spec` is not block-special.
`ENXIO`	if the device identified by `spec` does not exist.
`ENOTDIR`	if `dir` is not a directory.
`EBUSY`	if `dir` is currently mounted on, is someone's current working directory, or is otherwise busy.
`EBUSY`	if the device identified by `spec` is currently mounted.
`EBUSY`	if there are no more mount-table entries.

APPLICATION USAGE

The function `mount` is not recommended for use by application-programs.

SEE ALSO

UMOUNT(BA_SYS).

CAVEATS

The external variable errno will be set to EAGAIN rather than EBUSY when the system mount-table is full.

Additional optional arguments will be added to the mount function. New bit-patterns will be added to the set of possible values of the argument rwflag. Some of these patterns will be used to indicate if an optional argument is present.

NAME

open — open for reading or writing

SYNOPSIS

```
#include <fcntl.h>

int open(path, oflag, mode)
char *path;
int oflag, mode;
```

DESCRIPTION

The function `open` opens a file-descriptor for the named file.

The argument `path` points to a path-name naming a file.

The function `open` sets the file-status flags according to `oflag`. The `<fcntl.h>` header file defines the symbolic names of flags. The values of `oflag` are constructed by ORing flags from the following list (only one of the first three flags below may be used):

`O_RDONLY` Open for reading only.

`O_WRONLY` Open for writing only.

`O_RDWR` Open for reading and writing.

`O_NDELAY` This flag may affect subsequent reads and writes [see READ(BA_SYS) and WRITE(BA_SYS)].

When opening a FIFO with `O_RDONLY` or `O_WRONLY` set:

If `O_NDELAY` is set:

An `open` for reading-only returns without delay. An `open` for writing-only returns an error if no process currently has the file open for reading.

If `O_NDELAY` is clear:

An `open` for reading-only blocks until a process opens the file for writing. An `open` for writing-only blocks until a process opens the file for reading.

When opening a file associated with a communication line:

If `O_NDELAY` is set:

The `open` returns without waiting for carrier.

If `O_NDELAY` is clear:

The `open` blocks until carrier is present.

`O_APPEND` Set the file-pointer to the end of the file prior to each write.

`O_TRUNC` If the file exists, its length is truncated to 0 and the mode and owner are unchanged.

`O_CREAT` If the file exists, this flag has no effect; otherwise, the file is created, the owner-ID of the file is set to the effective-user-ID of the process, the group-ID of the file is set to the effective-group-ID of the process, and the access-permission-bits [see CHMOD(BA_SYS)] of the file-mode are set to the value of `mode` modified as follows [see CREAT(BA_SYS)]:

> The file-mode bits are ANDed with the complement of the process's file-mode-creation-mask [see UMASK(BA_SYS)]. Thus, `open` clears each bit in the file-mode whose corresponding bit in the file-mode-creation-mask is set.

`O_EXCL` If the file exists and both `O_EXCL` and `O_CREAT` are set, `open` will fail.

The file-pointer used to mark the current position within the file is set to the beginning of the file.

The new file-descriptor will be the lowest-numbered file-descriptor available and will remain open across calls to any EXEC(BA_SYS) routines [see FCNTL(BA_SYS)].

RETURN VALUE

If successful, `open` returns an open file-descriptor; otherwise, it returns −1 and `errno` indicates the error.

ERRORS

The function `open` fails and `errno` equals:

`ENOTDIR` if a component of the path-prefix is not a directory.

`ENOENT` if `O_CREAT` is not set and the named file does not exist, or a component of the path-name should exist but does not.

`EACCES` if a component of the path-prefix denies search permission; or if the file does not exist and the directory that would contain the file does not permit writing; or if the `oflag` permission is denied for the named file.

`EISDIR` if the named file is a directory and the `oflag` permission is write or read/write.

`EROFS` if the named file resides on a read-only file system and the `oflag` permission is write or read/write.

`EMFILE` if this process has {OPEN_MAX} file-descriptors currently open.

`ENXIO` if the named file is a character-special or block-special file and the device associated with this special file does not exist; or if `O_NDELAY` is set, the named file is a FIFO, `O_WRONLY` is set and no process has the file open for reading.

`ETXTBSY` if the file is a pure procedure (shared text) file that is being executed and `oflag` specifies write or read/write permission.

EEXIST	if O_CREAT and O_EXCL are set, and the named file exists.
EINTR	if a signal was caught during the open operation.
ENFILE	if the system-file-table is full, there are {SYS_OPEN} files open.
ENOSPC	if the directory to contain the file cannot be extended, the file does not exist, and O_CREAT is specified.

APPLICATION USAGE

Normally, applications should use the *stdio* routines to open, close, read and write files. Thus, applications should use the FOPEN(BA_SYS) *stdio* routine rather than using the OPEN(BA_SYS) routine.

SEE ALSO

CLOSE(BA_SYS), CREAT(BA_SYS), DUP(BA_SYS), FCNTL(BA_SYS), LSEEK(BA_SYS), READ(BA_SYS), WRITE(BA_SYS).

CAVEATS

Enforcement-mode file and record-locking features will be added:

> The function open will set errno to EAGAIN if the file exists, enforcement-mode file and record-locking is set and there are outstanding record-locks on the file [see CHMOD(BA_SYS)].

NAME

pause — suspend process until signal

SYNOPSIS

```
int pause()
```

DESCRIPTION

The function `pause` suspends the calling-process until it receives a signal. The signal must be one that is not currently set to be ignored by the calling-process.

RETURN VALUE

If the signal causes termination of the calling-process, `pause` will not return. In case of error, `pause` returns -1 and `errno` equals `EINTR`.

ERRORS

The function `pause` fails and `errno` equals:

`EINTR` if the signal is *caught* by the calling-process and control is returned from the signal-catching function, the calling-process resumes execution from the point of suspension.

SEE ALSO

ALARM(BA_SYS), KILL(BA_SYS), SIGNAL(BA_SYS), WAIT(BA_SYS).

NAME

pipe — create an interprocess channel

SYNOPSIS

```
int pipe(fildes)
int fildes[2];
```

DESCRIPTION

The function `pipe` creates an I/O mechanism called a *pipe* and returns two file-descriptors, `fildes[0]` and `fildes[1]`. The file associated with `fildes[0]` is opened for reading, the file associated with `fildes[1]` is opened for writing, and the `O_NDELAY` flag is cleared.

Up to {PIPE_MAX} bytes of data are buffered by the pipe before the writing-process is blocked. A read-only file-descriptor `fildes[0]` accesses the data written to `fildes[1]` on a first-in-first-out, FIFO, basis.

RETURN VALUE

If successful, `pipe` returns 0; otherwise, it returns -1 and `errno` indicates the error.

ERRORS

The function `pipe` fails and `errno` equals:

`EMFILE`	if {OPEN_MAX}-1 or more file-descriptors are currently open for this process.
`ENFILE`	if more than {SYS_OPEN} files would be open in the system.

SEE ALSO

READ(BA_SYS), WRITE(BA_SYS).

NAME

popen, pclose — initiate pipe to/from a process

SYNOPSIS

```
#include <stdio.h>

FILE *popen(command, type)
char *command, *type;

int pclose(stream)
FILE *stream;
```

DESCRIPTION

The function `popen` creates a pipe between the calling program and the command to be executed.

The arguments to `popen` are pointers to null-terminated strings containing, respectively, a command line [see SYSTEM(BA_SYS)] and an I/O mode, either `r` for reading or `w` for writing.

The function `popen` returns a stream pointer such that one can write to the standard input of the command, if the I/O mode is `w` by writing to the file `stream`; and one can read from the standard output of the command, if the I/O mode is `r` by reading from the file `stream`.

A stream opened by `popen` should be closed by `pclose`, which waits for the associated process to terminate and returns the exit status of the command.

Because open files are shared, a type `r` command may be used as an input filter and a type `w` command as an output filter.

RETURN VALUE

If files or processes cannot be created or if `command` cannot be executed, `popen` returns a `NULL` pointer.

If `stream` is not associated with a *popened* command, `pclose` returns −1.

APPLICATION USAGE

The FSEEK(BA_SYS) routine should not be used with a stream opened by `popen`.

SEE ALSO

FCLOSE(BA_SYS), FOPEN(BA_SYS), PIPE(BA_SYS), SYSTEM(BA_SYS), WAIT(BA_SYS).

NAME

read — read from file

SYNOPSIS

```
int read(fildes, buf, nbyte)
int fildes;
char *buf;
unsigned nbyte;
```

DESCRIPTION

The function `read` attempts to read `nbyte` bytes from the file associated with `fildes` into the buffer pointed to by `buf`.

The argument `fildes` is an open file-descriptor [see **file-descriptor** in **Definitions**].

On devices capable of seeking, `read` starts at a position in the file given by the file-pointer associated with `fildes`. Upon return from `read`, the file-pointer is incremented by the number of bytes actually read.

Devices incapable of seeking, such as terminals, always read from the current position. The value of a file-pointer associated with such a file is undefined.

If successful, `read` returns the number of bytes read and stored in the buffer; this number may be less than `nbyte` if the file is associated with a communication-line [see IOCTL(BA_SYS) and TERMIO(BA_ENV)], or if the number of bytes left in the file is less than `nbyte` bytes or if the file is a pipe or a special file. When end-of-file is reached, `read` returns 0.

When attempting to read from an empty pipe (or FIFO):

> If the pipe is no longer open for writing, `read` returns 0, indicating end-of-file.
>
> If `O_NDELAY` is clear, `read` blocks until data is written to the file or the file is no longer open for writing.

When attempting to read a file associated with a character-special file that has no data currently available:

> If `O_NDELAY` is clear, `read` blocks until data is available.

The function `read` reads data previously written to a file. If any portion of an ordinary-file prior to the end-of-file has not been written, `read` returns bytes with value 0. For example, the LSEEK(BA_SYS) routine allows the file-pointer to be set beyond the end of existing data in the file. If data are later written at this point, subsequent reads in the gap between the previous end of data and newly written data will return bytes with value 0 until data are written into the gap.

RETURN VALUE

If successful, `read` returns the number of bytes actually read; otherwise, it returns -1 and `errno` indicates the error.

ERRORS

The function `read` fails and `errno` equals:

`EBADF`	if `fildes` is not a valid file-descriptor open for reading.
`EINTR`	if a signal was caught during the `read` operation.
`EIO`	if a physical I/O error has occurred.
`ENXIO`	if the device associated with the file-descriptor is a block-special or character-special file and the file-pointer value is out of range.

APPLICATION USAGE

Normally, applications should use the *stdio* routines to open, close, read and write files. Thus, an application that used the FOPEN(BA_SYS) *stdio* routine to open a file should use the FREAD(BA_SYS) *stdio* routine rather than the READ(BA_SYS) routine to read it.

SEE ALSO

CREAT(BA_SYS), DUP(BA_SYS), FCNTL(BA_SYS), IOCTL(BA_SYS), OPEN(BA_SYS), POPEN(BA_SYS).

CAVEATS

When no data are present at the time of the read on a pipe, FIFO, or *tty-line* with the `O_NDELAY` flag set, `read` returns -1, rather than 0, and `errno` equals `EAGAIN`.

Enforcement-mode file and record-locking will be added:

When trying to read from an ordinary-file with enforcement-mode file and record-locking set [see CHMOD(BA_SYS)], and the segment of the file to be read has a blocking write-lock (i.e., a write-lock owned by another process):

If `O_NDELAY` is set, `read` returns -1 and `errno` equals `EAGAIN`.

If `O_NDELAY` is clear, `read` sleeps until the blocking write-lock is removed.

The function `read` fails and `errno` equals:

`EAGAIN`	if enforcement-mode file-locking and record-locking was set, `O_NDELAY` was set, and there was a blocking write-lock.
`ENOLCK`	if the system record-lock table was full, so `read` could not go to sleep until the blocking write-lock was removed.

NAME

setgid — set group-ID

SYNOPSIS

```
int setgid(gid)
int gid;
```

DESCRIPTION

The function `setgid` sets the real-group-ID and effective-group-ID of the calling-process.

If the effective-user-ID of the calling-process is super-user, set the real-group-ID and effective-group-ID to `gid`.

If the effective-user-ID of the calling-process is not super-user, but its real-group-ID equals `gid`, set the effective-group-ID to `gid`.

RETURN VALUE

If successful, `setgid` returns 0; otherwise, it returns -1 and `errno` indicates the error.

ERRORS

The function `setgid` fails and `errno` equals:

`EPERM` if the real-group-ID of the calling-process is not equal to `gid` and its effective-user-ID is not super-user.

`EINVAL` if `gid` is out of range.

SEE ALSO

EXEC(BA_SYS), GETGID(BA_SYS). GETUID(BA_SYS). SETUID(BA_SYS).

NAME

setpgrp — set process-group-ID

SYNOPSIS

```
int setpgrp()
```

DESCRIPTION

The function `setpgrp` sets the process-group-ID of the calling-process to the process-ID of the calling-process and returns the new process-group-ID.

RETURN VALUE

If successful, `setpgrp` returns the new process-group-ID.

SEE ALSO

EXEC(BA_SYS), FORK(BA_SYS), GETPID(BA_SYS), KILL(BA_SYS), SIGNAL(BA_SYS).

NAME

setuid — set user-ID

SYNOPSIS

```
int setuid(uid)
int uid;
```

DESCRIPTION

The function `setuid` sets the real-user-ID and effective-user-ID of the calling-process.

If the effective-user-ID of the calling-process is super-user, set the real-user-ID and effective-user-ID to `uid`.

If the effective-user-ID of the calling-process is not super-user, but its real-user-ID equals `uid`, set the effective-user-ID to `uid`.

If the effective-user-ID of the calling-process is not super-user, but the saved set-user-ID from an EXEC(BA_SYS) routine equals `uid`, set the effective-user-ID to `uid`.

RETURN VALUE

If successful, `setuid` returns 0; otherwise, it returns -1 and `errno` indicates the error.

ERRORS

The function `setuid` fails and `errno` equals:

`EPERM` if the real-user-ID of the calling-process is not equal to `uid` and its effective-user-ID is not super-user.

`EINVAL` if `uid` is out of range.

SEE ALSO

EXEC(BA_SYS), GETGID(BA_SYS), GETUID(BA_SYS), SETGID(BA_SYS).

NAME

signal — specify what to do upon receipt of a signal

SYNOPSIS

```
#include <signal.h>

int (*signal(sig, func))()
int sig;
int (*func)();
```

DESCRIPTION

The function `signal` allows the calling-process to choose one of three ways in which it is possible to handle the receipt of a specific signal.

The argument `sig` specifies the signal and the argument `func` specifies the choice. The argument `sig` can be assigned any one of the following signals except `SIGKILL`:

`SIGALRM`	alarm clock
`SIGFPE`	floating point exception*
`SIGHUP`	hangup
`SIGILL`	illegal instruction (not reset when caught)*
`SIGINT`	interrupt
`SIGKILL`	kill (cannot be caught or ignored)
`SIGPIPE`	write on a pipe with no one to read it
`SIGQUIT`	quit*
`SIGSYS`	bad argument to routine*
`SIGTERM`	software termination signal
`SIGTRAP`	trace trap (not reset when caught)*
`SIGUSR1`	user-defined signal 1
`SIGUSR2`	user-defined signal 2

For portability, application-programs should use or catch *only* the signals listed above; other signals are hardware and implementation-dependent and may have very different meanings or results across systems (For example, the UNIX System V signals `SIGEMT`, `SIGBUS`, `SIGSEGV`, and `SIGIOT` are implementation-dependent and are not listed above). Specific implementations may have other implementation-dependent signals.

---

* The default action for these signals is an abnormal process termination. See `SIG_DFL`.

The argument `func` is assigned one of three values: `SIG_DFL`, `SIG_IGN`, or an *address* of a signal-catching function. The following actions are prescribed by these values:

`SIG_DFL` Terminate process upon receipt of a signal.

Upon receipt of the signal `sig`, the receiving process is to be terminated with all of the consequences outlined in EXIT(BA_SYS). In addition, if `sig` is one of the signals marked with an asterisk above, implementation-dependent abnormal process termination routines, such as a core dump, may be invoked.

`SIG_IGN` Ignore signal.

The signal `sig` is to be ignored.

NOTE: The signal `SIGKILL` cannot be ignored.

address Catch signal.

Upon receipt of the signal `sig`, the receiving process executes the signal-catching function pointed to by `func`. The signal number `sig` is the only argument passed to the signal-catching function. Additional arguments may be passed to the signal-catching function for hardware-generated signals. Before entering the signal-catching function, the value of `func` for the caught signal is set to `SIG_DFL` unless the signal is `SIGILL`, or `SIGTRAP`.

The function `signal` will not catch an invalid function argument, `func`, and results are undefined when an attempt is made to execute the function at the bad address.

Upon return from the signal-catching function, the receiving process resumes execution at the point at which it was interrupted, except for implementation defined signals where this may not be true.

When a signal to be caught occurs during a non-atomic operation such as a call to a READ(BA_SYS), WRITE(BA_SYS), OPEN(BA_SYS), or IOCTL(BA_SYS) routine on a slow device (such as a terminal); or occurs during a PAUSE(BA_SYS) routine; or occurs during a WAIT(BA_SYS) routine that does not return immediately, the signal-catching function will be executed and then the interrupted routine may return a -1 to the calling-process with `errno` set to `EINTR`.

NOTE: The signal `SIGKILL` cannot be caught.

A call to `signal` cancels a pending signal `sig` except for a pending `SIGKILL` signal.

RETURN VALUE

If successful, `signal` returns the previous value of the argument `func` for the specified signal `sig`; otherwise, it returns `(int(*)())-1` and `errno` indicates the error.

ERRORS

The function `signal` fails and `errno` equals:

`EINVAL` if `sig` is an illegal signal number or `SIGKILL`.

APPLICATION USAGE

Signals may be sent by the system to an application-program (user-level process) or signals may be sent by one user-level process to another using the KILL(BA_SYS) routine. An application-program can catch signals and specify the action to be taken using the function `signal`. The signals that a portable application-program may *send* are:

`SIGKILL, SIGTERM, SIGUSR1, SIGUSR2.`

For portability, application-programs should use only the symbolic names of signals rather than their values and use only the set of signals defined here. Specific implementations may have additional signals.

SEE ALSO

KILL(BA_SYS), PAUSE(BA_SYS), WAIT(BA_SYS), SETJMP(BA_LIB).

CAVEATS

`SIGABRT` will be added to the `<signal.h>` header file [see ABORT(BA_SYS)].

A macro `SIG_ERR` will be defined by the `<signal.h>` header file to represent the return value `(int(*)())-1` of the function `signal` in case of error.

The end-user level utility KILL(BU_CMD) will be changed to use symbolic signal names rather than numbers.

In keeping with the proposed **ANSI X3J11** standard, the argument `func` will be declared as type pointer to a function returning `void`.

The following functions will be added to enhance the signal facility:

`sigset, sighold, sigrelse, sigignore, sigpause.`

These functions will give a calling-process control over the disposition of a specified signal that follows a signal that has been caught. When a signal has been caught, the system will hold (defer) a succeeding signal of the type specified should it occur. Similarly, processes will be able to establish critical regions of code where an incoming-signal is deferred so the critical region can be executed without losing the signal. Finally, a calling process will be able to suspend if a specified signal has not yet occurred.

NAME

sleep — suspend execution for interval

SYNOPSIS

```
unsigned sleep(seconds)
unsigned seconds;
```

DESCRIPTION

The function `sleep` suspends the current-process from execution for the number of seconds specified by the argument `seconds`. The actual suspension-time may be less than that requested for two reasons:

1. because scheduled wakeups occur at fixed 1-second intervals (on the second, according to an internal clock) and
2. because any signal caught will terminate `sleep` following execution of the signal-catching routine.

Also, the suspension-time may be longer than requested by an arbitrary amount due to the scheduling of other activity in the system.

The function `sleep` sets an alarm signal and pauses until it (or some other signal) occurs. The previous state of the alarm signal is saved and restored. The calling-process may have set up an alarm signal before calling `sleep`. If the argument `seconds` exceeds the time until such an alarm signal would occur, the process sleeps only until the alarm signal would have occurred. The alarm signal-catching routine of the calling-process is executed just before `sleep` returns. But if the suspension-time is less than the time till such alarm, the prior alarm time remains unchanged.

RETURN VALUE

If successful, `sleep` returns the *unslept* amount (the requested time minus the time actually slept) in case the caller had an alarm set to go off earlier than the end of the requested suspension-time or premature arousal due to another caught signal; otherwise, `sleep` returns `0`.

SEE ALSO

ALARM(BA_SYS), PAUSE(BA_SYS), SIGNAL(BA_SYS).

NAME

stat, fstat — get file-status information

SYNOPSIS

```
#include <sys/types.h>
#include <sys/stat.h>

int stat(path, buf)
char *path;
struct stat *buf;

int fstat(fildes, buf)
int fildes;
struct stat *buf;
```

DESCRIPTION

The function `stat` obtains information about the status of the file named by the path-name pointed to by `path`. Neither read, write, nor execute permission of the named file is required, but all directories listed in the path-name leading to the file must be searchable.

The function `fstat` obtains the status information about an open file associated with the file-descriptor `fildes` [see **file-descriptor** in **Definitions**].

The argument `buf` points to a structure `stat` which contains file-status information and includes the following members:

```
ushort st_mode;  /* file-mode */
ino_t  st_ino;   /* i-node number */
dev_t  st_dev;   /* file-system-identifier */
dev_t  st_rdev;  /* device-identifier, only */
                 /* for character-special */
                 /* or block-special files */
short  st_nlink; /* number of links */
ushort st_uid;   /* file-owner user-ID */
ushort st_gid;   /* file-group user-ID */
off_t  st_size;  /* file-size in bytes */
time_t st_atime; /* time data last accessed */
time_t st_mtime; /* time data last modified */
time_t st_ctime; /* time file-status last */
                 /* changed, in seconds since */
                 /* 00:00:00 GMT 1 Jan 70 */
```

The `<sys/types.h>` header file defines the types `ushort`, `ino_t`, `dev_t`, `off_t`, and `time_t`.

`st_mode` This field is the file-mode [see MKNOD(BA_SYS)].

`st_ino` This field uniquely identifies the file in a given file-system.

`st_dev` This field uniquely identifies the file-system holding the file. The field has no more significance, but the USTAT(BA_SYS) routine uses it to get more information about the file-system. Together, `st_ino` and `st_dev` uniquely identify ordinary-files.

`st_rdev` This field should not be used by application-programs. The field is valid for block-special or character-special files and has significance only on the system where the file was configured.

`st_nlink` This field should not be used by application-programs.

`st_size` For ordinary-files, this field is the address of the end of the file; for pipes or FIFOs, it is the count of the data currently in the file; for block-special or character-special files, it is undefined.

`st_atime` This field is the time when file-data was last accessed. The following routines change this field:

CREAT(BA_SYS), LOCKF(BA_SYS), MKNOD(BA_SYS), PIPE(BA_SYS), UTIME(BA_SYS), READ(BA_SYS).

`st_mtime` This field is the time when file-data was last modified. The following routines change this field:

CREAT(BA_SYS), MKNOD(BA_SYS), PIPE(BA_SYS), UTIME(BA_SYS), WRITE(BA_SYS).

`st_ctime` This field is the time when file status was last changed. The following routines change this field:

CHMOD(BA_SYS), CHOWN(BA_SYS), CREAT(BA_SYS), LINK(BA_SYS), MKNOD(BA_SYS), PIPE(BA_SYS), UNLINK(BA_SYS), UTIME(BA_SYS), WRITE(BA_SYS).

RETURN VALUE

If successful, both `stat` and `fstat` return 0; otherwise, they return -1 and `errno` indicates the error.

ERRORS

The function `stat` fails and `errno` equals:

`ENOTDIR` if a component of the path-prefix is not a directory.

`ENOENT` if the named file does not exist.

`EACCES` if a component of the path-prefix denies search permission.

The function `fstat` fails and `errno` equals:

`EBADF` if `fildes` is not a valid open file-descriptor.

SEE ALSO

CHMOD(BA_SYS), CHOWN(BA_SYS), CREAT(BA_SYS), LINK(BA_SYS), MKNOD(BA_SYS), PIPE(BA_SYS), READ(BA_SYS), TIME(BA_SYS), UNLINK(BA_SYS), UTIME(BA_SYS), WRITE(BA_SYS).

NAME

stime — set time

SYNOPSIS

```
int stime(tp)
long *tp;
```

DESCRIPTION

The function `stime` sets the system time and date. The argument `tp` points to the value of time in seconds since 00:00:00 GMT Jan. 1, 1970.

RETURN VALUE

If successful, `stime` returns `0`; otherwise, it returns `-1` and `errno` indicates the error.

ERRORS

The function `stime` fails and `errno` equals:

`EPERM` if the effective-user-ID of the calling-process is not super-user.

SEE ALSO

TIME(BA_SYS).

NAME

sync — update super-block

SYNOPSIS

```
void sync()
```

DESCRIPTION

The function `sync` causes all information in transient memory that updates a file-system to be written out to the file-system. This includes modified super-blocks, modified i-nodes, and delayed block I/O.

The function `sync` should be used by programs which examine a file-system.

The writing, although scheduled, is not necessarily complete upon return from the function `sync`.

APPLICATION USAGE

The function `sync` is not recommended for use by application-programs.

NAME

system — issue a command

SYNOPSIS

```
#include <stdio.h>

int system(string)
char *string;
```

DESCRIPTION

The function `system` causes the argument `string` to be given as input to a command interpreter and execution process. That is, the argument `string` is interpreted as a command, and then the command is executed.

Commands

A *blank* is a tab or a space.

A *word* is a sequence of characters excluding blanks.

A *parameter-name* is a sequence of letters, digits, or underscores beginning with a letter or underscore. A *parameter* is a parameter-name, a digit, or any of the characters `?`, `$`, or `!`.

A *simple-command* is a sequence of non-blank words separated by blanks. The first word specifies the path-name or file-name of the command to be executed. Except as specified below, the remaining words are passed as arguments to the invoked command. The command-name is passed as argument 0 [see EXEC(BA_SYS)]. The *value* of a simple-command is its exit *status* if it terminates normally, or (octal) `200`+*status* if it terminates abnormally [see WAIT(BA_SYS)].

A *pipeline* is a sequence of two or more simple-commands separated by the character `|`. The standard output of each simple-command (except the last simple-command in the sequence) is connected by a *pipe* [see PIPE(BA_SYS)] to the standard input of the next simple-command. Each simple-command is run as a separate process; the command execution process waits for the last simple-command to terminate. The exit status of a pipeline is the exit status of the last command.

A *command* is either a simple-command or a *list* enclosed in parentheses: `(` *list* `)`. Unless otherwise stated, the value returned by a command is that of the last simple-command executed in the command.

A *list* is a command or a pipeline or a sequence of commands and pipelines separated by the characters `;` or `&` or the character-pairs `&&` or `||`. Of these, the characters `;` and `&`, which have equal precedence, have a precedence lower than that of the character-pairs `&&` and `||`, which have equal precedence. A *list* may optionally be terminated by the characters `;` or `&`.

A series of commands and/or pipelines separated by the character `;` are executed sequentially, while commands and pipelines terminated by the character `&` are executed asynchronously.

The character-pair `&&` or `||` causes the command or pipeline following it to be executed only if the preceding pipeline returns a zero (non-zero) exit status. An arbitrarily long sequence of newlines may appear in a *list*, instead of the character `;`, to delimit commands.

Comments

A word beginning with the character `#` causes that word and all the following characters up to a new-line to be ignored.

Command Substitution

The standard output from a command bracketed by grave-accents (the character `) may be used as part or all of a word; trailing new-lines are removed.

Parameter Substitution

The character `$` is used to introduce substitutable keyword-parameters.

`$`{*parameter*} The value, if any, of the *parameter* is substituted. The braces are required only when *parameter* is followed by a letter, digit, or underscore that is not to be interpreted as part of its name.

Keyword-parameters (also known as variables) may be assigned values by writing:

parameter-name = *value*

The following parameters are automatically set:

Parameter	*Description*
?	The decimal value returned by the last synchronously executed command in this call to `system`.
$	The process-number of this process.
!	The process-number of the last background command invoked in this call to `system`.

The following parameters are used by the command execution process:

Parameter	*Description*
`HOME`	The initial working (home) directory, initially set from the 6th-field in the `/etc/passwd` file [see PASSWD(BA_ENV)].
`PATH`	The search path for commands (see **Execution** below).

Blank Interpretation

After parameter and command substitution, the results of substitution are scanned for internal field separator characters (*space*, *tab* and *new-line*) and split into distinct arguments where such characters are found. Explicit null arguments ("" or '') are retained. Implicit null arguments (those resulting from parameters that have no values) are removed.

File Name Generation

Following substitution, each word in the command is scanned for the characters `*`, `?`, and `[`. If one of these characters appears the word is regarded as a *pattern*. The word is replaced with alphabetically sorted file-names that match the pattern. If no file-name is found that matches the pattern, the word is left unchanged. The character `.` at the start of a file-name or immediately following the character `/`, as well as the character `/` itself, must be matched explicitly.

Parameter	*Description*
`*`	Matches any string, including the null string.
`?`	Matches any single character.
`[...]`	Matches any one of the enclosed characters. A pair of characters separated by the character `-` matches any character lexically between the pair, inclusive. If the first character following the opening `[` is the character `!` any character *not* enclosed is matched.

Quoting

The following characters have special meaning and cause termination of a word unless enclosed in quotation marks as explained below:

`;` `&` `(` `)` `|` `<` `>` *newline space tab*

A character may be *quoted* (i.e., made to stand for itself) by preceding it with the character `\`. The character-pair `\`*new-line* is ignored. All characters enclosed between a pair of single quote marks (`' '`), except a single quote, are quoted. Inside double quote marks (`" "`), parameter and command substitution occurs and the character `\` quotes the characters `\`, `*`, `"`, and `$`.

Input/Output

Before a command is executed, its input and output may be redirected using a special notation. The following may appear anywhere in a simple-command, or may precede or follow a command and are *not* passed on to the invoked command; substitution occurs before *word* or *digit* is used:

Notation	*Description*
<*word*	Use file *word* as standard input (file-descriptor `0`).
>*word*	Use file *word* as standard output (file-descriptor `1`). If the file does not exist it is created; otherwise, it is truncated to zero length.
>>*word*	Use file *word* as standard output. If the file exists, output is appended to it (by first seeking to the end-of-file); otherwise, the file is created.
<&*digit*	Use the file associated with file-descriptor *digit* as standard input. Similarly for the standard output using >&*digit*.
`<&-`	The standard input is closed. Similarly for the standard output using `>&-`.

If a digit precedes any of the above, the digit specifies the file-descriptor to be associated with the file (instead of the default `0` or `1`). For example:

`... 2>&1`

associates file-descriptor `2` with the file currently associated with file descriptor `1`.

The order in which redirections are specified is significant. Redirections are evaluated left-to-right. For example:

`... 1>`*xxx* `2>&1`

first associates file-descriptor `1` with file *xxx*. It associates file-descriptor `2` with the file associated with file-descriptor `1` (i.e., *xxx*). If the order of redirections were reversed, file-descriptor `2` would be associated with the terminal (assuming file-descriptor `1` had been) and file-descriptor `1` would be associated with file *xxx*.

If a command is followed by the character `&` the default standard input for the command is the empty file `/dev/null`. Otherwise, the environment for the execution of a command contains the file-descriptors of the invoking process as modified by input/output specifications.

Environment

The *environment* [see EXEC(BA_SYS)] is a list of parameter-name-value pairs passed to an executed program in the same way as a normal argument list. On invocation, the environment is scanned and a parameter is created for each name found, giving it the corresponding value.

The environment for any simple-command may be augmented by prefixing it with one or more assignments to parameters. For example:

```
TERM=450 cmd;
```

Signals

The `SIGINT` and `SIGQUIT` signals for an invoked command are ignored if the command is followed by the character `&`; otherwise signals have the values inherited by the command execution process from its parent.

Execution

The above substitutions are carried out each time a command is executed. A new process is created and an attempt is made to execute the command via the EXEC(BA_SYS) routines.

The parameter `PATH` defines the search path for the directory containing the command. The character `:` separates path-names. The default path is `:/bin:/usr/bin` (specifying the current directory, `/bin`, and `/usr/bin`, in that order). NOTE: The current directory is specified by a null path-name, which can appear immediately after the equal sign or between the colon delimiters anywhere else in the path-list. If the command-name contains the character `/` the search path is not used. Otherwise, each directory in the path is searched for an executable file.

Conventionally, `system` has been implemented with the Bourne shell, SH(BU_CMD) [see **Commands and Utilities**]. The current definition of `system` is not intended to preclude that or its implementation by another command-line interpreter that provides the minimum functionality described here. Of course, any implementation may provide a superset of the functionality described.

RETURN VALUE

If successful, `system` returns the exit status of the last simple-command executed. Errors, such as syntax errors, cause a non-zero return value and execution of the command is abandoned.

FILES

`/dev/null`

APPLICATION USAGE

If possible, applications should use the `system`, which is easier to use and supplies more functions, rather than the FORK(BA_SYS) and EXEC(BA_SYS) routines.

SEE ALSO

DUP(BA_SYS), EXEC(BA_SYS), FORK(BA_SYS), PIPE(BA_SYS), SIGNAL(BA_SYS), ULIMIT(BA_SYS), UMASK(BA_SYS), WAIT(BA_SYS).

NAME

time — get time

SYNOPSIS

```
long time((long *) 0)

long time(tloc)
long *tloc;
```

DESCRIPTION

The function `time` returns the value of time in seconds since 00:00:00 GMT, Jan. 1, 1970.

As long as `tloc` is not a null-pointer, the return value is also stored in the location to which `tloc` points.

The actions of `time` are undefined if `tloc` points to an invalid address.

RETURN VALUE

If successful, `time` returns the value of time; otherwise, it returns -1.

SEE ALSO

STIME(BA_SYS).

NAME

times — get process and child-process elapsed times

SYNOPSIS

```
#include <sys/types.h>
#include <sys/times.h>

long times(buffer)
struct tms *buffer;
```

DESCRIPTION

The function `times` fills the structure pointed to by `buffer` with time-accounting information. The action of `times` is undefined if `buffer` points to an illegal address.

The following are the contents of the structure `tms`, which is defined by the `<sys/times.h>` header file to include:

```
time_t  tms_utime;
time_t  tms_stime;
time_t  tms_cutime;
time_t  tms_cstime;
```

This information comes from the calling-process and each of its terminated child-processes for which it has executed a WAIT(BA_SYS) routine. All times are defined in units of 1/{CLK_TCK}'s of a second.

The type `time_t` is defined by the `<sys/types.h>` header file.

The value of `tms_utime` is the CPU time used while executing instructions in the user-space of the calling-process.

The value of `tms_stime` is the CPU time used by the system on behalf of the calling-process.

The value of `tms_cutime` is the sum of the `tms_utime` and `tms_cutime` of the child-processes.

The value of `tms_cstime` is the sum of the `tms_stime` and `tms_cstime` of the child-processes.

RETURN VALUE

If successful, `times` returns the elapsed real time, in units of 1/{CLK_TCK}'s of a second, since an arbitrary point in the past (e.g., system start-up time). This point does not change from one invocation of `times` to another. When `times` fails, it returns -1.

SEE ALSO

EXEC(BA_SYS), FORK(BA_SYS), TIME(BA_SYS), WAIT(BA_SYS).

NAME

ulimit — get and set user limits

SYNOPSIS

```
long ulimit(cmd, newlimit)
int cmd;
long newlimit;
```

DESCRIPTION

The function `ulimit` provides for control over process limits.

Values available for the argument `cmd` are:

1 Get the file size limit of the process. The limit is in units of 512-byte blocks and is inherited by child-processes. Files of any size can be read.

2 Set the file size limit of the process equal to `newlimit`. Any process may decrease this limit, but only a process with an effective-user-ID of super-user may increase the limit.

RETURN VALUE

If successful, `ulimit` returns a non-negative value; otherwise, it returns -1, it does *not* change the limit, and `errno` indicates the error.

ERRORS

The function `ulimit` fails and `errno` equals:

`EPERM` if a process with an effective-user-ID other than super-user attempts to increase its file size limit.

SEE ALSO

WRITE(BA_SYS).

NAME

umask — set and get file-mode-creation-mask

SYNOPSIS

```
int umask(cmask)
int cmask;
```

DESCRIPTION

The function `umask` sets the process's file-mode-creation-mask [see CREAT(BA_SYS)] equal to `cmask` and returns the previous value of the mask. Only the *owner*, *group*, *other* permission-bits of `cmask` and the file-mode-creation-mask are used.

RETURN VALUE

If successful, `umask` returns the previous value of the file-mode-creation-mask.

SEE ALSO

CHMOD(BA_SYS), CREAT(BA_SYS), MKNOD(BA_SYS), OPEN(BA_SYS).

NAME

umount — unmount a file system

SYNOPSIS

```
int umount(spec)
char *spec;
```

DESCRIPTION

The function `umount` requests that a previously mounted file system contained on the block-special device identified by `spec` be unmounted.

The argument `spec` points to a path-name. After unmounting the file-system, the directory upon which the file-system was mounted reverts to its ordinary interpretation.

The function `umount` may be invoked only by the super-user.

RETURN VALUE

If successful, `umount` returns 0; otherwise, it returns -1 and `errno` indicates the error.

ERRORS

The function `umount` fails and `errno` equals:

`EPERM`	if the process's effective-user-ID is not super-user.
`ENXIO`	if the device identified by `spec` does not exist.
`ENOTDIR`	if a component of the path-prefix is not a directory.
`ENOENT`	if the named file does not exist.
`ENOTBLK`	if the device identified by `spec` is not block-special.
`EINVAL`	if the device identified by `spec` is not mounted.
`EBUSY`	if a file on the device identified by `spec` is busy.

APPLICATION USAGE

The function `umount` is not recommended for use by application-programs.

SEE ALSO

MOUNT(BA_SYS).

NAME

uname — get name of current operating system

SYNOPSIS

```
#include <sys/utsname.h>

int uname(name)
struct utsname *name;
```

DESCRIPTION

The function `uname` stores information identifying the current operating system in the structure pointed to by `name`.

The `<sys/utsname.h>` header file defines the structure that `uname` uses and that includes the following members:

```
char sysname[ {SYS_NMLN} ];
char nodename[ {SYS_NMLN} ];
char release[ {SYS_NMLN} ];
char version[ {SYS_NMLN} ];
char machine[ {SYS_NMLN} ];
```

The function `uname` returns a null-terminated character string naming the current operating system in the character array `sysname`.

Similarly, the character array `nodename` contains the name that the system is known by on a communications network.

The members `release` and `version` further identify the operating system.

The member `machine` contains a standard name that identifies the hardware that the operating system is running on.

RETURN VALUE

If successful, `uname` returns a non-negative value; otherwise, it returns −1 and `errno` indicates the error.

NAME

unlink — remove directory entry

SYNOPSIS

```
int unlink(path)
char *path;
```

DESCRIPTION

The function `unlink` removes the directory entry named by the path-name pointed to by the argument `path`. When all links to a file have been removed and no process has the file open, the space occupied by the file is freed and the file ceases to exist. If one or more processes have the file open when the last link is removed, space occupied by the file is not released until all references to the file have been closed.

RETURN VALUE

If successful, `unlink` returns 0; otherwise, it returns -1 and `errno` indicates the error.

ERRORS

The function `unlink` fails and `errno` equals:

`ENOTDIR`	if a component of the path prefix is not a directory.
`ENOENT`	if the named file does not exist.
`EACCES`	if a component of the path-prefix denies search permission.
`EACCES`	if the directory containing the link to be removed denies write permission.
`EPERM`	if the named file is a directory and the effective-user-ID of the process is not super-user.
`EBUSY`	if the entry to be unlinked is the mount point for a mounted file system.
`ETXTBSY`	if the entry to be unlinked is the last link to a pure procedure (shared text) file that is being executed.
`EROFS`	if the entry to be unlinked is part of a read-only file system.

SEE ALSO

CLOSE(BA_SYS), LINK(BA_SYS), OPEN(BA_SYS).

NAME

ustat — get file system statistics

SYNOPSIS

```
#include <sys/types.h>
#include <ustat.h>

int ustat(dev, buf)
int dev;
struct ustat *buf;
```

DESCRIPTION

The function `ustat` returns information about a mounted file system.

The argument `dev` is a device number identifying a device containing a mounted file-system. The value of `dev` comes from the field `st_dev` of the structure `stat` [see STAT(BA_SYS)].

The argument `buf` points to a `ustat` structure that includes the following elements:

```
daddr_t f_tfree;     /* total free blocks */
ino_t   f_tinode;    /* number of free i-nodes */
char    f_fname[6];  /* file-system name or null */
char    f_fpack[6];  /* file-system pack or null */
```

The last two fields, `f_fname` and `f_fpack` may not have significant information on all systems, and, in that case, will contain the null character.

RETURN VALUE

If successful, `ustat` returns 0; otherwise, it returns -1 and `errno` indicates the error.

ERRORS

The function `ustat` fails and `errno` equals:

`EINVAL` if `dev` is not the device number of a device containing a mounted file-system.

SEE ALSO

STAT(BA_SYS).

NAME

utime — set file access and modification times

SYNOPSIS

```
#include <sys/types.h>

int utime(path, times)
char *path;
struct utimbuf *times;
```

DESCRIPTION

The function `utime` sets the access and modification times of the file named by the path-name pointed to by `path`; hence, `utime` updates the time of the last file-status change (`st_ctime`) for that file [see STAT(BA_SYS)].

If `times` is `NULL`, the access and modification times are set to the current time; a process must be the owner of the file or have write permission to do this. If `times` is not `NULL`, it must point to a `utimbuf` structure (see below) and the access and modification times are set to the values in that structure; only the owner of the file or the super-user may do this.

RETURN VALUE

If successful, `utime` returns 0; otherwise, it returns -1 and `errno` indicates the error.

ERRORS

The function `utime` fails and `errno` equals:

`ENOENT`	if the named file does not exist.
`ENOTDIR`	if a component of the path-prefix is not a directory.
`EACCES`	if a component of the path-prefix denies search permission, or if the effective-user-ID is not super-user and not the owner of the file and `times` is `NULL` and write access is denied.
`EPERM`	if the effective-user-ID is not super-user and not the owner of the file and `times` is not `NULL`.
`EROFS`	if the file-system containing the file is mounted read-only.

APPLICATION USAGE

Application-programs must declare the structure `utimbuf` as follows:

```
struct utimbuf {
        time_t actime;  /* access time */
        time_t modtime; /* modification time */
};
```

The structure `utimbuf` gives times in seconds since 00:00:00 GMT Jan. 1, 1970. The `<sys/types.h>` header file defines the type `time_t`.

SEE ALSO

STAT(BA_SYS).

NAME

wait — wait for child-process to stop or terminate

SYNOPSIS

```
int wait(stat_loc)
int *stat_loc;

int wait((int *)0)
```

DESCRIPTION

The function `wait` suspends the calling-process until one of the immediate children terminates. If a child-process terminates prior to the call to `wait`, return is immediate.

If `stat_loc` (taken as an integer) is non-zero, 16-bits of information called *status* are stored in the low-order 16-bits of the location pointed to by `stat_loc`. The status differentiates between stopped and terminated child-processes and if the child-process terminated, identifies the cause of termination and passes useful information to the parent-process as follows:

> If the child-process terminated due to a call to the EXIT(BA_SYS) routine, the low-order 8-bits of status will be zero and the next 8-bits will contain the low-order 8-bits of the argument that the child-process passed to the EXIT(BA_SYS) routine.
>
> If the child-process terminated due to a signal, the low-order 7-bits (i.e., bits 177) will contain the number of the signal that caused the termination. Also, if abnormal-process-termination routines [see SIGNAL(BA_SYS)] successfully completed, the low-order eighth-bit (i.e., bit 200) will be set. The next 8-bits of status will be zero.

If a parent-process terminates without waiting for its child-processes to terminate, a special system process inherits them [see EXIT(BA_SYS)].

The function `wait` fails and its actions are undefined if the argument `stat_loc` points to an illegal address.

RETURN VALUE

If `wait` returns due equals the receipt of a signal, it returns -1 to the calling-process and `errno` to `EINTR`.

If `wait` returns due to a terminated child-process, it returns the process-ID of the child-process to the calling-process; otherwise, it returns immediately with a value of -1 and `errno` indicates the error.

ERRORS

The function `wait` fails and `errno` equals:

`ECHILD` if the calling-process has no more unwaited-for child-processes.

SEE ALSO

EXEC(BA_SYS), EXIT(BA_SYS), FORK(BA_SYS), SIGNAL(BA_SYS).

NAME

write — write on a file

SYNOPSIS

```
int write(fildes, buf, nbyte)
int fildes;
char *buf;
unsigned nbyte;
```

DESCRIPTION

The function `write` attempts to write `nbyte` bytes from the buffer pointed to by `buf` to the file associated with the file-descriptor, `fildes`.

The argument `fildes` is an open file-descriptor [see **file-descriptor** in **Definitions**].

On devices capable of seeking, the actual writing of data proceeds from the position in the file indicated by the file-pointer associated with `fildes`. Upon returning from `write`, the file-pointer is incremented by the number of bytes actually written.

On devices incapable of seeking, such as a terminal, writing always takes place starting at the current position. The value of a file-pointer associated with such a device is undefined [see OPEN(BA_SYS)].

If the `O_APPEND` flag of the file status flags is set, the file-pointer is set to the end of the file prior to each `write` operation.

If a `write` requests that more bytes be written than there is room for (e.g., beyond the user process's file size limit [see ULIMIT(BA_SYS)] or the physical end of a medium), only as many bytes as there is room for are written. For example, suppose there is space for 20 bytes more in a file before reaching a limit; a `write` of 512-bytes will return 20-bytes. The next `write` of a non-zero number of bytes will give a failure return (except as noted for pipes and FIFOs below).

If a `write` to a pipe (or FIFO) of {PIPE_BUF} bytes or less is requested and less than `nbytes` bytes of free space is available in the pipe, one of the following occurs:

> If `O_NDELAY` is clear, the process blocks until at least `nbytes` of space is available in the pipe and then the `write` takes place, or
>
> If `O_NDELAY` is set, the process does *not* block and `write` returns `0`.

A `write` request to a pipe (or FIFO) of more than {PIPE_BUF} bytes behaves differently. Because it is not atomic, a `write` to a pipe (or FIFO) of `nbytes` greater than {PIPE_BUF} bytes should be used only when two cooperating processes, one reader and one writer, are using a pipe.

If a `write` to a pipe (or FIFO) of more than {PIPE_BUF} bytes is requested, one of the following occurs:

If `O_NDELAY` is clear, the process blocks if the pipe is full. As space becomes available in the pipe, the data from the `write` request are written piecemeal, in multiple smaller amounts until the request is fulfilled. Thus, data from a `write` request of more than {PIPE_BUF} bytes may be interleaved on arbitrary byte boundaries with data written by other processes.

If `O_NDELAY` is set and the pipe is full, the process does *not* block and `write` returns `0`.

If `O_NDELAY` is set and the pipe is not full, the process does *not* block and as much data as currently fits in the pipe is written and `write` returns the number of bytes written. In this case, only part of the data are written, but what data are written are *not* interleaved with data from other processes.

In contrast to a `write` of more than {PIPE_BUF} bytes, data from a `write` of {PIPE_BUF} bytes or less is *never* interleaved in the pipe with data from other processes.

RETURN VALUE

If successful, `write` returns the number of bytes written; otherwise, it returns -1, it does *not* change the file-pointer, and `errno` indicates the error.

ERRORS

The function `write` fails and `errno` equals:

`EBADF`	if `fildes` is not a valid file descriptor open for writing.
`EPIPE` and	`SIGPIPE` signal if an attempt is made to write to a pipe that is not open for reading by any process.
`EFBIG`	if an attempt was made to write a file that exceeds the process's file size limit or the system's maximum file size [see ULIMIT(BA_SYS)].
`EINTR`	if a signal was caught during the `write` operation.
`ENOSPC`	if there is no free space remaining on the device holding the file.
`EIO`	if a physical I/O error has occurred.
`ENXIO`	if the device associated with the file-descriptor is a block-special or character-special file and the file-pointer value is out of range.

APPLICATION USAGE

Normally, applications should use the *stdio* routines to open, close, read and write files. Thus, if an application had used the FOPEN(BA_SYS) *stdio* routine to open a file, it would use the FWRITE(BA_SYS) *stdio* routine rather than the WRITE(BA_SYS) routine to write it.

SEE ALSO

CREAT(BA_SYS), DUP(BA_SYS), LSEEK(BA_SYS), OPEN(BA_SYS), PIPE(BA_SYS), ULIMIT(BA_SYS).

CAVEATS

Enforcement-mode file and record-locking will be added:

A `write` to an ordinary-file blocks if enforcement-mode file and record-locking is set, and there is a record-lock owned by another process on the segment of the file to be written.

If `O_NDELAY` is not set, `write` sleeps until the blocking record-lock is removed.

The function `write` fails and `errno` equals:

`EAGAIN`	if enforcement-mode file-locking and record-locking was set, `O_NDELAY` was set and there was a blocking record-lock.
`EDEADLK`	if `write` should go to sleep and cause a deadlock to occur.
`ENOLCK`	if the system record-lock table was full, so `write` could not go to sleep until the blocking record-lock was removed.

Chapter 6

Kernel Extension Routines

NAME

acct — enable or disable process accounting

SYNOPSIS

```
int acct(path)
char *path;
```

DESCRIPTION

The function `acct` enables or disables the system-process accounting-routine. If the routine is enabled, for each process that terminates, an accounting-record will be written on an accounting-file. One of two things can cause termination:

1. a call to the EXIT(BA_SYS) routine, or
2. a signal [see SIGNAL(BA_SYS)].

The effective-user-ID of the calling-process must be super-user to use this function.

The argument `path` points to a path-name naming the accounting-file. The format of an accounting-file produced as a result of calling `acct` has records in the format defined by the structure `acct` in `<sys/acct.h>` which defines the following data-type:

```
comp_t /* floating point - 13-bit fraction, */
       /*                  3-bit exponent */
```

and defines the following members in the structure `acct`:

```
char    ac_flag;      /* accounting flag */
char    ac_stat;      /* exit status */
ushort  ac_uid;       /* accounting user-ID */
ushort  ac_gid;       /* accounting group-ID */
dev_t   ac_tty;       /* control typewriter */
time_t  ac_btime;     /* beginning time */
comp_t  ac_utime;     /* user-time in CLKTCKs */
comp_t  ac_stime;     /* system-time in CLKTCKs */
comp_t  ac_etime;     /* elapsed-time in CLKTCKs */
comp_t  ac_mem;       /* memory usage */
comp_t  ac_io;        /* chars transferred */
comp_t  ac_rw;        /* blocks read or written */
char    ac_comm[8];   /* command name */
```

and defines the following symbolic names:

```
AFORK  /* has executed fork, but no exec */
ASU    /* used super-user privileges */
ACCTF  /* record type: 00 = acct */
```

The `AFORK` flag is set in `ac_flag` when the FORK(BA_SYS) routine is executed and reset when an EXEC(BA_SYS) routine is executed. The `ac_comm` field is inherited from the parent process when a child process is created with the FORK(BA_SYS) routine and is reset when the EXEC(BA_SYS) routine is executed. The variable `ac_mem` is a cumulative record of memory usage and is incremented each time the system charges the process with a clock tick.

If no errors occur during the call, the accounting routine is enabled if `path` is non-zero and is disabled if `path` is zero.

RETURN VALUE

If successful, `acct` returns 0; otherwise, it returns -1 and `errno` indicates the error.

ERRORS

The function `acct` fails and `errno` equals:

`EPERM`	if the effective user of the calling-process is not super-user.
`EBUSY`	if an attempt is being made to enable accounting when it is already enabled.
`ENOTDIR`	if a component of the path-prefix is not a directory.
`ENOENT`	if one or more components of the accounting file path-name do not exist.
`EACCES`	if the file named by `path` is not an ordinary file.
`EROFS`	if the named file resides on a read-only file system.

SEE ALSO

EXIT(BA_SYS), SIGNAL(BA_SYS).

NAME

chroot — change root directory

SYNOPSIS

```
int chroot(path)
char *path;
```

DESCRIPTION

The function `chroot` causes the named-directory to become the root-directory, the starting point for `path` searches for path-names beginning with the character `/`. The user's working directory is unaffected by `chroot`.

The argument `path` points to a path-name naming a directory.

The effective-user-ID of the process must be super-user to change the root directory.

The `..` entry in the root directory is interpreted to mean the root-directory itself. Thus, `..` cannot be used to access files outside the sub-tree rooted at the root-directory.

RETURN VALUE

If successful, `chroot` returns 0; otherwise, it returns -1 and `errno` indicates the error.

ERRORS

The function `chroot` fails, it does *not* change the root-directory, and `errno` equals:

`ENOTDIR`	if any component of the path-name is not a directory.
`ENOENT`	if the named directory does not exist.
`EPERM`	if the effective-user-ID is not super-user.

SEE ALSO

CHDIR(BA_SYS).

NAME

msgctl — message-control-operations

SYNOPSIS

```
#include <sys/types.h>
#include <sys/ipc.h>
#include <sys/msg.h>

int msgctl(msqid, cmd, buf)
int msqid, cmd;
struct msqid_ds *buf;
```

DESCRIPTION

The function `msgctl` provides a variety of message-control-operations as specified by `cmd`. The following values for `cmd` and the message-control-operations they specify are available:

`IPC_STAT` Put the current value of each member of the `msqid_ds` structure in the structure pointed to by `buf`.

`IPC_SET` Setthe following members of the `msqid_ds` structure to the corresponding value found in the structure pointed to by `buf`:

```
msg_perm.uid
msg_perm.gid
msg_perm.mode /* only low 9-bits */
msg_qbytes
```

Only a process with an effective-user-ID equal to either super-user or to either `msg_perm.cuid` or `msg_perm.uid` in the `msqid_ds` structure can execute this `cmd`, and only super-user can raise the value of `msg_qbytes`.

`IPC_RMID` Remove the message-queue-identifier specified by `msqid` from the system and destroy the message-queue and `msqid_ds` structure. Only a process whose effective-user-ID equals either super-user or either `msg_perm.cuid` or `msg_perm.uid` in the `msqid_ds` structure can execute this `cmd`.

RETURN VALUE

If successful, `msgctl` returns 0; otherwise, it returns -1 and `errno` indicates the error.

ERRORS

The function `msgctl` fails and `errno` equals:

`EINVAL` if `msqid` is not a valid message-queue-identifier; or `cmd` is not a valid command.

`EACCES` if `cmd` is `IPC_STAT` and the calling-process does not have read permission.

`EPERM` if `cmd` is `IPC_RMID` or `IPC_SET` and the effective-user-ID of the calling-process does not equal either super-user or either msg_perm.cuid or msg_perm.uid in the msqid_ds structure.

EPERM if cmd is IPC_SET, an attempt is being made to increase the value of msg_qbytes, and the effective-user-ID of the calling-process does not equal super-user.

SEE ALSO

MSGGET(KE_SYS), MSGOP(KE_SYS).

NAME

msgget — get message-queue

SYNOPSIS

```
#include <sys/types.h>
#include <sys/ipc.h>
#include <sys/msg.h>

int msgget(key, msgflg)
key_t key;
int msgflg;
```

DESCRIPTION

The function `msgget` returns the message-queue-identifier associated with the argument `key`.

A message-queue-identifier with its associated `msqid_ds` structure and message-queue are created for `key` if one of the following are true:

if `key` equals `IPC_PRIVATE`.

if `key` does not already have a message-queue-identifier associated with it, and `(msgflg&IPC_CREAT)` is true.

Upon creation, the data structure associated with the new message-queue-identifier is initialized as follows:

Set `msg_perm.cuid` and `msg_perm.uid` to the effective-user-ID of the calling-process;

Set `msg_perm.cgid`, and `msg_perm.gid` to the effective-group-ID of the calling-process;

Set the low-order 9-bits of `msg_perm.mode` to the low-order 9-bits of `msgflg`;

Set `msg_qnum`, `msg_lspid`, `msg_lrpid`, `msg_stime`, and `msg_rtime` to `0`;

Set `msg_ctime` to the current-time;

Set `msg_qbytes` to the system-limit.

RETURN VALUE

If successful, `msgget` returns a message-queue-identifier (a non-negative integer); otherwise, it returns `-1` and `errno` indicates the error.

ERRORS

The function `msgget` fails and `errno` equals:

`EACCES` if a message-queue-identifier exists for `key`, but operation-permission as set by the low-order 9-bits of `msgflg` is denied.

`ENOENT` if a message-queue-identifier does not exist for `key` and `(msgflg&IPC_CREAT)` is "false".

ENOSPC if a message-queue-identifier is to be created but the system-imposed limit on the maximum number of allowed message-queue-identifiers system-wide would be exceeded.

EEXIST if a message-queue-identifier exists for the argument `key` but `((msgflg&IPC_CREAT)&&(msgflg&IPC_EXCL))` is "true".

SEE ALSO

MSGCTL(KE_SYS), MSGOP(KE_SYS).

NAME

msgop — message operations

SYNOPSIS

```
#include <sys/types.h>
#include <sys/ipc.h>
#include <sys/msg.h>

int msgsnd(msqid, msgp, msgsz, msgflg)
int msqid;
struct mymsg *msgp;
int msgsz, msgflg;

int msgrcv(msqid, msgp, msgsz, msgtyp, msgflg)
int msqid;
struct mymsg *msgp;
int msgsz;
long msgtyp;
int msgflg;
```

DESCRIPTION

The function `msgsnd` sends a message to the queue associated with the message-queue-identifier specified by `msqid`.

The argument `msgp` points to a user-defined buffer that must contain first a field of type `long integer` to specify the type of the message, and then a data portion to hold the text of the message. The structure below is an example of what this user-defined buffer might look like.

```
struct mymsg {
    long mtype;      /* message type */
    char mtext[];    /* message text */
}
```

The structure member `mtype` is a positive integer that can be used by the receiving-process for message selection (see `msgrcv` below).

The structure member `mtext` is any text of length `msgsz` bytes. The argument `msgsz` can range from 0 to a system-imposed maximum.

The argument `msgflg` specifies the action to take if any or all of the following are true:

The number of bytes already on the queue equals `msg_qbytes`.

The total number of messages on all queues system-wide equals the system-imposed limit.

These actions are as follows:

If (msgflg&IPC_NOWAIT) is "true", the message is *not* sent and the calling-process returns immediately.

If (msgflg&IPC_NOWAIT) is "false", the calling-process suspends execution until one of the following occurs:

- The condition responsible for the suspension no longer exists, in which case the message is sent.
- The message-queue-identifier msqid is removed from the system [see MSGCTL(KE_SYS)]. When this occurs, errno equals EIDRM and -1 is returned.
- The calling-process receives a signal that is to be caught. In this case the message is not sent and the calling-process resumes execution in the manner prescribed in the SIGNAL(BA_SYS) routine.

Upon successful completion, the following actions are taken with respect to the msqid_ds structure:

msg_qnum is increased by 1.

msg_lspid is set to the process-ID of the calling-process.

msg_stime is set to the current time.

The function msgrcv reads a message from the queue associated with the message queue identifier specified by msqid and places it in the user-defined buffer pointed to by msgp. The buffer must contain a message type field followed by the area for the message text (see the structure mymsg above).

The structure member mtype is the received message's type as specified by the sending-process.

The structure member mtext is the text of the message.

The argument msgsz specifies the size in bytes of mtext. The received message is truncated to msgsz bytes if it is larger than msgsz and (msgflg&MSG_NOERROR) is "true". The truncated part of the message is lost and no indication of the truncation is given to the calling-process.

The <sys/msg.h> header file defines the symbolic name MSG_NOERROR.

The argument msgtyp specifies the type of message requested as follows:

If msgtyp = 0, the first message on the queue is received.

If msgtyp > 0, the first message of type msgtyp is received.

If msgtyp < 0, the first message of the lowest type that is less than or equal to the absolute value of msgtyp is received.

The argument msgflg specifies the action to be taken if a message of the desired type is not on the queue.

These actions are as follows:

If `(msgflg&IPC_NOWAIT)` is "true", the calling-process immediately returns with -1 and `errno` equals `ENOMSG`.

If `(msgflg&IPC_NOWAIT)` is "false", the calling-process suspends execution until one of the following occurs:

- A message of the desired type is placed on the queue.
- The message-queue-identifier `msqid` is removed from the system. When this occurs, `errno` equals `EIDRM` and -1 is returned.
- The calling-process receives a signal that is to be caught. In this case a message is not received and the calling-process resumes execution in the manner prescribed in SIGNAL(BA_SYS).

Upon successful completion, the following actions are taken with respect to the `msqid_ds` structure:

`msg_qnum` is decremented by 1.

`msg_lrpid` is set to the process-ID of the calling-process.

`msg_rtime` is set to the current time.

RETURN VALUE

If successful, `msgsnd` returns 0.

If successful, `msgrcv` returns the number of bytes put in the buffer `mtext`.

Otherwise, both `msgsnd` and `msgrcv` return -1 and `errno` indicates the error.

ERRORS

The function `msgsnd` fails, it does *not* send any messages, and `errno` equals:

`EINVAL` if `msqid` is not a valid message-queue-identifier; or if `mtype` is less than 1; or if `msgsz` is less than 0 or greater than the system-imposed limit.

`EACCES` if the calling-process is denied operation-permission.

`EAGAIN` if the message cannot be sent for one of the reasons cited above and `(msgflg&IPC_NOWAIT)` is "true".

`EINTR` if `msgsnd` was interrupted by a signal.

`EIDRM` if the message-queue-identifier `msgid` has been removed from the system.

The function `msgrcv` fails, it does *not* receive any messages, and `errno` equals:

`EINVAL` if `msqid` is not a valid message-queue-identifier; or if `msgsz` is less than `0`.

`EACCES` if the calling-process is denied operation-permission.

`EINTR` if `msgrcv` was interrupted by a signal.

`EIDRM` if the message-queue-identifier `msqid` has been removed from the system.

`E2BIG` if the length of `mtext` exceeds `msgsz` and `(msgflg&MSG_NOERROR)` is "false".

`ENOMSG` if the queue does not contain a message of the desired type and `(msgtyp&IPC_NOWAIT)` is "true".

SEE ALSO

MSGCTL(KE_SYS), MSGGET(KE_SYS), SIGNAL(BA_SYS).

NAME

nice — change priority of a process

SYNOPSIS

```
int nice(incr)
int incr;
```

DESCRIPTION

The function `nice` adds the value of `incr` to the nice-value of the calling-process. A process's *nice-value* is a positive number for which a more positive value results in lower CPU priority.

The system imposes an implementation-specific, maximum process-nice-value of `2*{NZERO}-1` and a minimum process-nice-value of `0`. If adding `incr` to the process's current nice-value causes the result to be above or below these limits, the process's nice-value is set to the corresponding limit.

RETURN VALUE

If successful, `nice` returns the process's new nice-value minus `{NZERO}`.

ERRORS

The function `nice` fails, it does *not* change the process's nice-value, and `errno` equals:

`EPERM` if `incr` is negative or greater than `2*{NZERO}` and the effective-user-ID of the calling-process is not super-user.

SEE ALSO

EXEC(BA_SYS).

NAME

plock — lock process, text, or data in memory

SYNOPSIS

```
#include <sys/lock.h>

int plock(op)
int op;
```

DESCRIPTION

The function `plock` allows the calling-process to lock its text segment (text lock), its data segment (data lock), or both its text and data segments (process lock) into memory. Locked segments are immune to all routine swapping. The function `plock` also allows these segments to be unlocked. The effective-user-ID of the calling-process must be super-user to use this call. The argument `op` specifies the following, which are defined by the `<sys/lock.h>` header file:

`PROCLOCK`	lock text and data segments into memory (process lock)
`TXTLOCK`	lock text segment into memory (text lock)
`DATLOCK`	lock data segment into memory (data lock)
`UNLOCK`	remove locks

RETURN VALUE

If successful, `plock` returns 0 to the calling-process; otherwise, it returns −1 and `errno` indicates the error.

ERRORS

The function `plock` fails, it does *not* perform the requested operation, and `errno` equals:

`EPERM`	if the effective-user-ID of the calling-process is not super-user.
`EINVAL`	if `op` is `PROCLOCK` and a process-lock, a text-lock, or a data-lock already exists on the calling-process.
`EINVAL`	if `op` is `TXTLOCK` and a text-lock, or a process-lock already exists on the calling-process.
`EINVAL`	if `op` is `DATLOCK` and a data-lock, or a process-lock already exists on the calling-process.
`EINVAL`	if `op` is `UNLOCK` and the calling-process has no locks on it.

APPLICATION USAGE

The function `plock` should not be used by most applications. Only programs that must have the type of real-time control it provides should use it.

SEE ALSO

EXEC(BA_SYS), EXIT(BA_SYS), FORK(BA_SYS).

NAME

profil — execution time profile

SYNOPSIS

```
void profil(buff, bufsiz, offset, scale)
char *buff;
int bufsiz, offset, scale;
```

DESCRIPTION

The argument `buff` points to an area of memory whose length (in bytes) is given by `bufsiz`. After the call to `profil`, the user's program counter (pc) is examined each clock tick ({CLK_TCK} times per second); `offset` is subtracted from it, and the result multiplied by `scale`. If the resulting number corresponds to an entry inside `buff`, that entry is incremented. An "entry" is defined as a series of bytes with length `sizeof(short)`.

The scale is interpreted as an unsigned, fixed-point fraction with binary point at the left: `0177777` (octal) gives a 1-1 mapping of pc's to words in `buff`; `077777` (octal) maps each pair of instruction words together. `02`(octal) maps all instructions onto the beginning of `buff` (producing a non-interrupting core clock).

Profiling is turned off by giving a `scale` of `0` or `1`. It is rendered ineffective by giving a `bufsiz` of `0`. Profiling is turned off when an EXEC(BA_SYS) routine is executed, but remains on in both child and parent after a call to the FORK(BA_SYS) routine. Profiling will be turned off if an update in `buff` would cause a memory fault.

RETURN VALUE

Not defined.

APPLICATION USAGE

The function `profil` would normally be used by an application program only during development of a program to analyze the program's performance.

NAME

ptrace — process trace

SYNOPSIS

```
int ptrace(request, pid, addr, data)
int request, pid, data;
```

DESCRIPTION

The function `ptrace` provides a means by which a parent-process may control the execution of a child-process. Its primary use is for the implementation of breakpoint debugging. The child-process behaves normally until it encounters a signal [see SIGNAL(BA_SYS)] at which time it enters a stopped state and its parent is notified via the WAIT(BA_SYS) routine. When the child is in the stopped state, its parent can examine and modify its *core-image* using `ptrace`. Also, the parent can cause the child either to terminate or continue, with the possibility of ignoring the signal that caused it to stop.

The data type of `addr` depends upon the `request` passed `ptrace`.

The argument `request` determines the precise action to be taken by `ptrace` and is one of the following:

0 This request must be issued by the child-process if it is to be traced by its parent. It turns on the child's trace flag that stipulates that the child should be left in a stopped state upon receipt of a signal rather than the state specified by `func` [see SIGNAL(BA_SYS)]. The arguments `pid`, `addr`, and `data` are ignored, and a return value is not defined for this request. Peculiar results will ensue if the parent does not expect to trace the child.

The remainder of the requests can only be used by the parent-process. For each, `pid` is the process-ID of the child. The child must be in a stopped state before these requests are made.

1, 2 With these requests, the word at location `addr` in the address space of the child-process is returned to the parent-process. If instruction (I) and data (D) space are separated, request 1 returns a word from I-space, and request 2 returns a word from D-space. If I-space and D-space are not separated either request 1 or request 2 may be used with equal results. The argument `data` is ignored. These two requests fail if `addr` is not the start address of a word, in which case -1 is returned to the parent-process and the parent's `errno` equals `EIO`.

3 With this request, the word at location `addr` in the child's *user-area* in the system's address space is returned to the parent-process.

The argument `data` is ignored. This request fails if `addr` is not the start address of a word or is outside the *user-area*, in which case -1 is returned to the parent-process and the parent's `errno` equals `EIO`.

4, 5 With these requests, the value of `data` is written into the address space of the child at location `addr`. If I-space and D-space are separated, request 4 writes a word into I-space, and request 5 writes a word into D-space. If I-space and D-space are not separated, either request 4 or request 5 may be used with equal results. Upon successful completion, the value written into the address space of the child is returned to the parent.

These two requests fail if `addr` is a location in a pure procedure space and another process is executing in that space, or `addr` is not the start address of a word. Upon failure -1 is returned to the parent-process and the parent's `errno` equals `EIO`.

6 With this request, a few entries in the child's *user-area* can be written.

The value of `data` is written and `addr` is the location of the entry. Entries that can be written are implementation-specific but might include general registers portions of the *processor-status-word*.

7 This request causes the child to resume execution. If `data` is 0, all pending signals including the one that caused the child to stop are canceled before it resumes execution.

If `data` is a valid signal number, the child resumes execution as if it had incurred that signal, and any other pending signals are canceled. The argument `addr` must equal 1 for this request. Upon successful completion, the value of `data` is returned to the parent. This request fails if `data` is not 0 or a valid signal number, in which case -1 is returned to the parent-process and the parent's `errno` equals `EIO`.

8 This request causes the child to terminate with the same consequences as the EXIT(BA_SYS) routine.

9 This request is implementation-dependent but if operative, it is used to request single-stepping through the instructions of the child.

To forestall possible fraud, `ptrace` inhibits the set-user-ID facility on subsequent EXEC(BA_SYS) routines. If a traced process calls and EXEC(BA_SYS) routine, it will stop before executing the first instruction of the new image showing signal `SIGTRAP`.

RETURN VALUE

Upon failure, `ptrace` returns -1. Return values on successful completion are specific to the request type (see above).

ERRORS

In general, `ptrace` fails and `errno` equals:

`EIO` if `request` is an illegal number. See the summary for each request type above.

`ESRCH` if `pid` identifies a child that does not exist or has not executed a `ptrace` with request `0`.

APPLICATION USAGE

The function `ptrace` should not be used by application-programs. It is only used by software debugging programs and it is hardware-dependent.

When `ptrace` is used to read a word from the address space of the child-process, `request` 1, 2 or 3, the data read and value returned by `ptrace` could be -1. In this case, a return value of -1 would not indicate an error.

SEE ALSO

EXEC(BA_SYS), SIGNAL(BA_SYS), WAIT(BA_SYS).

NAME

semctl — semaphore-control-operations

SYNOPSIS

```
#include <sys/types.h>
#include <sys/ipc.h>
#include <sys/sem.h>

int semctl(semid, semnum, cmd, arg)
int semid, cmd;
int semnum;
union semun {
     int val;
     struct semid_ds *buf;
     ushort *array;
  } arg;
```

DESCRIPTION

The function `semctl` provides a variety of semaphore-control-operations, as specified by `cmd`, that are executed with respect to the semaphore specified by `semid` and `semnum`. The `<sys/sem.h>` header file defines the symbolic names for values of `cmd`. The level of permission required for each operation is shown with each command below:

`GETVAL` Return the value of `semval` (Requires read permission).

`SETVAL` Set `semval` to `arg.val` (Requires alter permission). Successfully executing this `cmd` clears the `semadj` value corresponding to the specified semaphore in all processes.

`GETPID` Return the value of `sempid` (Requires read permission).

`GETNCNT` Return the value of `semncnt` (Requires read permission).

`GETZCNT` Return the value of `semzcnt` (Requires read permission).

The following `cmds` operate on each `semval` in the set of semaphores.

`GETALL` Return `semvals` in the array pointed to by `arg.array` (Requires read permission).

`SETALL` Set `semval` values according to the array pointed to by `arg.array` (Requires alter permission). Successfully executing this `cmd` clears the `semadj` values corresponding to each specified semaphore in all processes.

The following `cmds` are also available:

`IPC_STAT` Put the current value of each member of the `semid_ds` structure in the structure pointed to by `arg.buf` (Requires read permission).

`IPC_SET` Set the following members of the `semid_ds` structure to the corresponding value found in the structure pointed to by `arg.buf`:

```
sem_perm.uid
sem_perm.gid
sem_perm.mode /* only low 9-bits */
```

Only a process with an effective-user-ID equal to either super-user or to either `sem_perm.cuid` or `sem_perm.uid` in the `semid_ds` structure can execute this `cmd`.

`IPC_RMID` Remove the semaphore-identifier specified by `semid` from the system and destroy the set of semaphores and the `semid_ds` structure. Only a process with an effective-user-ID equal to either super-user or to either `sem_perm.cuid` or `sem_perm.uid` in the `semid_ds` structure can execute this `cmd`.

RETURN VALUE

If successful, the value `semctl` returns depends on `cmd` as follows:

`GETVAL`	the value of `semval`.
`GETPID`	the value of `sempid`.
`GETNCNT`	the value of `semncnt`.
`GETZCNT`	the value of `semzcnt`.
All others	a value of `0`.

Otherwise, `shmctl` returns `-1` and `errno` indicates the error.

ERRORS

The function `semctl` fails and `errno` equals:

`EINVAL` if `semid` is not a valid semaphore-identifier; or `semnum` is less than `0` or greater than `sem_nsems`; or `cmd` is not a valid command.

`EACCES` if the calling-process is denied operation-permission.

`EPERM` if `cmd` is `IPC_RMID` or `IPC_SET` and the effective-user-ID of the calling-process does not equal either super-user or either `sem_perm.cuid` or `sem_perm.uid` in the `semid_ds` structure.

`ERANGE` if `cmd` is `SETVAL` or `SETALL` and `semval` would exceed the system imposed maximum.

SEE ALSO

SEMGET(KE_SYS), SEMOP(KE_SYS).

NAME

semget — get set of semaphores

SYNOPSIS

```
#include <sys/types.h>
#include <sys/ipc.h>
#include <sys/sem.h>
int semget(key, nsems, semflg)
key_t key;
int nsems, semflg;
```

DESCRIPTION

The function `semget` returns the semaphore-identifier associated with the argument `key`.

A semaphore-identifier with its associated `semid_ds` structure and its set of `nsems` semaphores are created for `key` if one of the following are true:

if `key` equals `IPC_PRIVATE`.

if `key` does not already have a semaphore-identifier associated with it, and `(semflg&IPC_CREAT)` is "true".

Upon creation, the `semid_ds` structure is initialized as follows:

In the operation-permissions structure, set `sem_perm.cuid` and `sem_perm.uid` to the effective-user-ID of the calling-process; while setting `sem_perm.cgid` and `sem_perm.gid` to the effective-group-ID of the calling-process.

Set the low-order 9-bits of `sem_perm.mode` to the low-order 9-bits of `semflg`.

Set `sem_nsems` is set to the value of `nsems`.

Set `sem_otime` to `0`, and set `sem_ctime` to the current time.

The data structure for each semaphore in the set is not initialized.

The function `semctl` with the command `SETVAL` or `SETALL` initializes each semaphore.

RETURN VALUE

If successful, `semget` returns a semaphore-identifier (a non-negative integer); otherwise, it returns -1 and `errno` indicates the error.

ERRORS

The function `semget` fails and `errno` equals:

`EACCES` if a semaphore-identifier exists for `key`, but operation-permission set by the low-order 9-bits of `semflg` is denied.

`EEXIST` if a semaphore-identifier exists for the argument `key` but `((semflg&IPC_CREAT)&&(semflg&IPC_EXCL))` is "true".

ENOENT if a semaphore-identifier does not exist for the argument key and (semflg&IPC_CREAT) is "false".

ENOSPC if a semaphore-identifier is to be created but the system-imposed limit on the maximum number of allowed semaphores system-wide would be exceeded.

EINVAL if nsems is either less than or equal to 0 or greater than the system-imposed limit, or a semaphore-identifier exists for key, but the number of semaphores in the set associated with it is less than nsems and nsems is not equal to 0.

SEE ALSO

SEMCTL(KE_SYS), SEMOP(KE_SYS).

NAME

semop — semaphore operations

SYNOPSIS

```
#include <sys/types.h>
#include <sys/ipc.h>
#include <sys/sem.h>

int semop(semid, sops, nsops)
int semid;
struct sembuf *sops;
unsigned nsops;
```

DESCRIPTION

The function `semop` automatically performs an user-defined array of semaphore-operations on the set of semaphores associated with the semaphore-identifier specified by the argument `semid`.

The argument `sops` points to a user-defined array of semaphore-operation structures.

The argument `nsops` is the number of such structures in the array.

Each structure, `sembuf`, includes the following members:

```
short sem_num;    /* semaphore number */
short sem_op;     /* semaphore operation */
short sem_flg;    /* operation flags */
```

Each semaphore operation specified by `sem_op` is performed on the corresponding semaphore specified by `semid` and `sem_num`.

The variable `sem_op` specifies one of three semaphore operations:

1. If `sem_op` is a negative integer and the calling-process has alter permission, one of the following occurs:

   - If `semval` is greater than or equal to the absolute value of `sem_op`, the absolute value of `sem_op` is subtracted from `semval`. Also, if `(sem_flg&SEM_UNDO)` is "true", the absolute value of `sem_op` is added to the calling-process's `semadj` value for the specified semaphore [see EXIT(BA_SYS) in EFFECTS(KE_ENV)]. The `<sys/sem.h>` header file defines the symbolic name `SEM_UNDO`.

   - If `semval` is less than the absolute value of `sem_op` and `(sem_flg&IPC_CREAT)` is "true", `semop` returns immediately.

   - If `semval` is less than the absolute value of `sem_op` and `(sem_flg&IPC_CREAT)` is "false", `semop` increments the `semncnt` associated with the specified semaphore and suspends execution of the calling-process until one of the following occurs:

- The value of semval becomes greater than or equal to the absolute value of sem_op. When this occurs, the value of semncnt associated with the specified semaphore is decremented, the absolute value of sem_op is subtracted from semval and, if (sem_flg&SEM_UNDO) is "true", the absolute value of sem_op is added to the calling-process's semadj value for the specified semaphore.
- The semid for which the calling-process is awaiting action is removed from the system [see SEMCTL(KE_SYS)]. When this occurs, errno is set equal to EIDRM, and a value of -1 is returned.
- The calling-process receives a signal that is to be caught. When this occurs, the value of semncnt associated with the specified semaphore is decremented, and the calling-process resumes execution in the manner prescribed in the routines defined in SIGNAL(BA_SYS).

2. If sem_op is a positive integer and the calling-process has alter permission, the value of sem_op is added to semval and, if (sem_flg&SEM_UNDO) is "true", the value of sem_op is subtracted from the calling-process's semadj value for the specified semaphore.
3. If sem_op is 0 and the calling-process has read permission, one of the following occurs:
   - If semval is 0, semop returns immediately.
   - If semval is not equal to 0 and (sem_flg&IPC_CREAT) is "true", semop returns immediately.
   - If semval is not equal to 0 and (sem_flg&IPC_CREAT) is "false", semop increments the semzcnt associated with the specified semaphore and suspends execution of the calling-process until one of the following occurs:
     - The value of semval becomes 0, at which time the value of semzcnt associated with the specified semaphore is decremented.
     - The semid for which the calling-process is awaiting action is removed from the system. When this occurs, errno is set equal to EIDRM, and a value of -1 is returned.
     - The calling-process receives a signal that is to be caught. When this occurs, the value of semzcnt associated with the specified semaphore is decremented, and the calling-process resumes execution in the manner prescribed in the routines defined in SIGNAL(BA_SYS).

RETURN VALUE

If successful, `semop` returns 0; otherwise, it returns −1 and `errno` indicates the error.

ERRORS

The function `semop` fails and `errno` equals:

`EINVAL` if `semid` is not a valid semaphore-identifier; or the number of individual semaphores for which the calling-process requests a `SEM_UNDO` would exceed the limit.

`EACCES` if the calling-process is denied operation-permission.

`EAGAIN` if the operation would result in suspension of the calling-process but `(sem_flg&IPC_CREAT)` is "true".

`EFBIG` if `sem_num` is less than 0 or greater than or equal to the number of semaphores in the set associated with `semid`.

`E2BIG` if `nsops` is greater than the system-imposed maximum.

`ENOSPC` if the limit on the number of individual processes requesting a `SEM_UNDO` would be exceeded.

`ERANGE` if an operation would cause a `semval` to overflow the system-imposed limit, or an operation would cause a `semadj` value to overflow the system-imposed limit.

`EINTR` if `semop` was interrupted by a signal.

`EIDRM` if semaphore-identifier `semid` was removed from the system.

Upon successful completion, the value of `sempid` for each semaphore specified in the array pointed to by `sops` is set to the process-ID of the calling-process.

SEE ALSO

EXEC(BA_SYS), EXIT(BA_SYS), FORK(BA_SYS), SEMCTL(KE_SYS), SEMGET(KE_SYS).

NAME

shmctl — shared-memory-control-operations

SYNOPSIS

```
#include <sys/types.h>
#include <sys/ipc.h>
#include <sys/shm.h>

int shmctl(shmid, cmd, buf)
int shmid, cmd;
struct shmid_ds *buf;
```

DESCRIPTION

The function `shmctl` provides a variety of shared-memory-control-operations as specified by `cmd`. The following values for `cmd` are available:

`IPC_STAT` Put the current value of each member of the `shmid_ds` structure in the structure pointed to by `buf`.

`IPC_SET` Set the following members of the `shmid_ds` structure to the corresponding value found in the structure pointed to by `buf`:

```
shm_perm.uid
shm_perm.gid
shm_perm.mode /* only low 9-bits */
```

Only a process whose effective-user-ID equals either super-user or either `shm_perm.cuid` or `shm_perm.uid` in the `shmid_ds` structure can execute this `cmd`.

`IPC_RMID` Remove the shared-memory-identifier specified by `shmid` from the system and destroy the shared-memory-segment and `shmid_ds` structure associated with it. Only a process whose effective-user-ID equals either super-user or either `shm_perm.cuid` or `shm_perm.uid` in the `shmid_ds` structure can execute this `cmd`.

RETURN VALUE

If successful, `shmctl` returns 0; otherwise, it returns -1 and `errno` indicates the error.

ERRORS

The function `shmctl` fails and `errno` equals:

`EINVAL` if `shmid` is not a valid shared-memory-identifier; or `cmd` is not a valid command.

`EACCES` if `cmd` is `IPC_STAT` and the calling-process does not have read permission.

`EPERM` if `cmd` is `IPC_RMID` or `IPC_SET` and the effective-user-ID of the calling-process does not equal either super-user or either `shm_perm.cuid` or `shm_perm.uid` in the `shmid_ds` structure.

APPLICATION USAGE

The functions `shmctl`, `shmget`, and `shmat` and `shmdt` are hardware-dependent and may not be present on all systems. The shared-memory-routines should not be used by applications except when extreme performance considerations demand them.

SEE ALSO

SHMGET(KE_SYS), SHMOP(KE_SYS).

NAME

shmget — get shared-memory-segment

SYNOPSIS

```
#include <sys/types.h>
#include <sys/ipc.h>
#include <sys/shm.h>

int shmget(key, size, shmflg)
key_t key;
int size, shmflg;
```

DESCRIPTION

The function `shmget` returns the shared-memory-identifier associated with the argument `key`.

A shared-memory-identifier with its associated `shmid_ds` structure and shared-memory-segment of at least `size` bytes are created for `key` if one of the following are true:

if `key` equals `IPC_PRIVATE`.

if `key` does not already have a shared-memory-identifier associated with it and `(shmflg&IPC_CREAT)` is "true".

Upon creation, the data structure associated with the new shared-memory-identifier is initialized as follows:

Set `shm_perm.cuid` and `shm_perm.uid` to the effective-user-ID of the calling-process.

Set `shm_perm.cgid` and `shm_perm.gid` to the effective-group-ID of the calling-process.

Set the low-order 9-bits of `shm_perm.mode` to the low-order 9-bits of `shmflg`.

Set `shm_segsz` to the value of `size`.

Set `shm_lpid`, `shm_nattch`, `shm_atime`, and `shm_dtime` to `0`.

Set `shm_ctime` to the current time.

RETURN VALUE

If successful, `shmget` returns a shared-memory-identifier (a non-negative integer); otherwise, it returns -1 and `errno` indicates the error.

ERRORS

The function `shmget` fails and `errno` equals:

`EACCES` if a shared-memory-identifier exists for `key` but operation-permission set by the low-order 9-bits of `shmflg` is denied.

`EEXIST` if a shared-memory-identifier exists for the argument `key` but `((shmflg&IPC_CREAT)&&(shmflg&IPC_EXCL))` is "true".

`ENOENT` if a shared-memory-identifier does not exist for the argument `key` and `(shmflg&IPC_CREAT)` is "false".

`ENOSPC` if a shared-memory-identifier is to be created but the system-imposed limit on the maximum number of allowed shared-memory-identifiers system-wide would be exceeded.

`ENOMEM` if a shared-memory-identifier and associated shared-memory-segment are to be created but the amount of available physical memory is not sufficient to fill the request.

`EINVAL` if `size` is less than the system-imposed minimum or greater than the system-imposed maximum, or a shared-memory-identifier exists for `key` but the size of the segment associated with it is less than `size` and `size` is not zero.

APPLICATION USAGE

The functions `shmctl`, `shmget` and `shmat` and `shmdt` are hardware-dependent and may not be present on all systems. The shared memory routines should not be used by applications except when extreme performance considerations require them.

SEE ALSO

SHMCTL(KE_SYS), SHMOP(KE_SYS).

NAME

shmop — shared-memory-operations

SYNOPSIS

```
#include <sys/types.h>
#include <sys/ipc.h>
#include <sys/shm.h>

char *shmat(shmid, shmaddr, shmflg)
int shmid;
char *shmaddr
int shmflg;

int shmdt(shmaddr)
char *shmaddr
```

DESCRIPTION

The function `shmat` attaches the shared-memory-segment associated with the shared-memory-identifier specified by `shmid` to the data segment of the calling-process at the address specified by one of the following criteria:

> If `shmaddr` is zero, attach the shared-memory-segment at the first available address the system selects.
>
> If `shmaddr` is not zero and `(shmflg&SHM_RND)` is "true", attach the shared-memory-segment at the address specified by `(shmaddr-(shmaddr%SHMLBA))`, where `%` is the C language modulos operator.
>
> If `shmaddr` is not zero and `(shmflg&SHM_RND)` is "false", attach the shared-memory-segment at the address given by `shmaddr`.

The segment is attached for reading if `(shmflg&SHM_RDONLY)` is "true" and the calling-process has read permission; otherwise, if it is not true and the calling-process has read and write permission, the segment is attached for reading and writing.

The function `shmdt` detaches the shared-memory-segment located at the address given by `shmaddr` from the data segment of the calling-process.

The `<sys/shm.h>` header file defines the following symbolic names:

Name	*Description*
SHMLBA	segment low boundary address multiple
SHM_RDONLY	attach read-only (else read-write)
SHM_RND	round attach address to SHMLBA

RETURN VALUE

If successful, `shmat` returns the data segment start address of the attached shared-memory-segment.

If successful, `shmdt` returns `0`. Otherwise, `shmat` and `shmdt` return -1 and `errno` indicates the error.

ERRORS

The function `shmat` fails, it does *not* attach the shared-memory-segment, and `errno` equals:

`EACCES` if the calling-process is denied operation-permission.

`ENOMEM` if the available data space is not large enough to accommodate the shared-memory-segment.

`EINVAL` if `shmid` is not a valid shared-memory-identifier; or if `shmaddr` is non-zero and the address specified by `(shmaddr-(shmaddr%SHMLBA))` is illegal; or if `shmaddr` is non-zero and `(shmflg&SHM_RND)` is "false" and `shmaddr` is an illegal-address.

`EMFILE` if the number of shared-memory-segments attached to the calling-process would exceed the system-imposed limit.

The function `shmdt` fails, it does *not* detach the shared-memory-segment, and `errno` equals:

`EINVAL` if `shmaddr` is not the data-segment-start-address of a shared-memory-segment.

APPLICATION USAGE

The functions `shmctl`, `shmget`, `shmat`, and `shmdt` are hardware dependent and may not be present on all systems. The shared-memory-routines should not be used by applications except when extreme performance considerations require them.

SEE ALSO

EXEC(BA_SYS), EXIT(BA_SYS), FORK(BA_SYS), SHMCTL(KE_SYS), SHMGET(KE_SYS).

Part III

Library Routines

Chapter 7

Base Library Routines

NAME

abs — return integer absolute value

SYNOPSIS

```
int abs(i)
int i;
```

DESCRIPTION

The function `abs` returns the absolute value of its integer operand.

APPLICATION USAGE

In two-complement representation, the absolute value of the negative integer with largest magnitude {INT_MIN} is undefined. Some implementations may catch this as an error but others may ignore it.

SEE ALSO

FLOOR(BA_LIB).

NAME

j0, j1, jn, y0, y1, yn — Bessel functions

SYNOPSIS

```
#include <math.h>

double j0(x)
double x;

double j1(x)
double x;

double jn(n, x)
int n;
double x;

double y0(x)
double x;

double y1(x)
double x;

double yn(n, x)
int n;
double x;
```

DESCRIPTION

The functions `j0` and `j1` return Bessel functions of `x` of the 1st kind of orders *0* and *1* respectively. The function `jn` returns the Bessel function of `x` of the 1st kind of order `n`.

The functions `y0` and `y1` return Bessel functions of `x` of the 2nd kind of orders *0* and *1* respectively. The function `yn` returns the Bessel function of `x` of the 2nd kind of order `n`. For the functions `y0`, `y1` and `yn`, the argument `x` must be positive.

RETURN VALUE

Non-positive arguments cause `y0`, `y1` and `yn` to return the value `-HUGE` and to set `errno` to `EDOM`. In addition, a message for a `DOMAIN` error is printed on the standard error output.

Arguments too large in magnitude cause the functions `j0`, `j1`, `y0` and `y1` to return zero and to set `errno` to `ERANGE`. In addition, a message for a `TLOSS` error is printed on the standard error output [see MATHERR(BA_LIB)].

APPLICATION USAGE

These error-handling procedures are changed by the MATHERR(BA_LIB) routine.

SEE ALSO

MATHERR(BA_LIB).

NAME

bsearch — binary search on a sorted table

SYNOPSIS

```
char *bsearch(key, base, nel, width,  compar)
char *key;
char *base;
unsigned nel, width;
int (*compar)();
```

DESCRIPTION

The function `bsearch` is a binary search routine. It returns a pointer into a table indicating where a datum may be found. The table must be previously sorted in increasing order according to a user-provided comparison function, `compar` [see QSORT(BA_SYS)].

The argument `key` points to a datum instance to be sought in the table.

The argument `base` points to the element at the base of the table.

The argument `nel` is the number of elements in the table.

The argument `width` is the size of an element in bytes.

The argument `compar` is the name of the comparison function, which is called with two arguments of type `char` that point to the elements being compared. The `compar` function must return an integer less than, equal to or greater than zero, as the first argument is to be considered less than, equal to or greater than the second.

RETURN VALUE

A `NULL` pointer is returned if the key cannot be found in the table.

APPLICATION USAGE

The pointers to the key and the element at the base of the table, `key` and `base`, should be of type pointer-to-element and cast to type pointer-to-character.

The comparison function need not compare every byte, so arbitrary data may be contained in the elements in addition to the values being compared.

Although declared as type pointer-to-character, the value returned should be cast into type pointer-to-element.

EXAMPLE

The following example searches a table containing pointers to nodes consisting of a string and its length. The table is ordered alphabetically on the string in the node pointed to by each entry.

This code fragment reads in strings; it either finds the corresponding node and prints out the string and its length or it prints an error message.

```
#include <stdio.h>
#include <search.h>

#define TABSIZE 1000

struct node {                    /* these are in the table */
    char *string;
    int length;
};
struct node table[TABSIZE];      /* table to be searched */
    . . .
{
    struct node *node_ptr, node;
  int node_compare( );           /* routine to compare 2 nodes */
  char str_space[20];            /* space to read string into */
      . . .
      node.string = str_space;
    while (scanf("%s", node.string) != EOF) {
        node_ptr = (struct node *)bsearch((char *)(&node),
          (char *)table, TABSIZE,
          sizeof(struct node), node_compare);
        if (node_ptr != NULL) {
            (void)printf("string = %20s, length = %d\n",
              node_ptr->string, node_ptr->length);
        } else {
            (void) printf("not found: %s\n", node.string);
        }
    }
}
/*
    This routine compares two nodes based on an
    alphabetical ordering of the string field.
*/
int node_compare(node1, node2)
struct node *node1, *node2;
{
    return strcmp(node1->string, node2->string);
}
```

SEE ALSO

HSEARCH(BA_LIB), LSEARCH(BA_LIB), QSORT(BA_LIB), TSEARCH(BA_LIB).

NAME

clock — report CPU time used

SYNOPSIS

```
long clock( )
```

DESCRIPTION

The function `clock` returns the amount of CPU time (in microseconds) used since the first call to `clock`. The time reported is the sum of the user and system times of the calling-process and its terminated child-processes for which it has executed the WAIT(BA_SYS) or SYSTEM(BA_SYS) routine.

APPLICATION USAGE

The value returned by `clock` is defined in microseconds for compatibility with systems that have CPU clocks with much higher resolution.

SEE ALSO

TIMES(BA_SYS), WAIT(BA_SYS), SYSTEM(BA_SYS).

NAME

toupper, tolower, _toupper, _tolower, toascii — translate characters

SYNOPSIS

```
#include <ctype.h>

int toupper(c)
int c;

int tolower(c)
int c;

int _toupper(c)
int c;

int _tolower(c)
int c;

int toascii(c)
int c;
```

DESCRIPTION

The functions `toupper` and `tolower` have as domain the range of the GETC(BA_LIB) routine: the integers from `-1` through `255`. If the argument of `toupper` represents a lower-case letter, the result is the corresponding upper-case letter. If the argument of `tolower` represents an upper-case letter, the result is the corresponding lower-case letter. All other arguments in the domain are returned unchanged.

The macros `_toupper`, `_tolower`, and `_toascii` are defined by the `<ctype.h>` header file. The macros `_toupper` and `_tolower` accomplish the same thing as `toupper` and `tolower` but have restricted domains and are faster. The macro `_toupper` requires a lower-case letter as its argument; its result is the corresponding upper-case letter. The macro `_tolower` requires an upper-case letter as its argument; its result is the corresponding lower-case letter. Arguments outside the domain cause undefined results.

The macro `toascii` yields its argument with all bits turned off that are not part of a standard **ASCII** character; it is intended for compatibility with other systems.

SEE ALSO

CTYPE(BA_LIB), GETC(BA_LIB).

NAME

crypt, setkey, encrypt — generate string encoding

SYNOPSIS

```
char *crypt(key, salt)
char *key, *salt;

void setkey(key)
char *key;

void encrypt(block, edflag)
char *block;
int edflag;
```

DESCRIPTION

The function `crypt` is a string-encoding function.

The argument `key` is a string to be encoded. The argument `salt` is a two-character string chosen from the set `[a-zA-Z0-9./]`; this string is used to perturb the encoding algorithm, after which the string that `key` points to is used as the key to repeatedly encode a constant string. The returned value points to the encoded string. The first two characters are the salt itself.

The functions `setkey` and `encrypt` provide (rather primitive) access to the encoding algorithm. The argument to the entry `setkey` is a character array of length 64 containing only the characters with numerical value 0 and 1. If this string is divided into groups of 8, the low-order bit in each group is ignored; this gives a 56-bit key. This is the key that will be used with the above mentioned algorithm to encode the string `block` with the function `encrypt`.

The argument to the entry `encrypt` is a character array of length 64 containing only the characters with numerical value 0 and 1. The argument array is modified in place to a similar array representing the bits of the argument after having been subjected to the encoding algorithm using the key set by `setkey`.

If the argument `edflag` is zero, the argument is encoded.

APPLICATION USAGE

The return value of the function `crypt` points to static data that are overwritten by each call.

NAME

ctermid — generate file name for terminal

SYNOPSIS

```
#include <stdio.h>

char *ctermid(s)
char *s;
```

DESCRIPTION

The function `ctermid` generates the path-name of the controlling terminal for the current process and stores it in a string.

If the argument `s` is a `NULL` pointer, the string is stored in an internal static area which will be overwritten at the next call to `ctermid`. The address of the static area is returned. Otherwise, `s` is assumed to point to a character array of at least `L_ctermid` elements; the path name is placed in this array and the value of `s` is returned. The constant `L_ctermid` is defined by the `<stdio.h>` header file.

APPLICATION USAGE

The difference between the TTYNAME(BA_LIB) routine and the function `ctermid` is that the TTYNAME(BA_LIB) routine must be passed a file-descriptor and returns the name of the terminal associated with that file-descriptor, while the function `ctermid` returns a string (e.g., `/dev/tty`) that will refer to the terminal if used as a file-name. Thus the TTYNAME(BA_LIB) routine is useful only if the process already has at least one file open to a terminal.

SEE ALSO

TTYNAME(BA_LIB).

NAME

ctime, localtime, gmtime, asctime, tzset — convert date and time to string

SYNOPSIS

```
#include <time.h>

char *ctime(clock)
long *clock;

struct tm *localtime(clock)
long *clock;

struct tm *gmtime(clock)
long *clock;

char *asctime(tm)
struct tm *tm;

extern long timezone;

extern int daylight;

extern char *tzname[2];

void tzset( )
```

DESCRIPTION

The function `ctime` converts a long integer, pointed to by `clock`, giving the time in seconds since 00:00:00 GMT, January 1, 1970 [see TIME(BA_SYS)] and returns a pointer to a 26-character string in the following form:

```
Sun Sep 16 01:03:52 1973
```

All the fields have constant width.

The functions `localtime` and `gmtime` return pointers to the structure `tm`, described below:

> The function `localtime` corrects for the time-zone and possible Daylight Savings Time.
>
> The function `gmtime` converts directly to Greenwich Mean Time (GMT), which is the time the system uses.

The function `asctime` converts a `tm` structure to a 26-character string, as shown in the above example, and returns a pointer to the string.

The external `long` variable `timezone` contains the difference, in seconds, between GMT and local standard time (in EST, `timezone` is `5*60*60`); the external variable `daylight` is non-zero only if the standard USA Daylight Savings Time conversion should be applied. The program compensates for the peculiarities of this conversion in 1974 and 1975; if necessary, a table for these years can be extended.

The <time.h> header file declares all the functions, the external variables and the tm structure, which includes the following members:

```
int tm_sec;     /* number of seconds past */
                /* the minute (0-59) */
int tm_min;     /* number of minutes past */
                /* the hour (0-59) */
int tm_hour;    /* current hour (0-23) */
int tm_mday;    /* day of month (1-31) */
int tm_mon;     /* month of year (0-11) */
int tm_year;    /* current year -1900 */
int tm_wday;    /* day of week (Sunday=0) */
int tm_yday;    /* day of year (0-365) */
int tm_isdst; /* daylight savings time flag */
```

The value of `tm_isdst` is non-zero if Daylight Savings Time is in effect.

If an environment variable named `TZ` is present, `asctime` uses the contents of the variable to override the default time-zone. The value of `TZ` must be a three-letter time-zone name, followed by an optional minus sign (for zones east of Greenwich) and a series of digits representing the difference between local time and Greenwich Mean Time in hours; this is followed by an optional three-letter name for a daylight time-zone. For example, the setting for New Jersey would be `EST5EDT`. The effects of setting `TZ` are thus to change the values of the external variables `timezone` and `daylight`. In addition, the time-zone names contained in the external variable

```
char *tzname[2] = { "EST", "EDT" };
```

are set from the environment variable `TZ`. The function `tzset` sets these external variables from `TZ`; the function `tzset` is called by `asctime` and may also be called explicitly by the user.

APPLICATION USAGE

The return values point to static data that is overwritten by each call.

SEE ALSO

TIME(BA_SYS), GETENV(BA_LIB).

CAVEATS

The argument `clock` to the functions `ctime`, `localtime` and `gmtime` will be defined by the <sys/types.h> header file as pointer to `time_t`.

The number in `TZ` will be defined as an optional minus sign followed by two hour-digits and two minute-digits, `hhmm`, to represent fractional time-zones.

NAME

isalpha, isupper, islower, isdigit, isxdigit, isalnum, isspace, ispunct, isprint, isgraph, iscntrl, isascii — classify characters

SYNOPSIS

```
#include <ctype.h>

int isalpha(c)
int c;

int isupper(c)
int c;

int islower(c)
int c;

int isdigit(c)
int c;

int isxdigit(c)
int c;

int isalnum(c)
int c;

int isspace(c)
int c;

int ispunct(c)
int c;

int isprint(c)
int c;

int isgraph(c)
int c;

int iscntrl(c)
int c;

int isascii(c)
int c;
```

DESCRIPTION

These macros, which are defined by the `<ctype.h>` header file, classify character-coded integer values. Each is a predicate returning non-zero for true, zero for false. The function `isascii` is defined on all integer values; the rest are defined only where `isascii` is true and on the single non-ASCII value `EOF`, which is defined by the `<stdio.h>` header file and represents end-of-file.

`isalpha(c)` c is a letter.

`isupper(c)` c is an upper-case letter.

`islower(c)`	c is a lower-case letter.
`isdigit(c)`	c is a digit `[0-9]`.
`isxdigit(c)`	c is a hexadecimal digit `[0-9]`, `[A-F]` or `[a-f]`.
`isalnum(c)`	c is an alphanumeric (letter or digit).
`isspace(c)`	c is a space, tab, carriage-return, new-line, vertical-tab or form-feed.
`ispunct(c)`	c is a punctuation mark (neither control nor alpha-numeric nor space).
`isprint(c)`	c is a printing character, **ASCII** code `040` (space) through `0176` (tilde).
`isgraph(c)`	c is a printing character, like `isprint` except false for space.
`iscntrl(c)`	c is a delete character (`0177`) or an ordinary control-character (less than `040`).
`isascii(c)`	c is an **ASCII** character, code between `0` and `0177` inclusive.

RETURN VALUE

If the argument to any of these macros is not in the domain of the function, the result is undefined.

SEE ALSO

FOPEN(BA_SYS), **ASCII character set** in **Definitions.**

NAME

drand48, erand48, lrand48, nrand48, mrand48, jrand48, srand48, seed48, lcong48 — generate uniformly distributed pseudo-random numbers

SYNOPSIS

```
double drand48()

double erand48(xsubi)
unsigned short xsubi[3];

long lrand48()

long nrand48(xsubi)
unsigned short xsubi[3];

long mrand48()

long jrand48(xsubi)
unsigned short xsubi[3];

void srand48(seedval)
long seedval;

unsigned short *seed48(seed16v)
unsigned short seed16v[3];

void lcong48(param)
unsigned short param[7];
```

DESCRIPTION

This family of functions generates pseudo-random numbers using the well-known linear congruential algorithm and 48-bit integer arithmetic.

Functions `drand48` and `erand48` return non-negative double-precision floating-point values uniformly distributed over the interval $[0.0,1.0)$.

Functions `lrand48` and `nrand48` return non-negative long integers uniformly distributed over the interval $[0,2^{31})$.

Functions `mrand48` and `jrand48` return signed long integers uniformly distributed over the interval $[-2^{31},2^{31})$.

Functions `srand48`, `seed48` and `lcong48` are initialization entry points, one of which should be called before calling `drand48`, `lrand48` or `mrand48`. While not recommended, constant default initializer values are supplied automatically if `drand48`, `lrand48` or `mrand48` is called without first calling an initialization entry point. Functions `erand48`, `nrand48` and `jrand48` need *no* initialization entry point called first.

All the routines generate a sequence of 48-bit integer values, X_i, according to the linear congruential formula:

$$X_{n+1} = (aX_n + c)_{mod\ m} \quad n \geqslant 0$$

The parameter $m = 2^{48}$; hence 48-bit integer arithmetic is performed.

Unless `lcong48` is called, the multiplier a and the addend c are:

$$a = 5DEECE66D_{16} = 273673163155_8$$
$$c = B_{16} = 13_8$$

The value returned by any of the functions `drand48`, `erand48`, `lrand48`, `nrand48`, `mrand48` or `jrand48` is computed by first generating the next 48-bit X_i in the sequence. Then the appropriate number of bits, according to the type of data item to be returned, are copied from the high-order (leftmost) bits of X_i and transformed into the returned value.

The functions `drand48`, `lrand48` and `mrand48` store the last 48-bit X_i generated in an internal buffer; that is why they must be initialized prior to being invoked. The functions `erand48`, `nrand48` and `jrand48` require the calling program to provide storage for the successive X_i values in the array specified as an argument when the functions are invoked. That is why these routines do not have to be initialized; the calling program merely has to place the desired initial value of X_i into the array and pass it as an argument. By using different arguments, functions `erand48`, `nrand48` and `jrand48` allow separate modules of a large program to generate several **independent** streams of pseudo-random numbers. In other words, the sequence of numbers in each stream will **not** depend upon how many times the routines have been called to generate numbers for the other streams.

The initializer function `srand48` sets the high-order 32-bits of X_i to the {LONG_BIT} bits contained in its argument. The low-order 16-bits of X_i are set to the arbitrary value $330E_{16}$.

The initializer function `seed48` sets the value of X_i to the 48-bit value specified in the argument array. In addition, the previous value of X_i is copied into a 48-bit internal buffer, used only by `seed48`, and a pointer to this buffer is the value returned by `seed48`.

The initialization function `lcong48` allows the user to specify the initial X_i, the multiplier a and the addend c. Argument array elements `param[0-2]` specify X_i, `param[3-5]` specify the multiplier a, and `param[6]` specifies the 16-bit addend c. After `lcong48` has been called, a subsequent call to either `srand48` or `seed48` will restore the *standard* multiplier and addend values, a and c, specified earlier.

APPLICATION USAGE

The pointer returned by `seed48`, which can just be ignored if not needed, is useful if a program is to be restarted from a given point at some future time. Use the pointer to get at and store the last X_i value and then use this value to reinitialize via `seed48` when the program is restarted.

SEE ALSO

RAND(BA_LIB).

NAME

erf, erfc — error function and complementary error function

SYNOPSIS

```
#include <math.h>

double erf(x)
double x;

double erfc(x)
double x;
```

DESCRIPTION

The function `erf` returns the error function of `x`, defined as follows:

$$\frac{2}{\sqrt{\pi}}\int_{0}^{x} e^{-t^2} dt$$

The function `erfc` returns `1.0-erf(x)`.

APPLICATION USAGE

The function `erfc` is provided because of the extreme loss of relative accuracy if `erf(x)` is called for large `x` and the result subtracted from `1.0`.

SEE ALSO

EXP(BA_LIB).

NAME

exp, log, log10, pow, sqrt — exponential, logarithm, power, square root functions

SYNOPSIS

```
#include <math.h>

double exp(x)
double x;

double log(x)
double x;

double log10(x)
double x;

double pow(x, y)
double x, y;

double sqrt(x)
double x;
```

DESCRIPTION

The function `exp` returns e^x.

The function `log` returns the natural logarithm of `x`. The value of `x` must be positive.

The function `log10` returns the logarithm base ten of `x`. The value of `x` must be positive.

The functions `pow` returns x^y. If `x` is zero, `y` must be positive. If `x` is negative, `y` must be an integer.

The function `sqrt` returns the non-negative square root of `x`. The value of `x` may not be negative.

RETURN VALUE

The function `exp` returns `HUGE` when the correct value would overflow or `0` when the correct value would underflow and sets `errno` to `ERANGE`.

The functions `log` and `log10` `return` `−HUGE` and set `errno` to `EDOM` when `x` is non-positive. A message indicating `DOMAIN` error (or `SING` error when `x` is `0`) is printed on the standard error output.

The function `pow` returns `0` and sets `errno` to `EDOM` when `x` is `0` and `y` is non-positive, or when `x` is negative and `y` is not an integer. In these cases a message indicating `DOMAIN` error is printed on the standard error output. When the correct value for `pow` would overflow or underflow, `pow` returns `±HUGE` or `0` respectively and sets `errno` to `ERANGE`.

The function `sqrt` returns `0` and sets `errno` to `EDOM` when `x` is negative. A message indicating `DOMAIN` error is printed on the standard error output.

APPLICATION USAGE

These error-handling procedures are changed by the MATHERR(BA_LIB) routine.

SEE ALSO

HYPOT(BA_LIB), MATHERR(BA_LIB), SINH(BA_LIB).

CAVEATS

A macro `HUGE_VAL` will be defined by the `<math.h>` header file. This macro will call a function which will either return $+\infty$ on a system supporting the **IEEE P754** standard or +{MAXDOUBLE} on a system that does not support the **IEEE P754** standard.

The function `exp` will return `HUGE_VAL` when the correct value overflows.

The functions `log` and `log10` will return `-HUGE_VAL` when `x` is not positive.

The function `sqrt` will return `-0` when the value of `x` is `-0`.

The return value of `pow` will be negative `HUGE_VAL` when an illegal combination of input arguments is passed to `pow`.

NAME

floor, ceil, fmod, fabs — floor, ceiling, remainder, absolute value functions

SYNOPSIS

```
#include <math.h>

double floor(x)
double x;

double ceil(x)
double x;

double fmod(x, y)
double x, y;

double fabs(x)
double x;
```

DESCRIPTION

The function `floor` returns the largest integer (as a double-precision number) not greater than `x`.

The function `ceil` returns the smallest integer not less than `x`.

The function `fmod` returns the floating-point remainder of the division of `x` by `y`, zero if `y` is zero or if `x/y` would overflow. Otherwise the number is f with the same sign as `x`, such that $x = iy + f$ for some integer i, and $|f| < |y|$.

The function `fabs` returns the absolute value of `x`, i.e., $|x|$.

SEE ALSO

ABS(BA_LIB).

CAVEATS

The function `fmod` will return `x` if `y` is zero or if `x/y` would overflow.

NAME

frexp, ldexp, modf — manipulate parts of floating-point numbers

SYNOPSIS

```
double frexp(value, eptr)
double value;
int *eptr;

double ldexp(value, exp)
double value;
int exp;

double modf(value, iptr)
double value, *iptr;
```

DESCRIPTION

Every non-zero number can be written uniquely as $x*2^n$, where the *mantissa* (fraction) x is in the range $0.5 \leqslant |x| < 1.0$ and the *exponent* n is an integer. The function `frexp` returns the mantissa of a `double value` and stores the exponent indirectly in the location pointed to by `eptr`. If `value` is `0`, both results returned by `frexp` are `0`.

The function `ldexp` returns the quantity `value*`2^{exp}.

The function `modf` returns the fractional part of `value` and stores the integral part indirectly in the location pointed to by `iptr`. Both the fractional and integer parts have the same sign as `value`.

RETURN VALUE

If `ldexp` would cause overflow, ±`HUGE` is returned (according to the sign of `value`) and `errno` is set to `ERANGE`.

If `ldexp` would cause underflow, `0` is returned and `errno` is set to `ERANGE`.

CAVEATS

A macro `HUGE_VAL` will be defined by the `<math.h>` header file This macro will call a function which will either return +∞ on a system supporting the **IEEE P754** standard or +{MAXDOUBLE} on a system that does not support the **IEEE P754** standard.

The return value of `ldexp` will be ±`HUGE_VAL` (according to the sign of `value`) in case of overflow.

NAME

ftw — walk a file tree

SYNOPSIS

```
#include <ftw.h>

int ftw(path, fn, param)
char *path;
int (*fn)();
int param;
```

DESCRIPTION

The function `ftw` recursively descends the directory hierarchy rooted in `path` visiting each directory before visiting any of its descendants. For each object in the hierarchy, `ftw` calls a user-defined function `fn` passing it three arguments. The first argument passed is a character pointer to a null-terminated string containing the name of the object. The second argument passed to `fn` is a pointer to a `stat` structure [see STAT(BA_SYS)] containing information about the object, and the third argument passed is an integer flag. Possible values of the flag, defined by the `<ftw.h>` header file, are `FTW_F` for a file, `FTW_D` for a directory, `FTW_DNR` for a directory that cannot be read and `FTW_NS` for an object for which `stat` could not successfully be executed. If the integer is `FTW_DNR`, descendants of that directory will not be processed. If the integer is `FTW_NS`, the contents of the `stat` structure are undefined.

The function `ftw` uses one file-descriptor for each level in the tree. The argument `param` limits the number of file-descriptors to be in the range of 1 to {OPEN_MAX}. The function `ftw` will run more quickly if `param` is at least as large as the number of levels in the tree.

RETURN VALUE

The tree traversal continues until the tree is exhausted or `fn` returns a non-zero value or `ftw` detects some error (such as an I/O error). If the tree is exhausted, `ftw` returns `0`. If `fn` returns a non-zero value, `ftw` stops its tree traversal and returns whatever value `fn` returned.

If `ftw` detects an error other than `EACCES` (see `FTW_DNR` and `FTW_NS` above), it returns -1 and `errno` equals the type of error. The external variable `errno` may contain the error values that are possible when a directory is opened [see OPEN(BA_SYS)] or when the STAT(BA_SYS) routine is executed on a directory or file.

APPLICATION USAGE

Because `ftw` is recursive, it is possible for it to terminate with a memory fault when applied to very deep file structures.

SEE ALSO

STAT(BA_SYS), MALLOC(BA_SYS).

NAME

gamma — log gamma function

SYNOPSIS

```
#include <math.h>

double gamma(x)
double x;

extern int signgam;
```

DESCRIPTION

The function `gamma` returns $\ln(|\Gamma(x)|)$, where $\Gamma(x)$ is defined as:

$$\int_0^\infty e^{-t} t^{x-1} dt$$

The sign of $\Gamma(x)$ is returned in the external integer `signgam`. The argument x may not be a non-positive integer.

The following C program fragment might be used to calculate Γ:

```
    if ((y = gamma(x)) > LN_MAXDOUBLE)
        error();
    y = signgam * exp(y);
```

RETURN VALUE

For non-positive integer arguments, `gamma` returns `HUGE` and `errno` equals `EDOM`. A message indicating `SING` error is printed on the standard error output [see MATHERR(BA_LIB)].

If the correct value overflows, `gamma` returns `HUGE` and `errno` equals `ERANGE`.

APPLICATION USAGE

These error-handling procedures are changed by the MATHERR(BA_LIB) routine.

SEE ALSO

EXP(BA_LIB), MATHERR(BA_LIB).

CAVEATS

A macro `HUGE_VAL` will be defined by the `<math.h>` header file. This macro calls a function returning either $+\infty$ on a system that does support the **IEEE P754** standard or +{MAXDOUBLE} on a system that does *not* support the **IEEE P754** standard.

If the correct value overflows, `gamma` returns `HUGE_VAL`.

NAME

getc, getchar, fgetc, getw — get character or word from a stream

SYNOPSIS

```
#include <stdio.h>

int getc(stream)
FILE *stream;

int getchar()

int fgetc(stream)
FILE *stream;

int getw(stream)
FILE *stream;
```

DESCRIPTION

The function `getc` returns as an integer the next character (i.e., byte) from the named input stream `stream` and sets the file-pointer, if defined, ahead one character in `stream`. The function `getchar` is defined as `getc(stdin)`. Both `getc` and `getchar` are macros.

The function `fgetc` behaves like `getc`, but is a function instead of a macro. The function `fgetc` runs more slowly than `getc` but it takes less space per invocation and its name can be passed as an argument to a function.

The function `getw` reads the next word (i.e., integer) from the named input stream, `stream` and sets the file-pointer, if defined, to point to the next word. The size of a word is the size of an integer and varies from machine to machine. The function `getw` needs no special alignment in the file.

RETURN VALUE

These functions return `EOF` at end-of-file or on an error. Because `EOF` is an integer constant, use the FERROR(BA_SYS) routines to detect these errors

APPLICATION USAGE

If the integer value returned by `getc`, `getchar` or `fgetc` is assigned to a character variable and then compared against the integer constant `EOF`, the comparison may never succeed because sign-extension of a character on widening to integer is machine-dependent.

Because word-length and byte-ordering are machine-dependent, files written using `putw` may not be read using `getw` on a different processor.

Because it is implemented as a macro, `getc` incorrectly treats `stream` when it has side-effects. In particular, `getc(*f++)` does not work sensibly, and `fgetc` should be used instead.

SEE ALSO

FCLOSE(BA_SYS), FERROR(BA_SYS), FOPEN(BA_SYS), FREAD(BA_SYS), GETS(BA_LIB), PUTC(BA_LIB), SCANF(BA_LIB).

NAME

getenv — return value for environment name

SYNOPSIS

```
char *getenv(name)
char *name;
```

DESCRIPTION

The function `getenv` searches the environment list for a string of the form:

```
name = value
```

and returns a pointer to `value` in the current environment if such a string is present. Otherwise, it returns a `NULL` pointer.

SEE ALSO

EXEC(BA_SYS), SYSTEM(BA_SYS), PUTENV(BA_LIB).

NAME

getopt — get option letter from argument vector

SYNOPSIS

```
int getopt(argc, argv, optstring)
int argc;
char *argv[ ], *optstring;

extern char *optarg;
extern int optind, opterr;
```

DESCRIPTION

The function `getopt` is a command-line parser. It returns the next option letter in `argv` that matches a letter in `optstring`. The function `getopt` stores the `argv` index of the next argument to be processed in the external variable `optind`, which is initialized to 1 before first calling `getopt`.

The argument `optstring` is a string of recognized option letters; if a letter is followed by a colon, the option is expected to have an argument that may or may not be separated from it by white space.

The function `getopt` sets `optarg` to point to the start of the option argument.

When all options are processed (i.e., up to the first non-option argument), `getopt` returns `EOF`. The special option `--` may be used to delimit the end of the options; `EOF` will be returned and `--` will be skipped.

RETURN VALUE

The function `getopt` prints an error message on `stderr` and returns a question-mark (`?`) when it gets an option letter not in `optstring`. Setting `opterr` to a 0 disables this error message.

EXAMPLE

The following code fragment shows how one can process the arguments for a command takes the mutually exclusive options `a` and `b` and the options `f` and `o`, both of which require arguments:

```
main (argc, argv)
int argc;
char *argv [ ];
{
    int c;
    int bflg, aflg, errflg;
    char *ifile;
    char *ofile;
    extern char *optarg;
    extern int optind;
    . . .
    while ((c = getopt(argc, argv, "abf:o:")) != EOF)
        switch (c) {
        case 'a': if (bflg)
                      errflg++;
                  else
                      aflg++;
                  break;
        case 'b': if (aflg)
                      errflg++;
                  else
                      bproc( );
                  break;
        case 'f': ifile = optarg;
                  break;
        case 'o': ofile = optarg;
                  break;
        case '?': errflg++;
        }
    if (errflg) {
        fprintf(stderr, "usage: . . . ");
        exit(2);
    }
    for ( ; optind < argc; optind++) {
        if (access(argv[optind], 4)) {
    . . .
}
```

CAVEATS

The function `getopt` will be enhanced to enforce all rules of the UNIX System V Command Syntax Standard (see below). All *new* UNIX System V commands will conform to the command syntax standard described here. Existing commands will migrate toward the new standard if they do not already meet it. Applications with command-like user-interfaces may want to conform to this standard.

The following rules form the UNIX System V standard for command syntax:

RULE 1: Command names must be between two and nine characters.

RULE 2: Command names must include lower-case letters and digits only.

RULE 3: Option names must be a single character in length.

RULE 4: All options must be delimited by the - character.

RULE 5: Options with no arguments may be grouped behind one delimiter.

RULE 6: The first option-argument following an option must be preceded by white space.

RULE 7: Option arguments cannot be optional.

RULE 8: Groups of option arguments following an option must be separated by commas or separated by white space and quoted.

RULE 9: All options must precede operands on the command line.

RULE 10: The characters -- may be used to delimit the end of the options.

RULE 11: The order of options relative to one another should not matter.

RULE 12: The order of operands may matter and position-related interpretations should be determined on a command-specific basis.

RULE 13: The - character preceded and followed by white space should be used only to mean standard input.

The function `getopt` is the command-line parser that will enforce the rules of this command syntax standard.

NAME

gets, fgets — get a string from a stream

SYNOPSIS

```
#include <stdio.h>

char *gets(s)
char *s;

char *fgets(s, n, stream)
char *s;
int n;
FILE *stream;
```

DESCRIPTION

The function `gets` reads characters from the standard input stream, `stdin`, into the array pointed to by `s` until a new-line character is read or an end-of-file occurs. The new-line character is discarded and the string is terminated with a null character.

The function `fgets` reads characters from `stream` into the array pointed to by `s` until `n-1` characters are read or a new-line character is read and transferred to `s` or an end-of-file occurs. The string is then terminated with a null-character.

RETURN VALUE

If end-of-file occurs and no characters were read, neither `gets` nor `fgets` transfer characters to `s` and they return a `NULL` pointer; if a read error occurs (such as trying to use these functions on a file that is not open for reading), they return a `NULL` pointer; otherwise, they return `s`.

APPLICATION USAGE

Reading too long a line through `gets` may cause `gets` to fail. The use of `fgets` is recommended.

SEE ALSO

FERROR(BA_SYS), FOPEN(BA_SYS), FREAD(BA_SYS), GETC(BA_LIB), SCANF(BA_LIB).

NAME

hsearch, hcreate, hdestroy — manage hash search tables

SYNOPSIS

```
#include <search.h>

ENTRY *hsearch(item, action)
ENTRY item;
ACTION action;

int hcreate(nel)
unsigned nel;

void hdestroy( )
```

DESCRIPTION

The function `hsearch` is a hash-table search routine. It returns a pointer into a hash table indicating the location at which an entry can be found. The comparison function used by `hsearch` is `strcmp` [see STRING(BA_LIB)].

The argument `item` is a structure of type `ENTRY` (defined by the `<search.h>` header file) containing two character pointers:

`item.key` points to the comparison key,
`item.data` points to any other data to be associated with that key.

(Pointers to types other than `char` should be cast to pointer-to-character.)

The argument `action` is a member of an enumeration type `ACTION`, defined by the `<search.h>` header file, indicating the disposition of the entry if it cannot be found in the table.

`ENTER` indicates that the item should be inserted in the table at an appropriate point. Given a duplicate of an existing item, the new item is not entered, and `hsearch` returns a pointer to the existing item.

`FIND` indicates that no entry should be made. Unsuccessful resolution is indicated by the return of a `NULL` pointer.

The function `hcreate` allocates sufficient space for the table and must be called before `hsearch` is used. The value of `nel` is an estimate of the maximum number of entries that the table will contain. This number may be adjusted upward by the algorithm in order to obtain certain mathematically favorable circumstances.

The function `hdestroy` destroys the search table and may be followed by another call to `hcreate`.

RETURN VALUE

Either if the action is `FIND` and the item can not be found or if the action is `ENTER` and the table is full, `hsearch` returns a `NULL` pointer.

If sufficient space for the table cannot be allocated, `hcreate` returns `0`.

APPLICATION USAGE

Both `hsearch` and `hcreate` use the MALLOC(BA_SYS) routines to allocate space.

EXAMPLE

The example reads in strings followed by two numbers and stores them in a hash table, then reads in strings and finds the entry in the table and prints it.

```
#include <stdio.h>
#include <search.h>

struct info {              /* these are in the table */
    int age, room;         /* apart from the key. */
};
#define NUM_EMPL 5000      /* # of elements in the table */

main()
{
    /* space for strings */
    char string_space[NUM_EMPL*20];
    /* space for employee info */
    struct info info_space[NUM_EMPL];
    /* next avail space for strings */
    char *str_ptr = string_space;
    /* next avail space for info */
    struct info *info_ptr = info_space;
    ENTRY item, *found_item, *hsearch();
    char name_to_find[30];   /* name to look for in table */
    int i = 0;

    /* create table */
    (void) hcreate(NUM_EMPL);
    while (scanf("%s%d%d", str_ptr, &info_ptr->age,
        &info_ptr->room) != EOF && i++ < NUM_EMPL) {
        /* put info in structure, and structure in item */
        item.key = str_ptr;
        item.data = (char *)info_ptr;
        str_ptr += strlen(str_ptr) + 1;
        info_ptr++;
        /* put item into table */
        (void) hsearch(item, ENTER);
    }
    /* access table */
    item.key = name_to_find;
    while (scanf("%s", item.key) != EOF) {
        if ((found_item = hsearch(item, FIND)) != NULL) {
        /* if item is in the table */
        (void) printf("found %s, age = %d, room = %d\n",
            found_item->key,
            ((struct info *)found_item->data)->age,
            ((struct info *)found_item->data)->room);
        } else {
        (void) printf("no such employee %s\n",
            name_to_find)
        }
    }
}
```

SEE ALSO

MALLOC(BA_SYS), BSEARCH(BA_LIB), LSEARCH(BA_LIB), STRING(BA_LIB), TSEARCH(BA_LIB).

CAVEATS

The restriction of having only one hash search table active at any given time will be removed.

NAME

hypot — Euclidean distance function

SYNOPSIS

```
#include <math.h>

double hypot(x, y)
double x, y;
```

DESCRIPTION

The function `hypot` returns `sqrt(x * x + y * y)`, taking precautions against unwarranted overflows.

RETURN VALUE

If the correct value overflows, `hypot` returns `HUGE` and `errno` equals `ERANGE`.

These error-handling procedures are changed by the MATHERR(BA_LIB) routine.

SEE ALSO

MATHERR(BA_LIB).

CAVEATS

A macro `HUGE_VAL` will be defined by the `<math.h>` header file. This macro will call a function which will either return +∞ on a system supporting the **IEEE P754** standard or +{MAXDOUBLE} on a system that does not support the **IEEE P754** standard.

If the correct value overflows, `hypot` will return `HUGE_VAL`.

NAME

lsearch, lfind — linear search and update

SYNOPSIS

```
#include <search.h>

char *lsearch(key, base, nelp, width, compar)
char *key;
char *base;
unsigned *nelp;
unsigned width;
int (*compar)();

char *lfind(key, base, nelp, width, compar)
char *key;
char *base;
unsigned *nelp;
unsigned width;
int (*compar)();
```

DESCRIPTION

The function `lsearch` is a linear search routine. It returns a pointer into a table indicating where a datum may be found. If the datum does not occur, it is added at the end of the table.

The function `lfind` is the same as `lsearch` except that if the datum is not found, it is not added to the table. Instead, a `NULL` pointer is returned.

The argument `key` points to the datum to be sought in the table.

The argument `base` points to the first element in the table.

The argument `nelp` points to an integer variable containing the current number of elements in the table. The variable pointed to by `nelp` is incremented if the datum is added to the table.

The argument `width` is the size of an element in bytes.

The argument `compar` is the name of the comparison function that the user must supply (`strcmp`, for example). It is called with two arguments that point to the elements being compared. The function must return zero if the elements are equal and non-zero otherwise.

RETURN VALUE

If the searched for datum is found, both `lsearch` and `lfind` return a pointer to it; otherwise, `lfind` returns `NULL` and `lsearch` returns a pointer to the newly added element.

APPLICATION USAGE

The function `lfind` was added in UNIX System V Release 2.0.

The pointers to the key and the element at the base of the table should be of type pointer-to-element and cast to type pointer-to-character.

The comparison function need not compare every byte, so arbitrary data may be contained in the elements in addition to the values being compared.

Although declared as type pointer-to-character, the value returned should be cast into type pointer-to-element.

Space for the table must be managed by the application-program. Undefined results can occur if there is not enough room in the table to add a new item.

EXAMPLE

This fragment will read in ≤ `TABSIZE` strings of length ≤ `ELSIZE` and store them in a table, eliminating duplicates.

```
#include <stdio.h>
#include <search.h>

#define TABSIZE 50
#define ELSIZE 120

     char line[ELSIZE], tab[TABSIZE][ELSIZE], *lsearch( );
     unsigned nel = 0;
     int strcmp( );
     . . .
     while (fgets(line, ELSIZE, stdin) != NULL &&
          nel < TABSIZE)
               (void) lsearch(line, (char *)tab, &nel,
                    ELSIZE, strcmp);
     . . .
```

SEE ALSO

BSEARCH(BA_LIB), HSEARCH(BA_LIB), TSEARCH(BA_LIB).

CAVEATS

A `NULL` pointer will be returned by the function `lsearch` with `errno` set appropriately, if there is not enough room in the table to add a new item.

NAME

matherr — error-handling function

SYNOPSIS

```
#include <math.h>

int matherr(x)
struct exception *x;
```

DESCRIPTION

The function `matherr` is invoked by math library routines when errors are detected. Users may define their own procedures for handling errors, by including a function named `matherr` in their programs. The function `matherr` must be of the form described above. When an error occurs, a pointer to the `exception` structure `x` will be passed to the user-supplied `matherr` function. This structure, which is defined by the `<math.h>` header file, includes the following members:

```
int type;
char *name;
double arg1, arg2, retval;
```

The element `type` is an integer describing the type of error that has occurred from the following list defined by the `<math.h>` header file:

`DOMAIN`	argument domain error.
`SING`	argument singularity.
`OVERFLOW`	overflow range error.
`UNDERFLOW`	underflow range error.
`TLOSS`	total loss of significance.
`PLOSS`	partial loss of significance.

The element `name` points to a string containing the name of the routine that incurred the error. The elements `arg1` and `arg2` are the first and second arguments with which the routine was invoked.

The element `retval` is set to the default value that will be returned by the routine unless the user's `matherr` function sets it to a different value.

If the user's `matherr` function returns non-zero, no error message will be printed, and `errno` will not be set.

If the function `matherr` is not supplied by the user, the default error-handling procedures, described with the math library routines involved, will be invoked upon error. If the user does not supply the function `matherr`, the default error-handling procedures, described with the math library routines involved, will be invoked upon error. These procedures are also summarized in the table below. In every case, `errno` is set to `EDOM` or `ERANGE` and the program continues.

ERRORS

DEFAULT ERROR HANDLING PROCEDURES						
	Types of Errors					
type	DOMAIN	SING	OVERFLOW	UNDERFLOW	TLOSS	PLOSS
errno	EDOM	EDOM	ERANGE	ERANGE	ERANGE	ERANGE
BESSEL:	–	–	–	–	M, 0	*
y0, y1, yn	M, –H	–	–	–	–	–
EXP:	–	–	H	0	–	–
LOG, LOG10:						
(arg < 0)	M, –H	–	–	–	–	–
(arg = 0)	–	M, –H	–	–	–	–
POW:	–	–	±H	0	–	–
neg ** non-int 0 ** non-pos	M, 0	–	–	–	–	–
SQRT:	M, 0	–	–	–	–	–
GAMMA:	–	M, H	H	–	–	–
HYPOT:	–	–	H	–	–	–
SINH:	–	–	±H	–	–	–
COSH:		–	H	–	–	–
SIN, COS, TAN:	–	–	–	–	M, 0	*
ASIN, ACOS, ATAN2:	M, 0	–	–	–	–	–

ABBREVIATIONS

*	As much as possible of the value is returned.
M	Message is printed (EDOM error).
H	HUGE is returned.
–H	–HUGE is returned.
±H	+HUGE or –HUGE is returned.
0	0 is returned.

EXAMPLE

```
#include <math.h>

int matherr(x)
register struct exception *x;
{
     switch (x->type) {
     case DOMAIN:
          /* change sqrt to return sqrt(-arg1), not 0 */
          if (!strcmp(x->name, "sqrt")) {
               x->retval = sqrt(-x->arg1);
               return (0);  /* print message and set errno */
          }
     case SING:
          /* SING or other DOMAIN errs, print message and abort */
          fprintf(stderr, "domain error in %s\n", x->name);
          abort();
     case PLOSS:
          /* print detailed error message */
          fprintf(stderr, "loss of significance in %s(%g) = %g\n",
               x->name, x->arg1, x->retval);
          return (1);   /* take no other action */
     }
     return (0); /* all other errors, execute default procedure */
}
```

CAVEATS

The math functions which return `HUGE` or ±`HUGE` on overflow will return `HUGE_VAL` or ±`HUGE_VAL` respectively.

NAME

memccpy, memchr, memcmp, memcpy, memset — memory operations

SYNOPSIS

```
#include <memory.h>

char *memccpy(s1, s2, c, n)
char *s1, *s2;
int c, n;

char *memchr(s, c, n)
char *s;
int c, n;

int memcmp(s1, s2, n)
char *s1, *s2;
int n;

char *memcpy(s1, s2, n)
char *s1, *s2;
int n;

char *memset(s, c, n)
char *s;
int c, n;
```

DESCRIPTION

These functions operate as efficiently as possible on memory areas (arrays of characters bounded by a count, not terminated by a null character). They do not check for the overflow of any receiving memory area.

The function `memccpy` copies characters from memory area `s2` into `s1`, stopping after the first occurrence of character `c` has been copied or after `n` characters have been copied, whichever comes first. It returns a pointer to the character after the copy of `c` in `s1`, or a `NULL` pointer if `c` was not found in the first `n` characters of `s2`.

The function `memchr` returns a pointer to the first occurrence of character `c` in the first `n` characters of memory area `s`, or a `NULL` pointer if `c` does not occur.

The function `memcmp` compares its arguments, looking at the first `n` characters only. It returns an integer less than, equal to or greater than `0`, according as `s1` is lexicographically less than, equal to or greater than `s2`.

The function `memcpy` copies `n` characters from memory area `s2` to `s1`. It returns `s1`.

The function `memset` sets the first `n` characters in memory area `s` to the value of character `c`. It returns `s`.

APPLICATION USAGE

All these functions are defined by the `<memory.h>` header file.

The function `memcmp` uses native character comparison. The sign of the value returned when one of the characters has its high-order bit set is implementation-dependent.

Character movement is performed differently in different implementations. Thus overlapping moves may be unpredictable.

SEE ALSO

STRING(BA_LIB).

CAVEATS

The declarations in the `<memory.h>` header file will be moved to the `<string.h>` header file.

NAME

mktemp — make a unique file-name

SYNOPSIS

```
char *mktemp(template)
char *template;
```

DESCRIPTION

The function `mktemp` replaces the contents of the string pointed to by `template` by a unique file-name and returns `template`. The string in `template` should look like a file-name with six trailing `X`s; `mktemp` replaces the `X`s with a letter and the current process-ID. The letter is chosen so that the resulting name does not duplicate an existing file.

RETURN VALUE

The function `mktemp` returns the pointer `template`. If a unique name cannot be created, `template` points to a null-string.

SEE ALSO

GETPID(BA_SYS), TMPFILE(BA_LIB), TMPNAM(BA_LIB).

CAVEATS

The function `mktemp` returns a `NULL` pointer if a unique name cannot be created.

NAME

perror — system error messages

SYNOPSIS

```
void perror(s)
char *s;

extern int errno;

extern char *sys_errlist[ ];

extern int sys_nerr;
```

DESCRIPTION

The function `perror` produces a message on the standard error output describing the last error encountered during a call to a function.

The string pointed to by the argument `s` is printed first, then a colon and a blank, then the message and a new-line. To be of most use, the argument string should include the name of the program that incurred the error.

The error number is taken from the external variable `errno`, which is set when errors occur but not cleared when successful calls are made.

If given a null-string, `perror` prints only the message and a new-line.

The array of message strings `sys_errlist` is provided to make messages consistent. The variable `errno` can be used as an index in this array to get the message string without the new-line.

The external variable `sys_nerr` is the largest message number provided for in the array; it should be checked because new error codes may be added to the system before they are added to the array.

CAVEATS

New error handling routines will be added to support the UNIX System V error message standard as a tool for application-developers to use. The UNIX System V Error Message Standard is designed to apply to: firmware/diagnostics, the operating system, networks, commands, languages and, when appropriate, applications. All *new* UNIX System V error messages will follow the standard, and existing error messages will be modified over time. The standard UNIX System V error message as seen by the end-user may have up to five informational elements:

Element	*Description*
LABEL	source of the error.
SEVERITY	one of at least 4 severity codes.
PROBLEM	description of the problem.
ACTION	error-recovery action.
TAG	unique error message identifier.

Each element is described in more detail below.

The standard specifies the information important in error-recovery, but does not specify the format in which to deliver the information. For example, with a graphical user-interface, the **LABEL** might be presented as an icon. An operating system error message meeting the standard information requirements is shown below with, **OS** as the **LABEL**, **HALT** as the **SEVERITY**, **Timeout Table Overflow** as the **PROBLEM**, **See Administration Manual** as the **ACTION**, and **OS-136** as the **TAG**.

OS: HALT: Timeout Table Overflow.
TO FIX: See Administration Manual. OS-136

The standard allows systematic omission of one or more elements in specific environments that do not need them for successful error-recovery. For example, while operating system errors need all five elements, a firmware error message can omit the **ACTION** because an expert service person is typically the user of this message and the **ACTION** may be too long to store in firmware. Software that obviously puts the user in a special environment (e.g., a spreadsheet program) where the user sees only errors from that environment may omit the **LABEL**. Because a primary use of the **TAG** is for reporting or to point to on-line documentation, it may be omitted when appropriate (e.g., when there is no on-line documentation).

LABEL This element of the message identifies the error source (e.g., OS, UUCP, application-program-name, etc.) and could double as a pointer to documentation.

SEVERITY This element of the message indicates the consequences of the error for the user. Four levels of severity (which can be expanded by system builders who want additional distinctions) are outlined below.

- **HALT** indicates that the processor, OS, application, or database is corrupted and that processing should be stopped immediately to rectify the problem. This severity indicates an emergency.
- **ERROR** indicates that a condition that may soon interfere with resource use has occurred. This severity indicates that corrective action is needed.
- **WARNING** indicates an aberrant condition (e.g., stray hardware interrupt, free file space is low) that should be monitored, but needs no immediate action.
- **INFO** gives information about a user request or about the state of the system (e.g., a printer taken off-line).

PROBLEM This element of the message clearly describes the error condition. In much of today's software, this element is the only one provided in the message.

ACTION This element of the message describes the first step to be taken in the error-recovery process. For OS errors, this section of the message might be one of five standard strings:

1. **See Hardware Vendor**
2. **See Software Vendor**
3. **See Administrator Procedure**
4. **See Operator Procedure**
5. **See Manual**

These strings should be clearly identified as action to be taken (e.g., by preceding them with the prefix: **TO FIX:**).

TAG This is a unique identifier for the message, used both internally and to obtain online documentation for the message *on those systems that have capacity to store such information.*

NAME

printf, fprintf, sprintf — print formatted output

SYNOPSIS

```
#include <stdio.h>

int printf(format [ , arg ]...)
char *format;

int fprintf(stream, format [ , arg ]...)
FILE *stream;
char *format;

int sprintf(s, format [ , arg ]...)
char *s, *format;
```

DESCRIPTION

The function `printf` places output on the standard output stream `stdout`.

The function `fprintf` places output on the named output stream `stream`.

The function `sprintf` places output, followed by the null-character (`\0`) in consecutive bytes starting at `*s`. The user must ensure that enough storage is available. Each function returns the number of characters transmitted (not including the `\0` in the case of `sprintf`) or a negative value if an output error occurred.

Each function converts, formats and prints its `args` under control of `format`, a character-string containing the following three types of objects:

1. plain-characters that are simply copied to the output stream;
2. escape-sequences that represent non-graphic characters; and
3. conversion-specifications.

The following escape-sequences produce the associated action on display devices capable of the action:

`\b` Backspace.
Moves the printing position to one character before the current position, unless the current position is the start of a line.

`\f` Form Feed.
Moves the printing position to the initial printing position of the next logical page.

`\n` New line.
Moves the printing position to the start of the next line.

`\r` Carriage return.
Moves the printing position to the start of the current line.

`\t` Horizontal tab.
Moves the printing position to the next implementation-defined horizontal tab position on the current line.

`\v` Vertical tab.
Moves the printing position to the start of the next implementation-defined vertical tab position.

The character `%` introduces each conversion-specification. After `%`, the following appear in sequence:

Zero or more *flags* to modify the meaning of the conversion-specification.

An optional string of decimal digits to specify a minimum *field-width*. If the converted value has fewer characters than the field-width, it is padded on the left (or right, if the left-adjustment flag (`-`), described below, has been given) to the field-width.

A *precision* to sets the minimum number of digits appearing in `d`, `o`, `u`, `x`, or `X` conversions (the field is padded with leading zeros), the number of digits appearing after the decimal-point in `e` and `f` conversions, the maximum number of significant digits in `g` conversion; or the maximum number of characters printed from a string in `s` conversion. The precision takes the form of a dot (`.`) followed by a decimal digit string; a null-digit-string is treated as zero.

An optional `l` (ell) to specify that a following `d`, `o`, `u`, `x` or `X` conversion-character applies to a long integer `arg`. An `l` before any other conversion-character is ignored.

A conversion-character to indicate the type of conversion to be applied (see below).

The *flag* characters and their meanings are:

- `-` Left-justify the result of the conversion within the field.
- `+` Begin the result of a signed conversion with a sign (`+` or `-`).
- *blank* Prepend a *blank* to the result if the first character of a signed conversion is not a sign (i.e., ignore the blank-flag if the `+`-flag also appears).
- `#` Convert the value to an *alternate form*; for `c`, `d`, `s` and `u` conversions, the flag has no effect; for `o` conversion, it increases the precision to force the first digit of the result to be a zero; for `x` or `X` conversion, `0x` or `0X` is prepended to a non-zero result; for `e`, `E`, `f`, `g` and `G` conversions, the result always contains a decimal-point, even if no digits follow the point (normally, a decimal-point appears in the result of these conversions only if a digit follows it); for `g` and `G` conversions, trailing zeroes are *not* removed from the result as they normally are.

A *field-width* or *precision* may be indicated by an asterisk (*) instead of a digit string. In this case, an integer `arg` supplies the field-width or precision. The `arg` actually converted is not fetched until the conversion letter is seen, so any `args` specifying field-width or precision must come *before* any `arg` to be converted.

Each conversion-character fetchs zero or more `args`. The results are undefined if there are insufficient `args` for the format. If the format is exhausted while `args` remain, the excess `args` are ignored.

The conversion-characters and their meanings are:

`%` Print a `%`; no argument is converted.

`c` Print the character `arg`.

`d,o,u,x,X` Convert the integer `arg` to signed decimal (`d`), unsigned octal (`o`), unsigned decimal (`u`) or unsigned hexadecimal notation (`x` and `X`). The `x` conversion uses the letters `abcdef` and the `X` conversion uses the letters `ABCDEF`. The *precision* of `arg` specifies the minimum number of digits to appear. If the value being converted can be represented in fewer digits than the specified minimum, it will be expanded with leading zeroes. The default precision is `1`. The result of converting a zero value with a precision of `0` is a null-string.

`e,E` Convert the float or double `arg` to the style `[-]`*d*`.`*ddd*`e±`*dd*, where there is one digit before the decimal-point and the number of digits after it is equal to the precision. When the precision is missing, six digits are produced; if the precision is `0`, no decimal-point appears. The `E` conversion-character produces a number with `E` instead of `e` introducing the exponent.

The exponent always contains at least two digits. However, if the value to be printed is greater than or equal to `1E+100`, additional exponent digits will be printed as necessary.

`f` Convert the float or double `arg` to decimal notation in the style `[-]`*ddd*`.`*ddd*, where the number of digits after the decimal-point is equal to the *precision* specification. If the precision is omitted from `arg`, six digits are output; if the precision is explicitly `0`, no decimal-point appears.

`g,G` Print the float or double `arg` in style `f` or `e` (or in style `E` in the case of a `G` conversion-character), with the precision-specifying the number of significant digits. The style used depends on the value converted: style `e` will be used only if the exponent resulting from the conversion is less than `-4` or greater than the precision. Trailing zeroes are removed from the result. A decimal-point appears only if it is followed by a digit.

s The `arg` is taken to be a string (character pointer) and characters from the string are printed until a null-character (`\0`) is encountered or the number of characters indicated by the *precision* specification of `arg` is reached. If the precision is omitted from `arg`, it is taken to be infinite, so all characters up to the first null-character are printed. A `NULL` value for `arg` will yield undefined results.

If the character after the `%` is not a valid conversion-character, the results of the conversion are undefined.

In no case does a non-existent or small field-width cause truncation of a field; if the result of a conversion is wider than the field-width, the field is simply expanded to contain the conversion result. Characters generated by `printf` and `fprintf` are printed as if the PUTC(BA_LIB) routine had been called.

RETURN VALUE

The functions `printf`, `fprintf`, and `sprintf` return the number of characters transmitted, or return -1 if an error was encountered.

EXAMPLE

To print a date and time in the form `Sunday, July 3, 10:02`, where `weekday` and `month` are pointers to null-terminated strings:

```
printf("%s, %s %d, %d:%.2d",
        weekday, month, day, hour, min);
```

To print π to 5 decimal places:

```
printf("pi = %.5f", 4 * atan(1.0));
```

SEE ALSO

PUTC(BA_LIB), SCANF(BA_LIB), FOPEN(BA_SYS).

CAVEATS

The function `printf` will make available character-string-representations for ∞ and "not a number" (NaN: a symbolic entity encoded in floating point format) to support the **IEEE P754** standard.

NAME

putc, putchar, fputc, putw — put character or word onto a stream

SYNOPSIS

```
#include <stdio.h>

int putc(c, stream)
int c;
FILE *stream;

int putchar(c)
int c;

int fputc(c, stream)
int c;
FILE *stream;

int putw(w, stream)
int w;
FILE *stream;
```

DESCRIPTION

The function `putc` writes character `c` onto named output stream, `stream`, where the file-pointer, if defined, points. Both `putc` and `putchar` are macros, and `putchar` is defined as `putc(c, stdout)`.

The function `fputc` behaves like `putc`, but is a function instead of a macro. The function `fputc` runs more slowly than `putc` but it takes less space per invocation and its name can be passed as an argument to a function.

The function `putw` writes the word (i.e., integer `w` onto the named output stream, `stream`, where the file-pointer, if defined, points). The size of a word is the size of an integer and varies from machine to machine. The function `putw` neither assumes nor causes special alignment in the file.

RETURN VALUE

On success, `putc`, `fputc`, and `putchar` each return the value they have written. On failure, they return the constant `EOF`. This occurs if `stream` is not open for writing or if it cannot grow. The function `putw` returns non-zero if an error occurs; otherwise, it returns zero.

APPLICATION USAGE

Because it is implemented as a macro, `putc` incorrectly treats `stream` when it has side-effects. In particular, `putc(c, *f++);` may not work sensibly, and `fputc` should be used instead.

Because word-length and byte-ordering are machine-dependent, files written using `putw` may not be read using `getw` on a different processor.

SEE ALSO

FCLOSE(BA_SYS), FERROR(BA_SYS), FOPEN(BA_SYS), FREAD(BA_SYS), PRINTF(BA_LIB), PUTS(BA_LIB), SETBUF(BA_LIB).

NAME

putenv — change or add value to environment

SYNOPSIS

```
int putenv(string)
char *string;
```

DESCRIPTION

The argument `string` points to a string of the the following form:

```
name = value
```

The function `putenv` makes the value of the environment variable `name` equal to `value` by altering an existing variable or creating a new one. In either case, the string pointed to by `string` becomes part of the environment, so altering the string will change the environment. The space used by `string` is no longer used once a new string-defining `name` is passed to the function `putenv`.

RETURN VALUE

The function `putenv` returns non-zero if it was unable to obtain enough space for an expanded environment, otherwise zero.

APPLICATION USAGE

The function `putenv` was added in UNIX System V Release 2.0.

The function `putenv` manipulates the environment pointed to by `environ`, and can be used in conjunction with `getenv`. However, `envp`, the third argument to `main`, is not changed [see EXEC(BA_SYS)].

A potential error is to call the function `putenv` with a pointer to an automatic variable as the argument and to then exit the calling function while `string` is still part of the environment.

SEE ALSO

EXEC(BA_SYS), MALLOC(BA_SYS), GETENV(BA_LIB).

NAME

puts, fputs — put a string on a stream

SYNOPSIS

```
#include <stdio.h>

int puts(s)
char *s;

int fputs(s, stream)
char *s;
FILE *stream;
```

DESCRIPTION

The function `puts` writes the null-terminated string `s` points to followed by a new-line character, onto the standard output stream, `stdout`.

The function `fputs` writes the null-terminated string `s` points to onto the named output stream, `stream`.

Neither function writes the terminating null-character.

RETURN VALUE

On success, both `puts` and `fputs` return the number of characters written, and both return `EOF` on error. This occurs if they try to write on a file that is not open for writing.

APPLICATION USAGE

The function `puts` appends a new-line character while `fputs` does not.

SEE ALSO

FERROR(BA_SYS), FOPEN(BA_SYS), FREAD(BA_SYS), PRINTF(BA_LIB), PUTC(BA_LIB).

NAME

qsort — quicker sort

SYNOPSIS

```
void qsort(base, nel, width, compar)
char *base;
unsigned nel, width;
int (*compar)( );
```

DESCRIPTION

The function `qsort` is a general-sorting algorithm that sorts a table of data in place.

The argument `base` points to the element at the base of the table.

The argument `nel` is the number of elements in the table.

The argument `width` is the size of an element in bytes.

The argument `compar` is the name of the user-supplied comparison function, which is called with two arguments that point to the elements being compared. The comparison function must return an integer less than, equal to or greater than zero, according as the first argument is to be considered is less than, equal to or greater than the second.

APPLICATION USAGE

The pointer to the base the table should be of type pointer-to-element, and cast to type pointer-to-character.

The comparison function need not compare every byte, so arbitrary data may be contained in the elements in addition to the values being compared.

The relative order in the output of two items which compare as equal is unpredictable.

SEE ALSO

BSEARCH(BA_LIB), LSEARCH(BA_LIB), STRING(BA_LIB).

NAME

rand, srand — simple random-number generator

SYNOPSIS

```
int rand( )

void srand(seed)
unsigned int seed;
```

DESCRIPTION

The function `rand` uses a multiplicative congruential random-number generator with period 2^{32} that returns successive pseudo-random numbers in the range from 0 to 32767.

The function `srand` uses the argument `seed` as a seed for a new sequence of pseudo-random numbers to be returned by subsequent calls to the function `rand`. If `srand` is then called with the same seed value, the sequence of pseudo-random numbers will be repeated. If `rand` is called before any calls to `srand` have been made, the same sequence will be generated as when `srand` is first called with a seed value of 1.

APPLICATION USAGE

The DRAND48(BA_LIB) routine provides a much more elaborate random-number generator.

The following functions define the semantics of `rand` and `srand`.

```
static unsigned long int next = 1;
int rand( )
{
        next = next * 1103515245 + 12345;
        return ((unsigned int)(next/65536) % 32768);
}
void srand(seed)
unsigned int seed;
{
        next = seed;
}
```

Specifying the semantics makes it possible to reproduce the behavior of programs that use pseudo-random sequences. This facilitates the testing of portable applications in different implementations.

SEE ALSO

DRAND48(BA_LIB).

NAME

regexp — regular-expression compile and match routines

SYNOPSIS

```
#define INIT declarations
#define GETC( ) getc code
#define PEEK( ) peekc code
#define UNGETC( ) ungetc code
#define RETURN(ptr) return code
#define ERROR(val) error code
#include <regexp.h>

char *compile(instring, expbuf, endbuf, eof)
char *instring, *expbuf, *endbuf;
int eof;

int step(string, expbuf)
char *string, *endbuf;

advance(string, expbuf)
char *string, *expbuf;

extern char *loc1, *loc2, *locs;
```

DESCRIPTION

These functions are general-purpose regular-expression matching routines to be used in programs that perform regular-expression matching. These functions are defined by the `<regexp.h>` header file.

The function `compile` takes a regular-expression as input and produces a compiled-expression that `step` or `advance` can use.

The functions `step` and `advance` do pattern-matching given a character-string and a compiled-expression as input.

A regular-expression, *re*, specifies a set of character-strings. A member of this set of strings is said to be *matched* by the *re*. Some characters have special meaning when used in an *re*; other characters stand for themselves.

The regular-expressions that `regexp` uses are constructed as follows:

Expression	*Meaning*
c	the character *c* where *c* is not a special character.
c	the character *c* where *c* is any character, except a digit in the range `1-9`.
^	the beginning of the line being compared.
$	the end of the line being compared.
.	any character in the input.

`[`*s*`]`	any character in the set *s*, where *s* is a sequence of characters and/or a range of characters (e.g., `[`*c*`-`*c*`]`).
`[^`*s*`]`	any character not in the set *s*, where *s* is defined as above.
r`*`	zero or more successive occurrences of regular-expression *r*. The longest match is chosen.
rx	the occurrence of regular-expression *r* followed by the occurrence of regular-expression *x*. (Concatenation)
r`\{`*m*`,`*n*`\}`	any number of *m* through *n* successive occurrences of regular-expression *r*. The regular-expression *r*`\{`*m*`\}` matches exactly *m* occurrences; *r*`\{`*m*`,\}` matches at least *m* occurrences.
`\(`*r*`\)`	the regular-expression *r*. When `\`*n* (where *n* is a number greater than zero) appears in a constructed regular-expression, it stands for regular-expression *x* where *x* is the nth regular-expression enclosed in `\(` and `\)` strings that appeared earlier in the constructed regular-expression. For example, `\(`*r*`\)`*x*`\(`*y*`\)`*z*`\2` is the concatenation of regular-expressions *rxyzy*.

Characters that have special meaning except when they appear within square brackets, `[ ]`, or are preceded by `\` are: `.`, `*`, `[`, `\`. Other special characters, such as `$` have special meaning in more restricted contexts.

The character `^` at the beginning of an expression permits a successful match only immediately after a new-line, and the character `$` at the end of an expression requires a trailing new-line.

Two characters have special meaning only when used within square brackets. The character `-` denotes a range, `[`*c*`-`*c*`]`, unless it is just after the opening bracket or before the closing bracket, `[-`*c*`]` or `[`*c*`-]` in which case it has no special meaning. When used within brackets, the character `^` means *complement of* if it immediately follows the open bracket, `[^`*c*`]`, elsewhere between brackets, `[`*c*`^]`, it stands for the ordinary character `^`.

The special meaning of the `\` operator can be escaped *only* by preceding it with another `\` (e.g., `\\`).

Programs must declare the following five macros before the `#include <regexp.h>` statement. The function `compile` uses the macros `GETC`, `PEEKC`, and `UNGETC` to operate on the regular-expression given as input.

`GETC()`	returns the next character in the regular-expression. Successive calls to `GETC()` return successive characters of the regular-expression.
`PEEKC()`	returns the next character in the regular-expression. Successive calls to `PEEKC()` return the same character, which also is the next character `GETC()` returns.

`UNGETC( )` causes the next call to `GETC( )` and `PEEKC( )` to return the argument `c`. No more than one character of pushback is ever needed and this character is guaranteed to be the last character `GETC( )` reads. The value of the macro `UNGETC(c)` is always ignored.

`RETURN(ptr)` is used on normal exit from `compile`. The argument `ptr` points to the character after the last character of the compiled-expression. This is useful to programs managing memory allocation.

`ERROR(val)` is the abnormal return from `compile`. The argument `val` is an error number [see **ERRORS** below for meanings]. This call should never return.

The syntax of a call to `compile` is as follows:

```
compile(instring,expbuf,endbuf,eof)
```

The first parameter `instring` is never used explicitly by `compile`, but is useful for programs pass different pointers to input characters. It is sometimes used in the `INIT` declaration (see below). Programs which call functions to input characters or have characters in an external array can pass down a value of `((char*)0)` for this parameter.

The next parameter `expbuf` is a character pointer. It points to the place where the compiled-expression will be placed.

The parameter `endbuf` is one more than the highest address where the compiled-expression may be placed. If the compiled-expression cannot fit in `(endbuf-expbuf)` bytes, a call to `ERROR(50)` is made.

The parameter `eof` is the character which marks the end of the regular-expression. For example, *re/*.

Each program that includes the `<regexp.h>` header file must have a `#define` statement for `INIT`. It is used for dependent declarations and initializations. Most often it is used to set a register variable to point to the beginning of the regular-expression so that this register variable can be used in the declarations for `GETC( )`, `PEEKC( )`, and `UNGETC( )`. Otherwise it can be used to declare external variables that might be used by `GETC( )`, `PEEKC( )` and `UNGETC( )`. See **EXAMPLES** below.

The first parameter to `step` points to a string of characters to be checked for a match. This string should be null-terminated.

The second parameter, `expbuf`, is the compiled-expression produced by calling `compile`.

The function `step` returns non-zero if some sub-string of `string` matches the regular-expression in `expbuf` and zero if there is no match. If there is a match, two external character pointers are set as a side effect to the call to `step`. The variable `loc1` points to the first character that matched the regular-expression; the variable `loc2` points to the character after the last character that matches the regular-expression. Thus if the regular-expression matches the entire input string, `loc1` points to the first character of `string` and `loc2` points to the null at the end of `string`.

The function `advance` returns non-zero if the initial substring of `string` matches the regular-expression in `expbuf`. If there is a match, an external character pointer, `loc2`, is set as a side-effect. The variable `loc2` points to the next character in `string` after the last character that matched.

When `advance` gets a * or `\{ \}` sequence in the regular-expression, it moves its pointer to the string to be matched as far as possible and recursively calls itself trying to match the rest of the string to the rest of the regular-expression. As long as there is no match, `advance` backs up along the string until it finds a match or reaches the point in the string that initially matched the * or `\{ \}`. It is sometimes desirable to stop this backing-up before reaching the inital point in the string. If the external character pointer `locs` equals the point in the string at sometime during the backing-up, `advance` stops the backing-up and returns zero.

The external variables `circf`, `sed`, and `nbra` are reserved.

RETURN VALUE

The function `compile` uses the macro `RETURN` on success and the macro `ERROR` on failure, see above. The functions `step` and `advance` return non-zero on a successful match and zero if there is no match.

ERRORS

11	range endpoint too large.
16	bad number.
25	*digit* out of range.
36	illegal or missing delimiter.
41	no remembered search string.
42	`\( \)` imbalance.
43	too many `\(`.
44	more than 2 numbers given in `\{ \}`.
45	} expected after `\`.
46	first number exceeds second in `\{ \}`.
49	`[ ]` imbalance.
50	regular-expression overflow.

EXAMPLES

The following shows how an application-program might use the regular-expression macros and calls:

```
#define INIT           register char *sp = instring;
#define GETC()         (*sp++)
#define PEEKC()        (*sp)
#define UNGETC(c)      (--sp)
#define RETURN(c)      return;
#define ERROR(c)       regerr()

#include <regexp.h>
  ...
     (void) compile(*argv, expbuf, &expbuf[ESIZE],'\0');
  ...
     if (step(linebuf, expbuf))
         succeed();
```

NAME

scanf, fscanf, sscanf — convert formatted input

SYNOPSIS

```
#include <stdio.h>

int scanf(format [ , pointer ]...)
char *format;

int fscanf(stream, format [ , pointer ]...))
FILE *stream;
char *format;

int sscanf(s, format [ , pointer ]...)
char *s, *format;
```

DESCRIPTION

The function `scanf` reads from the standard input stream, `stdin`.

The function `fscanf` reads from the named input stream, `stream`.

The function `sscanf` reads from the character-string, `s`.

Each function reads characters, interprets them according to a control-string, `format` described below, and stores the converted input where a set of `pointer` arguments indicates.

The control-string usually contains conversion-specifications, which direct interpretation of input sequences. The control-string may contain:

1. White-space characters (blanks, tabs, new-lines, or form-feeds) which, except in two cases described below, cause input to be read up to the next non-white-space character.

2. Ordinary character (not `%`), which must match the next character of the input stream.

3. Conversion-specifications, composed of the character `%`, an optional assignment suppressing the character `*`, a decimal-digit-string specifying an optional numerical maximum field-width, an optional letter `l` (ell) or `h` indicating the size of the receiving variable, and a conversion-code.

A conversion-specification directs the conversion of the next input field; the result is placed in the variable pointed to by the corresponding argument unless assignment suppression was indicated by the character `*`. The suppression of assignment provides a way of describing an input field which is to be skipped. An input field is defined as a string of non-space characters; it extends to the next inappropriate character or until the maximum field-width, if one is specified, is exhausted. For all descriptors except the character `[` and the character `c`, white space leading an input field is ignored.

The conversion-code indicates the interpretation of the input field; the corresponding `pointer` argument usually must be of a restricted type. For a suppressed field, no `pointer` argument is given.

The following conversion-codes are legal:

`%` a single `%` is expected; no assignment is done.

`d` a decimal integer is expected; the corresponding argument should be an integer pointer.

`u` an unsigned decimal integer is expected; the corresponding argument should be an unsigned integer pointer.

`o` an octal integer is expected; the corresponding argument should be an integer pointer.

`x` a hexadecimal integer is expected; the corresponding argument should be an integer pointer.

`e,f,g` a floating point number is expected; the next field is converted accordingly and stored through the corresponding argument, which should be a pointer to a `float`. The input format for floating point numbers is an optionally signed string of digits, possibly containing a decimal-point; followed by an optional exponent field consisting of an `E` or an `e`, followed by an optionally signed integer.

`s` a character-string is expected; the corresponding argument should be a pointer to an array of characters large enough to accept the string and a terminating `\0`, to be added automatically. The input field is terminated by a white-space character.

`c` a character is expected; the corresponding argument should be a character pointer. The normal skip over white space is suppressed in this case; to read the next non-space character, use `%1s`. If a field-width is given, the corresponding argument should point to a character array; the indicated number of characters is read.

`[` indicates string data; the corresponding argument must point to a character array large enough to hold the data field and the terminating `\0` which will be added automatically. The normal skip over leading white space is suppressed. The left bracket is followed by a set of characters called the *scanset* and a right bracket; the input field is the maximal sequence of input characters consisting only of characters in the scanset. At least one character must match for this conversion to be considered successful. The circumflex (`^`), when it is the first character in the scanset, serves as a complement operator defining the scanset as the set of all characters *not* contained in the rest of the scanset string.

Some conventions are used to construct the scanset. The construct *first*-*last* represents a range of characters; thus, `[0123456789]` may be expressed `[0-9]`. For this convention, *first* must be lexically less than or equal to *last*, or else the dash will stand for itself. The character `-` also stands for itself whenever it is the first or the last character in the scanset. To include the right square bracket as an element of the scanset (i.e., *not* as the closing bracket) it must appear as the first character (possibly preceded by a circumflex) of the scanset.

If an invalid conversion-character follows the `%`, the results of the operation are unpredictable.

The conversion-characters `d`, `u`, `o`, and `x` may be preceded by `l` or `h` to indicate that a pointer to `long` or to `short` rather than to `int` is in the argument list. Similarly, the conversion-characters `e`, `f`, and `g` may be preceded by `l` to indicate that a pointer to `double` rather than to `float` is in the argument list. Other conversion-characters ignore the `l` or `h` modifier.

The `scanf` conversion stops at end of file, at the end of the control-string or when an input character conflicts with the control-string. In the latter case, the offending character is left unread in the input stream.

RETURN VALUE

These functions return the number of successfully matched and assigned input items; this number can be zero in the event of an early conflict between an input character and the control-string. If the input ends before the first conflict or conversion, `EOF` is returned.

APPLICATION USAGE

Trailing white space (including a new-line) is left unread unless matched in the control-string.

The success of literal matches and suppressed assignments is not directly determinable.

EXAMPLE

The call to the function `scanf`:

```
int i, n; float x; char name[50];
n = scanf("%d%f%s", &i, &x, name);
```

with the input line:

```
25 54.32E-1 thompson
```

assigns to `n` the value `3`, to `i` the value `25`, to `x` the value `5.432`, and `name` contains `thompson\0`.

The call to the function `scanf`:

```
int i; float x; char name[50];
(void) scanf("%2d%f%*d %[0-9]", &i, &x, name);
```

with the input line:

```
56789 0123 56a72
```

assigns `56` to `i`, `789.0` to `x`, skips `0123`, and puts the string `56\0` in `name`. The next call to `getchar` [see GETC(BA_LIB)] returns `a`.

SEE ALSO

GETC(BA_LIB), PRINTF(BA_LIB), STRTOD(BA_LIB), STRTOL(BA_LIB).

CAVEATS

The function `scanf` will make available character string representations for ∞ and "not a number" (NaN: a symbolic entity encoded in floating point format) to support the **IEEE P754** standard.

NAME

setbuf — assign buffering to a stream

SYNOPSIS

```
#include <stdio.h>

void setbuf(stream, buf)
FILE *stream;
char *buf;

int setvbuf(stream, buf, type, size)
FILE *stream;
char *buf;
int type, size;
```

DESCRIPTION

The function `setbuf` may be used after a stream is opened but before it is read or written. If `buf` is the `NULL` pointer, input/output is completely unbuffered; otherwise `setbuf` causes the array pointed to by `buf` to be used instead of an automatically allocated buffer. A constant `BUFSIZ`, defined by the `<stdio.h>` header file, tells how big an array is needed:

```
char buf[BUFSIZ];
```

By default, terminal-output is line-buffered and all other input/output is fully buffered, except the standard error stream, `stderr`, which is normally unbuffered.

APPLICATION USAGE

A common source of error is allocating buffer space as an *automatic* variable in a code block, and then failing to close the stream in the same block.

SEE ALSO

FOPEN(BA_SYS), MALLOC(BA_SYS), GETC(BA_LIB), PUTC(BA_LIB), SETBUF(BA_LIB).

NAME

setjmp, longjmp — non-local goto

SYNOPSIS

```
#include <setjmp.h>

int setjmp(env)
jmp_buf env;

void longjmp(env, val)
jmp_buf env;
int val;
```

DESCRIPTION

These functions are useful for dealing with errors and interrupts encountered in a low-level subroutine of a program.

The function `setjmp` saves its stack environment in `env` (whose type, `jmp_buf`, is defined by the `<setjmp.h>` header file) for later use by `longjmp`. The function `setjmp` returns the value `0`.

The function `longjmp` restores the environment saved by the last call to `setjmp` with the corresponding `env`.

After `longjmp` is completed, program execution continues as if the corresponding call to `setjmp` (the caller of which must not itself have returned in the interim) had just returned `val`. All accessible data have values as of the time `longjmp` was called.

RETURN VALUE

When called by the calling-process, `setjmp` returns `0`.

The function `longjmp` does not return from where it was called, but rather, program execution continues as if the previous call to `setjmp` returned `val`. That is, when `setjmp` *returns* as a result of calling `longjmp`, `setjmp` returns `val`. However, `longjmp` cannot cause `setjmp` to return `0`. If `longjmp` is called with a `val` of `0`, `setjmp` returns `1`.

APPLICATION USAGE

The behavior is undefined when `longjmp` is called without `env` having been primed by calling `setjmp`, or when the last such call was in a function which has since returned.

Register variables may have unpredictable values when the call to `longjmp` is in a different function from the corresponding call to `setjmp`.

SEE ALSO

SIGNAL(BA_SYS).

NAME

setvbuf — assign buffering to a stream

SYNOPSIS

```
#include <stdio.h>

int setvbuf(stream, buf, type, size)
FILE *stream;
char *buf;
int type, size;
```

DESCRIPTION

The function `setvbuf` may be used after `stream` is opened but before it is read or written. The value of `type` determines how `stream` is buffered. Legal values for `type`, defined by the `<stdio.h>` header file, are:

- `_IOFBF` causes input/output to be fully buffered
- `_IOLBF` causes output to be line-buffered; the buffer is flushed when a new-line is written or the buffer is full or input is requested.
- `_IONBF` causes input/output to be completely unbuffered.

If `buf` is not the `NULL` pointer, the array it points to will be used for buffering instead of an automatically allocated buffer. The argument `size` specifies the size of the buffer to be used. The constant `BUFSIZ` in the `<stdio.h>` header file is suggested as a good buffer size. If input/output is unbuffered, `buf` and `size` are ignored.

By default, terminal-output is line-buffered and all other input/output is fully buffered, except the standard error stream, `stderr`, which is normally unbuffered.

RETURN VALUE

If the value for `type` or `size` is illegal, `setvbuf` returns a non-zero value; otherwise, it returns zero.

APPLICATION USAGE

The function `setvbuf` was added in UNIX System V Release 2.0.

A common source of error is allocating buffer space as an *automatic* variable in a code block, and then failing to close the stream in the same block.

SEE ALSO

FOPEN(BA_SYS), MALLOC(BA_SYS), GETC(BA_LIB), PUTC(BA_LIB), SETBUF(BA_LIB).

NAME

sinh, cosh, tanh — hyperbolic functions

SYNOPSIS

```
#include <math.h>

double sinh(x)
double x;

double cosh(x)
double x;

double tanh(x)
double x;
```

DESCRIPTION

The functions `sinh`, `cosh`, and `tanh` return, respectively, the hyperbolic sine, cosine and tangent of their argument.

RETURN VALUE

The functions `sinh` and `cosh` return `HUGE`, and `sinh` may return `-HUGE` for negative `x`, when the correct value would overflow and set `errno` to `ERANGE`.

APPLICATION USAGE

These error-handling procedures are changed by the MATHERR(BA_LIB) routine.

SEE ALSO

MATHERR(BA_LIB).

CAVEATS

A macro `HUGE_VAL` will be defined by the `<math.h>` header file. This macro will call a function which will either return +∞ on a system supporting the **IEEE P754** standard or +{MAXDOUBLE} on a system that does not support the **IEEE P754** standard.

The functions `sinh` and `cosh` will return `HUGE_VAL` (`sinh` will return `-HUGE_VAL` for negative `n`) when the correct value overflows.

NAME

ssignal, gsignal — software signals

SYNOPSIS

```
#include <signal.h>

int (*ssignal(sig, action))()
int sig,(*action)();

int gsignal(sig)
int sig;
```

DESCRIPTION

The functions `ssignal` and `gsignal` implement a software facility similar to the SIGNAL(BA_SYS) routine.

Software signals available to programs are described in SIGNAL(BA_SYS).

A call to `ssignal` associates a procedure, `action`, with the software signal `sig`; a call to `gsignal` raises the software signal, `sig`. Raising a software signal causes the action established for that signal to be taken.

The first argument, `sig`, to the function `ssignal`, is a signal number in the range `1-15` for which an action is to be established. The second argument, `action`, defines the action; it is either the name of a (user-defined) function `action` or one of the manifest constants `SIG_DFL` (default) or `SIG_IGN` (ignore). The function `ssignal` returns the action previously established for that signal type; if no action has been established or the signal is illegal, `ssignal` returns `SIG_DFL`.

The function `gsignal` raises the signal identified by its argument, `sig`:

> If an action has been established for `sig`, then `action` is reset to `SIG_DFL` and `action` is entered with `sig`. The function `gsignal` returns the value `action` returns.
>
> If the action for `sig` is `SIG_IGN`, `gsignal` returns 1 and takes no other action.
>
> If the action for `sig` is `SIG_DFL`, `gsignal` returns 0 and takes no other action.
>
> If `sig` has an illegal value or no action was ever specified for `sig`, `gsignal` returns 0 and takes no other action.

SEE ALSO

SIGNAL(BA_SYS).

NAME

strcat, strncat, strcmp, strncmp, strcpy, strncpy, strlen, strchr, strrchr, strpbrk, strspn, strcspn, strtok — string operations

SYNOPSIS

```
#include <string.h>

char *strcat(s1, s2)
char *s1, *s2;

char *strncat(s1, s2, n)
char *s1, *s2;
int n;

int strcmp(s1, s2)
char *s1, *s2;

int strncmp(s1, s2, n)
char *s1, *s2;
int n;

char *strcpy(s1, s2)
char *s1, *s2;

char *strncpy(s1, s2, n)
char *s1, *s2;
int n;

int strlen(s)
char *s;

char *strchr(s, c)
char *s;
int c;

char *strrchr(s, c)
char *s;
int c;

char *strpbrk(s1, s2)
char *s1, *s2;

int strspn(s1, s2)
char *s1, *s2;

int strcspn(s1, s2)
char *s1, *s2;

char *strtok(s1, s2)
char *s1, *s2;
```

DESCRIPTION

The arguments `s1`, `s2` and `s` point to strings (arrays of characters terminated by a null-character).

The functions `strcat`, `strncat`, `strcpy`, `strncpy` and `strtok` all alter `s1`, and do not check for overflow of the array pointed to by `s1`.

The function `strcat` appends a copy of `s2` to the end of `s1`.

The function `strncat` appends at most `n` characters. Each returns a pointer to the null-terminated result.

The function `strcmp` compares its arguments and returns an integer less than, equal to or greater than `0`, according as `s1` is lexicographically less than, equal to or greater than `s2`.

The function `strncmp` compares at most `n` characters of its arguments.

The function `strcpy` copies `s2` to `s1`, stopping after the null-character has been copied and returns `s1`.

The functions `strncpy` copies exactly `n` characters, truncating `s2` or adding null-characters to `s1` if necessary and returns `s1`. The result will not be null-terminated if the length of `s2` is `n` or more.

The function `strlen` returns the number of characters in `s`, not including the terminating null-character.

The function `strchr` (or `strrchr`) returns a pointer to the first (last) occurrence of character `c` in `s`, or a `NULL` pointer if `c` does not occur in `s`. The terminating null-character is considered to be part of the string.

The function `strpbrk` returns a pointer to the first occurrence in `s1` of any character from `s2`, or a `NULL` pointer if no character from `s2` occurs in `s1`.

The function `strspn` (or `strcspn`) returns the length of the initial segment of `s1` which consists entirely of characters from (not from) `s2`.

The function `strtok` considers `s1` to consist of a sequence of zero or more text tokens separated by spans of one or more separator-characters from `s2`. The first call (with pointer `s1` specified) returns a pointer to the first character of the first token, and will have written a null-character into `s1` immediately following the returned token. The function keeps track of its position in the string between separate calls, so that subsequent calls (which must be made with the first argument a `NULL` pointer) will work through `s1` immediately following that token. In this way subsequent calls will work through `s1`, returning a pointer to the first character of each subsequent token. A null-character will have been written into `s1` by `strtok` immediately following the token. The separator-string `s2` may be different from call to call. When no token remains in `s1`, a `NULL` pointer is returned.

APPLICATION USAGE

All these functions are declared by the `<string.h>` header file.

Both `strcmp` and `strncmp` use native character comparison. The sign of the value returned when one of the characters has its high-order bit set is implementation-dependent.

Character movement is performed differently in different implementations. Thus overlapping moves may yield surprises.

SEE ALSO

MEMORY(BA_LIB).

CAVEATS

The type of argument `n` to `strncat`, `strncmp` and `strncpy` and the type of value returned by `strlen` will be declared through the `typedef` facility in a header file as `size_t`.

NAME

strtod, atof — convert string to double-precision number

SYNOPSIS

```
double strtod(str, ptr)
char *str, **ptr;

double atof(str)
char *str;
```

DESCRIPTION

The function `strtod` returns as a double-precision floating-point number the value represented by the character string pointed to by `str`. The string is scanned up to the first unrecognized character.

The function `strtod` recognizes an optional string of *white-space* characters [as defined by `isspace` in CTYPE(BA_LIB)], then an optional sign, then a string of digits optionally containing a decimal point, then an optional `e` or `E` followed by an optional sign, followed by an integer.

If the value of `ptr` is not `((char **)0)`, a pointer to the character terminating the scan is returned in the location pointed to by `ptr`. If no number can be formed, `*ptr` is set to `str`, and 0 is returned.

The function call `atof(str)` is equivalent to:

```
strtod(str, (char **)0)
```

RETURN VALUE

If the correct value would cause overflow, ±`HUGE` is returned (according to the sign of the value) and `errno` is set to `ERANGE`.

If the correct value would cause underflow, zero is returned and `errno` is set to `ERANGE`.

APPLICATION USAGE

The function `strtod` was added in UNIX System V Release 2.0.

SEE ALSO

CTYPE(BA_LIB), SCANF(BA_LIB), STRTOL(BA_LIB).

CAVEATS

A macro `HUGE_VAL` will be defined by the `<math.h>` header file. This macro will call a function which will either return +∞ on a system that supports the **IEEE P754** standard or +{MAXDOUBLE} on a system that does not support the **IEEE P754** standard.

If the correct value overflows, ±`HUGE_VAL` will be returned (according to the sign of the value).

NAME

strtol, atol, atoi — convert string to integer

SYNOPSIS

```
long strtol(str, ptr, base)
char *str, **ptr;
int base;

long atol(str)
char *str;

int atoi(str)
char *str;
```

DESCRIPTION

The function `strtol` returns as a long integer the value represented by the character string pointed to by `str`. The string is scanned up to the first character inconsistent with the base. Leading *white-space* characters [as defined by `isspace` in CTYPE(BA_LIB)] are ignored.

If the value of `ptr` is not `((char **)0)`, a pointer to the character terminating the scan is returned in the location pointed to by `ptr`. If no integer can be formed, that location is set to `str` and zero is returned.

If `base` is positive, but not greater than `36`, it is used as the base for conversion. After an optional leading sign, leading zeros are ignored and `0x` or `0X` is ignored if `base` is `16`.

If `base` is zero, the string itself determines the base in the following way: After an optional leading sign, a leading zero causes octal-conversion and a leading `0x` or `0X` hexadecimal-conversion; otherwise, decimal-conversion is used.

Truncation from `long` to `int` can, of course, take place upon assignment or by an explicit cast.

The function call `atol(str)` is equivalent to:

```
strtol(str, (char **)0, 10)
```

The function call `atoi(str)` is equivalent to:

```
(int)strtol(str, (char **)0, 10)
```

RETURN VALUE

If `ptr` is a null-pointer, `strtol` returns the value of the string `str` as a long integer.

If `ptr` is not `NULL`, `strtol` returns the value of the string `str` as a long integer, and a pointer to the character terminating the scan is returned in the location `ptr` points to. If no integer can be formed, that location is set to `str` and `strtol` returns `0`.

APPLICATION USAGE

Overflow conditions are ignored.

SEE ALSO

CTYPE(BA_LIB), SCANF(BA_LIB), STRTOD(BA_LIB).

CAVEATS

Error handling will be added to `strtol`.

NAME

swab — swap bytes

SYNOPSIS

```
void swab(from, to, nbytes)
char *from, *to;
int nbytes;
```

DESCRIPTION

The function `swab` copies `nbytes` bytes pointed to by `from` to the array pointed to by `to`, exchanging adjacent even and odd bytes. It is useful for carrying binary data between machines with different low-order/high-order byte arrangements.

The argument `nbytes` should be even and non-negative. If the argument `nbytes` is odd and positive, the function `swab` uses `nbytes-1` instead. If the argument `nbytes` is negative, the function `swab` does nothing.

NAME

tmpfile — create a temporary file

SYNOPSIS

```
#include <stdio.h>

FILE *tmpfile()
```

DESCRIPTION

The function `tmpfile` creates a temporary file using a name generated by the TMPNAM(BA_LIB) library routine, and returns a corresponding pointer to the `FILE` structure associated with the stream [see **stdio-stream** in **Definitions**]. The temporary file will automatically be deleted when the process that opened it terminates or the temporary file is closed. The temporary file is opened for update (`w+`) [see FOPEN(BA_SYS)].

RETURN VALUE

If the temporary file cannot be opened, an error message is written and a `NULL` pointer is returned.

SEE ALSO

CREAT(BA_SYS), UNLINK(BA_SYS), FOPEN(BA_SYS), MKTEMP(BA_LIB), TMPNAM(BA_LIB).

NAME

tmpnam, tempnam — create a name for a temporary file

SYNOPSIS

```
#include <stdio.h>

char *tmpnam(s)
char *s;

char *tempnam(dir, pfx)
char *dir, *pfx;
```

DESCRIPTION

These functions create file-names that can safely be used for a temporary file.

The function `tmpnam` always generates a file-name using the path-prefix defined as `P_tmpdir` by the `<stdio.h>` header file. If `s` is `NULL`, `tmpnam` stores its result in an internal static area and returns a pointer to that area. The next call to `tmpnam` destroys the contents of the area. The function `tmpnam` stores its result in an array of at least `L_tmpnam` bytes, where `L_tmpnam` is a constant defined by the `<stdio.h>` header file. If `s` is not `NULL`, `tmpnam` stores its result in the array pointed to by `s` and returns `s`.

The function `tempnam` allows the user to control the choice of a directory. If defined in the user's environment, the value of the environmental variable `TMPDIR` is used as the name of the desired temporary file directory. The argument `dir` points to the name of the directory in which the file is to be created. If `dir` is `NULL` or points to a string that is not a name for an appropriate directory, `tempnam` uses the path-prefix defined as `P_tmpdir` by the `<stdio.h>` header file. If that directory is not accessible, the directory `/tmp` is used as a last resort.

The function `tempnam` uses the MALLOC(BA_SYS) routine to get space for the constructed file-name, and returns a pointer to this area. Thus, any pointer value `tempnam` returns may serve as an argument to the function `free` defined in MALLOC(BA_SYS). If `tempnam` cannot return the expected result for any reason, for example, the MALLOC(BA_SYS routine failed or none of the above-mentioned attempts to find an appropriate directory succeeded, `tempnam` returns a `NULL` pointer.

APPLICATION USAGE

Many applications prefer their temporary-files to have certain favorite initial letter sequences in their names. Use the argument `pfx` for this. This argument may be `NULL` or point to a string of up to five characters to be used as the first few characters of the temporary-file name.

The functions `tmpnam` and `tempnam` create a different file-name each time they are called.

Files created using these functions and either the FOPEN(BA_SYS) routine or the CREAT(BA_SYS) routine are temporary only in the sense that they reside in a directory intended for temporary use, and their names are unique. The user is responsible for using the UNLINK(BA_SYS) routine to remove the file when done.

If called more than {TMP_MAX} times in a single process, these functions start recycling previously used names.

Between the time a file-name is created and the file is opened, some other process can create a file with the same name. This can never happen if that other process uses these functions or `mktemp`, and the file-names are chosen so as to render duplication by other means unlikely.

SEE ALSO

CREAT(BA_SYS), UNLINK(BA_SYS), FOPEN(BA_SYS), MALLOC(BA_SYS), MKTEMP(BA_LIB), TMPFILE(BA_LIB).

NAME

sin, cos, tan, asin, acos, atan, atan2 — trigonometric functions

SYNOPSIS

```
#include <math.h>

double sin(x)
double x;

double cos(x)
double x;

double tan(x)
double x;

double asin(x)
double x;

double acos(x)
double x;

double atan(x)
double x;

double atan2(y, x)
double y, x;
```

DESCRIPTION

The functions `sin`, `cos` and `tan` return respectively the sine, cosine and tangent of their argument, `x`, measured in radians.

The function `asin` returns the arc-sine of `x` in the range $-\pi/2$ to $\pi/2$.

The function `acos` returns the arc-cosine of `x` in the range 0 to π.

The function `atan` returns the arc-tangent of `x` in the range $-\pi/2$ to $\pi/2$.

The function `atan2` returns the arc-tangent of `y/x` in the range $-\pi$ to π, using the signs of both `y` and `x` to get the quadrant of the return value.

RETURN VALUE

Both `sin` and `cos` lose accuracy when their argument is far from zero. For arguments sufficiently large, these functions return zero when there would otherwise be a complete loss of significance, and a `TLOSS` error message is printed on the standard error output [see MATHERR(BA_LIB)]. For arguments causing only partial loss of significance, a `PLOSS` error occurs but no message is printed. In both cases, `errno` equals `ERANGE`.

If the magnitude of the argument to `asin` or `acos` is greater than one, they return `0`, print a `DOMAIN` error message on the standard error output, and `errno` equals `EDOM`.

If both arguments to `atan2` are zero, it returns `0`, prints a `DOMAIN` error message on the standard error output, and `errno` equals `EDOM`.

APPLICATION USAGE

These error-handling procedures are changed by the MATHERR(BA_LIB) routine.

SEE ALSO

MATHERR(BA_LIB).

NAME

tsearch, tfind, tdelete, twalk — manage binary search trees

SYNOPSIS

```
#include <search.h>

char *tsearch(key, rootp, compar)
char *key;
char **rootp;
int (*compar)( );

char *tfind(key, rootp, compar)
char *key;
char **rootp;
int (*compar)( );

char *tdelete(key, rootp, compar)
char *key;
char **rootp;
int (*compar)( );

void twalk(root, action)
char *root;
void(*action)( );
```

DESCRIPTION

The functions `tsearch`, `tfind`, `tdelete`, and `twalk` manipulate binary search trees. All comparisons are done with a user-supplied function, `compar`. The comparison function is called with two arguments, the pointers to the elements being compared. It returns an integer less than, equal to or greater than `0`, according to whether the first argument is to be considered less than, equal to or greater than the second argument. The comparison function need not compare every byte, the elements may contain arbitrary data in addition to the values being compared.

The function `tsearch` can build and access the tree. The argument `key` points to a datum to be accessed or stored. If a datum in the tree equals `*key` (the value pointed to by `key`), `tsearch` returns a pointer to this found datum. Otherwise, `tsearch` inserts `*key`, and returns a pointer to it. Only pointers are copied, so the calling routine must store the data. The argument `rootp` points to a variable that points to the root of the tree. A `NULL` value for the variable pointed to by `rootp` denotes an empty tree; in this case, the variable is set to point to the datum which will be at the root of the new tree.

Like `tsearch`, `tfind` searchs for a datum in the tree, and returns a pointer to it if found. However, if it is not found, `tfind` returns a `NULL` pointer. The arguments for `tfind` are the same as for `tsearch`.

The function `tdelete` deletes a node from a binary search tree. The arguments are the same as for `tsearch`. The variable pointed to by `rootp` is changed if the deleted node was the root of the tree.

The function `twalk` traverses a binary search tree. The argument `root` is the root of the tree to be traversed. (Any node in a tree may be used as the root for a walk below that node.) The argument `action` names a user-defined routine to be called at each node. This routine is, in turn, called with three arguments.

The first argument is the address of the node being visited.

The second argument is a value from an enumeration data type, `VISIT` defined by the `<search.h>` header file. The values `preorder`, `postorder`, `endorder`, indicate whether this is the first, second or third time that the node has been visited (during a depth-first, left-to-right traversal of the tree), or the value `leaf` indicates that the node is a leaf.

The third argument is an integer that identifies the level of the node in the tree, with the root being level zero.

RETURN VALUE

If enough space is not available to create a new node, `tsearch` returns a `NULL` pointer.

If `rootp` is `NULL` on entry, `tsearch`, `tfind` and `tdelete` return a `NULL` pointer.

If the datum is found, both `tsearch` and `tfind` return a pointer to it. If not, `tfind` returns `NULL`, and `tsearch` returns a pointer to the inserted item. If the node is not found, `tdelete` returns a pointer to the parent of the deleted node, or a `NULL` pointer.

APPLICATION USAGE

The function `tfind` was added in UNIX System V Release 2.0.

The pointers to the key and the root of the tree must be of type pointer-to-element, and cast to type pointer-to-character. Similarly, although declared as type pointer-to-character, the value returned should be cast to type pointer-to-element.

The argument `root` to `twalk` is one level of indirection less than the argument `rootp` to `tsearch` and `tdelete`.

There are two nomenclatures used to refer to the order in which tree nodes are visited. The function `tsearch` uses preorder, postorder and endorder to respectively refer to visiting a node before any of its children, after its left child and before its right, and after both its children. The alternate nomenclature uses preorder, inorder and postorder to refer to the same visits, which could result in some confusion over the meaning of postorder.

If the calling function alters the pointer to the root, results are unpredictable.

EXAMPLE

The following code reads in strings and stores structures containing a pointer to each string and a count of its length. It then walks the tree, printing out the stored strings and their lengths in alphabetical order.

```
#include <search.h>
#include <stdio.h>

struct node {  /* pointers to these are stored in the tree */
    char *string;
    int length;
};
char string_space[10000]; /* space to store strings */
struct node nodes[500];   /* nodes to store */
struct node *root = NULL; /* this points to the root */

main( )
{
    char *strptr = string_space;
    struct node *nodeptr = nodes;
    void print_node( ), twalk( );
    int i = 0, node_compare( );

    while (gets(strptr) != NULL && i++ < sizeof(nodes [0]) {
        /* set node */
        nodeptr->string = strptr;
        nodeptr->length = strlen(strptr);
        /* put node into the tree */
        (void) tsearch((char *)nodeptr, &root, node_compare);
        /* adjust pointers, to not overwrite tree */
        strptr += nodeptr->length + 1;
        nodeptr++;
    }
    twalk(root, print_node);
}
/* This routine compares two nodes, based on an */
/* alphabetical ordering of the string field. */
int node_compare(node1, node2)
struct node *node1, *node2;
{
    return strcmp(node1->string, node2->string);
}
/* This routine prints out a node, the */
/* first time twalk encounters it. */
void print_node(node, order, level)
struct node **node;
VISIT order;
int level;
{
    if (order == preorder || order == leaf) {
        (void) printf("string = %20s,  length = %d\n",
            (*node)->string, (*node)->length);
    }
}
```

SEE ALSO

BSEARCH(BA_LIB), HSEARCH(BA_LIB), LSEARCH(BA_LIB).

NAME

ttyname, isatty — find name of a terminal

SYNOPSIS

```
char *ttyname(fildes)
int fildes;

int isatty(fildes)
int fildes;
```

DESCRIPTION

The function `ttyname` returns a pointer to a string containing the null-terminated path-name of the terminal-device associated with file-descriptor, `fildes`.

The function `isatty` returns 1 if `fildes` is associated with a terminal-device, 0 otherwise.

RETURN VALUE

The function `ttyname` returns a null-pointer if `fildes` does not describe a terminal device.

APPLICATION USAGE

The return value points to static data that is overwritten by each call.

NAME

ungetc — push character back into input stream

SYNOPSIS

```
#include <stdio.h>

int ungetc(c, stream)
int c;
FILE *stream;
```

DESCRIPTION

The function `ungetc` inserts the character `c` into the buffer associated with an input `stream`. That character, `c`, will be returned by the next call to the GETC(BA_LIB) routine on that `stream`. The function `ungetc` returns `c`, and leaves the file corresponding to `stream` unchanged.

One character of pushback is guaranteed, provided something has already been read from the stream and the stream is actually buffered.

If `c` equals `EOF`, `ungetc` does nothing to the buffer and returns `EOF`.

The FSEEK(BA_SYS) routine erases all memory of inserted characters.

RETURN VALUE

If successful, `ungetc` returns `c`; `ungetc` returns `EOF` if it cannot insert the character.

SEE ALSO

FSEEK(BA_SYS), GETC(BA_LIB), SETBUF(BA_LIB).

NAME

vprintf, vfprintf, vsprintf — print formatted output of a varargs argument list

SYNOPSIS

```
#include <stdio.h>
#include <varargs.h>

int vprintf(format, ap)
char *format;
va_list ap;

int vfprintf(stream, format, ap)
FILE *stream;
char *format;
va_list ap;

int vsprintf(s, format, ap)
char *s, *format;
va_list ap;
```

DESCRIPTION

The functions `vprintf`, `vfprintf`, and `vsprintf` are the same as `printf`, `fprintf`, and `sprintf` respectively, except they are called with an argument list `ap` of type `va_list` as defined by the `<varargs.h>` header file.

The `<varargs.h>` header file defines the type `va_list` and a set of macros for advancing through a list of arguments whose number and types may vary. The argument `ap` is used with the `<varargs.h>` header file macros `va_start`, `va_arg` and `va_end`. The **EXAMPLE** section below shows their use with `vprintf`.

The macro `va_alist` is used as the parameter list in a function definition as in the function called `error` in the example below.

The macro `va_dcl` is the declaration for `va_alist` and should not be followed by a semicolon.

The macro `va_start(ap)`, where `ap` is of type `va_list`, must be called before any attempt to traverse and access the list of arguments.

Calls to `va_arg(ap, atype)` traverse the argument list. Each execution of `va_arg` expands to an expression with the value of the next argument in the list `ap`. The argument `atype` is the type that the returned argument is expected to be.

The macro `va_end(ap)` must be executed when all desired arguments have been accessed. (The argument list in `ap` can be traversed again if `va_start` is called again after `va_end`).

APPLICATION USAGE

The functions `vprintf`, `vfprintf` and `vsprintf` were added in UNIX System V Release 2.0.

EXAMPLE

The following shows how `vfprintf` can be used to write an error routine. In it, `va_arg` is executed first to return the function name passed to `error` and it is called again to retrieve the format passed to `error`. The remaining `error` arguments, `arg1`, `arg2`, ..., are given to `vfprintf` in `ap`.

```
#include <stdio.h>
#include <varargs.h>
...
/*
 *   error should be called like
 *          error(function_name, format, arg1, arg2...);
 */
void error(va_alist)
va_dcl
{
     va_list ap;
     char *fmt;

     va_start(ap);
     /* print out name of function causing error */
     (void) fprintf(stderr, "ERR in %s:
     fmt = va_arg(ap, char *);
     /* print out remainder of message */
     (void) vfprintf(stderr, fmt, ap);
     va_end(ap);
     (void) abort( );
}
```

SEE ALSO

PRINTF(BA_LIB).

Chapter 8

Software Development Library

NAME

a64l, l64a — convert between long integer and base-64 ASCII string

SYNOPSIS

```
long a64l(s)
char *s;

char *l64a(l)
long l;
```

DESCRIPTION

These routines are used to maintain numbers stored in *base-64* **ASCII** characters. In this notation, up to six characters can represent a `long` integer; with each character being a radix-64 digit.

The characters used to represent radix-64 digits are `.` for 0, `/` for 1, `0` through `9` for 2 through 11, `A` through `Z` for 12 through 37, and `a` through `z` for 38 through 63.

The routine `a64l` takes a pointer to a null-terminated base-64 representation and returns a corresponding `long` value. If the string pointed to by `s` contains more than six characters, `a64l` will use the first six.

The routine `l64a` takes a `long` argument and returns a pointer to the corresponding base-64 representation. If the argument is `0`, `l64a` returns a pointer to a null-string.

APPLICATION USAGE

The value returned by `l64a` may be a pointer into a static buffer, which would therefore be overwritten by each call.

NAME

assert — verify program assertion

SYNOPSIS

```
#include <assert.h>

void assert(expression)
int expression;
```

DESCRIPTION

The macro `assert` is useful for putting diagnostics into programs. When it is executed, if `expression` is false (zero), `assert` prints

`assertion failed: expression, file` *xyz*, `line` *nnn*

on the standard error output and aborts. In the error message, *xyz* is the name of the source file and *nnn* the source line number of the `assert` statement.

SEE ALSO

ABORT(BA_SYS).

APPLICATION USAGE

Compiling with the pre-processor option `-DNDEBUG` or with the pre-processor control statement `#define NDEBUG` ahead of the `#include <assert.h>` statement will stop assertions from being compiled into the program.

NAME

getgrent, getgrgid, getgrnam, setgrent, endgrent, fgetgrent — get group file entry

SYNOPSIS

```
#include <grp.h>
#include <stdio.h>

struct group *getgrent( )

struct group *getgrgid(gid)
int gid;

struct group *getgrnam(name)
char *name;

void setgrent( )

void endgrent( )

struct group *fgetgrent(f)
FILE *f;
```

DESCRIPTION

The routines `getgrent`, `getgrgid` and `getgrnam` each return pointers to an object with the following structure containing the broken-out fields of a line in the `/etc/group` file. Each line contains a `group` structure, defined in the `<grp.h>` header file. The structure contains at least the following members:

```
char *gr_name; /* the name of the group */
int gr_gid;    /* the numerical group-ID */
char **gr_mem; /* pointer array to member names */
```

The routine `getgrent` when first called returns a pointer to the first `group` structure in the file; thereafter, it returns a pointer to the next `group` structure in the file; thus, successive calls search the entire file.

The routine `getgrgid` searches the file for a group-ID matching `gid` and returns a pointer to the particular structure in which to find it.

The routine `getgrnam` searches the file for a group-name matching *name* and returns a pointer to the particular structure in which to find it.

If an end-of-file or an error occurs on reading, these functions return a NULL pointer.

The routine `setgrent` rewinds the group-file to allow repeated searches.

The routine `endgrent` closes the group-file when processing is done.

The routine `fgetgrent` returns a pointer to the next `group` structure in the file `f`; this file must have the format of `/etc/group`.

RETURN VALUE

A NULL pointer is returned on end of file or an error.

FILES

`/etc/group`

SEE ALSO

GETLOGIN(SD_LIB), GETPWENT(SD_LIB).

APPLICATION USAGE

All information may be contained in a static area, so it should be copied if it is to be saved.

NAME

getlogin — get login-name

SYNOPSIS

```
char *getlogin( );
```

DESCRIPTION

The routine `getlogin` returns a pointer to the login-name as found in the file `/etc/utmp`. It may be used in conjunction with the routine `getpwnam` [see GETPWENT(SD_LIB)] to locate the correct password-file entry when the same user-ID is shared by several login-names.

If `getlogin` is called within a process that is not attached to a terminal, it returns a NULL pointer. The correct procedure for determining the login-name is to call `getlogin` and if it fails to call `getpwuid`.

RETURN VALUE

Returns a NULL pointer if `name` is not found.

FILES

`/etc/utmp`

SEE ALSO

GETGRENT(SD_LIB), GETPWENT(SD_LIB).

APPLICATION USAGE

The return value may point to static data that is overwritten by each call.

NAME

getpass — read a password

SYNOPSIS

```
char *getpass(prompt)
char *prompt;
```

DESCRIPTION

The routine `getpass` reads up to a new-line or an `EOF` from the file `/dev/tty`, after prompting on the standard error output with the null-terminated string `prompt` and disabling echoing. A pointer is returned to a null-terminated string of at most 8 characters. If `/dev/tty` cannot be opened, a NULL pointer is returned. An interrupt will terminate input and send an interrupt signal to the calling program before returning.

FILES

`/dev/tty`

APPLICATION USAGE

The return value points to static data that is overwritten by each call.

NAME

getpwent, getpwuid, getpwnam, setpwent, endpwent, fgetpwent — get password file entry

SYNOPSIS

```
#include <pwd.h>
#include <stdio.h>

struct passwd *getpwent( )

struct passwd *getpwuid(uid)
int uid;

struct passwd *getpwnam(name)
char *name;

void setpwent( )

void endpwent( )

struct passwd *fgetpwent(f)
FILE *f;
```

DESCRIPTION

Each of the functions `getpwent`, `getpwuid` and `getpwnam` returns a pointer to a structure containing the broken-out fields of a line in the `/etc/passwd` file. Each line in the file contains a `passwd` structure, declared in the `<pwd.h>` header file. The structure contains at least the following members:

```
char *pw_name;      /* login-name */
char *pw_passwd;    /* encrypted-password */
int  pw_uid;        /* numerical user-ID */
int  pw_gid;        /* numerical group-ID */
char *pw_dir;       /* initial-working-directory */
char *pw_shell;     /* command-interpreter */
```

The function `getpwent` when first called returns a pointer to the first `passwd` structure in the file; thereafter, it returns a pointer to the next `passwd` structure in the file; so successive calls can be used to search the entire file.

The function `getpwuid` searches the file for a user-ID matching `uid` and returns a pointer to the particular structure in which to find it.

The function `getpwnam` searches the file for a login-name matching `name` and returns a pointer to the particular structure in which to find it.

If an end-of-file or an error occurs on reading, these functions return a NULL pointer.

The function `setpwent` rewinds the password-file to allow repeated searches.

The function `endpwent` closes the password-file when processing is done.

The function `fgetpwent` returns a pointer to the next `passwd` structure in the file `f`, which must have the format of `/etc/passwd`.

RETURN VALUE

A NULL pointer is returned on end-of-file or error.

FILES

`/etc/passwd`

SEE ALSO

GETLOGIN(SD_LIB), GETGRENT(SD_LIB).

APPLICATION USAGE

All information may be contained in a static area, so it should be copied if it is to be saved.

NAME

getutent, getutid, getutline, pututline, setutent, endutent, utmpname — access utmp file entry

SYNOPSIS

```
#include <utmp.h>

struct utmp *getutent( )

struct utmp *getutid(id)
struct utmp *id;

struct utmp *getutline(line)
struct utmp *line;

void pututline(utmp)
struct utmp *utmp;

void setutent( )

void endutent( )

void utmpname(file)
char *file;
```

DESCRIPTION

Each of the routines `getutent`, `getutid` and `getutline` returns a pointer to a structure, which is defined in the header file `<utmp.h>`. The structure contains at least the following members:

```
char    ut_user[ ];   /* user login-name */
char    ut_id[ ];     /* /etc/inittab ID */
char    ut_line[ ];   /* device-name */
short   ut_pid;       /* process-ID */
short   ut_type;      /* type of entry */
```

In addition, (at least) the following type values for `ut_type` are defined:

`EMPTY`, `RUN_LVL`, `BOOT_TIME`, `OLD_TIME`, `NEW_TIME`, `INIT_PROCESS`, `LOGIN_PROCESS`, `USER_PROCESS`, `DEAD_PROCESS`, `ACCOUNTING`.

The routine `getutent` reads in the next entry from the `/etc/utmp` file. It opens the file if it is not already open and it fails if it reaches the end of the file.

The routine `getutid` searches forward from the current point in the `/etc/utmp` file; if the `ut_type` value of the structure `id` is `RUN_LVL`, `BOOT_TIME`, `OLD_TIME` or `NEW_TIME`, then it stops when it finds an entry with a `ut_type` matching the `ut_type` of the structure `id`. If the `ut_type` value is `INIT_PROCESS`, `LOGIN_PROCESS`, `USER_PROCESS`, or `DEAD_PROCESS`, then it stops when it finds an entry whose type is one of these four and whose `ut_id` field matches the `ut_id` field of `id`. If the end-of-file is reached without a match, `getutid` fails.

The routine `getutline` searches forward from the current point in the `/etc/utmp` file until it finds an entry of the type `LOGIN_PROCESS` or `USER_PROCESS` which also has a `ut_line` value matching that of `line`. If the end-of-file is reached without a match, `getutline` fails.

The routine `pututline` writes out the supplied `/etc/utmp` structure into the `/etc/utmp` file. It uses `getutid` to search forward for the proper place if it finds that it is not already at the proper place. It is expected that normally the user of `pututline` will have searched for the proper entry using one of the above routines. If so, `pututline` will not search. If `pututline` does not find a matching slot for the new entry, it will add a new entry to the end of the file.

The routine `setutent` resets the input stream to the beginning of the file. To examine the entire file, it must be reset before each search for a new entry.

The routine `endutent` closes the currently open file.

The routine `utmpname` allows the user to change the name of the file examined by these routines, from `/etc/utmp` to any other file, usually this other file is `/etc/wtmp`. If the file does not exist, this will not show up until the first attempt to reference the file because `utmpname` does not open the file; it just closes the old file if it is currently open and saves the new file-name.

RETURN VALUE

A NULL pointer is returned upon failure to read, whether for permissions or having reached the end of file, or upon failure to write.

FILES

`/etc/utmp`
`/etc/wtmp`

APPLICATION USAGE

The most current entry is saved in a static structure that must be copied before making further accesses.

Each call to either `getutid` or `getutline` sees the routine examine the static structure before performing more I/O. If the contents of the static structure match what it is searching for, it looks no further. For this reason, to use `getutline` to search for multiple occurrences, it is necessary to zero out the static after each success, or `getutline` will just return the same pointer over and over again.

There is one exception to the rule about removing the structure before doing further reads. If the user modifies the contents of the static structure returned by `getutent`, `getutid`, or `getutline`, and passes the pointer back to `pututline`, the implicit read done by `pututline` (if it finds that it is not already at the correct place in the file) does not hurt the contents.

The `sizeof` operator finds the sizes of the arrays in the structure.

NAME

MARK — profile within a function

SYNOPSIS

```
#define MARK
#include <prof.h>

void MARK(name)
```

DESCRIPTION

The macro `MARK` will introduce a mark called `name` that will be treated the same as a function entry point. Execution of the mark will add to a counter for that mark, and program-counter time spent will be accounted to the immediately preceding mark or to the function if there are no preceding marks within the active function.

The identifier `name` may be any combination of letters, numbers or underscores. Each `name` in a single compilation must be unique, but may be the same as any ordinary program symbol.

For marks to be effective, the symbol `MARK` must be defined before the header file `<prof.h>` is included. This may be defined by a preprocessor directive as in the synopsis, or by a command line argument, i.e.:

```
cc -p -DMARK foo.c
```

If `MARK` is not defined, the `MARK(name)` statements may be left in the source files containing them and will be ignored.

EXAMPLE

In this example, marks can be used to determine how much time is spent in each loop. Unless this example is compiled with `MARK` defined on the command line, the marks are ignored.

```
#include <prof.h>

foo( )
{
        int i, j;
       ...
        MARK(loop1);
        for (i = 0; i < 2000; i++) {
            ...
        }
        MARK(loop2);
        for (j = 0; j < 2000; j++) {
            ...
        }
}
```

SEE ALSO

PROFIL(KE_SYS), MONITOR(SD_LIB), PROF(SD_CMD).

NAME

monitor — prepare execution profile

SYNOPSIS

```
#include <mon.h>

void monitor(lowpc, highpc, buffer, bufsize, nfunc)
int (*lowpc)(), (*highpc)();
WORD *buffer;
int bufsize, nfunc;
```

DESCRIPTION

The routine `monitor` is an interface to the `profil` system service routine [see PROFIL(KE_SYS)]; `lowpc` and `highpc` are the addresses of two functions; `buffer` is the address of a (user supplied) array of `bufsize` `WORD`s (`WORD` is defined in the `<mon.h>` header file). The `monitor` routine arranges to record a histogram of periodically sampled values of the program-counter, and of counts of calls of certain functions, in the buffer. The lowest address sampled is that of `lowpc` and the highest is just below `highpc`; `lowpc` may not equal `0` for this use of `monitor`. At most `nfunc` call counts can be kept; only calls of functions compiled with the profiling option `-p` of `cc` are recorded.

An executable program created by using the `-p` option with `cc` automatically includes calls for the `monitor` routine with default parameters; therefore `monitor` need not be called explicitly except to gain fine control over profiling.

For the results to be significant, especially where there are small, heavily used routines, it is suggested that the buffer be no more than a few times smaller than the range of locations sampled.

To profile the entire program, it is sufficient to use the following:

```
externintetext();
...
monitor((int(*)())2,etext,buf,bufsize,nfunc);
```

The routine `etext` lies just above all the program text.

To stop execution monitoring and write the results, use the following:

```
monitor((int(*)())0,(int(*)())0,0,0,0);
```

The command `prof` [see PROF(SD_CMD)] can then be used to examine the results.

The name of the file written by `monitor` is controlled by the environmental variable `profdir`. If `PROFDIR` is not set, then the file `mon.out` is created in the current directory. If `PROFDIR` is set to the null-string, then no profiling is done and no output file is created. Otherwise, the value of `PROFDIR` is used as the name of the directory in which to create the output file. If `PROFDIR` is `dirname`, then the output file is named dirname/*pid*.mon.out, where *pid* is the program's process-ID. (When monitor is called automatically by using the -p option of cc, the file created is dirname/*pid.progname*, where *progname* is the name of the program).

FILES

mon.out

SEE ALSO

PROFIL(KE_SYS), CC(SD_CMD), PROF(SD_CMD).

NAME

nlist — get entries from name list

SYNOPSIS

```
#include &lt;nlist.h&gt;

int nlist(filename, nl)
char *filename;
struct nlist *nl;
```

DESCRIPTION

The routine `nlist` examines the name list in the executable file whose name is pointed to by `filename`, and selectively extracts a list of values and puts them in the array of `nlist` structures pointed to by `nl`. The name-list `nl` consists of an array of structures containing names of variables, types and values. The list is terminated with a null-name; that is, a null-string is in the name position of the structure. Each variable-name is looked up in the name-list of the file. If the name is found, the type and value of the name are inserted in the next two fields. The type field will be set to 0 unless the file was compiled with the `-g` option of `cc`. If the name is not found, both entries are set to 0.

This function is useful for examining the system name-list kept in the `namelist` file. In this way programs can obtain system-addresses that are up to date.

RETURN VALUE

Returns -1 upon error; otherwise returns 0.

All value entries are set to 0 if the file cannot be read or if it does not contain a valid name-list.

NAME

putpwent — write password file entry

SYNOPSIS

```
#include <pwd.h>

int putpwent(p, f)
struct passwd *p;
FILE *f;
```

DESCRIPTION

The routine `putpwent` is the inverse of `getpwent`. Given a pointer to a password structure created by `getpwent` (or `getpwuid` or `getpwnam`), `putpwent` writes a line on the file `f`, which must h the format of `/etc/passwd`.

RETURN VALUE

Returns a non-zero value if an error was detected during its operation, otherwise returns `0`.

SEE ALSO

GETPWENT(SD_LIB).

NAME

sputl, sgetl — access long integer data in a machine-independent fashion.

SYNOPSIS

```
void sputl(value, buffer)
long value;
char *buffer;

long sgetl(buffer)
char *buffer;
```

DESCRIPTION

The routine `sputl` takes the four bytes of the long integer `value` and places them in memory starting at the address pointed to by `buffer`. The ordering of the bytes is the same across all machines.

The routine `sgetl` retrieves the four bytes in memory starting at the address pointed to by `buffer` and returns the long integer value in the byte ordering of the host machine.

The combination of `sputl` and `sgetl` provides a machine-independent way of storing long numeric data in a file in binary form without conversion to characters.

A program which uses these functions must be compiled with the object file library, by using the `-lld` option of `cc`.

Part IV

Environment

Chapter 9

Base System Environment

NAME

devcon — system console interface

SYNOPSIS

`/dev/console`

DESCRIPTION

`/dev/console` is a generic name given to the system console. It is usually linked to a particular machine-dependent special file, and provides a basic I/O interface to the system console through the *termio* interface [see TERMIO(BA_ENV)].

SEE ALSO

TERMIO(BA_ENV).

NAME

devnul — the null file

SYNOPSIS

`/dev/null`

DESCRIPTION

Data written on a null special file are discarded.

Read operations from a null special file always return 0 bytes.

Output of a command is written to the special file `/dev/null` when the command is executed for its side effects and not for its output.

SEE ALSO

FILSYS(BA_ENV).

NAME

devtty — controlling terminal interface

SYNOPSIS

`/dev/tty`

DESCRIPTION

The file `/dev/tty` is, in each process, a synonym for the control-terminal associated with the process group of that process, if any. It is useful for programs that wish to be sure of writing messages on the terminal no matter how output has been redirected [see SYSTEM(BA_SYS)]. It can also be used for programs that demand the name of a file for output when typed output is desired and as an alternative to identifying what terminal is currently in use.

APPLICATION USAGE

Normally, application programs should not need to use this file interface. The standard input, standard output and standard error files should be used instead. These file are accessed through the `stdin`, `stdout` and `stderr` *stdio* interfaces [see **stdio-stream** in **Definitions**].

SEE ALSO

TERMIO(BA_ENV).

NAME

envvar — environmental variables

DESCRIPTION

When a process begins execution, the EXEC(BA_SYS) routines make available an array of strings called the *environment* [see also SYSTEM(BA_SYS)]. By convention, these strings have the form `variable=value`, for example, `PATH=/bin/usr/bin`. These environmental variables provide a way to make information about an end-user's environment available to programs. The following environmental variables can be used by applications and are expected to be set in the target run-time environment.

Variable	*Use*
`HOME`	Full path-name of the user's home-directory, the user's initial-working-directory [see PASSWD(BA_ENV)].
`PATH`	Colon-separated ordered list of path-names that determine the search sequence used in locating files [see SYSTEM(BA_SYS)].
`TERM`	The kind of terminal for which output is prepared. This information is used by applications that may exploit special capabilities of the terminal.
`TZ`	Time-zone information. `TZ` must be a three-letter, local time-zone abbreviation, followed by a number (an optional minus sign, for time-zones east of Greenwich, followed by a series of digits) that is the difference in hours between this time-zone and Greenwich Mean Time. This may be followed by an optional three-letter daylight local time-zone. For example, `EST5EDT` for Eastern Standard, Eastern Daylight Savings Time.

Other variables might be set in a particular environment but are not required to be included in the Base System.

SEE ALSO

EXEC(BA_SYS), SYSTEM(BA_SYS), FILSYS(BA_ENV).

CAVEATS

The number in `TZ` will be defined as an optional minus sign followed by two hour digits and two minute digits, `hhmm`, in order to represent fractional time-zones.

NAME

errors — error code and condition definitions

SYNOPSIS

```
#include <errno.h>

extern int errno;
```

DESCRIPTION

The numerical value represented by the symbolic name of an error condition is assigned to the external variable `errno` for errors that occur when executing a system service routine or general library routine.

The component definitions list possible error conditions for each routine and the meaning of the error in that *context*. The order in which possible errors are listed is not significant and does not imply precedence. The value of `errno` should be checked only *after* an error has been indicated; that is, when the return value of the component indicates an error, and the component definition specifies that `errno` will be set. A program that checks the value of `errno` must include the `<errno.h>` header file. The `errno` value 0 is reserved; no error condition will be equal to zero.

Additional error conditions may be defined by Extensions to the Base System or by particular implementations.

The following list describes the *general* meaning of each error:

`E2BIG` Argument list too long
An argument list longer than {ARG_MAX} bytes was presented to a member of the EXEC(BA_SYS) family of routines.

`EACCES` Permission denied
An attempt was made to access a file in a way forbidden by the protection system.

`EAGAIN` Resource temporarily unavailable, try again later,
For example, the FORK(BA_SYS) routine failed because the system's process table is full.

`EBADF` Bad file number
Either a file-descriptor specifies no open file, or a read (respectively, write) request was made to a file that is open only for writing (respectively, reading).

`EBUSY` Device or resource busy
An attempt was made to mount a device that was already mounted or an attempt was made to dismount a device on which there is an active file (open file, current directory, mounted-on file, active text segment). It will also occur if an attempt is made to enable accounting when it is already enabled. The device or resource is currently unavailable.

`ECHILD` No child processes
The WAIT(BA_SYS) routine was executed by a process that had no existing or unwaited-for child processes.

`EDEADLK` Deadlock avoided
The request would have caused a deadlock; the situation was detected and avoided.

`EDOM` Math argument
The argument of a function in the math package is out of the domain of the function.

`EEXIST` File exists
An existing file was specified in an inappropriate context (e.g., a call to the LINK(BA_SYS) routine).

`EFAULT` Bad address
The system encountered a hardware fault in attempting to use an argument of a routine. For example, `errno` potentially may be set to `EFAULT` any time a routine that takes a pointer argument is passed an invalid address, if the system can detect the condition. Because systems will differ in their ability to reliably detect a bad address, on some implementations passing a bad address to a routine will result in undefined behavior.

`EFBIG` File too large
The size of a file exceeded the maximum file size, {FCHR_MAX} [see ULIMIT(BA_SYS)].

`EINTR` Interrupted system service
An asynchronous signal (such as interrupt or quit), which the user has elected to catch, occurred during a system service routine. If execution is resumed after processing the signal, it will appear as if the interrupted routine returned this error condition.

`EINVAL` Invalid argument
Some invalid argument (e.g., dismounting a non-mounted device; mentioning an undefined signal in a call to the SIGNAL(BA_SYS) or KILL(BA_SYS) routine). Also set by math routines.

`EIO` I/O error
Some physical I/O error has occurred. This error may, in some cases, occur on a call following the one to which it actually applies.

`EISDIR` Is a directory
An attempt was made to write on a directory.

`EMFILE` Too many open files in a process
No process may have more than {OPEN_MAX} file descriptors open at a time.

`ENLINK` Too many links
An attempt to make more than the maximum number of links, {LINK_MAX}, to a file.

`ENFILE` Too many open files in the system
The system file table is full (i.e., {SYS_OPEN} files are open, and temporarily no more *opens* can be accepted).

`ENODEV` No such device
An attempt was made to apply an inappropriate operation to a device (e.g., read a write-only device).

`ENOENT` No such file or directory
A file-name is specified and the file should exist but does not, or one of the directories in a path-name does not exist.

`ENOEXEC` Exec format error
A request is made to execute a file which, although it has the appropriate permissions, does not start with a valid format.

`ENOLCK` No locks available
There are no more locks available. The system lock table is full.

`ENOMEM` Not enough space
During execution of an EXEC(BA_SYS) routine, a program asks for more space than the system is able to supply. This is not a temporary condition; the maximum space size is a system parameter. The error may also occur if the arrangement of text, data, and stack segments requires too many segmentation registers, or if there is not enough swap space during execution of the FORK(BA_SYS) routine.

`ENOSPC` No space left on device
While writing an ordinary file or creating a directory entry, there is no free space left on the device.

`ENOTBLK` Block device required
A non-block file was specified where a block device was required (e.g., in a call to the MOUNT(BA_SYS) routine).

`ENOTDIR` Not a directory
A non-directory was specified where a directory is required (e.g., in a path-prefix or in a call to the CHDIR(BA_SYS) routine).

`ENOTTY` Not a character device
A call was made to the IOCTL(BA_SYS) routine specifying a file that is not a special character device.

`ENXIO` No such device or address
I/O on a special file specifies a subdevice which does not exist, or exists beyond the limits of the device. It may also occur when, for example, a tape drive is not on-line or no disk pack is loaded on a drive.

`EPERM` No permission match
Typically this error indicates an attempt to modify a file in some way forbidden except to its owner or super-user. It is also returned for attempts by ordinary users to do things allowed only to the super-user.

`EPIPE` Broken pipe
A write on a pipe for which there is no process to read the data. This condition normally generates a signal; the error is returned if the signal is ignored.

`ERANGE` Result too large
The value of a function in the math package is not representable within machine precision.

`EROFS` Read-only file system
An attempt to modify a file or directory was made on a device mounted read-only.

`ESPIPE` Illegal seek
A call to the LSEEK(BA_SYS) routine was issued to a pipe.

`ESRCH` No such process
No process can be found corresponding to that specified by `pid` in the KILL(BA_SYS) or PTRACE(KE_SYS) routine.

`ETXTBSY` Text file busy
An attempt was made to execute a pure-procedure program that is currently open for writing. Also an attempt to open for writing a pure-procedure program that is being executed.

`EXDEV` Cross-device link
A link to a file on another device was attempted.

APPLICATION USAGE

Because a few routines may not have an error return value, an application may set `errno` to zero, call the routine, and then check `errno` again to see if an error has occurred.

NAME

file system — directory tree structure

DESCRIPTION

Directory Tree Structure

Below is a diagram of the minimal directory tree structure expected to be on any UNIX System V operating system.

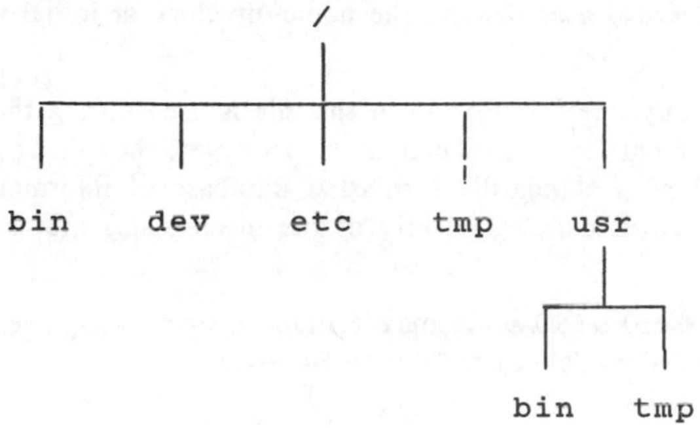

The following guidelines apply to the contents of these directories:

- `/bin`, `/dev`, `/etc`, and `/tmp` are primarily for the use of the system. Most applications should never *create* files in any of these directories, though they may read and execute them. Applications, as well as the system, can use `/usr/bin` and `/usr/tmp`.
- `/bin` holds executable system-commands (utilities), if any.
- `/dev` holds special device files.
- `/etc` holds system-data-files, such as `/etc/passwd`.
- `/tmp` holds temporary files created by utilities in `/bin` and by other system-processes.
- `/usr/bin` holds (user-level) executable application and system-commands.
- `/usr/tmp` holds temporary files created by applications and the system.

Some Extensions to the Base System will have additional requirements on the tree structure when the Extension is installed on a system. Directory tree requirements specific to an Extension will be identified when the Extension is defined in detail.

System Data Files

The Base System Definition specifies only these system-resident data files:

```
/etc/passwd
/etc/profile
```

The `/etc/passwd` and `/etc/profile` files are owned by the system and are readable but not writable by ordinary users.

The format and contents of `/etc/passwd` are defined on PASSWD(BA_ENV). This is a generally useful file, readable by applications, that makes available to application programs some basic information about end-users on a system. It has one entry for each user. Minimally, each user's entry contains a string that is the name by which the user is known on the system, a numerical user-ID, and the home-directory or initial-working-directory of the user.

Conventionally, the information in this file is used during the initialization of the environment for a particular user. However, the `/etc/passwd` file is also useful as a standardly formatted database of information about users, which can be used independently of the mechanisms that maintain the data file.

The `/etc/profile` file may contain a string assignment of the `PATH` and `TZ` variables defined in ENVVAR(BA_ENV).

CAVEATS

The following directory structure and guidelines are proposed for applications ("add-ons") that are to be installed on a system:

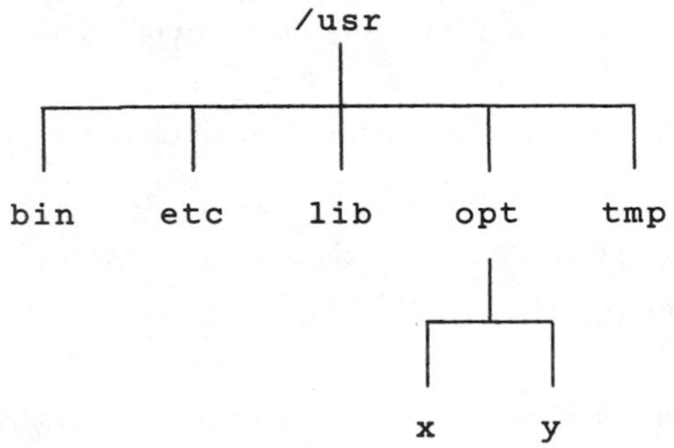

- `/usr/etc` would hold data and log files for commands in `/usr/bin`.
- `/usr/lib` would hold any executable files for commands in `/usr/bin`.
- `/usr/opt` would hold sub-directories for each add-on to hold data files private to the add-on (e.g., add-on `x`)
- `/usr/opt/x` would hold files and/or directories private to add-on `x`, `/usr/opt/y` would hold files and/or directories private to add-on `y`.

NAME

passwd — password file

SYNOPSIS

/etc/passwd

DESCRIPTION

The file /etc/passwd contains the following information for each user:

name
encrypted password (may be empty)
numerical user-ID
numerical group-ID (may be empty)
free field
initial-working-directory
program to use as command interpreter (may be empty)

This ASCII file resides in directory /etc. It has general read permission and can be used, for example, to map *numerical user-IDs* to *names*.

Each field within each user's entry is separated from the next by a colon. Fields 2, 4, and 7 may be empty. However, if they are not empty, they must be used for their stated purpose. Field 5 is a free field that is implementation-specific. Fields beyond 7 are also free but may be standardized in the future. Each user's entry is separated from the next by a new-line.

The *name* is a character string that identifies a user. Its composition should follow the same rules used for file-names.

By convention, the last element in the path-name of the initial-working-directory is typically *name*.

SEE ALSO

CRYPT(BA_LIB).

NAME

termio — general terminal interface

SYNOPSIS

```
#include <termio.h>

ioctl(fildes, request, arg)
struct termio *arg;

ioctl(fildes, request, arg)
int arg;
```

DESCRIPTION

The `termio` facility offers a general interface for asynchronous communications ports that is hardware-independent and that has the common features discussed in this section.

When a terminal file is opened, it normally causes the process to wait until a connection is established. Typically, these files are opened by the system initialization process and become the *standard input*, *standard output*, and *standard error* files [see **stdio-stream** in **Definitions**]. The very first terminal file opened by the process-group-leader but not already associated with a process-group becomes the *control-terminal* for that process-group. The control-terminal plays a special role in handling quit and interrupt signals [see below]. The control-terminal is inherited by a new process during a FORK(BA_SYS) or EXEC(BA_SYS) operation. A process can break this association by changing its process-group with the SETPGRP(BA_SYS) routine.

A terminal associated with one of these files ordinarily operates in full-duplex mode. This means characters may be typed at any time, even while output is occurring. Characters are only lost when the system's character input buffers become completely full, or when an input line exceeds {MAX_CHAR}, the maximum allowable number of input characters. When the input limit is reached, all the saved characters may be thrown away without notice.

Normally, terminal input is processed in units of lines. A line is delimited by the new-line (**ASCII LF**) character, end-of-file (**ASCII EOT**) character, or end-of-line character. This means that a program attempting to read will be suspended until an entire line has been typed. Also, no matter how many characters may be requested in a read, at most one line will be returned. It is not, however, necessary to read a whole line at once; any number of characters may be requested in a read, even one, without losing information.

Some characters have special meaning when input. For example, during input, *erase* and *kill* processing is normally done. The **ERASE** character erases the last character typed, except that it will not erase beyond the beginning of the line. Typically, the default **ERASE** character is the character **#**. The **KILL** character kills (deletes) the entire input line, and optionally outputs a new-line character. Typically, the default **KILL** character is the character **@**. Both characters operate on a key-stroke basis independently of any backspacing or tabbing.

Special Characters.
Some characters have special functions on input. These functions and their typical default character values are summarized below:

INTR (Typically, rubout or **ASCII DEL**) generates an *interrupt* signal, which is sent to all processes with the associated control-terminal. Normally, each such process is forced to terminate, but arrangements may be made either to ignore the signal or to receive a trap to an agreed-upon location [see SIGNAL(BA_SYS)].

QUIT (Typically, control-\ or **ASCII FS**) generates a *quit* signal. Its treatment is identical to the interrupt signal except that, unless a receiving process has made other arrangements, it will not only be terminated but the abnormal termination routines will be executed.

ERASE (Typically, the character #) erases the preceding character. It will not erase beyond the start of a line, as delimited by an **EOF**, **EOL** or **NL** character.

KILL (Typically, the character @) deletes the entire line, as delimited by an **EOF**, **EOL** or **NL** character.

EOF (Typically, control-d or **ASCII EOT**) may be used to generate an **EOF**, from a terminal. When received, all the characters waiting to be read are immediately passed to the program, without waiting for a new-line, and the **EOF** is discarded. Thus, if there are no characters waiting, which is to say the **EOF** occurred at the beginning of a line, zero characters will be passed back, which is the standard end-of-file indication.

NL (**ASCII LF**) is the normal line delimiter. It can not be changed or escaped.

EOL (Typically, **ASCII NUL**) is an additional line delimiter, like **NL**. It is not normally used.

STOP (Typically, control-s or **ASCII DC3**) is used to temporarily suspend output. It is useful with CRT terminals to prevent output from disappearing before it can be read. While output is suspended, **STOP** characters are ignored and not read.

START (Typically, control-q or **ASCII DC1**) is used to resume output suspended by a **STOP** character. While output is not suspended, **START** characters are ignored and not read. The **START/STOP** characters can not be changed or escaped.

MIN Used to control terminal I/O during raw mode (`ICANON` off) processing [see the **MIN/TIME Interaction** section below].

TIME Used to control terminal I/O during raw mode (`ICANON` off) processing [see the **MIN/TIME Interaction** section below].

The **ERASE, KILL** and **EOF** characters may be entered literally, their special meaning escaped, by preceding them with the escape character. In this case, no special function is performed and the escape character is not read as input.

When one or more characters are written, they are transmitted to the terminal as soon as previously-written characters have finished typing. Input characters are echoed by putting them in the output queue as they arrive. If a process produces characters more rapidly than they can be typed, it will be suspended when its output queue exceeds some limit. When the queue has drained down to some threshold, the program is resumed.

When a modem disconnect is detected, a *hang-up* signal, `SIGHUP`, is sent to all processes that have this terminal as the control-terminal. Unless other arrangements have been made, this signal causes the processes to terminate. If the hang-up signal is ignored, any subsequent read returns with an end-of-file indication. Thus, programs that read a terminal and test for end-of-file can terminate appropriately when hung up on.

IOCTL(BA_SYS) Requests.

The primary IOCTL(BA_SYS) requests to a terminal have the form:

```
ioctl(fildes, request, arg)
struct termio *arg;
```

The requests using this form are:

`TCGETA` Get the parameters associated with the terminal and store in the structure `termio` referenced by `arg`.

`TCSETA` Set the parameters associated with the terminal from the structure `termio` referenced by `arg`. The change is immediate.

`TCSETAW` Wait for the output to drain before setting the new parameters. This form should be used when changing parameters that will affect output.

`TCSETAF` Wait for the output to drain, then flush the input queue and set the new parameters.

Additional IOCTL(BA_SYS) requests to a terminal have the form:

```
ioctl(fildes, request, arg)
int arg;
```

The requests using this form are:

`TCSBRK` Wait for the output to drain.
If `arg` is `0`, then send a break (zero bits for 0.25 seconds).

`TCXONC` Start/stop control.
If `arg` is `0`, suspend output; if `1`, restart suspended output.

`TCFLSH` Flush queues
If `arg` is `0`, flush the input queue; if `1`, flush the output queue; if `2`, flush both the input and output queues.

Several IOCTL(BA_SYS) requests apply to terminal files and use the structure `termio` which is defined by the `<termio.h>` header file. The structure `termio` includes the following members:

```
unsigned short c_iflag;   /* input modes */
unsigned short c_oflag;   /* output modes */
unsigned short c_cflag;   /* control modes */
unsigned short c_lflag;   /* local modes */
char           c_line;    /* line-discipline */
unsigned char  c_cc[NCC]; /* control chars */
```

The special control-characters are defined by the array `c_cc`. The symbolic name `NCC` is the size of the control-character array and is also defined by the `<termio.h>` header file. The relative positions, subscript names and typical default values for each entry are as follows:

0	VINTR	ASCII DEL
1	VQUIT	ASCII FS
2	VERASE	#
3	VKILL	@
4	VEOF	ASCII EOT
4	VMIN	
5	VEOL	ASCII NUL
5	VTIME	
6	reserved	
7	reserved	

Input Modes.

The following values for `c_iflag` define basic terminal input control:

`IGNBRK` Ignore break condition.
If `IGNBRK` is set, the break condition (a character framing error with data all zeros) is ignored (i.e., not put on the input queue and therefore not read by any process). Otherwise, see `BRKINT`.

`BRKINT` Signal interrupt on break.
If `BRKINT` is set, the break condition generates an interrupt signal and flushs both the input and output queues.

`IGNPAR` Ignore characters with parity errors.
If `IGNPAR` is set, characters with other framing and parity errors are ignored.

`PARMRK` Mark parity errors.
If `PARMRK` is set, a character with a framing or parity error which is not ignored is read as the three-character sequence: `0377, 0, X`, where `0377, 0` is a two-character flag preceding each sequence and `X` is the data of the character received in error. To avoid ambiguity in this case, if `ISTRIP` is not set, a valid character of `0377` is read as `0377, 0377`.

If PARMRK is not set, a framing or parity error which is not ignored is read as the character **ASCII NUL** (**ASCII** code 0).

INPCK Enable input parity check.
If INPCK is set, input parity checking is enabled.

If INPCK is not set, input parity checking is disabled allowing output parity generation without input parity errors.

ISTRIP Strip character.
If ISTRIP is set, valid input characters are first stripped to 7-bits, otherwise all 8-bits are processed.

INLCR Map NL to **ASCII CR** on input.
If INLCR is set, a received NL character is translated into a **ASCII CR** character.

IGNCR Ignore **ASCII CR**.
If IGNCR is set, a received **ASCII CR** character is ignored (not read).

ICRNL Map **ASCII CR** to NL on input.
If ICRNL is set, a received **ASCII CR** character is translated into a NL character.

IUCLC Map upper-case to lower-case on input.
If IUCLC is set, a received upper-case alphabetic character is translated into lower-case.

IXON Enable start/stop output control.
If IXON is set, start/stop output control is enabled. A received **STOP** character will suspend output and a received **START** character will restart output. All start/stop characters are ignored and not read.

IXANY Enable any character to restart output.
If IXANY is set, any input character, will restart output which has been suspended.

IXOFF Enable start/stop input control.
If IXOFF is set, the system will transmit **START/STOP** characters when the input queue is nearly empty/full.

The initial input control value is all bits clear.

Output Modes.
The following values for c_oflag define system treatment of output:

OPOST Postprocess output.
If OPOST is set, output characters are post-processed as indicated by the remaining flags; otherwise characters are transmitted without change.

OLCUC Map lower case to upper on output.
If OLCUC is set, a lower-case alphabetic character is transmitted as the corresponding upper-case character. This function is often used in conjunction with IUCLC.

ONLCR Map NL to ASCII CR-NL on output.
If ONLCR is set, the NL character is transmitted as the ASCII CR-NL character pair.

OCRNL Map ASCII CR to NL on output.
If OCRNL is set, the ASCII CR character is transmitted as the NL character.

ONOCR No ASCII CR output at column 0.
If ONOCR is set, no ASCII CR character is transmitted when at column 0 (first position).

ONLRET NL performs ASCII CR function.
If ONLRET is set, the NL character is assumed to do the carriage-return function; the column pointer will be set to 0 and the delays specified for ASCII CR will be used. Otherwise the NL character is assumed to do just the line-feed function; the column pointer will remain unchanged. The column pointer is also set to 0 if the ASCII CR character is actually transmitted.

OFILL Use fill-characters for delay.
If OFILL is set, fill-characters will be transmitted for delay instead of a timed delay. This is useful for high baud-rate terminals that need only a minimal delay.

OFDEL Fill is ASCII DEL, else ASCII NUL.
If OFDEL is set, the fill-character is ASCII DEL, otherwise ASCII NUL.

The delay-bits specify how long transmission stops to allow for mechanical or other movement when certain characters are sent to the terminal. In all cases a value of 0 indicates no delay. The actual delays depend on line-speed and system-load.

NLDLY New-line delay lasts about 0.10 seconds.

If ONLRET is set, the carriage-return delays are used instead of the new-line delays.

If OFILL is set, two fill-characters will be transmitted.

Select new-line delays:

NL0	New-Line character type 0
NL1	New-Line character type 1

CRDLY Carriage-return delay type 1 is dependent on the current column position, type 2 is about 0.10 seconds, and type 3 is about 0.15 seconds.

If `OFILL` is set, delay type 1 transmits two fill-characters, and type 2, four fill-characters.

Select carriage-return delays:

`CR0`	Carriage-return delay type 0
`CR1`	Carriage-return delay type 1
`CR2`	Carriage-return delay type 2
`CR3`	Carriage-return delay type 3

`TABDLY` Horizontal-tab delay type 1 is dependent on the current column position, type 2 is about 0.10 seconds, and type 3 specifies that tabs are to be expanded into spaces.

If `OFILL` is set, two fill-characters will be transmitted for any delay.

Select horizontal-tab delays:

`TAB0`	Horizontal-tab delay type 0
`TAB1`	Horizontal-tab delay type 1
`TAB2`	Horizontal-tab delay type 2
`TAB3`	Expand tabs to spaces.

`BSDLY` Backspace delay lasts about 0.05 seconds.

If `OFILL` is set, one fill-character will be transmitted.

Select backspace delays:

`BS0`	Backspace delay type 0
`BS1`	Backspace delay type 1

`VTDLY` Vertical-tab delay lasts about 2.0 seconds.

Select vertical-tab delays:

`VT0`	Vertical-tab delay type 0
`VT1`	Vertical-tab delay type 1

`FFDLY` Form-feed delay lasts about 2.0 seconds.

Select form-feed delays:

`FF0`	Form-feed delay type 0
`FF1`	Form-feed delay type 1

The initial output control value is all bits clear.

Control Modes.

The following values for `c_cflag` define hardware control for terminals:

`HUPCL` Hang up on last close.
If `HUPCL` is set, the modem control lines for the port will be lowered when the last process with the line open closes it or terminates. In other words, the data-terminal-ready signal will not be asserted.

`CLOCAL` Local line, else dial-up.
If `CLOCAL` is set, the line is assumed to be a local, direct connection with no modem control. Otherwise modem control is assumed.

Under normal circumstances, an OPEN(BA_SYS) operation will wait for the modem connection to complete. However, if the `O_NDELAY` flag is set, or `CLOCAL` is set, the OPEN(BA_SYS) operation will return immediately without waiting for the connection. For those files on which the connection has not been established, or has been lost, and for which `CLOCAL` is not set, both READ(BA_SYS) and WRITE(BA_SYS) operations will return a zero character count. For the READ(BA_SYS) operation, this is equivalent to an end-of-file condition. The initial hardware control value after the OPEN(BA_SYS) operation is implementation-dependent.

`CBAUD` Specify the baud-rate.
The zero baud-rate, `B0`, is used to hang up the connection. If `B0` is specified, the data-terminal-ready signal will not be asserted. Normally, this will disconnect the line. For any particular hardware, unsupported speed changes are ignored.

Select baud rate:

`B0`	`Hang up`
`B50`	`50 baud`
`B75`	`75 baud`
`B110`	`110 baud`
`B134`	`134.5 baud`
`B150`	`150 baud`
`B200`	`200 baud`
`B300`	`300 baud`
`B600`	`600 baud`
`B1200`	`1200 baud`
`B1800`	`1800 baud`
`B2400`	`2400 baud`
`B4800`	`4800 baud`
`B9600`	`9600 baud`
`B19200`	`19200 baud`
`B38400`	`38400 baud`

`CSIZE` Specify the character size in bits for both transmission and reception. This size does not include the parity-bit, if any.

Select character size:

`CS5`	5-bits
`CS6`	6-bits
`CS7`	7-bits
`CS8`	8-bits

`CSTOPB` Send two stop-bits, else one.
If `CSTOPB` is set, two stop-bits are used, otherwise one stop-bit. For example, at 110 baud, two stop-bits are normally used.

`CREAD` Enable receiver.
If `CREAD` is set, the receiver is enabled. Otherwise no characters will be received.

`PARENB` Enable parity.
If `PARENB` is set, parity generation and detection is enabled and a parity-bit is added to each character.

`PARODD` Specify odd parity, else even.
If parity is enabled, the `PARODD` flag specifies odd parity if set, otherwise even parity is used.

Local Modes and Line Discipline.

The line-discipline uses `c_lflag` to control terminal functions. The basic line-discipline, `c_line` set to `0`, provides the following:

`ISIG` Enable signals.
If `ISIG` is set, each input character is checked against the special control characters **INTR** and **QUIT**. If an input character matches one of these control characters, the function associated with that character is performed. If `ISIG` is not set, no checking is done. Thus these special input functions are possible only if `ISIG` is set. These functions may be disabled individually by changing the value of the control character to an unlikely or impossible value (e.g., `0377`).

`ICANON` Canonical input (**ERASE** and **KILL** processing).
If `ICANON` is set, canonical processing is enabled. This enables the **ERASE** and **KILL** edit functions, and the assembly of input characters into lines delimited by the **EOF**, **EOL** or **NL** characters. If `ICANON` is not set, read requests are satisfied directly from the input queue. A read will not be satisfied until at least **MIN** characters have been received or the time-out value **TIME** has expired between characters [see the **MIN/TIME Interaction** section below]. This allows fast bursts of input to be read efficiently while still allowing single character input. The **MIN** and **TIME** values are stored in the position for the **EOF** and **EOL** characters, respectively. The time-value is expressed in units of 0.10 seconds.

`XCASE` Canonical upper/lower presentation.
If both `XCASE` and `ICANON` are set, an upper-case letter is input by preceding it with the character `\`, and is output preceded by the character `\`.

With canonical upper/lower presentation, the following escape sequences are generated on output and accepted on input:

for:	**use:**
`	\'
¦	\!
~	\^
{	\(
}	\)
\	\\

`A` is input as `\a`, `\n` as `\\n`, and `\N` as `\\\n`.

`ECHO` Enable echo.
If `ECHO` is set, characters are echoed back to the terminal as received.

When `ICANON` is set, the following echo functions are possible:

`ECHOE` Echo the **ERASE** character as **ASCII BS-SP-BS**.
If both `ECHOE` and `ECHO` are set, the **ERASE** character is echoed as **ASCII BS-SP-BS**, which will clear the last character from a CRT screen.

If `ECHOE` is set but `ECHO` is not set, the **ERASE** character is echoed as **ASCII SP-BS**.

`ECHOK` Echo the **NL** character after the **KILL** character.
If `ECHOK` is set, the **NL** character will be echoed after the **KILL** character to emphasize that the line will be deleted. Note that an escape character preceding the **ERASE** character or the **KILL** character removes any special function.

`ECHONL` Echo the **NL** character.
If `ECHONL` is set, the **NL** character will be echoed even if `ECHO` is not set. This is useful for terminals set to local-echo (also called half-duplex). Because **ASCII EOT** is the default **EOF** character, the **EOF** character is not echoed unless escaped, to prevent terminals that respond to **ASCII EOT** from hanging up.

`NOFLSH` Disable flush after interrupt or quit.
If `NOFLSH` is set, the normal flush of the input and output queues associated with the quit and interrupt characters will not be done.

The initial line-discipline control value is all bits clear.

MIN/TIME Interaction.
MIN represents the minimum number of characters that should be received when the read is satisfied (i.e., the characters are returned to the user). **TIME** is a timer of 0.10 second granularity used to time-out bursty and short-term data transmissions.

The four possible values for **MIN** and **TIME** and their interactions follow:

1. **MIN** > 0, **TIME** > 0. In this case, **TIME** serves as an inter-character timer activated after receipt of the first character, and reset upon receipt of each character. **MIN** and **TIME** interact as follows:

   As soon as a character is received, the inter-character timer starts.

   If **MIN** characters are received before the inter-character timer expires, the read is satisfied.

   If the inter-character timer expires before **MIN** characters are received, the characters received to that point are returned to the user.

   A READ(BA_SYS) operation will sleep until the **MIN** and **TIME** mechanisms are activated by the receipt of the first character; thus, at least one character must be returned.

2. **MIN** > 0, **TIME** = 0. In this case, because **TIME** = 0, the timer plays no role and only **MIN** is significant. A READ(BA_SYS) operation is not satisfied until **MIN** characters are received.

3. **MIN** = 0, **TIME** > 0. In this case, because **MIN** = 0, **TIME** no longer serves as an inter-character timer, but now serves as a read timer that is activated as soon as the READ(BA_SYS) operation is processed (in canon). A READ(BA_SYS) operation is satisfied as soon as a single character is received or the timer expires, in which case, the READ(BA_SYS) operation will not return any characters.

4. **MIN** = 0, **TIME** = 0. In this case, return is immediate. If characters are present, they will be returned to the user.

SEE ALSO

FORK(BA_SYS), IOCTL(BA_SYS), SETPGRP(BA_SYS), SIGNAL(BA_SYS).

Chapter 10

Kernel Extension Environment

NAME

effects — effects of the Kernel Extension on the Base System.

DESCRIPTION

Kernel Extension Routines have the following effects on Base System Routines:

EXEC(BA_SYS)

The `AFORK` flag in the `ac_flag` field of the accounting record is turned off, and the `ac_comm` field is reset by executing an EXEC(BA_SYS) routine [see ACCT(KE_SYS)].

Any process-locks, data-locks, or text locks are removed and not inherited by the new process [see PLOCK(KE_SYS)].

Profiling is disabled for the new process [see PROFIL(KE_SYS)].

The shared-memory-segments attached to the calling-process will not be attached to the new process [see SHMOP(KE_SYS)].

The new process inherits these added attributes from the calling-process:

nice-value [see NICE(KE_SYS)];

`semadj` values [see SEMOP(KE_SYS)];

trace flag [see request 0 in PTRACE(KE_SYS)].

EXIT(BA_SYS)

An accounting record is written on the accounting file if the system's accounting routine is enabled [see ACCT(KE_SYS)].

Any process-locks, data-locks, or text-locks are removed [see PLOCK(KE_SYS)].

Each attached shared-memory-segment is detached and the value of `shm_nattch` in the data structure associated with its shared-memory-identifier is decremented by 1.

For each semaphore for which the calling-process has set a `semadj` value [see SEMOP(KE_SYS)], that `semadj` value is added to the `semval` of the specified semaphore.

FORK(BA_SYS)

The `AFORK` flag is turned on when the function `fork` is executed.

The child-process inherits these added attributes from the parent-process:

The `ac_comm` contents of the accounting record [see ACCT(KE_SYS)];

nice-value [see NICE(KE_SYS)];

profiling on/off status [see PROFIL(KE_SYS)];

all attached shared-memory-segments [see SHMOP(KE_SYS)].

The child-process differs from the parent-process in these other ways:

All `semadj` values are cleared [see SEMOP(KE_SYS)].

The child-process does not inherit process-locks, data-locks, and text-locks [see PLOCK(KE_SYS)].

SEE ALSO

ACCT(KE_SYS), NICE(KE_SYS), PLOCK(KE_SYS), PROFIL(KE_SYS), PTRACE(KE_SYS), SEMOP(KE_SYS), SHMOP(KE_SYS),

NAME

error — error codes and condition definitions

SYNOPSIS

```
#include <errno.h>

extern int errno;
```

DESCRIPTION

In addition to the values defined in the Base System for the external variable `errno` [see ERRNO(BA_ENV)], two additional error conditions are defined in the Kernel Extension:

`ENOMSG` No message of desired type.
An attempt was made to receive a message of a type that does not exist on the specified message queue.

`EIDRM` Identifier removed.
This error is returned to processes that resume execution because of the removal of an identifier [see MSGCTL(KE_SYS), SEMCTL(KE_SYS), and SHMCTL(KE_SYS)].

SEE ALSO

ERRNO(BA_ENV).

Chapter 11

Administered Systems Environment

NAME

sysinit — system initialization

SYNOPSIS

`/etc/inittab`

DESCRIPTION

This section is intended to provide some background information about the system-process-spawner (**init**), and about how a user is logged in (**getty** and **login**). The description here is a general one; there may be minor differences between different implementations of UNIX System V.

INIT

The **init**-process is invoked at system-initialization, as one of the steps in the boot procedure; its primary role is to create processes according to entries in the file `/etc/inittab`.

One kind of entry in this file specifies how the **getty**-process (see GETTY section below) is to be executed on the individual terminal lines available for users to log in. Other entries control the initiation of autonomous processes required by any particular system.

The system-administrator communicates with the **init**-process by executing the `init` command [see INIT(AS_CMD)]. (It is important to keep in mind the distinction between the two; here **init** refers to the special system-process, while `init` refers to the command that allows communication with the special system-process).

The **init**-process considers the system to be in a particular *run-level* at any given time. A *run-level* can be viewed as a software configuration of the system, where each configuration is defined by the collection of processes that are to be spawned. The specification of the *run-levels* (that is, the specification of the processes to be spawned by **init**) is defined in the `/etc/inittab` file. There are eight allowed *run-levels*, **0** to *6* and **s** (or **S**). The *run-level* may be changed when the administrator runs the `init` command.

When it is invoked at system-initialization, the first thing the **init**-process does is to look for the `/etc/inittab` file and see if there is an entry of the type `initdefault`. If there is, **init** uses the *run-level* specified in that entry as the initial *run-level* to enter. If this entry is not in `/etc/inittab`, then **init** requests that the user enter a *run-level* from the virtual system console, `/dev/console`.

The *run-level* **s** (**S**) corresponds to *SINGLE USER* level. This is the only *run-level* that does not require the existence of a properly formatted `/etc/inittab` file. If `/etc/inittab` doesn't exist, then by default **init** enters *SINGLE USER* level. (Note: Since other *run-levels* may also be configured for single-user, *SINGLE USER* level need not be the only level in which only one user is allowed on the system).

The levels **0** through **6** have no special meaning; they are defined by the entries in the `/etc/inittab` file.

Whenever a new *run-level* is entered, **init** scans the `/etc/inittab` file and processes all entries corresponding to that *run-level*. In addition, entry to and exit from *SINGLE USER* level results in some special actions, as follows:

1. When *SINGLE USER* level is entered in the boot-sequence, `/etc/inittab` is scanned for any entries of the type `sysinit`. These entries are processed before any other actions in state **s**.

2. The first time **init** leaves *SINGLE USER* level, it scans `/etc/inittab` for special entries of the type `boot` and `bootwait`. Entries of this type, for which the specified *run-level* matches the new *run-level* to be entered, are performed before any normal processing of `/etc/inittab` takes place.

In this way any special initialization of the operating system, such as mounting file systems, can take place before users are allowed onto the system.

In a normal operating environment (multi-user), the `/etc/inittab` file is usually set up so that **init** will create a process for each terminal on the system.

After it has spawned all of the processes specified by the `/etc/inittab` file, **init** waits for one of its child-processes to die, a powerfail signal, or until a request is made via the `init` command to change the system's *run-level*. When one of the above three conditions occurs, **init** re-examines the `/etc/inittab` file. New entries can be added to this file at any time; however, **init** still waits for one of the above three conditions to occur. To get an immediate response the `init` command may be invoked with the option `q` in order to force **init** to re-examine the `/etc/inittab` file.

When **init** is requested to change *run-level*s, all processes defined in the current *run-level*, that are undefined in the target *run-level*, are terminated. This is done by first sending the signal `SIGTERM` (which serves as a warning for processes that catch it), and, after a brief delay, sending the signal `SIGKILL`.

If **init** finds that it is continuously respawning an entry from `/etc/inittab` (more frequently than some specified rate), it will assume that there is an error in the command string, generate an error message on the system console, and refuse to respawn this entry until either some time has elapsed or it receives a directive from the `init` command. This prevents **init** from eating up system resources when someone makes a typographical error in the `/etc/inittab` file or a program is removed that is referenced in `/etc/inittab`.

GETTY

The **getty**-process is invoked by the **init**-process, to allow a user to login on a terminal-line. It is thus the **getty**-process that the user encounters when logging in to the system.

The actions of **getty** are controlled by entries in the file `/etc/gettydefs`. These entries specify what line speed should be used initially, what the login message should look like, what the initial tty settings are, and what speed to try next should the user indicate that the speed is inappropriate (by typing a **BREAK**-character).

If a null character (or framing error) is received, it is assumed to be the result of the user pushing the **BREAK**-key. This will cause **getty** to attempt the next speed in a sequence defined in `/etc/gettydefs`.

Finally, the **login** command is called to allow the user to complete logging in.

LOGIN

The **login** process is invoked by the **getty**-process, as described above, at the beginning of each terminal session. It is the means by which the user is identified to the system.

If the user has a password, **login** asks for it, and verifies its correctness. If system echoing has been enabled, it is turned off during the typing of the password. (However, echoing will continue to occur if local echo has been enabled).

If the login is not completed successfully within a certain period of time, (e.g., one minute) the user may be disconnected.

After a successful login, the user-ID, the group-ID, the working-directory, and the command-interpreter, are initialized.

SEE ALSO

GETTY(AS_CMD), LOGIN(AS_CMD), INIT(AS_CMD).

Part V

Definitions

Chapter 12

Base System Definitions

ASCII character set

The following maps of the **ASCII** character set give octal and hexadecimal equivalents for each character. Although the **ASCII** code does not use the eighth-bit in an octet, this bit should not be used for other purposes because codes for other languages may need to use it.

Octal map of **ASCII** character set.

000 nul	001 soh	002 stx	003 etx	004 eot	005 enq	006 ack	007 bel
010 bs	011 ht	012 nl	013 vt	014 np	015 cr	016 so	017 si
020 dle	021 dc1	022 dc2	023 dc3	024 dc4	025 nak	026 syn	027 etb
030 can	031 em	032 sub	033 esc	034 fs	035 gs	036 rs	037 us
040 sp	041 !	042 "	043 #	044 $	045 %	046 &	047 '
050 (	051)	052 *	053 +	054 ,	055 -	056 .	057 /
060 0	061 1	062 2	063 3	064 4	065 5	066 6	067 7
070 8	071 9	072 :	073 ;	074 <	075 =	076 >	077 ?
100 @	101 A	102 B	103 C	104 D	105 E	106 F	107 G
110 H	111 I	112 J	113 K	114 L	115 M	116 N	117 O
120 P	121 Q	122 R	123 S	124 T	125 U	126 V	127 W
130 X	131 Y	132 Z	133 [	134 \	135]	136 ^	137 _
140 `	141 a	142 b	143 c	144 d	145 e	146 f	147 g
150 h	151 i	152 j	153 k	154 l	155 m	156 n	157 o
160 p	161 q	162 r	163 s	164 t	165 u	166 v	167 w
170 x	171 y	172 z	173 {	174 ¦	175 }	176 ~	177 del

Hexadecimal map of **ASCII** character set.

00 nul	01 soh	02 stx	03 etx	04 eot	05 enq	06 ack	07 bel
08 bs	09 ht	0a nl	0b vt	0c np	0d cr	0e so	0f si
10 dle	11 dc1	12 dc2	13 dc3	14 dc4	15 nak	16 syn	17 etb
18 can	19 em	1a sub	1b esc	1c fs	1d gs	1e rs	1f us
20 sp	21 !	22 "	23 #	24 $	25 %	26 &	27 '
28 (	29)	2a *	2b +	2c ,	2d -	2e .	2f /
30 0	31 1	32 2	33 3	34 4	35 5	36 6	37 7
38 8	39 9	3a :	3b ;	3c <	3d =	3e >	3f ?
40 @	41 A	42 B	43 C	44 D	45 E	46 F	47 G
48 H	49 I	4a J	4b K	4c L	4d M	4e N	4f O
50 P	51 Q	52 R	53 S	54 T	55 U	56 V	57 W
58 X	59 Y	5a Z	5b [	5c \	5d]	5e ^	5f _
60 `	61 a	62 b	63 c	64 d	65 e	66 f	67 g
68 h	69 i	6a j	6b k	6c l	6d m	6e n	6f o
70 p	71 q	72 r	73 s	74 t	75 u	76 v	77 w
78 x	79 y	7a z	7b {	7c ¦	7d }	7e ~	7f del

directory
Directories organize files into a hierarchical system of files with directories as the nodes in the hierarchy. A directory is a file that catalogs the list of files, including directories (sub-directories), that are directly beneath it in the hierarchy. Entries in a directory file are called links. A link associates a file-identifier with a file-name. By convention, a directory contains at least two links, . (*dot*) and .. (*dot-dot*). The link called *dot* refers to the directory itself while *dot-dot* refers to its parent-directory. The root-directory, which is the top-most node of the hierarchy, has itself as its parent-directory. The path-name of the root directory is / and the parent-directory of the root-directory is /.

effective-user-ID and **effective-group-ID**
An active process has an effective-user-ID and an effective-group-ID that are used to determine file-access-permissions (see below). The effective-user-ID and effective-group-ID are equal to the process's real-user-ID and real-group-ID respectively, unless the process or one of its ancestors evolved from a file that had the set-user-ID bit or set-group-ID bit set [see EXEC(BA_SYS)]. In addition, they can be reset with the SETUID(BA_SYS) and SETGID(BA_SYS) routines, respectively.

environmental variables
When a process begins, an array of strings called the *environment* is made available by the EXEC(BA_SYS) routine [see also SYSTEM(BA_SYS)]. By convention, these strings have the form `variable=value`, for example, `PATH=:/bin:/usr/bin`. These environmental variables provide a way to make information about an end-user's environment available to programs [see ENVVAR(BA_ENV)].

file-access-permissions
Read, write, and execute/search permissions [see CHMOD(BA_SYS)] on a file are granted to a process if one or more of the following are true:

- The effective-user-ID of the process is super-user.
- The effective-user-ID of the process matches the user-ID of the owner of the file and the appropriate access-permission-bit of the *owner* portion of the file-mode is set.
- The effective-user-ID of the process does not match the user-ID of the owner of the file and the effective-group-ID of the process matches the group of the file and the appropriate access-permission-bit of the *group* portion of the file-mode is set.
- The effective-user-ID of the process does not match the user-ID of the owner of the file and the effective-group-ID of the process does not match the group-ID of the file and the appropriate access-permission-bit of the *other* portion of the file-mode is set.

Otherwise, the corresponding permissions are denied.

file-descriptor
A file-descriptor is a small integer used to identify a file for the purposes of doing I/O. The value of a file-descriptor is from 0 to {OPEN_MAX} - 1. An open file-descriptor is obtained from a call to the CREAT(BA_SYS), DUP(BA_SYS), FCNTL(BA_SYS), OPEN(BA_SYS), or PIPE(BA_SYS) routine. A process may have no more than {OPEN_MAX} file-descriptors open simultaneously.

A file-descriptor has associated with it information used in performing I/O on the file: a file-pointer that marks the current position within the file where I/O will begin; file-status and access-modes (e.g., read, write, read/write) [see OPEN(BA_SYS)]; and close-on-exec flag [see FCNTL(BA_SYS)]. Multiple file-descriptors may identify the same file. The file-descriptor is used as an argument by such routines as the READ(BA_SYS), WRITE(BA_SYS), IOCTL(BA_SYS), and CLOSE(BA_SYS) routines.

file-name
Strings consisting of 1 to {NAME_MAX} characters may be used to name an ordinary file, a special file or a directory. {NAME_MAX} must be at least 14. These characters may be selected from the set of all character values excluding the characters *null* and *slash* (/).

Note that it is generally unwise to use *, ?, !, [, or] as part of file-names because of the special meaning attached to these characters for file-name expansion by the command interpreter [see SYSTEM(BA_SYS)]. Other characters to avoid are the hyphen, blank, tab, <, >, backslash, single and double quotes, accent grave, vertical bar, caret, curly braces, and parentheses. It is also advisable to avoid the use of non-printing characters in file names.

implementation-specific constants
In detailed definitions of components, it is sometimes necessary to refer to constants that are implementation-specific, but which are not necessarily expected to be accessible to an application-program. Many of these constants describe boundary-conditions and system-limits.

In the SVID, for readability, these constants are replaced with symbolic names. These names always appear enclosed in curly brackets to distinguish them from symbolic names of other implementation-specific constants that are accessible to application-programs by header files. These names are not necessarily accessible to an application-program through a header file, although they may be defined in the documentation for a particular system.

In general, a portable application program should not refer to these constants in its code. For example, an application-program would not be expected to test the length of an argument list given to an EXEC(BS_SYS) routine to determine if it was greater than {ARG_MAX}.

The following lists implementation-specific constants used in component definitions:

Name	*Description*
{ARG_MAX}	max. length of argument to `exec`
{CHAR_BIT}	number of bits in a `char`
{CHAR_MAX}	max. integer value of a `char`
{CHILD_MAX}	max. number of processes per user-ID
{CLK_TCK}	number of clock ticks per second
{FCHR_MAX}	max. size of a file in bytes
{INT_MAX}	max. decimal value of an `int`
{LINK_MAX}	max. number of links to a single file
{LOCK_MAX}	max. number of entries in system lock table
{LONG_BIT}	number of bits in a `long`
{LONG_MAX}	max. decimal value of a `long`
{MAXDOUBLE}	max. decimal value of a `double`
{MAX_CHAR}	max. size of character input buffer
{NAME_MAX}	max. number of characters in a file-name
{OPEN_MAX}	max. number of files a process can have open
{PASS_MAX}	max. number of significant characters in a password
{PATH_MAX}	max. number of characters in a path-name
{PID_MAX}	max. value for a process-ID
{PIPE_BUF}	max. number bytes atomic in write to a pipe
{PIPE_MAX}	max. number of bytes written to a pipe in a write
{PROC_MAX}	max. number of simultaneous processes, system wide
{SHRT_MAX}	max. decimal value of a `short`
{STD_BLK}	number of bytes in a physical I/O block
{SYS_NMLN}	number of characters in string returned by `uname`
{SYS_OPEN}	max. number of files open on system
{TMP_MAX}	max. number of unique names generated by `tmpnam`
{UID_MAX}	max. value for a user-ID or group-ID
{USI_MAX}	max. decimal value of an `unsigned`
{WORD_BIT}	number of bits in a `word` or `int`
{CHAR_MIN}	min. integer value of a `char`
{INT_MIN}	min. decimal value of an `int`
{LONG_MIN}	min. decimal value of a `long`
{SHRT_MIN}	min. decimal value of a `short`

parent-process-ID

The parent-process-ID of a process is the process-ID of its creator. A new process is created by a currently active-process [see FORK(BA_SYS)].

path-name and **path-prefix**
In a C program, a path-name is a null-terminated character-string starting with an optional slash (/), followed by zero or more directory-names separated by slashes, optionally followed by a file-name. A null string is undefined and may be considered an error.

More precisely, a path-name is a null-terminated character-string as follows:

```
<path_name>::=<file_name>|<path_prefix><file_name>|/|.|..
<path_prefix>::=<rtprefix>|/<rtprefix>|empty
<rtprefix>::=<dirname>/|<rtprefix><dirname>/
```

where <file_name> is a string of 1 to {NAME_MAX} significant characters other than slash and null, and <dirname> is a string of 1 to {NAME_MAX} significant characters (other than slash and null) that names a directory. The result of names not produced by the grammar are undefined.

If a path-name begins with a slash, the path search begins at the root-directory. Otherwise, the search begins from the current-working-directory.

A slash by itself names the root-directory. The meanings of . and .. are defined under **directory**.

process-group-ID
Each active-process is a member of a process-group. The process-group is uniquely identified by a positive-integer, called the process-group-ID, which is the process-ID of the group-leader (see below). This grouping permits the signaling of related processes [see KILL(BA_SYS)].

process-group-leader
A process group leader is any process whose process-group-ID is the same as its process-ID. Any process may detach itself from its current process-group and become a new process-group-leader by calling the SETPGRP(BA_SYS) routine. A process inherits the process-group-ID of the process that created it [see FORK(BA_SYS) and EXEC(BA_SYS)].

process-ID
Each active-process in the system is uniquely identified by a positive-integer called a process-ID. The range of this ID is from 0 to {PID_MAX}. By convention, process-ID 0 and 1 are reserved for special system-processes.

real-user-ID and **real-group-ID**
Each user allowed on the system is identified by a positive-integer called a real-user-ID. Each user is also a member of a group. The group is identified by a positive-integer called the real-group-ID.

An active-process has a real-user-ID and real-group-ID that are set to the real-user-ID and real-group-ID, respectively, of the user responsible for the creation of the process. They can be reset with the SETUID(BA_SYS) and SETGID(BA_SYS) routines, respectively.

root-directory and **current-working-directory**
Each process has associated with it a concept of a root-directory and a current-working-directory for the purpose of resolving path searches. The root-directory of a process need not be the root-directory of the root file system.

special-processes
All special-processes are system-processes (e.g., a system's process-scheduler). At least process-IDs 0 and 1 are reserved for special-processes.

stdio-routines
A set of routines described as Standard I/O (*stdio*) routines constitute an efficient, user-level I/O buffering scheme. The complete set of Standard I/O, *stdio* routines is shown below [see also the definition of **stdio-stream** below]. Detailed component definitions of each can be found in either the Base System (BA_SYS) routines or the Base Library (BA_LIB) routines.

(BA_SYS) `clearerr`, `fclose`, `fdopen`, `feof`, `ferror`, `fileno`, `fflush`, `fopen`, `fread`, `freopen`, `fseek`, `ftell`, `fwrite`, `popen`, `pclose`, `rewind`.

(BA_LIB) `ctermid`, `fgetc`, `fgets`, `fprintf`, `fputc`, `fputs`, `fscanf`, `getc`, `getchar`, `gets`, `getw`, `printf`, `putc`, `putchar`, `puts`, `putw`, `scanf`, `setbuf`, `setvbuf`, `sprintf`, `tempnam`, `tmpfile`, `tmpnam`, `ungetc`, `vprintf`. `vfprintf`. `vsprintf`.

The Standard I/O routines and constants are declared in the `<stdio.h>` header file and need no further declaration. The following *functions* are implemented as macros and must not be redeclared: `getc`, `getchar`, `putc`, `putchar`, `ferror`, `feof`, `clearerr`, and `fileno`. The macros `getc` and `putc` handle characters quickly. The macros `getchar` and `putchar`, and the higher-level routines `fgetc`, `fgets`, `fprintf`, `fputc`, `fputs`, `fread`, `fscanf`, `fwrite`, `gets`, `getw`, `printf`, `puts`, `putw`, and `scanf` all use or act as if they use `getc` and `putc`; they can be freely intermixed.

The `<stdio.h>` header file also defines three symbolic constants used by the *stdio* routines:

> The defined constant `NULL` designates a nonexistent *null* pointer.
>
> The integer constant `EOF` is returned upon end-of-file or error by most integer functions that deal with streams (see the individual component definitions for details).
>
> The integer constant `BUFSIZ` specifies the size of the *stdio* buffers used by the particular implementation.

Any application-program that uses the *stdio* routines must include the `<stdio.h>` header file.

stdio-stream

A file with associated *stdio* buffering is called a *stream*. A stream is a pointer to a type `FILE` defined by the `<stdio.h>` header file. The FOPEN(BA_SYS) routine creates certain descriptive data for a stream and returns a pointer that identifies the stream in all further transactions with other *stdio* routines.

Most *stdio* routines manipulate either a stream created by the function `fopen` or one of three streams that are associated with three files that are expected to be open in the Base System [see TERMIO(BA_ENV)]. These three streams are declared in the `<stdio.h>` header file:

`stdin`	the standard input file.
`stdout`	the standard output file.
`stderr`	the standard error file.

Output streams, with the exception of the standard error stream `stderr`, are by default buffered if the output refers to a file and line-buffered if the output refers to a terminal. The standard error output stream `stderr` is by default unbuffered. When an output stream is unbuffered, information is queued for writing on the destination file or terminal as soon as written; when it is buffered, many characters are saved up and written as a block. When it is line-buffered, each line of output is queued for writing on the destination terminal as soon as the line is completed (that is, as soon as a new-line character is written or terminal input is requested). The SETBUF(BA_LIB) routines may be used to change the stream's buffering strategy.

super-user

A process is recognized as a super-user process and is granted special privileges if its effective-user-ID is `0`.

tty-group-ID

Each active-process can be a member of a terminal-group that shares a control terminal [see DEVTTY(BA_ENV)] and is identified by a positive-integer called the tty-group-ID. This grouping is used to terminate a group of related processes upon termination of one of the processes in the group [see EXIT(BA_SYS) and SIGNAL(BA_SYS)].

Chapter 13

Kernel Extension Definitions

ipc-permissions

The Kernel Extension includes three mechanisms for inter-process communication (ipc): messages, semaphores, and shared-memory. All of these use a common structure type, `ipc_perm`, to pass information used in determining permission to use an ipc-operation.

The `<ipc.h>` header file defines the `ipc_perm` structure that includes the following members:

```
ushort  cuid;     /* creator user-ID */
ushort  cgid;     /* creator group-ID */
ushort  uid;      /* user-ID */
ushort  gid;      /* group-ID */
ushort  mode;     /* r/w permission */
```

The `<ipc.h>` header file also defines the following symbolic constants:

Name	*Description*
IPC_CREAT	create entry if key does not exist
IPC_EXCL	fail if key exists
IPC_NOWAIT	error if request must wait
IPC_PRIVATE	private key
IPC_RMID	remove identifier
IPC_SET	set options
IPC_STAT	get options

message-queue-identifier

A message-queue-identifier `msqid` is a unique positive integer created by calling the MSGGET(KE_SYS) routine. Each `msqid` has a message-queue and a data structure `msqid_ds` associated with it. The `msqid_ds` structure contains the following members:

```
struct ipc_perm msg_perm;   /* operation perms */
ushort          msg_qnum;   /* no. of messages on q */
ushort          msg_qbytes; /* max no. of bytes on q */
ushort          msg_lspid;  /* pid, last msgsnd call */
ushort          msg_lrpid;  /* pid, last msgrcv call */
time_t          msg_stime;  /* last msgsnd time */
time_t          msg_rtime;  /* last msgrcv time */
time_t          msg_ctime;  /* last change time */
                            /* time in secs since */
                            /* 00:00:00 GMT 1 Jan 70 */
```

`msg_perm` an `ipc_perm` structure [see **ipc-permissions**] that specifies the message-operation-permission.

`msg_qnum` the number of messages currently on the queue.

`msg_qbytes` the maximum number of bytes allowed on the queue.

`msg_lspid` the process-ID of last process to use a `msgsnd` operation.

`msg_lrpid` the process-ID of last process to use a `msgrcv` operation.

`msg_stime` the time of last `msgsnd` operation.

`msg_rtime` the time of last `msgrcv` operation.

`msg_ctime` the time of last MSGCTL(KE_SYS) operation to change a member of the above structure.

message-operation-permissions

In the MSGOP(KE_SYS) and MSGCTL(KE_SYS) routines, the permission required for an operation is determined by the bit-pattern in `msg_perm.mode`, where the type of permission needed is interpreted as follows:

`00400`	Read by user
`00200`	Write by user
`00040`	Read by group
`00020`	Write by group
`00004`	Read by others
`00002`	Write by others

The Read and Write permissions on a `msqid` are granted to a process if one or more of the following are true:

- The effective-user-ID of the process is super-user.
- The effective-user-ID of the process matches `msg_perm.cuid` or `msg_perm.uid` in the `msqid_ds` structure and the appropriate bit of the *user* portion (`0600`) of `msg_perm.mode` is set.
- The effective-user-ID of the process does not match `msg_prm.cuid` or `msg_perm.uid`, and the effective-group-ID of the process matches `msg_perm.cgid` or `msg_perm.gid`, and the appropriate bit of the *group* portion (`0060`) of `msg_perm.mode` is set.
- The effective-user-ID of the process does not match `msg_perm.cuid` or `msg_perm.uid`, and the effective-group-ID of the process does not match `msg_perm.cgid` or `msg_perm.gid`, and the appropriate bit of the *other* portion (`0006`) of `msg_perm.mode` is set.

Otherwise, the corresponding permissions are denied.

semaphore-identifier

A semaphore-identifier `semid` is a unique positive integer created by calling the SEMGET(KE_SYS) routine. Each `semid` has a set of semaphores and a data structure `semid_ds` associated with it. The `semid_ds` structure contains the following members:

```
struct ipc_perm sem_perm;  /* operation perms */
ushort          sem_nsems; /* count of sems in set */
time_t          sem_otime; /* last operation time */
time_t          sem_ctime; /* last change time */
                           /* time in secs since */
                           /* 00:00:00 GMT 1 Jan 70 */
```

`sem_perm` — an `ipc_perm` structure [see **ipc-permissions**] that specifies the semaphore-operation-permission.

`sem_nsems` — the number of semaphores in the set. Each semaphore in the set is referenced by a positive integer, `sem_num`, that runs sequentially from `0` to the value of `sem_nsems-1`. `sem_otime` is the time of last SEMOP(KE_SYS) operation. `sem_ctime` is the time of last SEMCTL(KE_SYS) operation to change a member of the above structure.

A semaphore is a data structure with the following members:

```
ushort semval;  /* semaphore value */
short  sempid;  /* pid of last operation */
ushort semncnt; /* no. awaiting semval > cval */
ushort semzcnt; /* no. awaiting semval = 0 */
```

`semval` — a non-negative integer.

`sempid` — the process-ID of last process to use a semaphore operation on this semaphore.

`semncnt` — a count of the suspended-processes currently waiting for the `semval` of this semaphore exceed greater than its current value.

`semzcnt` — a count of the suspended-processes currently waiting for the `semval` of this semaphore exceed zero.

semaphore-operation-permissions

In the SEMOP(KE_SYS) and SEMCTL(KE_SYS) routines, the permission required for an operation is determined by the bit-pattern in `sem_perm.mode`, where the type of permission needed is interpreted as follows:

`00400`	Read by user
`00200`	Alter by user
`00040`	Read by group
`00020`	Alter by group
`00004`	Read by others
`00002`	Alter by others

The Read and Alter permissions on a `semid` are granted to a process if one or more of the following are true:

- The effective-user-ID of the process is super-user.
- The effective-user-ID of the process matches `sem_perm.cuid` or `sem_perm.uid` in the `semid_ds` structure and the appropriate bit of the *user* portion (`0600`) of `sem_perm.mode` is set.
- The effective-user-ID of the process does not match `sem_perm.cuid` or `sem_perm.uid`, and the effective-group-ID of the process matches `sem_perm.cgid` or `sem_perm.gid`, and the appropriate bit of the *group* portion (`0060`) of `sem_perm.mode` is set.

- The effective-user-ID of the process does not match `sem_perm.cuid` or `sem_perm.uid`, and the effective-group-ID of the process does not match `sem_perm.cgid` or `sem_perm.gid`, and the appropriate bit of the *other* portion (`0006`) of `sem_perm.mode` is set.

Otherwise, the corresponding permissions are denied.

shared-memory-identifier

A shared-memory-identifier `shmid` is a unique positive integer created by calling the SHMGET(KE_SYS) routine. Each `shmid` has a segment of memory (referred to as a shared-memory-segment) and a data structure `shmid_ds` associated with it. The `shmid_ds` structure contains the following members:

```
struct ipc_perm shm_perm;   /* operation perms */
int             shm_segsz;  /* size of segment */
ushort          shm_cpid;   /* pid, creator */
ushort          shm_lpid;   /* pid, last operation */
short           shm_nattch; /* no. of current attaches */
time_t          shm_atime;  /* last attach time */
time_t          shm_dtime;  /* last detach time */
time_t          shm_ctime;  /* last change time */
                            /* times in secs since */
                            /* 00:00:00 GMT 1 Jan 70 */
```

`shm_perm`	an `ipc_perm` structure [see **ipc-permissions**] that specifies the shared-memory-operation-permission.
`shm_segsz`	specifies the size of the shared-memory-segment.
`shm_cpid`	the process-ID of the creator of the shared-memory-identifier.
`shm_lpid`	the process-ID of last process to use a shared-memory operation.
`shm_nattch`	the number of processes with the segment currently attached.
`shm_atime`	the time of last `shmat` operation.
`shm_dtime`	the time of last `shmdt` operation.
`shm_ctime`	the time of last SHMCTL(KE_SYS) operation to change one of the members of the above structure.

shared-memory-operation-permissions

In the SHMOP(KE_SYS) and SHMCTL(KE_SYS) routines, the permission required for an operation is determined by the bit-pattern in `shm_perm.mode`, where the type of permission needed is interpreted as follows:

`00400`	Read by user
`00200`	Write by user
`00040`	Read by group
`00020`	Write by group
`00004`	Read by others
`00002`	Write by others

The Read and Write permissions on a shmid are granted to a process if one or more of the following are true:

- The effective-user-ID of the process is super-user.
- The effective-user-ID of the process matches shm_perm.cuid or sem_perm.uid in the shmid_ds structure and the appropriate bit of the *user* portion (0600) of shm_perm.mode is set.
- The effective-user-ID of the process does not match shm_perm.cuid or sem_perm.uid, and the effective-group-ID of the process matches shm_perm.cgid or sem_perm.gid, and the appropriate bit of the *group* portion (0060) of shm_perm.mode is set.
- The effective-user-ID of the process does not match shm_perm.cuid or sem_perm.uid, and the effective-group-ID of the process does not match shm_perm.cgid or sem_perm.gid, and the appropriate bit of the *other* portion (0006) of shm_perm.mode is set.

Otherwise, the corresponding permissions are denied.